Romantic New England Getaways

BY ANDREA BROX

Every effort has been made to insure the accuracy of the information provided.
However, prices, hours, and menus at inns and restaurants do change.
Sometimes too, these establishments are sold or close.
Readers should call or write ahead to avoid disappointment.
The maps provided in *Romantic New England Getaways* are designed
to help travelers get their bearings in a region.
They are not meant to take the place of a good local map.

Romantic New England Getaways
by Andrea Brox
Edited by Beverly Wood
Cover Design and Maps by Chris Jagmin
Cover photograph: the Gardner Room at the Four Chimneys Inn, Nantucket, MA
Cover Photograph by George Ross
Pleasant Street Press
Lexington, Massachusetts

ISBN No. 0-9636123-0-1
Copyright ©, 1993 Andrea Brox
Printed in the United States of America
For information address
Pleasant Street Press, 1644 Massachusetts Avenue, Suite 40, Lexington, MA 02173.

Brox, Andrea
    Romantic New England Getaways/by Andrea Brox
    p. cm.
    Includes indexes.
    ISBN 0-9636123-0-1
    1. New England – Tours. I. Title.
    F2.3.B77 1993
    917.404'43 – dc20   93-5825
                                             CIP

To my husband, John McCarthy,
and to my parents, Frank and Eleanor Brox

Summer

Fall

Winter

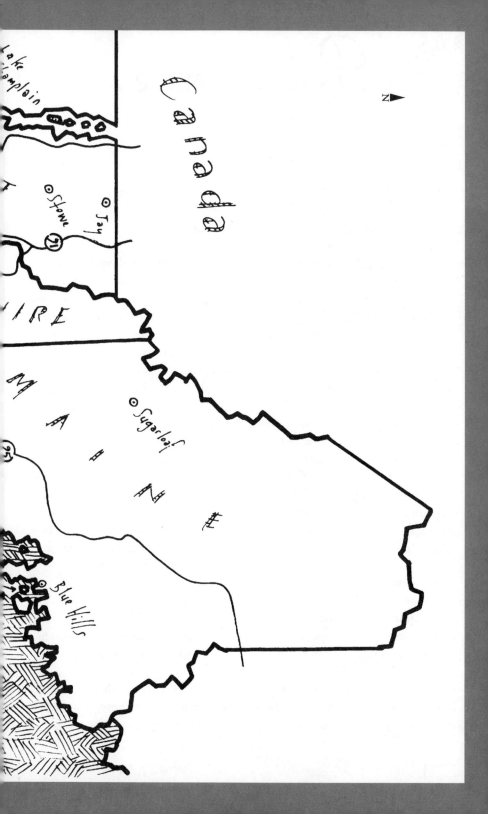

Romance.

Romance. The word is simple, yet the notion is not so easily defined. A candlelight dinner, an unexpected bouquet of roses, a sunset walk on a secluded beach. We all have images of the quintessential romantic scene. And the fact is, none of us is wrong.

A romantic moment doesn't have tangible prerequisites. Rather, it's a fleeting interlude that removes us from the mundane. It does, however, require that we be with our loved one. Romance, after all, can't be experienced alone. Moreover, it requires that we participate together in an extraordinary experience. It might be as simple as a shared soak in a hot bath or a sunset picnic in a local park. Or it could be as extravagant as a weekend escape to a country inn.

These romantic getaways, so often talked about and so infrequently spent, are fantastically special for many reasons. First and most importantly, the only agenda is to spend time together. But also, they provide a refreshing extended escape from our workaday lives. Unlike longer, planned holidays, these getaways feel almost clandestine

– as if we are stealing time. They are more unexpected, more frivolous, and so more romantic.

Enter *Romantic New England Getaways.* This guide is designed to unleash your imagination – to point you in the direction of romance. We have undertaken the truly awesome task of finding the most romantic locales in these six states. And while New England is home to hundreds of romantic spots, we chose only those that meet the criteria we consider essential for an amorous escape:

BEAUTY – whether it be awe-inspiring natural vistas or the charm of urban brownstones and manicured parks.

MEMORABLE ACCOMMODATIONS – places with charm and personality, from cozy B&Bs to elegant hotels.

GOOD RESTAURANTS – they needn't be high priced or fancy (although some are), but they must have ambiance, fine food, and an unhurried atmosphere.

DIVERSE ACTIVITIES – should there be a change in weather or mood, alternative options are important.

While some destinations included in *Romantic New England Getaways* are old favorites, such as Boston and Newport, many are on roads less traveled. Still other locations, like Nantucket and Block Island, are extolled for their off-season charm. Our aim is to ferret out the offbeat and unspoiled, because one of the most exciting components of a romantic holiday is finding your own special place.

Unlike most guidebooks that provide laundry lists of things to do, places to stay, and restaurants to visit, *Romantic New England Getaways* offers highly specialized (and personalized) information. It doesn't suggest where you could go, but specifically tells you where you should go for the perfect romantic retreat.

Destinations are categorized by season. Five locations are highlighted for summer, fall, winter, and spring. Each chapter contains four sections: a short introduction; descriptions of suggested accommodations; detailed daily activities from day hikes to museum trips, including restaurants to visit; and finally, directions and visitor information. Itineraries are planned from Friday night arrival through Sunday departure. Additional suggestions are included at the end of each chapter should you be lucky enough to escape for a three-or four-day weekend.

While the itinerary is specific, it is not intended to be rigid. You should consider it a guide to help optimally plan your trip. However, keep in mind that each weekend's suggested schedule has been carefully organized with significant thought to pacing, attraction schedules, and mood.

In addition to seasonal breakdowns, *Romantic New England Getaways* categorizes weekends according to personal interests. Because there is no one- size-fits-all getaway, we've identified four basic types of romantic individual (with accompanying icons):

THE CULTURAL ROMANTIC – prefers courting in art galleries, museums, and city streets, to wildflower fields.

THE ATHLETIC ROMANTIC – considers mutually sustained optimal heart rate the highest form of togetherness. Enjoys hiking, biking, and simply communing with nature.

THE HISTORIC ROMANTIC – waxes poetic about cemeteries, battlegrounds, and war vessels. Learning together is their most potent aphrodisiac.

THE GOURMET ROMANTIC – focus is food and wine. These connoisseurs enjoy all the finer things in life, and also take great pleasure in buying each other little trinkets between meals.

Of course some people enjoy a variety of activities; hiking and shopping and visiting museums. Most weekends offer several different types of activities. To help select the weekends that would most please you, appropriate icons appear at the beginning of each chapter.

A price index is also provided. Accommodations and restaurants are rated as:

$ inexpensive, less than $50 for a double room/less than $25 for dinner for two.

$$ moderate, less than $100 for a double room/less than $50 for dinner for two.

$$$ moderately expensive, less than $150 for a double room/less than $75 for dinner for two.

$$$$ expensive, more than $150 for a double room/more than $75 for dinner for two.

Although most people will splurge on a romantic weekend, not everyone has the same checkbook balance. While many romantic spots are indeed costly, some of the most charming hotels and restaurants are surprisingly moderate.

This guide also provides a romance rating of one to four hearts for restaurants and inns (lunch spots are excluded). Although the establishments detailed in *Romantic New England Getaways* are included precisely because they are romantic, even in this rarefied stratum, some are more conducive to romance than others.

So read, enjoy, and of course, amour! ♥

Quick Reference Guide

Inn	Location		Price	
1661 Inn	Block Island, Rhode Island	♥ ♥ ♥	$$-$$$$	🚲
Addison Choate Inn	Cape Ann, Massachusetts	♥ ♥	$$	🚲 🍴 📖
Antiques & Accommodations	Mystic and Stonington, Connecticut	♥ ♥ - ♥ ♥ ♥	$$-$$$$	🚲 🍴 📖
Apple Tree Inn	Lenox and the Berkshires, Massachusetts	♥ ♥	$$-$$$$	🚲 🍴 📖
Bayberry Heath	Block Island, Rhode Island	♥ ♥ ♥	$$	🚲
Black Lantern Inn	Jay and Montgomery, Vermont	♥ ♥	$$	🚲 📖
Blantyre	Lenox and the Berkshires, Massachusetts	♥ ♥ ♥ ♥	$$$$	🚲 🍴 📖
Blue Hill Inn	Down East–Blue Hill and Deer Isle, Maine	♥ ♥ ♥	$$-$$$	🚲 🍴
Boston Harbor Hotel	Boston, Massachusetts	♥ ♥	$$$$	🍴 📖
Boulders, The	Litchfield Hills, Connecticut	♥ ♥ ♥ ♥	$$$$	🍴 📖
Bow Street Inn	Portsmouth, New Hampshire	♥ - ♥ ♥	$$-$$$	🍴 📖
Breakfast at Tiasquam	Martha's Vineyard, Massachusetts	♥ ♥	$$-$$$	🚲 📖
Brehmer Graphics	Wellfleet, Massachusetts	♥	$$	🚲 🍴 📖
Brook Farm Inn	Lenox and the Berkshires, Massachusetts	♥	$$-$$$	🚲 🍴 📖
Cahoun Hollow Bed & Breakfast	Wellfleet, Massachusetts	♥ ♥	$$	🚲 🍴 📖

Centerboard Guest House	*Nantucket, Massachusetts*	♥ ♥ ♥	$$$	
Charlotte Inn	*Martha's Vineyard, Massachusetts*	♥ ♥ ♥ ♥	$$$$	
Cliff Lodge	*Nantucket, Massachusetts*	♥ ♥ ♥	$$$	
Cliffside Inn	*Newport, Rhode Island*	♥ ♥ ♥	$$$-$$$$	
Colonial Inn	*Concord and Lexington, Massachusetts*	♥	$$-$$$$	
Corner House	*Nantucket, Massachusetts*	♥ ♥ ♥	$$-$$$	
Eaglebrook at Grafton	*Grafton and Weston, Vermont*	♥ ♥	$$	
Eden Pines Inn	*Cape Ann, Massachusetts*	♥ ♥	$$-$$$	
Edson Hill Manor	*Stowe, Vermont*	♥ ♥	$$$	
Elm Tree Cottage	*Newport, Rhode Island*	♥ ♥ ♥	$$$-$$$$	
Fore the Rocks	*Jay and Montgomery, Vermont*	♥ ♥ ♥	$$	
Four Chimneys Inn	*Nantucket, Massachusetts*	♥ ♥	$$$-$$$$	
Gables, The	*Lenox and the Berkshires, Massachusetts*	♥ ♥ ♥	$$-$$$$	
Goose Cove Lodge	*Down East—Blue Hill and Deer Isle, Maine*	♥ ♥ - ♥ ♥ ♥	$$-$$$$	
Governor's House Inn	*Portsmouth, New Hampshire*	♥ ♥	$$-$$$	
Green Mountain Inn	*Stowe, Vermont*	♥ - ♥ ♥	$$-$$$	
Greenwoods Gate	*Litchfield Hills, Connecticut*	♥ ♥ ♥ ♥	$$$$	
Gundalow Inn	*Portsmouth, New Hampshire*	♥ ♥ - ♥ ♥ ♥	$$	
Haus Andreas	*Lenox and the Berkshires, Massachusetts*	♥ ♥	$$$-$$$$	
Hawthorne Inn	*Concord and Lexington, Massachusetts*	♥ ♥	$$-$$$$	
Herbert Hotel	*Sugarloaf and Kingfield, Maine*	♥	$$	

Name	Location	Rating	Price	Features
Hilltop Haven	*Litchfield Hills, Connecticut*	♡-♡♡	$-$$	✎ ⚘
Inn at Castle Hill	*Newport, Rhode Island*	♡-♡♡	$-$$$$	✎ 📖
Inn at the Brass Lantern	*Stowe, Vermont*	♡	$$-$$$	🚲 ⚘
Inn at Thorn Hill	*Jackson, New Hampshire*	♡♡	$$	🚲
Inn on Cove Hill	*Cape Ann, Massachusetts*	♡♡	$-$$	🚲 ✎ ⚘ 📖
Inn on Winter's Hill	*Sugarloaf and Kingfield, Maine*	♡♡	$$-$$$	🚲 ✎ ⚘ 📖
Ivy Lodge	*Newport, Rhode Island*	♡♡♡	$$-$$$	🚲 ✎ ⚘ 📖
John Peters Inn	*Down East — Blue Hill and Deer Isle, Maine*	♡♡♡	$$-$$$$	🚲 ✎ ⚘ 📖
Longfellow's Wayside Inn	*Concord and Lexington, Massachusetts*	♡	$$	🚲 ✎ ⚘ 📖
Manor House, The	*Litchfield Hills, Connecticut*	♡♡-♡♡♡	$$-$$$	🚲 ✎ ⚘ 📖
Mayflower Inn	*Litchfield Hills, Connecticut*	♡♡♡♡	$$$$	🚲 ✎ ⚘ 📖
Nestlenook Farm	*Jackson, New Hampshire*	♡♡♡	$$$-$$$$	🚲
North Hero House	*Lake Champlain Islands, Vermont*	♡-♡♡	$-$$	🚲
Notchland Inn	*Jackson, New Hampshire*	♡♡	$$-$$$	🚲
Old Tavern at Grafton	*Grafton and Weston, Vermont*	♡♡	$$	🚲 ✎ 📖
Outermost Inn	*Martha's Vineyard, Massachusetts*	♡♡♡	$$$-$$$$	🚲 ⚘ 📖
Paisley & Parsley	*Jackson, New Hampshire*	♡♡♡	$$	🚲
Pilgrim's Inn	*Down East – Blue Hill and Deer Isle, Maine*	♡♡♡	$$$	🚲 ✎
Pomegranate Inn	*Portland, Maine*	♡♡♡♡	$$	✎ ⚘ 📖
Portland Regency	*Portland, Maine*	♡-♡♡	$$-$$$	✎ ⚘ 📖
Randall's Ordinary	*Mystic and Stonington, Connecticut*	♡♡	$$-$$$	🚲 ✎ 📖
Ritz-Carlton	*Boston, Massachusetts*	♡♡♡♡	$$$$	✎ ⚘ 📖

Rose Apple Acres Farm	*Jay and Montgomery, Vermont*	♥	$$	🚲 🐾
Rowell's Inn	*Grafton and Weston, Vermont*	♥ ♥ ♥	$$$	🚲 🔑 🐾 📖
Sea Breeze, The	*Block Island, Rhode Island*	♥ ♥ ♥ ♥	$$$-$$$$	🚲 🔑 🐾 📖
Sea Cliff	*Wellfleet, Massachusetts*	♥ ♥ ♥	$$$$	🚲 🐾 📖
Seacrest Manor	*Cape Ann, Massachusetts*	♥	$$-$$$	🚲 🔑 🐾 📖
Shiverick Inn	*Martha's Vineyard, Massachusetts*	♥ ♥	$$-$$$$	🚲 🐾 📖
Shore Acres Inn	*Lake Champlain Islands, Vermont*	♥-♥ ♥	$$	🚲
Sise Inn	*Portsmouth, New Hampshire*	♥ ♥	$$-$$$$	🔑 🐾 📖
Steamboat Inn	*Mystic and Stonington, Connecticut*	♥ ♥ ♥ ♥	$$-$$$$	🚲 🔑 📖
Sugarloaf Mountain Hotel	*Sugarloaf and Kingfield, Maine*	♥-♥ ♥	$$-$$$$	🚲 📖
Ten Acres Lodge	*Stowe, Vermont*	♥ ♥	$$-$$$$	🚲 🐾
Ten Lyon St.	*Nantucket, Massachusetts*	♥ ♥ ♥	$$$	🔑 🐾 📖
Terrace Townhouse	*Boston, Massachusetts*	♥ ♥ ♥	$$	🔑 🐾 📖
Thomas Mott Homestead	*Lake Champlain Islands, Vermont*	♥	$$	🚲
Thorncroft Inn	*Martha's Vineyard, Massachusetts*	♥ ♥ ♥	$$-$$$$	🚲 🐾 📖
West End Inn	*Portland, Maine*	♥ ♥	$$	🔑 🐾 📖
Wilder Homestead Inn	*Grafton and Weston, Vermont*	♥ ♥	$$	🚲 🔑 📖

Spring

Boston, Massachusetts

Cape Ann, Massachusetts

Concord & Lexington, Massachusetts

Mystic & Stonington, Connecticut

Newport, Rhode Island

Boston, Massachusetts

*B*eans, Brahmins, banned books, and, of course, the Kennedys. Boston, the nation's 7th largest urban center, has many associations.

For those who've never visited Boston, let alone New England, it represents one of the last urban strongholds of polite society. While Boston is indeed a genteel place – filled with Victorian brownstones, cobblestone streets, and stalwart Yankees who live frugally "off the principal"– it is also a city brimming with cultural diversity.

The North End is Boston's Italian stronghold. Alive with pastry shops, cafés, and a never-ending string of religious festivals, it provides an old-world anchor. Conversely, the South End is a progressive neighborhood, home to much of Boston's gay and art communities. It is also an area most noted for its renaissance. Old brownstones, once boarded and worn, have in the past decade been transformed into truly regal residences.

Although not quite the equivalent of New York's Time Square, Kenmore Square is in constant motion. Between the neon night clubs, Fenway Park, and Boston University students swarming the streets, it is a true urban spectacle.

And of course there's the Back Bay and Beacon Hill, two neighborhoods that typify what the rest of the world imagines Boston to be. Gaslights dot brick sidewalks, and magnificent brownstones with bow front windows line the streets. The city's Brahmins really do live here, the swan boats still glide through the Public Garden's pond, and the Ritz Carlton still serves high tea complete with finger sandwiches.

What makes Boston such a vibrant and livable city, however, is not simply its gentility – for as a whole it is far from genteel – but rather, its vigorous embrace of old world values as well as all things modern, from rap music to spa cuisine.

Spring in Boston is particularly glorious. Unlike most cities that have bulldozed virtually all traces of greenery, Boston is unusually lush. Jonquils sprout in the Public Garden, magnolias sweeten the Back Bay air, sailboats drift along the Charles, and people crowd the outdoor cafés enjoying the season's first warm breezes.

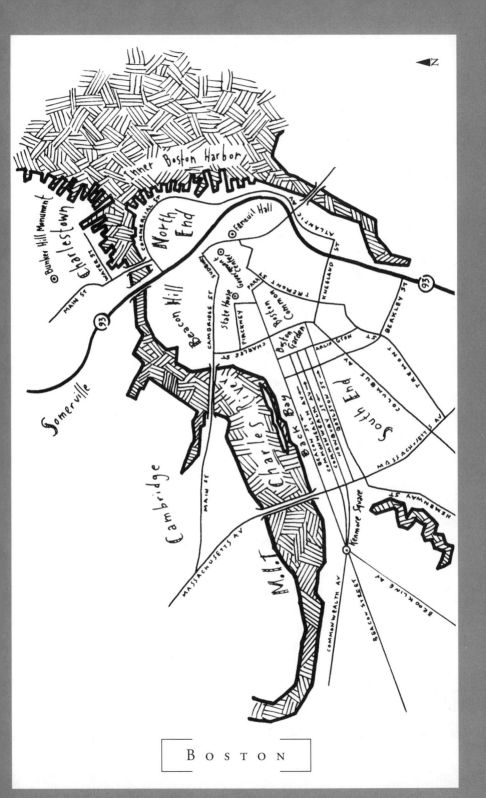

N

Inner Boston Harbor

Bunker Hill Monument

Charlestown

North End

Faneuil Hall

ATLANTIC ST

93

COMMERCIAL ST

WATER ST

MAIN ST

93

Beacon Hill

Somerville

Cambridge

State House

CAMBRIDGE ST

PINCKNEY

CHARLES ST

SUDBURY ST

Government Center

PARK ST

TREMONT ST

KNEELAND ST

BEAKLEY ST

93

Boston Common

Boston Garden

ARLINGTON

South End

TREMONT

COLUMBUS AV

BEACON ST

Back Bay

MARLBOROUGH ST

COMMONWEALTH AV

NEWBURY ST

BOYLSTON ST

MASS AV

MASSACHUSETTS AV

Charles R.

MAIN ST

MASSACHUSETTS AV

M.I.T.

COMMONWEALTH AV

Kenmore Square

HEMENWAY ST

BEACON STREET

BROOKLINE AV

BOSTON

Where To Stay

The Terrace Townhouse, ♡ ♡ ♡, $$, 60 Chandler St. 02116, 617/350-6520. If you don't need 24-hour room service or an on-site cocktail lounge, you won't find a more elegant place to stay in Boston. This B&B is a lovingly restored 1870 town house, which is resplendent in crystal chandeliers, Oriental rugs, and 18th and 19th century antiques. All four rooms have private baths and showers, with separate antique wash basins and marble sinks, ornamental fireplaces, and telephones. Be sure to ask for the "London Drawing Room," which has a queen-size, four-poster canopy bed draped in curtains, and is decorated with authentic English antiques.

Breakfast is served in rooms daily. Proprietor Gloria Belknap, a former caterer who attended La Varenne in Paris, prepares everything herself. Morning staples include fresh-squeezed orange juice, scones, yogurt, fresh fruits, and whatever entree strikes Gloria's fancy.

Common areas include a library and lovely roof deck with a view of the entire city. It's a great place to take your afternoon tea.

Nestled on a quiet, tree-lined street, The Terrace Townhouse is just a few blocks from the theater district, Newbury Street shopping, and downtown.

RATES PER NIGHT: $115-$140 May 1 - November 30, $105-$125 December 1 - April 30.

ACCOMMODATIONS: 4 rooms with private baths.

AMENITIES: Telephones in rooms.

RESTRICTIONS: No children under 14. No smoking. No pets.

The Ritz-Carlton, ♡ ♡ ♡ ♡, $$$$, 15 Arlington St. 02117, 617/536-1335. Some luxurious new hotels have opened in Boston over the past decade, but the Ritz is still *the* hotel. Just as the Plaza is the axis of uptown Manhattan, so is the Ritz – poised at the tip of Newbury Street and overlooking the Public Garden – the hub of Boston's trendiest district.

The Ritz has inspired a variety of romantic endeavors since it first opened in 1927: it's where Tennessee Williams wrote parts of "A Streetcar Named Desire," Richard Rodgers composed "Ten Cents a Dance," and Oscar Hammerstein developed the lyrics to "Edelweiss."

Although all the rooms are plush – decorated with French Provincial furnishings, imported fabrics, and fine pieces of art – be sure to ask for a fireplace suite overlooking the Public Garden. (Yes the fireplaces really work and the windows really open.) For an additional fee, the Ritz offers a "Romantic Holiday"; your room will come equipped with fresh flowers, a half-bottle of chilled champagne, and a selection of fruits and sweets.

However, it's not just the little touches, decor, or location that make the Ritz special; it simply exudes elegance. Here you can experience traditional afternoon tea, or nightly dancing to a live swing band. Granted, spending a weekend at the Ritz isn't something you'll probably do every year. But for a special getaway, its refinement and old world charm can't be surpassed.

RATES PER NIGHT: $600 for a one-bedroom suite overlooking the Public Garden (only the suites have fireplaces), $250-$350 for individual rooms.

ACCOMMODATIONS: 278 rooms with private baths, 47 suites with private baths.

AMENITIES: Two restaurants serving breakfast, lunch, high tea, and dinner. Roof deck restaurant serves drinks and dinner in season. Lounge with live entertainment. 24-hour room service. Health club. Televisions, telephones, and honor bars in rooms. Some suites with fireplaces.

RESTRICTIONS: Only small pets welcome.

Boston Harbor Hotel, ♡ ♡, $$$$, 70 Rowes Wharf 02110, 617/439-7000. Since the Boston Harbor Hotel burst on the scene in August 1987, it has been heralded as not only a grand luxury hotel, but also as an urban architectural triumph. Its rotunda-topped 80-foot arch spectacularly frames Boston Harbor and allows public access to the waterfront.

The hotel is indeed elegant – with its marbled lobby, crystal chandeliers, fine oil paintings, and deferential but not fawning help. Rooms reflect the quality you expect at any four-star accommodation – pleasant, understated decor and many amenities: honor bar, fluffy towels, and bathrobes. (There is no mistaking, however, that you are at a large hotel.) What gives Boston Harbor its real ambiance its its unmatched location. Where else can you open your windows to draw in fresh sea air, have views of the navy blue ocean dotted with yachts and fishing vessels, and catch a boat that takes you directly from your hotel to the airport – in seven minutes!

The Harbor View Café moves outdoors in spring, and in the evening twinkles with decorative lights. The nighttime panorama, with airplane lights shooting in and out of the sky and boats glimmering under the moonlight, is truly magical.

Room service is offered 24 hours a day. Why not take advantage? Order a nightcap and have the waiter set the aperitifs at your window-side table.

RATES PER NIGHT: $220-$340, $390-$580 for suites, $750 for Governor's Suite, $1,290 for Presidential Suite.

ACCOMMODATIONS: 230 rooms with private baths, 28 suites with private baths

AMENITIES: Restaurant serving breakfast, lunch, and dinner. Lounge. 24-hour room service. 24-hour pressing and laundry service. Health club. Televisions, telephones, and mini bar in rooms. Complimentary shoeshine.

RESTRICTIONS: None.

FRIDAY EVENING

Note: This evening is meant to be taken on foot. Hence there are few "in transit" references. Ask for a street map at your hotel. If you're staying at the Boston Harbor, take a cab to the Ritz, a central location. Or take the "T" (short for the Massachusetts Bay Transit Authority, Boston's subway system) there. From South Station, take the red line to Park Street, then the green line to Arlington Street. The Ritz is on the corner of Arlington and Newbury. You can walk to your destination from there.

Drinks

Hampshire House, Oak Room Bar and Café ♡ ♡ ♡ ♡, $$$, 84 Beacon St., 617/227-9600. Located at the foot of Beacon Hill and above the Bull & Finch (the bar on which Cheers was modeled), this is the perfect place to begin a weekend in Boston. The dark paneling, roaring fireplace, leather chairs, and tall paneled windows overlooking the Public Garden make you feel as if you've been whisked back to another era. (Don't worry about the tourists visiting Cheers, they'd rather comment on how none of the bartenders resembles Sam, than venture upstairs.) Hours: 5:00 P.M. - 12:00 P.M., closes earlier if business is slow.

Biba, ♡ ♡ ♡, $$$$, 272 Boylston St., 617/426-7878. This restaurant is considered by most critics to be among the best in the city, if not the country. And while this may be true, it can get a tad noisy for a romantic interlude. However, Biba's intimate ground-floor bar is a treat. The dark murals depicting well-fed people engaged in amorous pursuits, faux-painted mustard walls, and post-modern metal chandeliers all help give Biba its too-hip-to-live image. The scene, as well as the bar snacks, are not to be missed. Hours: 5:30 P.M. - 1:00 A.M., 2:00 A.M. on Saturdays.

Dinner

Hungry i, ♡ ♡ ♡ ♡, $$$, 71½ Charles St., 617/227-3524. A fabulously romantic setting, the Hungry i is tucked away in a small garden-level spot on the flat of Beacon Hill. To get there, walk through a narrow, roofed alley. Open the door and walk down into a long, dimly-lit, brick-walled room adorned with antique china.

The only two windows are of the diminutive, eye-level, cellar variety, giving the place a truly clandestine aura. In good weather you can dine on the i's back patio – even smaller than the dining room, it is nonetheless pleasant. Start your meal with a champagne cocktail (the Hungry i has no hard liquor license). The menu is short and specializes in French country cuisine; entrees primarily focus on fish and fowl. Although the food is good and attractively presented, the pièce de résistance is truly the ambiance. Hours: 6:00 P.M. - 9:30 P.M.

Davio's, ♥ ♥ ♥, $$-$$$, 269 Newbury St., 617/542-2121. If you're looking for al fresco dining under the stars, you won't find a place finer than Davio's. Located on Boston's most chic thoroughfare, Davio's is casually sophisticated with camel-colored canvas umbrellas and large black iron tables. Street musicians gently serenade and the scene shimmers with indirect light from nearby storefronts.

Moreover, Davio's serves great Northern Italian food. All pastas and sausage are homemade. And although the menu is fairly traditional, it has inventive twists. For example, veal scallopinne is served with sun-dried tomatoes, grilled endive, and roasted shallots. If you choose to eat indoors (don't unless the weather is inclement), head downstairs. Although it's more expensive than the upstairs café, the atmosphere is quiet and more intimate. Hours: 5:00 P.M. - 11:00 P.M.

Jasper's, ♥ ♥ ♥, $$$$, 240 Commercial St., Boston, 617/523-1126. In transit: This is the only recommendation outside the Back Bay. Your best bet is simply to take a cab from where you're having drinks. The ride should take no more than 10 minutes.

Gourmets should be advised that they haven't really eaten in Boston until they've eaten at Jasper's. Nationally regarded, Jasper's is considered the best restaurant in Boston. (Julia Child celebrated her 80th birthday here.) Chef Jasper White deftly mixes refined and hearty foods for his own unique version of New England cuisine.

The menu changes regularly. But some selections you might find include shrimp bisque, pear and celery root salad, and a tossed salad of endive and watercress with blue cheese and walnuts. White is most famous for his seafood entrees: among them, grilled lobster sausage, Maine rock crabcakes, and sauteed scallops served with rigatoni and a spinach and pine nut sauce.

The dessert menu is unusually extensive and includes some delicious fruit sorbets (the banana is sublime), ice cream, and hearty confections, such as chocolate poundcake with hazelnut ice cream.

Those used to a lot of flash and the unusual food combinations served at many of today's trendy restaurants could be disarmed by the simplicity of White's cuisine. Yet everything is cooked and served flawlessly.

Surprisingly, the interior is, if not quite forgettable, unremarkable. The walls are very pale peach and decorated with oversize antique French wine and liqueur posters. Hours: From 6:00 P.M. Closed Sunday and Monday. Reservations are a must.

Coffee / After Dinner Drinks

IN TRANSIT: You can walk to all the after dinner suggestions from any of the recommended restaurants, except Jasper's. The only spot to which you might consider taking a cab is Java. Just a bit off the beaten path, a cab would be safer if you're traveling late at night.

Java, ♥, $, 558 Tremont St., no phone. Located in Boston's South End, a culturally diverse neighborhood and stronghold of the city's gay community, Java is an urban phenomenon. A hangout for the neighborhood's artsy crowd, Java serves only coffee, fresh squeezed orange juice, and homemade sweets (when the owner is in the mood to bake). In a garden-level space, Java is appointed with some eye-catching modern furniture. A fireplace glows in the front room. And the back area, where the coffee bar is located, looks out onto a small garden.

Sidle up to the bar, place your order for caffe latte and then take a seat near the fireplace and sit back for some great people watching. You can linger over your coffee for hours and no one will bother you. About as funky as they come, Java is the perfect respite for the urban adventurer. Hours 3 P.M. - 11 P.M. (or thereabouts.)

Plaza Bar, ♥ ♥ ♥, $$$, Copley Plaza Hotel, 138 St. James St., 617/267-5300. This bar is an old-world classic. Walls are dark wood paneled, chairs are upholstered, and the ornately carved ceiling is painted in gold. Floor lamps cast a soft light, and waitresses quietly glide through the room in flowing black skirts. If you're looking for real class – along with some good nightly jazz music – the Plaza Bar is the place to find it. Hours: 5:00 P.M. - 2 A.M., Monday through Saturday. (Jacket and tie are recommended for men.)

SATURDAY MORNING

Historical Walk from Charlestown to Faneuil Hall.

In transit: From your hotel, take a cab to the corner of Main and Monument streets in Charlestown. (The T doesn't go to Charlestown.) Although you can take a bus, a cab is the most sensible alternative. The monument is visible from this intersection.

Walk uphill on Monument Street to the Bunker Hill Monument. As you walk, you'll notice the changing character of Charlestown: once a decidedly run-down, blue-collar and predominately Irish enclave, it's fast becoming a fashionable place to live.

The Bunker Hill Monument, a 221-foot granite obelisk, commemorates one of the first battles of the American Revolution and is a must visit for history buffs. The 294-step walk to the top is arduous, but worth it for the spectacular view of the city. A small museum, located at the base of monument, has dioramas of the battle.

From the monument, follow the red stripe in the street to the Charlestown Navy Yard and the U.S.S. Constitution. The walk takes about 10 minutes. The stripe, which may seem odd, represents Boston's Freedom Trail. Today, 14 sites are connected via the wide red stripe, thus making it simple for tourists to give themselves a walking tour of historic Boston.

The U.S.S. Constitution is the oldest surviving commissioned warship in the world. "Old Ironsides" was first launched in 1797 and fought against the Barbary pirates and the British in the war of 1812. It never lost a battle. Guides take visitors on tours throughout the ship, and additional exhibits and audio-visual displays help give a real sense of shipboard life in the 1800s.

Although the entire Navy Yard isn't open to the public, you can admire the exteriors of the still-standing 200-year-old brick Marine barracks, officers quarters, and Muster House.

Lunch

The Sail Loft, $$, 80 Atlantic Ave., 617/227-7280. In transit: From the Navy Yard, follow the Freedom Trail's red stripe over the Charlestown Bridge to Boston's North End and Commercial Street. But instead of following the Freedom Trail to Hull Street, continue down Commercial to Atlantic Avenue, which runs along Boston Harbor.

While it attracts the young executive singles crowd at night, The Sail Loft remains one of Boston's great casual restaurants – particularly at lunch when it's minus the hordes. Although there is no outdoor dining, it does have a small deck for cocktails, and picture windows offer a tremendous view of Boston Harbor as well as a glimpse of some impressive boats moored at a nearby dock. Polished wood floors and dark blue tables carry out the nautical theme. Although the menu includes typical lunch fare, e.g., sandwiches and burgers, the Loft is known for its fish. The onion rings and fries here are a treat as well. Hours: 11:30 A.M. - 10:00 P.M. Monday and Tuesday, 11:30 A.M. - 11:00 P.M. Wednesday through Saturday, 12:00 P.M. - 10:00 P.M. Sunday.

A café at Faneuil Hall.

In transit: To get to Faneuil Hall from Atlantic Avenue, walk down to the Marriott Long Wharf Hotel, on the corner of Atlantic Avenue and State Street. Walk through the underpass to Faneuil Hall, it's visible from the Marriott.

If you'd prefer to eat outdoors, Faneuil Hall, Boston's famous outdoor shopping and restaurant galleria, has some fun outdoor cafés that offer great people watching. Following are two of the best bets:

The Salty Dog, $$, Faneuil Hall, 617/742-2094. The Dog is a favorite with locals; it lacks the phony attempt-to-be-trendy ambiance so common at many Faneuil Hall eateries. Although the menu includes sandwiches and salads, this restaurant's claim to fame is its fried fish plates and hand-cut onion rings. It's always fun to sit outside under the Dog's bright blue umbrellas and watch the crowds stroll by. (If the outdoor café is closed because of weather, it's best to eat lunch elsewhere. You'll get the same good food inside, but the atmosphere is nowhere near as pleasant.) Hours: 11:00 A.M.. - 1:00 A.M. Monday through Saturday, 10:00 A.M. - 1:00 A.M. Sunday.

The Marketplace Café $$, Faneuil Hall, 617/227-9660. A little more sophisticated than many other outdoor cafés, this large breezy spot is in a prime

location at the tip of Faneuil Hall. Even if the weather is less than perfect, you'll find a lovely greenhouse that makes you feel as if you're outside. The menu ranges from herbed grilled chicken to fish and chips. Hours: 11:00 A.M. - 11:30 P.M. Monday through Thursday, 11:00 A.M. - 1:00 A.M. Friday, 10:00 A.M. - 1:00 A.M. Saturday, 10:00 A.M. - 11:30 P.M. Sunday.

SATURDAY AFTERNOON

Strolling Newbury Street.

In transit: You can catch a cab from Faneuil Hall or at the Marriott Long Wharf on Atlantic Avenue. If you prefer public transportation, take the T's Green Line inbound from Government Center. To get there, walk through Faneuil Hall from Atlantic Avenue. When you reach the end you'll see a long set of steps leading up to City Hall. At the top of those steps is the Government Center stop. Get off at Arlington Street; this runs perpendicular to Newbury.

Newbury Street is the nerve central of Boston's cultural and couture community. It is here that you'll find the bulk of the city's art galleries and boutiques, not to mention beautiful people.

Start at the Ritz-Carlton, at the corner of Arlington and Newbury Streets, and walk the length of the street to Massachusetts Avenue; round trip is about two miles. You'll notice the distinct, although not entirely dissimilar, flavors of the street's two ends. Arlington is all elegance and refinement, and Massachusetts Avenue has a decidedly "downtown", student-oriented flavor.

Following is a list of some of the more interesting shops and galleries along the street. All stores are open until at least 5 P.M. and many until 7 P.M.

Alan Bilzerian, 34 Newbury St., 617/536-1001. Considered to be the hippest clothing store in Boston, Bilzerian caters to the nontraditional dresser who wants to make a statement. A favorite with rock stars making stops in town, Bilzerian counts Mick Jagger and Bruce Springsteen as past customers.

La Ruche, 168 Newbury St., 617/536-6366. This exclusive home decoration store is an institution on Newbury Street. Known for its wonderful selection of French and Italian faïence dishes and kitchenware, trompe l'oeil furniture, and unusual linens, pillows, and lamps, it's a goldmine for the elegant knickknack junkie.

Essence, 39 Newbury St., 617/859-8009. You can take the romanticism of perfume to a new level by creating a unique fragrance. With more than 300 oils in stock – from Egyptian jasmine to French vanilla – this salon specializes in personally blending perfumes. On a trip to Boston, Madonna herself dropped by to get a scent custom mixed.

Her choice was a combination of African musk and vertiver.

Gargoyles Grotesques & Chimeras, 262 Newbury St., 617/536-2362. Bizarre name. Bizarre store. But definitely worth a visit. When you step into this tiny space, you'll feel as if you've entered an abandoned mausoleum. With all manner of gargoyles (decorative pieces – traditionally roof spouts – carved in the image of grotesque human or animal figures) and dried fallen leaves on the floor, the store has an eerie feel. But the wall hangings, candelabras, and statues are oddly fascinating. Not made from traditional stone, but plaster, the objects are surprisingly light. Romantic, you ask? Of course. There's nothing more fun than huddling together and sharing a good dose of fear.

Eastern Accent, 237 Newbury St., 617/266-9707. Eclectic, modern selection of art objects to wear and display – frames, vases, earrings, watches, and more. The store is small, but it's got a nice selection of merchandise. Great spot to purchase a frame for that perfect snapshot of the two of you.

Art Galleries

Barbara Krakow Gallery, 10 Newbury St., 617/262-4490. A long established avante-garde gallery, Krakow displays a range of local, national, international, and emerging artists.

Vose Galleries of Boston, 238 Newbury St., 617/536-6176. Run continuously by five generations of Voses, this is the grand dame of the city's traditionally-oriented galleries. It features primarily American artists from the colonial period through the early 20th century, especially the Boston School.

Society of Arts & Crafts, 175 Newbury St., 617/345-0033. Not a fine art gallery per se, but a serious craft gallery with works by local and national American artists. Wonderful spot for finding unusual pottery.

SATURDAY EVENING
Dinner

A trattoria in the North End, Boston's version of Little Italy. In transit: Take a cab to Hanover Street, the neighborhood's main thoroughfare. Tell the driver to let you off at Martignetti's. It's a well-known liquor store at the top of Hanover and an easy landmark. From there you can walk to your restaurant and tour the streets.

Note: Although in the past decade, many have complained of the North End's "yuppification," it is still an Italian stronghold. On summer evenings older women in their de rigueur black dresses sit on apartment stoops and discuss the day's events – in Italian. Men, young and old, chat outside cafés. And streets are filled with scents of tomato sauce and olive oil emanating from the many neighborhood restaurants.

Even though you're just a visitor, walking through the North End makes you feel part of a community, where neighbors *all* know each and mothers still call out windows for their children to come home for supper.

The North End is popular, not just for its local color, but for the plethora of good, reasonably priced restaurants. (Don't expect "new" Italian fare – sage foccaccia or radicchio with balsamic vinegar – at any of these restaurants.) Consequently most any place worth eating at is jammed on Saturday night. Since few of the area restaurants take reservations, it's not uncommon to see lines forming outside these trattorias. Not to worry, that's part of the atmosphere. Relax, lean back on a parked car and enjoy the scene.

Giacamo's, ♡ ♡, $$-$$$, 355 Hanover St. 617/523-9026. A relative newcomer to the North End scene, Giacomo's has quickly become one of the most popular neighborhood restaurants. Part of the reason is its warm atmosphere. Ambient lighting, brick walls, wood floors, and a few well-placed oil paintings make the place far more welcoming than many of the garden-variety, red-checkered tablecloth restaurants. But even if Giacomo's didn't have the feel of a cozy café, people would still flock because the food is so good.

Grilled fish and meats are its specialties, and even standard Italian fare is done with a light hand. If you're a seafood lover, try the linguine con frutte de mare (fruit of the sea) – clams, shrimp, scallops, lobster, tossed in a garlicky red sauce, served over a bed of pasta. Add a bottle of Valpolicella and some of Giacomo's crusty bread and you've got a memorable meal. Hours: 5:30 P.M. - 10:30 P.M. Monday through Saturday, 5:00 P.M. - 10:00 P.M. Sunday.

5 North Square, ♥ ♥, $$-$$$, 5 North Square, 617/720-1050. Don't let the Suzanne Somers photo plastered to the window scare you away. A cozy, little restaurant, 5 North Square has a modern look and a hearty, old-world menu. The downstairs dining room boasts large picture windows, thus making the most of the restaurant's location: a quiet cobblestone street next to Paul Revere's House. Decor is simple - embossed gray tin walls, wine-colored café curtains and tablecloths, and small oil lamps on each table. Although the upstairs dining room menu is the same, the atmosphere is slightly more formal with white walls and tablecloths and a few ornate mirrors and an antique-china filled hutch.

Food is reassuringly Italian – fettuccine Alfredo, linguine with clams sauce, chicken parmigiana. Daily specials, however, are more adventurous. The restaurant's owners, a husband and wife team who grew up in the North End, oversee the kitchen, and their attentive-ness shows: Everything truly tastes homemade. Hours: 5:30 P.M. - 10:30 P.M.

Coffee And Dessert

Part of the North End's romance is that it's so European. People stroll down the streets at night, hopping from café to café, sipping espresso and gossiping. After your meal, take a walk – perhaps down Hanover Street. Or you might stroll around North Square (from Hanover, turn right on Richmond Street, then left on North Street.)

Browse in the pastry shop windows. Peer into the the Italian social clubs: Off limits to nonmembers, the doors are usually open to reveal men playing cards and smoking cigars. And of course, work up an appetite for an Italian sweet and aperitif.

Caffe Paradiso, ♥ ♥, $, 255 Hanover St., 617/742-1768. This small café is the most well known espresso bar in the North End. Part of its claim to fame is that it has the only 2:00 A.M. liquor license in the area. Beyond that, all its gelati (Italian egg yolk-based ice cream) and sorbetti are homemade. The place is long and narrow and the mirrors on the wall give the impression that Paradiso is packed. And it usually is. Hours: 7:00 A.M. - 2:00 A.M.

Caffe Vittoria, ♥ ♥, $, 296 Hanover St., 617/227-7606. With dark marble tables and Venetian murals, this spot has a heavy-handed decor that so many Americans associate with "Italian." What gives Vittoria its charm is that it's not attempting to look ethnic, it just is. Witness the men gathered around tiny tables chattering in Italian and daintily sipping from espresso cups. Locals rub elbows with business people, students, and visitors alike, giving Vittoria a jovial, party-like atmosphere. Hours: 8:00 A.M. - 12:00 A.M.

If you still have some energy, stroll down to the waterfront. From Hanover Street, turn onto Richmond Street, to Waterfront Park. Wooden benches line the sidewalks and park, and are perfect perches for gazing at Boston Harbor.

In transit: From the park, you can catch a cab back to your hotel. They frequent Atlantic Avenue, the street at which Richmond dead ends. Or you can turn right on Atlantic and right on State Street toward Faneuil Hall, which swarms with cabs. For public transportation, walk through Faneuil Hall until you are facing the City Hall steps. Walk up the steps to the Government Center subway stop. However, if you're staying at the Boston Harbor Hotel, you just have a 10-minute walk up Atlantic Avenue.

Sunday Brunch

The Ritz Dining Room, ♡ ♡ ♡, $$$$, 15 Arlington St., 617/536-5700. In transit: From the Terrace Townhouse and Chandler Street, turn right onto Clarendon Street and walk down to Newbury. Turn right onto Newbury to the Ritz. From the Harbor, take a cab. You can also take the T from South Station to Park Street. Then take the green line inbound to Arlington Street.

On the second floor of the hotel, with picture windows overlooking the Public Garden, the Ritz Dining Room is tastefully ornate with crystal chandeliers and a gold-filagreed ceiling. If you're in the mood for something extravagant and formal (jacket and ties are required), there is no other brunch in Boston. The buffet offers more than 60 items, and includes a glass of champagne and a shrimp cocktail. Hours: 10:45 A.M. - 2:30 P.M.

St. Cloud, ♡ ♡ ♡, $$$, 557 Tremont St., 617/353-0202. In transit: From the Back Bay (Ritz and Terrace Town-house), walk south on Clarendon Street. The Cloud is on the corner of Clarendon and Tremont streets.

Although the St. Cloud is best known for its dinners, unbeknownst to many, its serves a wonderful brunch. You won't find a buffet or 25 different types of omelettes. The menu is relatively short, but selections range from eclectic egg dishes to granola and fresh fruit. If you're a waffle fan, the Cloud's version is delicately crisp, and topped with raspberries and warm syrup.

Ambiance is very New York, stark white walls, large colorful murals, and huge picture windows for surveying the street. Not surprisingly, the crowd is hip. The South End is much quieter than the Back Bay and Newbury Street, particularly on a Sunday. But that's what makes it so relaxing. A great place to stop on a sunny morning. Hours: 11:00 A.M. - 4:00 P.M.

SUNDAY AFTERNOON

Visit the Isabella Stewart Gardner Museum, 280 The Fenway, 617/566-1401. In transit: From the Arlington Street T station, take the green line's E train to the Museum stop. Walk down Museum Road past the west wing of the Museum of Fine Arts. Turn left on The Fenway to number 280.

The Gardner is Boston's most well-loved museum, and is considered to be among the finest private house museums in the world. The building, Fenway Court, a replica of a 15th century Venetian palazzo, was the home of the museum's namesake.

Elizabeth Stewart Gardner, a wealthy New York socialite who married a proper Bostonian, had an insatiable appetite for fine music and art; it is Gardner herself who actually formed the collection, designed the building, and ultimately endowed it. Both eclectic and eccentric, the museum includes works from Botticelli, Manet, Rembrandt, Rubens, Matisse, and Whistler. As Gardner requested in her will, all pieces remain in the spots that she chose for them. She lived in Fenway court until her death in 1924.

Be sure to take a break in the museum's four-story courtyard. With a profusion of flowering plants, fountains, and a mosaic floor from a second century Roman villa, it is one of the most picturesque and peaceful spots any-where. Hours: 12:00 P.M. - 6:30 P.M. Tuesday, 12:00 P.M.- 5:00 P.M. Wednesday through Sunday.

Walking Tour of Beacon Hill.

In transit: From the Museum T stop take the green line E train inbound to Arlington Street. Or you could ask a museum official to call you a taxi. (Cabs don't frequent the Fenway as they do other areas.) Another option is to walk five minutes to Longwood Avenue for a cab. When leaving the museum turn left. Then turn left on Palace Road to Longwood Avenue. Direct the cab driver to the Ritz-Carlton. From there you can begin a tour of Beacon Hill.

This is unquestionably the most well known neighborhood in Boston. It was settled by the city's elite Brahmins and is still home to a socially insular community. However, it is the best place to drink in the flavor of historical Boston. Save the cars and trendy restaurants, Beacon Hill, with its cobblestone streets, gas lanterns, brick sidewalks and 150-year old town houses, looks much the same as it did in the 19th century. Taking a walk here, especially at dusk – after the daytime hubbub and before the evening's hustle – is like taking a walk through the past. In fact, the experience can be almost eerie.

For history buffs, Beacon Hill is a veritable treasure trove. And while it is pleasant to simply wander the streets and snoop into people's windows or browse through Charles Street antique shops, you might find your walk more interesting if you have some historical information. Although you can find brochures at the Boston Visitors Centers, they are mostly rudimentary. A good source for detailed information on architecture and topography is the *Blue Guide for Boston and Cambridge*. It can be found at most book stores in the city.

Start your walk at the corner of Arlington and Newbury streets, head through the Public Garden, then up Beacon Street to the State House. Its gold dome is probably the singular most recognizable symbol of Boston architecture. The building, used by the Massachusetts legislature since 1798, was originally designed by Charles Bulfinch, and the cornerstone of the building was laid by then Governor Samuel Adams. Turn left just past the State House, then left again to walk under the State House portico. You are now on Mt. Vernon Street.

Number 85 Mt. Vernon is considered the grandest mansion on the hill. It is, however, a private residence and not open to the public. Built around 1800, it is distinguished by two Corinthian pillars at the door and a cobblestone driveway that leads to what once were stables.

Continue down to Louisburg Square, the most prestigious address in Beacon Hill, if not in all Boston. These homes are the 19th century versions of modern town houses.

Walk around the Square and follow Mt. Vernon Street to Charles, turn right on Charles and head up Pinckney Street. Although not quite as grand as Mt. Vernon, Pinckney has a quirky charm all its own. This street is the boundary between the Hill's prestigious south slope and the pedestrian north slope that leads to Cambridge Street.

Number 81 Pinckney was once the home of Louisa May Alcott, author of Little Women. Number 4 Pinckney was the home of another literary star, Henry David Thoreau. And Number 5, known as the Middleton-Glapion House, is believed to be the oldest house on the Hill, dating back to 1791. It is named after two free black men who originally bought the plot of land on which the house now stands.

On your way back down Pinckney, you might want to take a detour to West Cedar Street, one of the Hill's many charming side streets. From there, turn right onto Mt. Vernon, then left on Charles Street.

Charles Street is Beacon Hill's street of commerce. But in addition to a hardware store, two convenience markets, and pharmacy, you'll find a good selection of antique stores. Among the more notable:

Danish Country Antique Furniture, 138 Charles St., 617/227-1804. Emphasis is on simple blonde wood pieces – a r m o i r e s , tables, and bed frames. Many items are from the 18th century.

Richard Kazarian Antiques, 70 Charles St., 617/720-2758. This store specializes in quirky show-stopping pieces, e.g., iron candelabras. None of the merchandise is priced, just coded. But if you have to ask...

Marika's Antiques, 130 Charles St., 617/523-4520. A quintessential antique store that smells of dust and is crammed with merchandise. Worth a look for the interesting china, silver, and Oriental pieces.

Early Evening Snack

Caffe Bella Vita, $, 30 Charles St., 617/720-4505. In transit: Bella Vita is on the end of Charles Street nearest to the Boston Common. If you're walking toward the Common, it's on the right.

This simple café, with startling raspberry-colored walls is the kind of spot where locals come with a book, order an espresso, and sit for two hours. It's not that the food is so fabulous – the menu consists primarily of sandwiches, pastries, and gelati – but with picture windows that face Charles Street, it's the perfect place to enjoy the spectacle of urban life. Hours: 8:00 A.M. - midnight

Additional Activities

A Night with The Boston Pops, at Symphony Hall, 301 Massachusetts Ave., 617/266-1492. The Pops is a Boston institution, playing primarily show tunes and popular music. (Until recently it led by Oscar-winning conductor John Williams.) Going to the Pops is a relaxed event; the wooden seats are removed from the Symphony's main floor and are replaced with tables and chairs where refreshments are served. The Pops are in residence at Symphony Hall from early May to mid July. Hours: 8:00 P.M. Tuesday through Saturday, 7:30 P.M. Sunday.

Sunset Cruise around Boston Harbor, Bay State Cruises, 67 Long Wharf, 617/723-7800. Could there be a better way to end the day? On weekdays, boats depart at 5:30 P.M. and return at 7:15 P.M., on weekends they return at 8:15 P.M. Bay State also offers extended daytime tours and whale watches. (The cruises don't start until late April.)

Rollerblading along the Charles River. If you've never tried the nation's newest craze, the miles of smooth, paved paths along the Charles are the perfect place to perfect your technique. Beacon Hill Skate Shop (135 Charles St. South, 617/482-7400) rents skates for $10 a day. Ask for directions to the Charles from the store.

A Red Sox Night Game at Fenway Park, Ticket Office, 4 Yawkey Way, 617/267-8661. Even if you're not the biggest baseball fan, there's something magical about an evening under the lights of Fenway. Unlike many big league parks that are located off an interstate, Fenway is part of the urban scene. Originally built in 1912, it's considered one of the last remaining classic baseball parks. (Remember, Kevin Costner visited it in "Field of Dreams.") Arrive early just to catch the scene of souvenir sellers, hot sausage hawkers, and passersby.

Dinner at Hammersly Bistro, $$$, 578 Tremont St., 617/267-6068. Critics across the nation have been singing Hammersly's praises for years. Come see for yourself what all the talk is about. Ambiance is very much like a real French bistro – casually elegant and boisterous. Dress is informal, food is simple (roast chicken is a menu staple), but artfully prepared. Hours: 6:00 P.M. - 10:00 P.M. Monday through Saturday, 6:00 P.M. - 9:00 P.M. Sunday.

GETTING THERE

By AIR: All major airlines service Logan International Airport. The real trick to traveling by air is leaving the airport. Taxis and shuttles are an option, but traffic in the Callahan-Sumner Tunnel, which connects the airport to Boston proper, is notorious. A relaxed alternative, which also boasts a stunning approach to Boston, is the Airport Water Shuttle (800/235-6426). It runs year-round and departs from Logan Airport to Rowes Wharf every 15 minutes, Monday through Friday 6:00 A.M. - 8:00 P.M. and every 30 minutes on Saturday and Sunday from 12:15 - 7:45 P.M. The trip takes about seven minutes. A one-way adult fare is $7.

Be sure to stop for a drink at the Harborview Lounge at the Boston Harbor Hotel, which is built on Rowes Wharf. As its name implies, the lounge boasts a spectacular view of Boston Harbor. From there, catch a taxi to your hotel (if you're not staying at the Boston Harbor).

By CAR: If possible, travel by some other means. Everything you've ever heard about Boston drivers is true, and who needs that aggravation on a romantic getaway. If you must, downtown is accessible via I-93 and the Massachusetts Turnpike. Call your hotel for specific directions. One word of advice: park your car and don't drive again until you're ready to go home. One of

Boston's charms is its walkability, and the best way to appreciate the city's architecture is on foot. Be sure to buy a good street map once you arrive. If you get tired, use the subway, or call a cab.

BY TRAIN: Amtrak (800/USA-RAIL) has service directly into Boston via two stations, South Station and Back Bay. Get off at Back Bay if you're staying at the Ritz-Carlton or the Terrace Townhouse. Pack lightly and you can walk to either hotel. Cabs are also available from the stations. The Boston Harbor Hotel is a five-minute walk from South Station.

BY BUS: Plenty of bus lines travel to Boston: Bonanza (617/720-4110) from Rhode Island and southeastern Massachusetts, Concord Trailways (800/258-3722) from New Hampshire; Greyhound-Trailways (617/423-5810) nationwide, Peter Pan (617/426-7838) from central and western Massachusetts and New York City, and Plymouth & Brockton (800/328-9997) from southeastern Massachusetts.

TAXI/LIMOUSINES SERVICE: As with any city, there are a myriad of taxi and limousine companies. Taxis are plentiful, both at the airport and on the streets. If you'd rather call, than hail, try Checker Cab (617/497-9000) or Town Taxi (617/536-5000.) If you're looking for special limo service, consider Classic Limo (617/266-3980.) It offers (as the name suggests) classic limousines from the '30s and '40s, as well as late-model luxury cars, including Rolls Royces. For a traditional limo, try Commonwealth Limousine Service (617/787-5575).

INFORMATION: It's best to get your information on Boston before you visit. Write or call the Greater Boston Convention and Visitors Bureau, P.O. Box 490, Dept. IA, Boston, MA 02199, 617/536,4100. The bureau operates two information centers, one at Boston Common, 146 Tremont St., and at the Prudential Plaza, 800 Boylston St. Hours: 9:00 A.M. - 5:00 P.M. daily.

Cape Ann, Massachusetts

Cape Ann is known among New Englanders as "the other Cape." *The* Cape, of course, is Cape Cod, a place whose stature relies more on past mythology than present reality. Reminiscent of the rugged Maine coast, Cape Ann is smaller, quieter, and although it attracts tourists from around the world, has not succumbed to commercialism. It is still today, as it was 300 years ago, a quiet Yankee stronghold populated by fishermen, artists, and people who simply love the sea.

Essex, Manchester, Gloucester, and Rockport comprise Cape Ann. While Essex and Manchester are essentially residential communities, both Gloucester and Rockport cater to travelers.

America's oldest seaport, Gloucester is beautiful yet undeniably gritty. Still a vital port and fish processing town, its harbors are more crowded with trawlers than with yachts. Its culture is shaped by the Italian and Portuguese immigrants drawn to Gloucester's plentiful waters, as well as by artists drawn to its impressive coastline. In fact, Rocky Neck, a small harborside section of East Gloucester, has been designated America's oldest artist colony by the Smithsonian Institution.

Rockport too is known for its artist colony. Although Bearskin Neck is more commercial than Gloucester's version, the town itself is far quieter and retains the air of a summer playground for the well-to-do.

In addition to these artistic offerings, Cape Ann has a wealth of other cultural activities. Among them is the Gloucester Stage Company, whose artistic director is the award-wining playwright Israel Horovitz. Of the area's several historic museums, the most famous is Hammond Castle. It is the one-time home of Dr. John Hays Hammond, who is second only to Thomas Edison as the nation's greatest inventor.

For those interested in less cerebral pursuits, Cape Ann offers some excellent biking routes, coastal state parks for hiking, whale watches, and sailing adventures.

Despite all these activities, Cape Ann is still known to many as just a beach resort. However, it is equally (if not

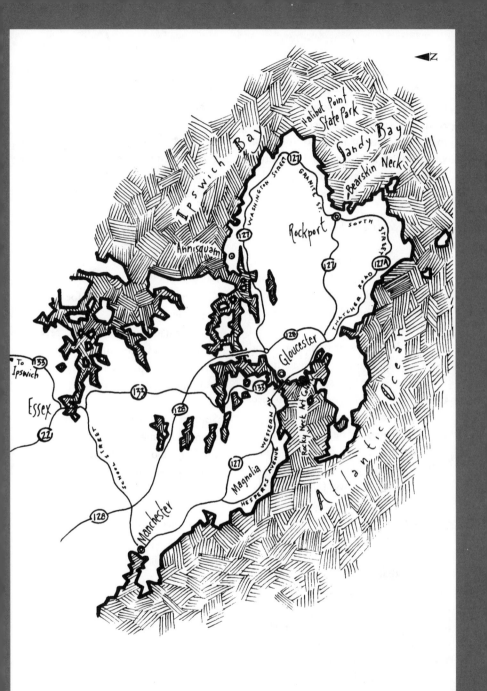

Ipswich Bay

Halibut Point State Park

Sandy Bay

Bearskin Neck

121

WASHINGTON STREET

GRANITE ST.

Rockport

SOUTH STREET

127

Annisquam

127

127A

THATCHER ROAD

128

Gloucester

To Ipswich

133

Atlantic Ocean

133

Essex

133

127

ROCKY NECK AV.

WESTERN AV.

127A

SCHOOL STREET

27

127

Magnolia

HESPERUS AVENUE

Rocky Neck Art Colony

128

Manchester

CAPE ANN

more) pleasant in the late spring and fall. (Note that many attractions don't open until May.) The crowds are gone. And the cooler temperatures will make you less inclined to spend all your time at the beach, and encourage you to explore some of the region's less obvious, but equally enticing, charms.

Where To Stay

The Seacrest Manor, ♡, $$-$$$, 131 Marmion Way, Rockport 01966 508/546-2211. Located on top of a rugged knoll on a quiet residential street, the Seacrest Manor offers commanding views of both woods and sea. Originally built as a private home, Seacrest, as its name suggests, has the feel of an English country house. Common rooms are pleasantly decorated, if a little frumpy. They include a well-stocked library, a dining room, and a living room that has huge windows and expansive ocean views. (Unfortunately, the living room also has some outdated dark wood paneling and acoustic ceiling tile that detracts from its graciousness.) All public rooms have fireplaces that are kept stoked on all but the warmest nights.

For the most part, guest rooms have a cozy, grandmotherly ambiance. Most are decorated with floral wallpaper and chenille bedspreads. Furniture includes some well-placed antiques mixed with a few 1960s motel-style pieces. If you can, choose room 7 or 8. Both have king-size beds, beautiful ocean views, and a private entrance to the second story deck.

Town & Country has called Seacrest's complimentary breakfast among the 50 best in the nation. It includes fresh squeezed orange juice, spiced Irish oatmeal, and a special selection that might be blueberry pancakes or bacon and eggs. In addition, tea is served every afternoon.

Civility is the byword for owners Leighton Saville and Dwight MacCormack. Their special services include men's shoeshines, complimentary morning papers (except Sunday), and nightly pillow mints.

Seacrest has a magnificently landscaped lawn. A tremendous oak sits outside the front door, and in the backyard are carefully tended gardens, overflowing with flowers.

RATES PER NIGHT: $76-$102. Seacrest Manor is open from April through November.

ACCOMMODATIONS: 6 rooms with private baths, 2 rooms share a bath; 3 rooms have private access to a porch or deck.

AMENITIES: Televisions in some rooms.

RESTRICTIONS: No children. No pets.

The Addison Choate Inn, ♥♥, $$, 40 Broadway, Rockport 01966, 508/546-7543. What the Addison Choate Inn lacks in an oceanside setting, it makes up for in country charm. This casually gracious inn features gleaming pumpkin pine floors, restored woodwork, and authentic antique furniture. Innkeepers Chris and Peter Kelleher have done a fine job making the place at once homey and elegant.

Common rooms include a split living room: on one side, a few cozy chairs are arranged by the fireplace, and on the other is a television and stereo. Among the nice touches are two wall hangings: an antique wedding-ring quilt and a framed Ming dynasty gold embroidered Mandarin silk suit.

Each of the eight guest rooms has its own character, but the most elegant is the Captain's Room. It includes a queen-size, fishnet canopy bed, deep-blue walls, Chinese lamps, oil paintings of ships, and hand-hooked rugs.

If you're looking for more space, consider the third-floor suite. It's the only room with a view of the ocean, albeit over several rooftops. Other amenities include a stereo system, and a bath with a deep-soaking tub and stained glass skylight.

For complete privacy, opt for the Stable House, a quaint three-room cottage behind the inn and overlooking the swimming pool. A bit more casual than the main house, its features include rough-hewn beams, terra-cotta floors, stained glass windows, and teak furniture, as well as a color television and a private picnic and barbecue area.

Each morning, Chris serves homemade muffins and other treats on the flower-filled porch. In inclement weather, she delivers breakfast in bed.

RATES PER NIGHT: $83-$87 June 15 through Columbus day, $84-$110 for suite, $100 for stable house.

ACCOMMODATIONS: 6 rooms with private baths, one two-room suite with bath, one private three-room suite.

AMENITIES: Air conditioning in some rooms. Television in carriage house. Outdoor pool.

RESTRICTIONS: No smoking. No pets.

The Eden Pines Inn, ♥♥, $$-$$$, Eden Pines Road, Rockport 01966, 508/546-2505. (Address from November through April is c/o 8 Cakebread Drive, Sudbury, MA 01776.) If Eden Pines Inn was any closer to the ocean, it would undoubtedly set sail. And even though the inn is not a ship, but a rambling turn-of-the century gray shingled beach house, it sits so precipitously close to the water, you're likely to think you are at sea.

The inn has a casual and comfortable ambiance that's an extension of innkeepers' Inge and John Sullivan's warmth. They are among a small group of innkeepers who really make guests feel like old friends.

When you enter the front door, you'll walk right into the living room, which is blessed with picture windows that face the Atlantic. The room itself has a large fieldstone fireplace, beige wall-to-wall carpeting, and comfortable upholstered furniture.

Adjacent to it is the airy breakfast room with sea grass floor mats, wicker furniture, and grass green curtains. It leads to two decks and a dipping pool. Although the inn is right on the ocean, the nearest beach is a 15-minute walk. The pool is great for cooling off when you're sunning on the deck.

All six guest rooms are pleasant and comfortable and have ocean views. Decor includes pastel carpeting, wicker and rattan furniture, and an occasional antique. Most baths are unusually large and done in Italian marble. Five rooms have private decks. Despite these amenities, the Sullivans aren't big on high fashion or country motifs. Their style is entirely uncontrived.

If you're looking for space and elegance, opt for room 6. It has a queen-size, canopy bed with flowing curtains, seafoam green carpeting, and muted floral curtains. Although slightly smaller, room 5, outfitted with white wicker furniture and decorated in shades of peach and mint, is equally cheery.

Each morning Inge and her daughter Carol bake muffins and coffeecakes for breakfast. Their efforts are augmented by cereals, fruit, yogurt, juice, and coffee. In the afternoon, usually about 3 o'clock, you're likely to find a plate of homemade cookies and pitchers of lemonade and ice tea.

In the early evening, the Sullivans provide drink set-ups. Because Rockport is a dry town, it's nice to have a cocktail on the deck before you head out to dinner.

RATES PER NIGHT: $100-$120, July through October; $80-$120 May, June, and October. Eden Pines is closed November through April.

ACCOMMODATIONS: 6 rooms with private baths. 5 rooms have private decks.

AMENITIES: Air conditioning. Dipping pool.

RESTRICTIONS: Smoking on outside decks only. No children under 10. No pets.

Inn on Cove Hill, ♡ ♡, $-$$, 37 Mount Pleasant St., Rockport 01966, 508/546-2701. For people who enjoy old homes, the Inn on Cove Hill is a treat. The house was built in 1791, and innkeepers Marjorie and John Pratt have gone to great lengths to maintain the building's integrity, and to give guests a sense of living in the past.

You enter the inn through a small vestibule that has an original spiral staircase leading to the second floor. To the left is the common room, the only community area in the inn. The Pratts restored the original wide pine floors and dentil molding and have decorated the room with authentic period furniture, including family heirlooms.

Like so many colonial homes, the inn has low ceilings, relatively small rooms, narrow halls, and steep stairs. Those who don't appreciate authenticity might find it a bit claustrophobic.

Marjorie is a stickler for detail, and has outfitted guest rooms with Oriental and hand-hooked rugs, quilts, and Federal period antiques or good reproductions. A few rooms that were added in the 19th century have Victorian furnishings—wicker chairs and white iron bedframes.

Room 8 has a great view of Rockport harbor, as well as a fishnet-lace canopy bed, a Danish pine armoire, and delicate mauve, blue, and white wallpaper. Another choice room is number 6, which has red and cream Laura Ashley wallpaper, white wainscoting, a lovely hand-hooked gray and nasturtium colored rug.

Although it's on the first floor and faces Rockport's main street, room 10 is a charmer. It has its own front porch with two cherry red rockers. The room, decorated in the Victorian style, includes a white iron bed, white wicker chairs, and a grand clawfoot tub in the bath.

For breakfast, John grinds fresh coffee and makes muffins from scratch. In warm weather the Pratts serve on the patio or, if guests prefer, on one of the upper decks that face the harbor. When it's cool, they deliver breakfast in bed.

RATES PER NIGHT: $46-$91 Memorial Day weekend through October, $43-$73 November to Memorial Day.

ACCOMMODATIONS: 9 rooms with private baths, 2 with shared bath.

AMENITIES: Televisions and fans in rooms.

RESTRICTIONS: No smoking. No pets.

FRIDAY EVENING

Strolling Rocky Neck.

In transit: From Rockport Center, follow Route 127 to Gloucester. At the rotary, turn onto East Main Street. There will be a sign indicating this is the way to Rocky Neck. From there, simply follow the signs. A central lot offers free parking.

With any luck, you will be able to arrive on Cape Ann before dusk. This will give you a chance to stroll Rocky Neck,

Gloucester's famous art colony. With seemingly hundreds of brightly colored fishing shacks cum studios, the place is truly unforgettable. Deemed the oldest art colony in the nation by the Smithsonian Institution, such greats as Winslow Homer and Milton Avery have painted and lived on this small shard of earth that juts into the sea.

Although some live here year round, in season (from Memorial to Labor day) about 30 artists set up camp. Naturally, most come to paint the sea. But you can find some photographers and tactile artists as well. Seasonal hours are from 10:00 A.M. to 10:00 P.M.

Strolling the streets and ducking in and out of little studios is a great way to find a beloved piece of original art –and–work up an appetite for supper.

Dinner

The Raven, ♡ ♡, $$-$$$, 197 East Main St., Gloucester, 508/281-3951. In transit: If you've parked your car, you can walk to the Raven. It will take about five minutes. At the intersection for East Main Street, turn left. The Raven is on the left.

If an ocean view isn't on your list of "must haves" tonight, The Raven is an interesting alternative. This funky storefront, reminiscent of a French café, serves inventive seafood and continental cuisine.

The single dining room is small and intimate, with deep-wine-colored decor.

Walls are adorned with oversized antique posters advertising French wine.

Begin with fried oysters served with wilted spinach and sesame ginger mayonnaise, or a salad of romaine and arugula with fried calamari, black olives, roasted pepper, and Caesar dressing.

Besides a selection of pastas, entrees include a fisherman's stew with saffron, and tenderloin Havana, which is served with black bean sauce, rice, and vegetables. Hours: 5:00 P.M. - 10:00 P.M. Tuesday through Sunday.

The Rudder, ♡, $$-$$$, 73 Rocky Neck Ave., Gloucester, 508/283-7967. In transit: If you're walking along Rocky Neck Avenue, The Rudder is at the end of the street on the right.

A fixture on Rocky Point for nearly three decades, The Rudder is an off-beat restaurant that is known as much for its impromptu entertainment as for its food. The Rudder is run by a mother and two daughters, any of whom might break into song or a baton twirling act at the drop of a hat. (The paid entertainment is a piano player and singer who's happy to take requests.)

Obviously, this is not the place to go if you're looking for some quiet conversation and longing gazes. But The Rudder is a fun, casual place–it's housed in a former fish-packing plant–that also happens to have an outside deck that sits right on the water.

The food is good and reliable, and the menu entirely traditional. Appetizers include New England clam chowder, French onion soup, and smoked mussels with horseradish cream. Although The Rudder does offer meat dishes, its specialty is fish. Selections range from baked stuffed shrimp to fried clams. Locals claim that the Rudder's baked sole with spinach stuffing is the best around. Hours: From 6:00 P.M. No reservations accepted. The Rudder also serves lunch and Sunday brunch. Open from April through mid October.

SATURDAY MORNING

Tour Rockport on the Cape Ann Trolley, Dock Square, 508/546-5950 or 508/546-2553. In transit: From Route 127, head straight on Broadway to Rockport center. At the end of the street, take a left. Dock Square is right in the center of downtown Rockport. Or from Marmion Way, turn right onto South Street and head back toward the center of town. South turns into Mt. Pleasant Street, which runs into Main Street and Dock Square.

This engine-red, open-air trolley may look hokey, but it's a great way to tour Rockport. The one-hour trip travels on several oceanside roads, providing a glorious view of some of Rockport's finer homes. A guide gives a nice overview of the town's history. (The tickets are good all day. You can get off at one of the 15 stops the trolley makes, then get back on

later in the day.) Hours: 10:00 A.M. - 6:00 P.M. on the hour. Weekends only in May, June, and September, and daily in July and August. Tickets: $5.

Visit Bearskin Neck; Tour Downtown Rockport on Foot. In transit: If you make a round-trip tour on the trolley, it will drop you off at its starting point, Dock Square. This square is at the tip of Bearskin Neck, and the perfect jumping off point for exploring Rockport on foot.

Bearskin Neck is Rockport's version of Rocky Neck. Although more polished and commercial, it is nonetheless picturesque. This harborside enclave is chock-full of artists' and craftsmen's studios, as well as small boutiques selling jewelry, pottery, and gourmet food. As might be expected, most of the artists who settle on Cape Ann do so to capture the landscape. If you're looking for something post modern, chances are slim that you'll find it. Most works are traditional.

If you're serious about buying, **visit the Rockport Art Association** (12 Main St., 508/546-6604). Home to 250 artist members, the association has changing exhibits. If you don't find something there, you can at least determine the artists you like, and then visit them at their studios. The RAA has a listing of all member artists, many of whom have studios in their homes.

After you've completed your tour of Bearskin Neck, take a scenic walk from Dock Square up Mount Pleasant Street to the Headlands. This rocky point, at the tip of Rockport Harbor, has benches for relaxing and paths for strolling. (This is a great spot for watching boats.) To get there, take a left on Norwood Avenue, then left again on Highland Avenue, and then walk through the shrubbery to the Headlands. You will have spectacular views of the Old Garden Beach, Straitsmouth Lighthouse, Sandy Bay, and Rockport Harbor. A paved path will take you back to Atlantic Avenue (it runs parallel to Norwood) and Mt. Pleasant Street.

Once back on Mt. Pleasant, head back toward Dock Square. Turn right on T Wharf for a view of Motif #1, arguably the most painted fishing shack in the world.

From the T Wharf, head back to Dock Square and Main Street to tour some of the shops. If you're an antique lover, don't miss Hanna Wingate, 11 Main St. (508/546-1008). Merchandise includes an unusual selection of quilts, mirrors, and furniture. If you're looking for books on the region, check out the Toad Hall Book Store, 51 Main St. (508/546-7323).

Lunch

My Place By the Sea, $$, Bearskin Neck, 508/546-9667. My place is blessed with the best perch on Bearskin Neck. Sitting at its very tip, the restaurant faces directly out into Rockport Harbor. If the weather is warm, try to sit on the lower outside deck. Views are great.

The restaurant's atmosphere is casual. You won't feel out of place in shorts and a T-shirt. Pale yellow walls, pink table clothes, and pastel green floors provide a summery feel.

Although the food isn't gourmet, it is good. Your best bet is to stick to the fish, you won't find it any fresher. My Place's seafood salad sandwich is particularly good, hearty and not too heavy on the mayo. You might also consider some poached mussels, chowder, or a boiled lobster. For landlubbers, there's also a selection of pasta and meat. If you're cutting down on fat, try a turkey burger. It's surprisingly tasty. Hours: 12:00 P.M.-3:00 P.M. Open mid May through October. My Place is also open for dinner.

SATURDAY AFTERNOON

Tour Hammond Castle, 80 Hesperus Ave., Gloucester, 508/283-7673 or 800/649-1930. In transit: From Rockport follow Route 127 to Gloucester. Continue on this route through Gloucester and continue on toward Magnolia and Manchester. About two miles past downtown Gloucester there's a small sign for Hammond Castle, just off the ground on the left side of the road. Turn left here, onto Hesperus Avenue. Hammond Castle is about a half mile on the left.

Dr. John Hays Hammond is second only to Thomas Edison as the nation's greatest inventor. Hammond, best known as the father of remote control, had more than 800 inventions and 400 U.S. patents to his name. An eccentric man, Hammond built a grand Medieval European castle on a rocky ledge overlooking the Atlantic Ocean. The castle houses his magnificent collection of Roman, Medieval, and Renaissance artifacts, as well as a 8,200 pipe organ, the largest ever built in a private home.

Hammond's collection is truly mind-boggling. It includes a Roman cathedral archway built with lava from Mt. Vesuvius, a 13th century sarcophagus, and a tile floor taken from the home of Christopher Columbus's son. The tour also includes a visit to Hammond's laboratory, where many of his inventions are on display.

After his death in 1965, the castle was opened to visitors. Hammond wanted the public to enjoy his vast collections. He is buried on the property, with two of his 35 cats. As per his request, poison ivy grows over the grave site. Admission $3.50. Hours: 9:00 A.M. - 5:00 P.M. daily. Tours are usually on the hour in season, but call ahead to verify.

Cruise on the Appledore Schooner, Tuna Wharf, Rockport, 508/546-9876. In transit: From Hammond Castle, head north on Route 127 to Rockport. At the "five corners" continue on Route 127/Broadway to end. Turn left onto Main Street and right onto Tuna Wharf.

If you enjoy the tranquility of sailing, don't miss a trip on the Appledore III. Built in 1984, to resemble the all-wood fishing schooners of the '20s and '30s, the Appledore circumnavigated the globe before she made her permanent home in Rockport.

Captain Vaughan Hawley and crew will sail the Appledore out of Rockport Harbor, past The Headlands to Straitsmouth Island, Whale Cove, Emerson Point, and the Twin Lighthouses of Thatcher's Island. The entire trip is 1½ hours. Tickets $18. Hours: 11:00 A.M., 1:00 P.M., 3:00 P.M., 5:00 P.M., and 7:00 P.M. The last sail of the day is a sunset cruise. Weekends only from mid May through mid June and daily from mid June through mid October.

Whale Watching on Yankee Fleet, 75w Essex Ave., Gloucester, 508/283-0313 or 800/942-5464. In transit: From Hammond Castle, follow Route 127 back into central Gloucester. Turn onto Route 133. Yankee Fleet is docked right at Gloucester Harbor and Route 133.

If you're looking for a little more excitement in your open-water adventure, you might prefer whale watching. Gloucester is considered one of the whale watching capitals of the world. Although many reputable vessels sail out of Gloucester Harbor, Yankee Fleet is considered one of the best operations.

This 4½ hour trip will voyage to the favorite feeding grounds of the humpback, finback, and minke whale. Scientists on board are available to offer expert commentary and answer questions. If you have a particularly keen interest, join the research scientists on the bridge and help them collect data. (The research ticket costs $15 more than regular admission.)

Sightings are virtually guaranteed. A scout ship heads out each morning at 6:00 A.M. to report whale locations by radio. You're also likely to see dolphins, porpoises, sharks, turtles, seabirds, and seals.

If you're seriously considering this option, you'll have to rearrange your morning. Consider skipping lunch at My Place, and having it instead on board ship. The food isn't fancy, but convenient. Or if you prefer, get a sandwich to go at Virgilio's (29 Main St., Gloucester, 508/283-5295) and bring it aboard. Hours: 8:30 A.M. and 1:00 P.M. Wednesday, Saturday, and Sunday, in spring and fall. Daily in summer. Admission: $20; research participant $35

SATURDAY EVENING
Dinner

Bistro at 2 Main St., ♥ ♥ ♥, $$$-$$$$, 2 Main St., Gloucester, 508/281-8055. In transit: From Rockport, follow Route 127 to Gloucester. Once you get into Gloucester center, Route 127 is known as Rogers Street. At the end of Rogers Street you'll see Washington Street on your right, and Tally's Auto Sales before

you. To the left is a public parking lot. Leave your car here. The Bistro is in the Blackburn Building, on the corner of Main and Washington streets. It's visible from the lot.

Frank Sinatra tunes wafting through the air set the tone for this intimate, eclectic restaurant, with brick walls, low ceilings, and startling country-scene wall murals.

Head chef Annalisa Tornberg, studied with nationally renowned Boston chefs Lydia Shire (Biba) and Jasper White (Jasper's). Her top-notch training shows in attention to peripherals: the basket of homemade breads including addictive olive oil bread sticks, the brilliant verdant salad, the potent coffee.

The menu is primarily new American. Yet in addition to cuisine from New England and the Southwest, it has influences from, among others, Thailand, Italy, and Mexico. Although items change seasonally, some appetizers you might find include oyster fritters, soft shredded pork tacos, and spiced crab cakes. (The latter are sublime.) Entrees include grilled sea scallops with roasted garlic lasagna, olives, and red pepper, as well as beef tenderloin with rosemary sauce and Romano mashed potatoes. Desserts are similarly inventive; among them are pear cobbler, pumpkin bread pudding, and warm beignets with ice cream and strawberry caramel sauce. They, like the entrees, change with the season. Hours: 5:30 P.M. - 10:00 P.M. Monday through Thursday, 5:30 P.M. - 11:00 P.M. Friday and Saturday.

White Rainbow, ♡ ♡ ♡, $$$$, 65 Main St., Gloucester, 508/281-0017. In transit: From Rockport, head north on Route 127 toward Gloucester. As you enter central Gloucester, 127 becomes Rogers Street. Main runs parallel with Rogers. You can park at the lot at the end of Rogers, or try your luck on Main.

When you ask most people on the North Shore to name the area's most elegant restaurant, invariably they will say "White Rainbow." The grand dame of local gourmet restaurants, it's still held in high regard. In fact, its only serious competition is the Bistro, located right down the street.

Unlike the Bistro, however, which has an eclectic menu, White Rainbow emphasizes French cuisine. (Look for lots of cream-based sauces.) For an appetizer, try lobster stew (for two), made with heavy cream, brandy, and spices, or Maui onion soup, which is made with Hawaiian Kula sweet onions simmered in chicken broth.

Entrees include grilled sea scallops served with scallop ravioli in a crabmeat cream sauce, and lobster de Montal, which is chunks of shelled lobster sautéed with scallions, exotic mushrooms, peppers, Armagnac, and cream. If you prefer meat, White Rainbow has

a selection of roasted and grilled items, including roast duck served with a Japanese barbecue sauce. A selection of French pastries is a nice (albeit caloric) ending to a classic meal.

Patrons can eat in the dining room, which has brick and granite walls decorated with oils by local artists, or in the more intimate and casual wine bar. (If you decide to eat dinner at the Bistro, you can come to the White Rainbow's wine bar for dessert and coffee.) Hours: Tuesday through Sunday 5:30 P.M. - 9:30 P.M. Saturday, 6:00 P.M. - 10:00 P.M.

After Dinner Entertainment

Attend a Play at the Gloucester Stage Company, 267 East Main St., Gloucester, 508/281-4099. In transit: From downtown Gloucester, head east on Rogers Street (it runs parallel to Main Street,) then turn right onto East Main Street. Follow signs for East Gloucester and Rocky Neck.

If you're unfamiliar with the Gloucester Stage Company, don't dismiss it as just a little community theater group. Established 14 years ago, it's still under the artistic direction of its founder, two-time OBIE award winner Israel Horovitz. Among Horovitz's Broadway credits are *The Indian Wants the Bronx* (starring Al Pacino) and *Park Your Car in Harvard Yard* (starring Jason Robards).

Horovitz's home base is this company. All his plays enjoy their world premiere on its stage, inside a converted fish processing plant. In addition to Horovitz's own work, the company performs a variety of modern plays from the likes of Harold Pinter, Herb Gardner, John Updike, and Sam Shepard.

Performances are typically held Wednesdays, Thursdays, and Fridays at 8:00 P.M. On Saturdays, it's common for Gloucester Stage to put on two evening shows. And on Sundays, shows are usually at 5:00 P.M. Tickets: $12-$18, depending on the day of the week.

Note: If you have your heart set on seeing a play, call for tickets when you are planning the trip.

SUNDAY MORNING

Bicycle Ride to Halibut Point State Park, Gott Avenue, Rockport. In transit: From Rockport center, follow Route 127 north. Look for signs to Pigeon Cove. Turn right on Gott Avenue to Halibut Point. You'll see signs. Halibut Point is less than three miles from Rockport center.

This 54-acre coastal state park encompasses an abandoned granite quarry now filled with water. (It's a little known fact that in the 1900s Rockport was one of the nation's granite capitals.) Halibut Point has splendid views of Ipswich Bay. On a clear day, you can see Crane's

Beach in Ipswich, the Isle of Shoals in New Hampshire, and Mt. Agamenticus Beach in Maine.

Amidst this dramatic setting you can walk along one of the many paths, explore the tidal pools, or just catch some sun on one of the large granite shelves. Self-guided trail brochures are available at the WWII Tower Building inside the park.

If you didn't bring bicycles or prefer not to bike, parking is available in the Gott Avenue parking lot for $5. Even if you don't bike, you can get some good exercise by walking through the park.

Lunch

Picnic at Halibut Point from Ellen's Harborside, $, 1-T Wharf, Rockport, 508/546-2512. In transit: You'll obviously have to get your sandwiches before you go for your bike ride. But Ellen's opens at 5:30 A.M., so you shouldn't have a problem. T Wharf is the wharf right in Rockport center that houses the red fishing shack Motif #1. If you're facing the water, the wharf is just to the right of Bearskin Neck.

This restaurant is a local institution. It serves up simple, reasonably-priced food in a down-home atmosphere. Locals claim Ellen's serves the best lobster roll in town. Thankfully, the restaurant offers take-out. Sandwiches come with pickles and chips.

If you want fruit, cookies, or other treats, take a short detour down Broadway (if you're in Dock Square, take an immediate left) to Tony's (508/546-7370). This great little fruit and vegetable store also sells baked goods and juices. If you're looking for junk food, a Richdale convenience store is just down the street.

Tom Shea's, $$-$$$, 122 Main St. (Route 133), Essex, 508/768-6931. In transit: From Halibut Point, continue on Route 127 toward Annisquam (away from Rockport center). Follow Route 127 into Gloucester, where it intersects with Route 133. Follow Route 133 into Essex. Tom Shea's is in Essex center, along with several other restaurants and antique shops. Or from Rockport center, follow Route 127 toward Gloucester to the intersection of Route 133.

If you're not in a picnic mood, but don't want to give up a peaceful water view, consider this popular restaurant, located on the edge of a salt marsh and the Ipswich River.

The atmosphere is a bit more formal than several of Shea's lobster shack neighbors. Yet decor is simple – whitewashed wood walls, wooden tables, large windows, and lots of plants. The food is similarly uncomplicated, but good. Boiled lobster, fried squid, fish and chips, seafood rolls, and shrimp in coconut beer butter are just a few of the staples. If you're a chowder fan, don't forget to try Shea's version. It's the best around.

Shea's can be crowded and noisy at night, because it's such a popular restaurants with locals. But at lunch you should be able to enjoy a peaceful meal. Hours: 11:30 A.M. - 4:00 P.M. Monday through Saturday, 11:00 A.M. - 2:00 P.M. Sunday.

SUNDAY AFTERNOON

Antique Shopping in Essex.

In transit: If you've made your way to Tom Shea's, you're in the heart of antique territory. But Shea's won't be happy if you leave your car in their parking lot. Move to a spot on the street. If you're coming from a picnic, simply follow directions to Tom Shea's (see above).

Although it may appear to be a sleepy, small town, Essex enjoys a national – indeed international – reputation as an antique mecca. Collectors from all over the globe visit the many Essex dealers who carry museum-quality pieces. All told, Essex boasts more than 50 antique dealers, most located within a one-mile stretch. Merchandise ranges from the nearly priceless to "attic" antiques.

Following are a few shops you should not miss:

Rider and Clarke, 144 Main St. (Route 133), 508/768-7441. One of Essex's premier shops, it specializes in 18th and 19th century American, English, and continental antiques. Merchandise includes furniture, paintings, decorations, and Oriental rugs. Even if you can't afford the stuff, it's fun to snoop.

Howard's Flying Dragon Antiques, 136 Main St. (Route 133), 508/768-7282. A tad dusty, but a treasure trove of affordable antiques. Look for everything from old post cards to grandma's mink stole. Also a huge selection of china and decorative pieces.

Walker Creek Furniture, 57 Eastern Ave. (Route 133), 508/768-7622. In transit: This shop is about a two-minute drive from the center of town. Follow Route 133 east toward Gloucester. Walker Creek is on the right.

Walker isn't an antique shop, but it's a must visit for anyone with an appreciation for fine furniture, all of which is made by one local craftsman. The workmanship is exquisite; surfaces are all hand-planed and finished. Most pieces – including chairs, tables, and hutches – have an elegant Shaker quality. If you don't see anything that suits you, Walker makes to order. In addition to furniture, the store carries a fine and well-priced selection of locally made crafts including rugs, quilts, baskets, stained glass, and pottery. Upstairs, the Goodwin Gallery shows paintings by local artists.

SUNDAY EVENING

Early Supper at Woodman's, ♥, $, 121 Main St., Essex, 508/768-6451 or 800/649-1773. In transit: Woodman's is in the middle of Essex center. If you're heading back into town from Walker's, it's on the left.

If you've spent three or more hours browsing the antique shops, you'll probably want a bite before you head for home. Most people consider a trip to Essex incomplete if it doesn't include a meal at Woodman's. A culinary landmark of sorts, it is here, in 1916, that Gramp Woodman threw some clams in a kettle of oil and fried the first clam.

Sit on one of Woodman's picnic benches, inside or out, and enjoy the taste treat for which they are famous. They also serve lobster and fish plates, as well as a tasty clam chowder. Don't expect any frills: Order at the bar and wait for your number to be called. If you can afford the calories, stop next door where Woodman's serves ice cream and frozen yogurt.

Farnham's, ♥, $, Eastern Avenue (Route 133), Essex (508/768-6643). In transit: Continue on Route 133 east, Farnham's is on the left.

Woodman's may be the most famous clam shack in New England, but ask any local and they'll tell you Farnham's serves better clams. The jury is still out, but Farnham's is a great spot if you're looking for some real small-town flavor. Don't forget to wash down your meal with a can of the locally made Twin Lights "tonic." (That's Yankee for soda.)

Visit the Cape Ann Historical Association, 21 Pleasant St., Gloucester, 508/283-0455. The association's museum has the world's largest collection of works by famed maritime painter Fitz Hugh Lane. It also has a nice collection of Revolutionary War artifacts, as well as those from the Gloucester fishing industry. The fishing exhibit includes mast figureheads, model schooners, and objects ranging from nets to foul weather gear. Admission $3. Hours: 10:00 A.M.- 5:00 P.M. Tuesday through Sunday.

Visit Beauport, 75 Eastern Point Blvd., Gloucester, 508/283-0800. Built by Roaring 20's collector and interior designer Henry Davis Sleeper, this summer retreat on Gloucester Harbor is a monument to style. The 40 rooms are filled with vast collections of American and European objects, and arranged in truly inspired compositions.

As a result of Beauport, Sleeper's reputation grew. He eventually moved beyond designing interiors for wealthy Gloucester residents to working for Hollywood celebrities – among them Joan Crawford and Frederic March. Admission $5. Hours: 10:00 A.M.- 4:00 P.M. Monday through Friday, mid May to mid September; 1:00 P.M.- 4:00 P.M. Saturday and Sunday mid September to mid October. Tours are on the hour.

Spend an Afternoon at **Crane's Beach**, Argilla Road, Ipswich, 508/356-4354. Cape Ann may have some beautiful beaches, but none can compare to Crane's in Ipswich. (The town is right next to Essex; Crane's is about a 15-minute ride from Essex center.) The four miles of white sandy beach and dune is just what the perfect beach looks like in your mind's eye. Parking is $3.25 weekdays and $3.75 weekends in spring, $6 weekdays and $10 weekends from Memorial Day through summer. (If you visit Cape Ann in summer, it's best to avoid Crane's in July. Then greenhead flies are a nuisance. If you're concerned about the flies, call the office. They're usually honest about the problem.)

Attend an Organ Concert at Hammond Castle, 80 Hesperus Ave., Gloucester, 508/283-2080 or 800/649-1930. You've toured the castle, now consider returning for an organ concert. The castle houses an 8,200 pipe organ, the largest ever built in a private home. Weekend concerts are held throughout the year. Call for information and reservations.

Attend Rockport Chamber Music Festival, C/o Rockport Art Association, 12 Main St., Rockport, 508/546-6604. Each June, the Rockport Art Association conducts a chamber music festival. In addition to scheduled concerts, patrons are invited to attend open rehearsals and lectures.

GETTING THERE

BY AIR: Boston's Logan International Airport is just 30 miles from Cape Ann. All major carriers travel to Logan.

BY CAR: From the south, take I-95 north to Route 128 north to the end. Follow Route 127A into Rockport. Route 128 can also be reached via the Massachusetts Turnpike and I-93.

BY TRAIN: The Massachusetts Bay Transit Authority (800/392-6100 inside Massachusetts, 800/872-7245 outside Massachusetts) has daily service from Boston's North Station to all of Cape Ann, including Rockport, Gloucester, Ipswich, and Manchester.

BY BUS: No bus service is available to Cape Ann, but the Cape Ann Transit Authority (C.A.T.A.) offers service among the communities. For a schedule, call 508/283-7916.

CAR RENTAL: Budget (617/787-8200), Sears (800/527-0770 or 617/787-8220), Avis (800/331-1212), Hertz (800/654-3131 or 617/569-7272), and American International (800/527-0202 or 617/569-3550) all have offices at Logan International Airport. In Rockport, call Thrifty Car Rental (508/281-2225.)

TAXI/LIMOUSINE SERVICE: Cape Ann Tours (508/546-5950) offers shuttle service direct from Logan to Rockport. One-way transportation for one to five passengers is $45. Also, MaDruga's Taxi (508/281-5550) in Gloucester and Horton's Taxi (508/546-6233) in Rockport.

INFORMATION: The Cape Ann Chamber of Commerce, 33 Commercial St., Gloucester 01930, (508/283-1601). Hours: 8:00 A.M.- 6:00 P.M. Monday through Friday, 10:00 A.M.-6:00 P.M. Saturday, 10:00 A.M.-4:00 P.M. Sunday from May through October. Off season hours are 8:00 A.M.-5:00 P.M. Monday through Friday.

Also, the Rockport Chamber of Commerce, P.O. Box 67, Rockport 01966, (508/546-5997). The Chamber has a year-round office that's open Monday through Friday at 3 Main St. and Pier Avenue. An information center is open on Upper Main Street /Route 127 from mid May to mid October. Hours: 11:00 A.M. - 5:00 P.M. Monday through Saturday, 1:00 P.M. - 5:00 P.M. Sunday.

Concord & Lexington, Massachusetts

Concord and Lexington. Their names are burned in your brain from countless elementary school textbooks. Forever connected by history as the birthplace of the American Revolution, these two Massachusetts towns are thriving communities today. Yet they maintain a strong link to the past and, combined, offer visitors an unparalleled chance to learn about our nation's earliest days.

Both towns have done an extraordinary job memorializing their history. Through museums, historic houses, and preserved sites and woodlands, you can relive the beginning of our nation, and develop a keen understanding of early American life. Visit the site where the British captured Paul Revere; tour Buckman Tavern, where the colonials gathered across from Lexington Green on the morning of the Revolution; and walk across the North Bridge, just as the Minutemen did on April 19, 1775, when they faced off against the Red Coats.

Giving flesh and blood to these memories is the town of Concord itself. (Lexington, though charming, appears a far more modern post-war suburb.) Streets are lined with well-preserved – and still-in- use–250-year-old houses. The common green is the very same on which colonists gathered. And the town meeting house (now the First Parish Unitarian Church), with its spiraling white steeple, presides over that green, just as it did in the days of John Hancock and Samuel Adams.

One of the reasons Concord holds on so strongly to its past is because that past is so glorious. Although known primarily in connection with the American Revolution, Concord played an equally significant role in early American literature and thought. Louisa May Alcott, Henry David Thoreau, and Ralph Waldo Emerson all lived and worked in Concord. And interestingly, they all lived here during the mid 1800s and were friends. In fact, it's well known among historians that Alcott had an unrequited teenage crush on Emerson, who was almost her father's age.

The homes of Alcott and Emerson are open to the public. Concord also houses a museum dedicated entirely to Thoreau that includes a replica of the house he built on Walden Pond.

Although Concord and Lexington attract tourists from all over the world, the towns are decidedly untouristy. You won't find lots of chic restaurants or fancy hotels. In fact, you won't find lots of any kinds of restaurants or hotels. As one local said of Concord, "It wants to have an international reputation, but it doesn't want anyone to visit."

Residents do want people to visit. They just don't want the towns to be overrun. Nor do they want their communities to be altered by the unbridled commerce to which so many tourist areas succumb. Thankfully, both Concord and Lexington are free from T-shirt stores and fudge shops. They remain as they have always been, simple Yankee communities.

WHERE TO STAY

The Hawthorne Inn, ♡ ♡, $$-$$$$, 462 Lexington Rd., Concord 01742, 508/369-5610. The pale pink stucco exterior looks surprisingly whimsical compared to its austere neighbors. However, the Hawthorne Inn is a Concord original, built in 1870 on land that was once owned by Ralph Waldo Emerson. The two majestic pine trees that shade the west side of the house were planted by the author himself.

Innkeepers Marilyn Mudry and Gregory Burch have done an admirable job giving the inn at once an old world and eclectic modern charm. The house is filled with a mix of period antiques, Japanese prints, South American artifacts, as well as paintings and soapstone carvings by Gregory.

While most inns have one or two prize rooms, all of Hawthorne's have equal charm. When guests arrive, Marilyn and Gregory show them all available rooms so that they can make their own decisions. If you've a penchant for sunshine, opt for one of the two rooms in Hawthorne's addition. Both have huge skylights and windows that look out on the lush back yard. The Sleepy Hollow room has a romantic lace canopy bed covered with a vibrant multicolored patchwork quilt that Marilyn made herself. (She made quilts for all the beds.)

On the second floor, the Musketequid room is the inn's most spacious. It has emerald green walls decorated with Japanese art, a floral couch, and an antique spool bed covered with a brilliant purple and blue quilt. If you're looking for something a bit less dramatic, consider the Concord room; it has a white iron bed, Danish pine armoire, antique Victorian settee, and pale pink walls.

Breakfast is served in Hawthorne's large and bright dining room, where guests sit family style at one long table. The menu is expanded continental and includes coffee, juice, cereals, yogurt, cheese, and home-baked goods.

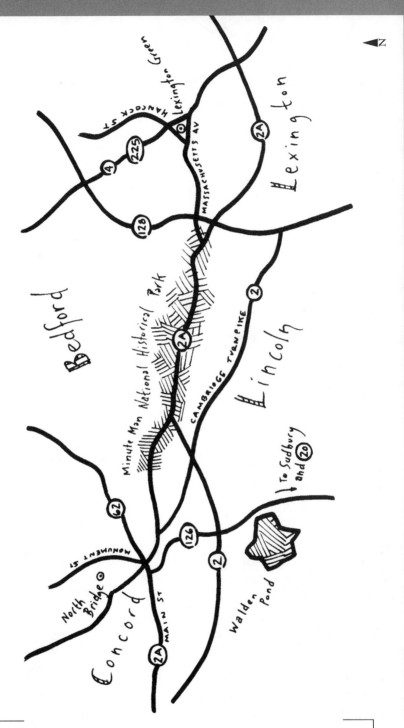

CONCORD & LEXINGTON

Marilyn and Gregory have a sense of peacefulness about them, which permeates the inn. They encourage guests to relax in the garden, and they keep plenty of books on hand, should anyone be interested in curling up with a local author. The two are also extraordinarily knowledgeable about the area, as well as Concord's history, and are a wonderful resource for suggesting what to see and do.

RATES PER NIGHT: $110-$160 April 1 through October 31, $85-$110 November 1 through March 31.

ACCOMMODATIONS: 7 rooms with private baths.

AMENITIES: Air conditioning.

RESTRICTIONS: No smoking. No pets.

The Colonial Inn, ♥, $$-$$$, 48 Monument Square, Concord 01742, 508/369-9200 or 800/370-9200. This rambling gray clapboard structure is an old-fashioned country inn that sits right on Concord Green. A hub of community activity, it's here local business people meet for lunch, young couples have their weddings, traditionalists enjoy high tea, and sports enthusiasts gather to catch a Red Sox game on television.

Built in 1716 as a private home, several additions were made to the house, even prior to the Revolution. What is now the central part of the inn was used as a storehouse during the war. In the early 1800s, the house passed to the Thoreau family. Henry David, the famed essayist and naturalist, lived here while he was attending Harvard. It wasn't until 1893 that the house was converted to an inn and opened to the public.

Today the Colonial Inn houses 54 guest rooms, all but 15 of which are in the modern motel-style Prescott Wing. Although these rooms are pleasant enough – with colonial reproduction furniture, ceramic lamps, and wing chairs – they are sterile and bland. However, some of the rooms in the main part of the inn are a treat. Many have original wide pine floorboards, rough-hewn ceiling beams, and handmade quilts.

Room 24 is the Colonial's best offering. With original wood floors, Wedgwood blue wainscoting, and an ornamental fireplace, the room has a sense of history. Furnishings include a king-size pencil post bed and two wing chairs. Another choice room is number 4. With rough-hewn ceiling beams, a hand-hooked rug, and dainty floral wallpaper, it offers a more rustic ambiance.

Breakfast is not included in the room price. But the Colonial has five dining rooms and serves breakfast, lunch, dinner, and tea. Don't be put off by the number of dining spots, all but the main Merchants Row room are small and intimate. The Colonial also has two bars. Both darkly paneled, they are fine places to relax at the end of the day.

RATES PER NIGHT: $85-$120 mid April through early September, $95-$130 early September through November 1, $75-$110 December to mid April.

ACCOMMODATIONS: 54 rooms with private baths

AMENITIES: Air conditioning, telephones, televisions in rooms. Five dining rooms. Breakfast, lunch, dinner, and tea are served.

RESTRICTIONS: No pets.

Longfellow's Wayside Inn, ♡, $$, Boston Post Road, Sudbury, MA 01776, 508/443-1776. In 1702, David How built a two-room house for his wife Hepzibah and the first two of their seven children. Fourteen years later, the state gave him permission to run a tavern and inn from his home. Today those two rooms, along with many other additions over the centuries, comprise Longfellow's Wayside Inn.

The inn is named after Henry Wadsworth Longfellow because he made the place famous in this book entitled *Tales From a Wayside Inn*. This notoriety, combined with the fact that the Wayside is the oldest operating inn in the United States, draws thousands of tourists to its doors annually.

Although the inn has a gift shop, waitresses dressed in quasi-colonial garb, and a relatively steady stream of tour bus groups, the Wayside has undeniable charm. Despite its sprawling appearance, the clay colored clapboard inn only houses 10 guest rooms. Of those rooms, 9 and 10 are the oldest, both dating back to the early 1700s. Room 9, which was open on our visit, had wide board wooden floorboards painted a soft gray, rough-hewn paneling, low beamed ceilings, and a king size bed covered with a chenille spread.

Other rooms are similarly appointed, though a bit brighter. Most have white walls with red or blue wainscoting, Oriental scatter rugs, and wing chairs. Several rooms have twin beds, so be sure to ask for a double room when making reservations.

A full breakfast, included in the price of the room, is served in the Tap Room. This part of the Wayside was built in 1796, and thus has an authentic tavern ambiance with unvarnished wooden floors, low ceilings, and fireplace with a beehive oven.

The Wayside sits on more than 100 acres of land, and has on its property a chapel, one-room schoolhouse, and grist mill where organically grown wheat and corn are ground and then used in all the inn's baked goods. All buildings are open to the public. In addition, the Wayside has lovely walking paths, and a rose and wildflower garden. They also keep a carriage and a few horses on hand to take guests on rides through the property.

Sudbury is about 15 minutes from Concord center. Yet this inn is recommended because of its historical significance. It's a great place to stay when planning an "all" history weekend.

RATES PER NIGHT: $70-$80.

ACCOMMODATIONS: 10 rooms with private baths.

AMENITIES: Telephones in rooms. Restaurant and bar. Air conditioning. Gift shop. Carriage rides.

RESTRICTIONS: No pets.

FRIDAY EVENING
Dinner

Aigo Bistro, ♥ ♥, $$-$$$, 84 Thoreau St. at Depot Square, Concord, 508/371-1333. In transit: From Monument Square in Concord center, turn onto Main Street. Go through the center. Then turn left onto Thoreau Street. Aigo Bistro is on the right at Depot Square, a small shopping complex.

Concord's first and only gourmet dining spot, Aigo Bistro (pronounced Eyego) has surprising sophistication for a casual country restaurant. Located inconspicuously on the second floor of a small shopping mall next to Concord's train station, Aigo's two dining rooms and bar–subtly colored in deep oranges, rusts, and greens – are a pleasant surprise. If you can, opt for the dining room to the right of the bar; it has huge windows overlooking the train tracks (it may not sound nice, but is). The terra cotta and glass candle lamps give the place a soft glow.

The menu is primarily southern French. (Aigo is French for garlic broth.) For starters, try fennel and tomato salad with olive oil and lemon, or pizza provençale with sun-dried tomatoes and tapenade. Entree staples include roasted garlic and rosemary monkfish with roasted vegetables and fried basil, as well as linguini with roasted bell peppers, tomato, and Parma ham. Aigo also has some interesting nightly specials, usually relying on the region's fresh fish. For meat lovers, Aigo has an outstanding leg of lamb, served with couscous, eggplant chips, and charred scallions.

Desserts run the gamut from old standards like chocolate mousse, to more exotic sweets, such as honey lavender ice cream with red fruit coulis, and red wine flan with fresh berries. Hours: 5:30 P.M. - 10:00 P.M. Tuesday through Sunday.

The Colonial Inn, ♥, $$-$$$, 48 Monument Square, Concord, 508/369-9200. In transit: The Colonial

Inn is in the heart of Concord Center, right at the Concord Green. It is impossible to miss.

The main dining room at the Colonial Inn isn't the most wildly romantic in the world. However, the inn is included here for several reasons. First, it is an authentic old country inn, and dinner here will help set the tone for your weekend. Second, the Colonial has several dining options, so if you don't feel like eating in the main dining room, you could opt for a light meal in their lounge or open-air porch (in warmer weather). And sometimes when the inn is crowded, several of the small, more intimate dining rooms are opened. The most interesting of these is the Thoreau Room, which has robin's egg blue wainscoting, white walls, a fireplace, and large windows that look out on the green. If it's open, be sure to ask for a table here.

Merchants Row, the main dining room, has a traditional look—dark gold and purple Concord grape wallpaper, wooden ceiling beams, and gas "look" wall lights. (An unfortunate concession to modern times is the acoustic ceiling tile.) Tables are covered with pink damask cloths and green napkins.

The menu relies on old-fashioned American favorites, and although not gourmet, has a pleasing down-home appeal. Appetizers include shrimp cocktail, baked clams casino, country paté, and New England clam chowder.

Entrees include a wide range of fish, beef, and chicken. If you're a seafood fan, consider the Colonial's broiled Cape Cod scallops, or baked Boston scrod. Or if you really want to go the old-fashioned route, try their chicken pot pie with vegetables baked in a cream sauce, or the North Atlantic lobster pie, with a brandied Newburg sauce and cornbread crust.

The Colonial takes the most pride in its desserts. A full-time pastry chef bakes a fresh assortment of sweets daily, as well as truly great Indian pudding. Other desserts include bread pudding, apple pie, and ice cream.

If you visit in May, the front porch might be open for dinner. You won't get the same menu as the dining room, but it's a real treat to look out on the green and watch the world go by. Its menu includes soups, salads, hamburgers, and sandwiches, as well as the inn's chicken pie, and homemade desserts. This light menu is also served in the inn's lounge. Hours: 5:00 P.M. - 9:30 P.M. Friday and Saturday, 5:00 P.M. - 9:00 P.M. Sunday through Thursday. The light menu is served 11:30 A.M. - 9:00 P.M. daily.

SATURDAY MORNING

Start Tour of Revolutionary Concord and Lexington at Minuteman National Park, Battle Road Visitors Center, Route 2A, Lexington, 508/862-7753. In transit: From the Concord

Green, follow Lexington Road to Route 2A toward Lexington. The Visitor's Center is on the left. The Hawthorne is on Lexington Road. From its driveway, turn right onto Lexington Road, to Route 2A. From Sudbury, take Route 20 east for about five miles, then take Route 126 north toward Concord. Once in Concord this route is known as Walden Street. Follow Walden to the end. Then turn right on Main Street which leads to the Concord. From there, follow above directions.

Most of us need a good brush up on American history. Thankfully the 22-minute film at the Minuteman National Park, offers an informative overview of the conflict between the colonists and the British that led up to the Revolution. The Visitors Center also offers several small exhibits pertaining to the Revolution. Hours: 8:30 A.M. - 5:00 P.M. Free.

Visit Lexington Green, Were the First Shots of the Revolution Were Fired. In transit: Continue along Route 2A toward Lexington. You'll eventually come to a light with a sign pointing left to Lexington Center. This is Waltham Street. Turn left onto Waltham Street. Follow it to the end. Then turn left onto Massachusetts Avenue. This is Lexington's main thoroughfare. Lexington Green is just ahead. Park at meters along the street, or in a municipal lot behind Massachusetts Avenue. You'll see signs for the lots.

If you're going to embark on a Revolutionary tour, it makes sense to follow the battle route as it unfolded on that fateful day, April 19, 1775. The Lexington Green is the site of the first skirmish between the British and the minutemen. (The minutemen were so named because they were specially trained soldiers who could respond to a call to arms and be on the town green within a minute.) A monument stands above the tomb of the seven Lexington soldiers who were slain in battle.

Visit the Hancock-Clarke House, 36 Hancock St., Lexington, 617/861-0928. In transit: A short walk from Lexington Green. Cross the street to the Lexington Chamber of Commerce Visitors Center. Continue on that sidewalk away from the town center. The Hancock-Clarke is on the left. The walk should take about five minutes. If you'd like a map, you can get one at the Visitor's Center.

In 1775 this house was a parsonage, home to minister Jonas Clarke and his family. It is also where John Hancock and Samuel Adams were visiting on the night of April 18. And it is to this home Paul Revere was dispensed to warn Hancock and Adams that, "The British are coming."

Today the house remains much as it looked during that period. It's furnished almost entirely with pieces from the Clarke and Hancock families. (Reverend John Hancock and Reverend Jonas

Clarke both served as ministers in Lexington and lived in the parsonage, but at different times. Reverend Hancock was John [first signer of the Declaration of Independence] Hancock's grandfather.) A guide offers regular tours throughout the house and provides insight into the events of Revolution eve, as well as life during the 1700s.

An exhibit displays one of John Hancock's silk vests, William Diamond's drums (the minuteman who drummed out orders on the morning of the Revolution), and pistols from the British Major Pitcairn. Hours: 10:00 A.M. - 5:00 P.M. Monday through Saturday, 1:00 P.M. - 5:00 P.M. Sunday. Admission $2.50.

Visit Buckman Tavern, Massachusetts Avenue (opposite Lexington Green), Lexington, 617/862-1703. In transit: Walk back down Hancock Street toward the Green. The Buckman Tavern is a yellow clapboard building right in front of the Visitors Center.

Among the most interesting historic houses in Lexington and Concord, the Buckman Tavern is the spot where a dozen minutemen gathered in the early morning of April 19 to hear news of the Red Coats' march. These minutemen, along with about 70 colonists, eventually gathered on the Green early that morning to await the British soldiers. Although their stand was meant to be a protest of British rule – not a fight against British rule – a single shot was fired and

the war was on. To this day historians debate about who shot first. Many believe someone inside the Buckman Tavern fired the shot to incite a battle.

A guided tour of the tavern, including its kitchen, parlor, and bed chambers, not only provides fascinating information about the start of the Revolution, but also about tavern life in general. Although the Buckman is associated with the war, it was also one of Lexington's most popular taverns, frequented by churchgoers, drovers, and minutemen alike.

The tap room boasts many original fixtures, including walls marked with chalk (that's how the bartender took orders) and the old front door with a bullet hole made by a British musket that was shot on the morning of the Lexington battle. Hours: 10:00 A.M. - 5:00 P.M. Monday through Saturday, 1:00 P.M. - 5:00 P.M. Sunday mid April through October. Admission $2.50.

Lunch

Bel Canto, $-$$, 1709 Massachusetts Ave., Lexington, 617/861-6556 In transit: From the Buckman Tavern, walk down Massachusetts Avenue into Lexington Center. Bel Canto is on the same side of the street as the tavern.

Famous for bringing thick crust pizza to Boston in the 70s, this outpost of the urban original still serves great pizza and

Italian dishes. The place is light and airy with butcher block wooden tables and plenty of windows and plants. In warm weather, you can sit on an outside deck overlooking Massachusetts Avenue.

You can order one of Bel Canto's pizza pies, or create one of your own. For a twist consider tuna, garlic, and fresh basil, or goat cheese, carrots, and broccoli. If you like your pizza more traditional, it has that too.

Bel Canto also has a nice selection of salads and calzones. (To the uninitiated, calzones are Italian style "sandwiches" –warm turnovers filled with a combination of meat, cheese, and vegetables.) Or, if you're looking for something not quite so Mediterranean, try the salad with chicken breast chunks and sugar snap peas tossed in a sweet red pepper dressing. Hours: From 11:00 A.M.

Goodies to Go, $, 1734 Massachusetts Ave., Lexington, 617/863-1704. In transit: Goodies is across the street from Bel Canto.

If you're visiting in warm weather, you may want to picnic. Goodies is a great spot for picking up supplies. Design your own gourmet sandwich on some of Goodies' home-baked breads. They also have a great selection of homemade cookies, muffins, and pastries, as well as imported and domestic crackers, juices, and sodas.

Enjoy your picnic right on Lexington Green and soak up the historic aura. Hours: 7:00 A.M. - 6:00 P.M. Monday through Saturday.

Walden Station, $-$$, 24 Walden St., Concord, 508/371-2233. In transit: From Lexington center, retrace your steps back to Concord. Head down Waltham Street. Turn right onto Route 2A. Take a short scenic detour down the Battle Road. It leads right back to 2A. At the fork, bear right and follow the sign to Concord Center. Turn left onto Main Street. Turn left onto Walden Street. The restaurant is on the right. Park either on the street, or at one of the marked municipal lots. There's a large lot behind Walden Street.

Walden Station looks like many casual restaurants – lots of brick, wood, and plants. But the place is immaculately clean and has a pleasant ambiance. It's decorated with firefighting memorabilia because the building once housed Concord's fire station. (A new modern station sits down the street.)

The menu is a mix of burgers, salads, sandwiches, and light meals that range from Louisiana catfish to chicken pesto quesadillas. The food isn't particularly inspired, but the ingredients are fresh and the plates well presented. Good bets are Walden's burgers – they're eight ounces of ground Angus beef. Hours: from 11:30 A.M.

Saturday Afternoon

*Continue Revolutionary Tour
with a Visit to North Bridge.*

In transit: From Lexington center, retrace your path back to Concord. Turn right onto Waltham Street, then right onto Route 2A to Concord. For an especially scenic route, consider taking a short detour down the Battle Road. It is the road on which the British marched to Concord, and is part of the 750-acre Minuteman National Park. It eventually veers back onto Route 2A. In Concord center, park on the street or in a lot.

If you're already in Concord, leave your car in Concord Center. Head up Main Street toward the Colonial Inn. Once at the Colonial Inn, turn right. This is Monument Street. The North Bridge is about an 8-minute walk (a half mile) from the inn. If the weather is bad, there is free parking by the bridge.

Although Lexington is the site of the Revolution's first skirmish, it is widely held that the North Bridge is where the battle actually began. It is the site of the first effective resistance, where minutemen from Concord and surrounding towns gathered in the belief that the British soldiers were trying to burn down Concord. The Red Coats met the colonists at the North Bridge. Each stood on opposite sides. As the colonists advanced, the British fired.

Although the original wooden planks have been replaced several times over the centuries, the bridge retains its same shape and form. On this site you will also see William Chester French's famous Minuteman statue that was sculpted for the 1875 centennial. (French is also the sculptor of the Lincoln Memorial in Washington D.C.)

A five-minute walk through rolling meadows, where the minutemen waited for the British, will take you to the North Bridge Visitors Center. It offers a short film and has displays of many Revolutionary artifacts. Talks are also offered every hour from 10:00 A.M. TO 4:00 P.M. daily, year-round except Christmas and New Year's Day.

Tour the Old Manse, Monument Street, 508/369-3909. In transit: The house is right next to the North Bridge.

Although famous because Ralph Waldo Emerson once lived here, during the Revolution the Manse was the parsonage of Reverend William Emerson, Ralph Waldo's grandfather. On the morning of the North Bridge battle, he and many of his followers watched the entire battle through the windows of the house. The Manse, thankfully,was left undisturbed. Hours: 10:00 A.M. - 5:00 P.M. Wednesday through Saturday, and Monday; 1:00 P.M. - 5:00 P.M. Sunday. Closed Tuesday. Open mid April through October. Limited winter hours. Admission: $4.

Visit the Old Hill Burying Ground, Monument Square and Lexington Road, Concord. In transit: Follow Monument Street back toward the center. Walk down to the end of the Concord Green, which is at the tip of Main Street. Old Hill is on the left, next to St. Bernard's Catholic Church.

It may seem morbid to visit a cemetery, but Old Hill is fascinating. Several revolutionary families are buried here. The stones are interesting reading and beautiful to look at. Grave rubbings are allowed.

Stroll through Concord Center.

In transit: Walk down Main Street, then turn left on Walden. Most of Concord's shops are located on these two streets.

Concord has a lovely town center. Although shopping doesn't have much to do with the American Revolution, a downtown peruse is a relaxing way to end the day. Following are a few of the center's more interesting stores:

Concord Hand Designs, 20 Main St., 508/371-2118. If you enjoy dried flowers, take a look into this small store. Most arrangements are pretty without being overly cute. There is also a small array of garden adornments. Don't worry if you can't fit your purchases in your suitcase, Concord Hand Design ships anywhere.

Perceptions, 67 Main St., 508/369-6797. A good spot for women looking for something different. Lots of artsy hand-painted women's clothing that manages to look sophisticated. Also nice selection of jewelry and prints.

Artful Image, 16A Walden St., 508/371-2353. Concord's premier fine craft shop, Artful Image carries ceramics, sculpture, jewelry, and wooden objects, as well as a supply of modern handmade quilts that utilize traditional designs.

Cooleys Marco Polo, 9 Walden St., 508/369-3692. This fine china, glass, and gift shop has been popular for decades. Although you might not be in the market for china on your visit, Cooleys has some nice mementos. Consider a cotton throw embossed with local historic scenes. These blue and cream colored blankets are specially made for the store.

SATURDAY EVENING
Drinks

The Village Forge Lounge at the Colonial Inn, ♡, $, 48 Monument Square, Concord, 508/369-9200. In transit: Walk up Main Street toward the Concord Green. The inn is at the end of the green.

With rough-hewn paneling and brick walls, ceiling beams, and dark wood furniture, the Village Forge has a cozy appeal. It's a casual spot, decorated with antique posters and authentic metal works tools. Not the kind of place for your Sunday best, but a great spot for relaxing before you change clothes for dinner.

Dinner

The Wayside Inn, ♡-♡ ♡, $$-$$$, Boston Post Road, Sudbury 01776, 508/443-8846. In transit: From Concord center, drive down Main Street. Turn left onto Walden Street. This turns into Route 126. Follow 126 to Route 20. At that intersection, turn right to Sudbury. Follow that road for about 5 miles. The sign for the Wayside Inn is on the right.

The Wayside Inn is known more for its dining room than its guest rooms. In fact, the Wayside has three public dining rooms, a tavern, and several rooms used for parties and private dining. Despite the many tourists attracted to the Wayside, there are two intimate spots where you can enjoy a quiet romantic meal.

If you really want to take a step back in time, arrange for a carriage ride around the Wayside's grounds. The antique carriage drawn by horses takes passengers around the inn's 100 plus pastoral acres.

The carriage will drop you at the inn's front door. From there, proceed either to the Tap Room or the Innkeepers' Dining Room. (The main dining room is pleasant, but as the newest addition to the inn, it doesn't have the same charm.) The Innkeepers Room, with antique wood paneling, a working fireplace, and only three tables, it is the inn's most intimate dining area. Although quite a bit larger, the Tap Room is equally cozy. Added to the original structure in 1796, it has wide wood floorboards, low beamed ceilings, and an ornamental paneled fireplace. Tables are set with brown and white checkered cloths and candles set in brown ceramic jugs.

As might be expected of America's oldest inn, the menu is strictly traditional. However, all of the Waysides food is fresh. The grist mill, just 300 yards from the inn, grinds the restaurant's flour from organic corn and wheat. And the Inn's acres of gardens produce much of its vegetables.

The menu changes slightly every day. But for appetizers you can usually find oysters on the half shell, New England clam chowder, and French onion soup. Entrees typically include roast prime rib, baked Nantucket scallops, and roast chicken with walnut cranberry stuffing.

If you want to continue the traditional theme into dessert, opt for the Wayside's authentic baked Indian pudding. Other sweets, all baked daily, include tapioca, deep dish apple pie, and strawberry shortcake. Hours: 5:00 P.M. - 9:00 P.M. Friday and Saturday, 5:00 P.M. - 8:30 P.M. Sunday through Thursday. Carriage rides are $5 per person.

Il Capriccio, ♡ ♡, $$$, 53 Prospect St., Waltham, 617/894-2234. In transit: From Concord center, drive down Main Street. Turn left onto Walden Street. Walden Street becomes Route 126. Follow Route 126 to the intersection of Route 17. Turn left onto Route 17, follow it into Waltham. Once in Waltham, Route 17 turns into Main Street. Turn right onto Prospect Street, which is in Waltham center. Il Capriccio is in a small storefront on the right. The trip from Concord should take about 20 minutes.

Wedged between a garage and Carl's Steak and Sub shop, Il Capriccio hardly looks the sort of place that would serve gourmet Italian food. Yet this tiny, inauspicious storefront is the darling of Boston food critics, and is considered one of the area's best Italian restaurants.

The interior is a refined oasis with gilt-trimmed sage green walls, and tables dressed in starched white clothes and decorated with a colorful bouquet of fresh flowers.

This elegant theme is also applied to the menu, which steers well clear of traditional "red sauce" dishes. Appetizers include crab cakes with mustard and herbs, as well as gravalox and tuna carpaccio with onions and capers. Entrees are equally ambitious:

gorgonzola ravioli in walnut sauce, squid ink gnocchi with squid in casserole, roast lamb medallions with red wine and green peppercorns.

If you can, save some room for dessert. Il Capriccio's hazelnut meringue torte or lemon mousse, accompanied by a hot cup of espresso, make a perfect ending to the meal. Hours: 6:00 P.M. - 9:15 P.M. Monday through Saturday.

SUNDAY MORNING

Canoe Trip down the Sudbury and Concord Rivers, South Bridge Boat House, Main Street, Concord, 508/369-9438. In transit: From the Concord Green, drive down Main Street through the center of town. At the fork, bear left. This is the continuation of Main Street. The boat house is on the right.

One of Concord's most popular recreational activities is a gentle canoe ride down the Concord River. With more than 18 miles of "canoeable" water, you can be guaranteed a tour free from noisy boaters. There is no better or more leisurely way to see historic Concord. A round trip from South Bridge to North Bridge takes you no more than two hours, and may take you by abundant wildlife – geese, ducks, turtles, and muskrats.

If you've never canoed before – it's easy. If you feel uncomfortable, the people at South Bridge are happy to give you pointers. Or, if you really feel like leading the life of leisure, hire a pontoon boat. The "captain" will escort you down the river and serve you lunch. The pontoon will only go out with a minimum of four people. However, if you pay $40 (the cost of 4) they'll take the two of you out alone. Hours: 9:00 A.M. - dusk, April 1 through November 1. Cost: $7.40 an hour or $36 a day for a canoe. Lunch-time pontoon tours are $10 a person, and dinner tours are $15.

Lunch

The Willow Pond Kitchen, $, Lexington Road, Concord, no phone. In transit: From South Bridge, follow Main Street through the center of town. At the rotary by the Green, turn right onto Lexington Road. At the fork, bear left to stay on Lexington. The Willow Pond is about a mile down on the left.

As Bette Davis might say, "What a dump!" But a trip to Concord wouldn't be complete without a visit to the locals' favorite restaurant. In business for more years than folks remember, Willow Pond serves old-fashioned, simple fare – hamburger plates, tomato and cheese sandwiches, steamers, and fried clams. However, what packs the parking lot on virtually every night of the week are its steamed lobsters. For $9.25, the Pond serves a 1-pound lobster with melted butter, French fries (or onion rings) and cole slaw. An unbelievable deal when you consider the price of

lobster at virtually every other restaurant in New England.

Decor is 40's diner – red check curtains, taxidermed animals, and tin napkin canisters on every table. The Pond also has its share of waitresses who are wide of girth and smart of mouth. But what else would you expect. Hours: from 11:30 A.M.

SUNDAY AFTERNOON

Begin Tour of literary Concord at The Wayside, 455 Lexington Road, Concord, 508/369-6975. In transit: From the parking lot of The Willow Pond, turn right on Lexington Road, back to Concord center. The Wayside is about $\frac{1}{4}$ mile on the right. To park, turn left onto Hawthorne Lane. A lot for the Wayside and the Orchard House is on the right.

Home to more writers than any other house in Concord, its notable inhabitants included Bronson and Louisa May Alcott, Nathaniel Hawthorne, and Margaret Lothrop. (Margaret is the author of the famous children's book *The Five Little Peppers.*)

A guided tour of the house gives visitors a glimpse at virtually all the rooms, arranged with original furniture from its various inhabitants. Among the more interesting rooms is Hawthorne's writing tower, an addition he built to the house to resemble a tower he saw in

Italy. It is here he did most of his writing, standing at a tall wooden desk that still sits in its original place. Hours: 9:30 A.M. - 5:00 P.M. Tours run roughly on the hour from 10:00 A.M. until 5:00 P.M. Open weekends only early April through mid May. Open daily, except Monday, mid-May through November 1. Admission: $1.

Visit the Orchard House, 399 Lexington Road, Concord, 508/369-4118. In transit: The Orchard House is right next door to The Wayside. Either walk along the sidewalk, or through the path in the woods. A guide can point the path out to you.

Longtime home of Bronson Alcott and his family, Orchard House is perhaps the most popular literary Concord home. Bronson's daughter, Louisa May, wrote Little Women here. And the house contains the Alcotts' real furniture. Some of their clothes even remain in the closets. But more importantly, the Alcotts were a fascinating family and played a large role not only in literature, but in the society of the day.

Bronson was a Transcendentalist whose ideas, particularly on education, were far in advance of his time. Although most of Bronson's endeavors were unsuccessful (he started several schools in which children learned through discussion and observation rather than by rote), he was the darling of the Concord literary circle. His supporters

included Emerson, Thoreau, and Hawthorne. His wife Abigail was a prominent advocate of women's rights and the abolition of slavery. And daughter May, although much less known than Louisa, was an accomplished artist. She, in fact, was one of Daniel Chester French's teachers.

Hours: 10:00 A.M. - 4:30 P.M. Monday through Saturday; 1:00 P.M. - 4:30 P.M. Sunday and holidays, from April 1 through mid September; 1:00 P.M. - 4:30 P.M. daily, from mid September through November 1; 1:00 P.M. - 4:30 P.M. Saturday and Sunday, November and March. Open by appointment only from December 1 to February 28/29. Admission: $3.50.

Visit Emerson House, 28 Cambridge Turnpike, Concord, 508/443-4661. In transit: From the parking lot, turn right onto Hawthorne Lane and follow it to the end. This is Cambridge Turnpike. Turn right onto Cambridge. The Emerson House is on the eft, across from the Concord Museum.

Although the contents of Emerson's study are housed across the street at the Concord Museum, the house contains all of Emerson's furniture and belongings, including many of his books. Emerson stored these, his most prized possessions, on detachable shelves made with handles so they could be easily removed from the house in case of fire.

A tour guides visitors through the entire house, offering details of Emerson's work and family life.

Hours: 10:00 A.M. - 4:30 P.M. Thursday through Saturday. 2:00 P.M. - 4:30 P.M. Sunday and holidays. Closed Monday through Wednesday. Open only mid April through October.

Early Evening Stroll around Walden Pond. In transit: From the Emerson House, continue down Cambridge Turnpike toward the center. Turn left onto Heywood Street (that's where the tourist information booth is located), then turn left onto Walden Street/ Route 126. Walden Pond is about two miles down on the right. Parking is on the left and costs $5.

Walden Pond is world famous. Although it is no more or less picturesque than any other pond in the New England woods, it does have a lot of history. It is here where Henry David Thoreau lived in a cabin for two years to contemplate life and discern its essential facts from nature. In his book, Walden, the product of this experiment, he tells about his life and thoughts. Published in the mid 1800s, the book has never been out of print.

A replica of Thoreau's cabin sits at the front of the parking lot. Walk around the dirt path that circles the pond's perimeter. Signs point to the cairn that commemorates the site of Thoreau's cabin.

SUNDAY EVENING
Early Dinner

Pizza at Pappa Razzi, ♥, $$, 768 Elm St., Concord, 508/371-0030. In transit: From the Walden Pond parking lot, turn right onto Route 126 back to Concord. At the intersection for Route 2, turn left. Continue west along Route 2 for about two miles. Pappa Razzi is on the right.

This big boisterous restaurant is a far cry from a staid colonial dining room. but if you're looking for a quick and delicious bite before you head home, you won't find a better restaurant in town. Once a Howard Johnson's, this spot, right off Route 2, has been miraculously transformed into a hip modern Italian eatery. Although the menu includes a variety of pasta, meat, and salads, the pizza is truly outstanding. No chewy pies globbed with mozzarella and canned tomato sauce here. This is strictly the thin crispy crust and fresh vegetable variety. Hours: 11:30 A.M. - 10:00 P.M., pizza and salad until 11:00 P.M. Sunday through Wednesday; 11:30 A.M. - 11:00 P.M., pizza and salad until 12:00 A.M. Thursday through Saturday.

Additional Activities

Visit the Great Meadows National Wildlife Refuge, Monsen Road, Concord, 508/443-4661. This refuge offers 2.7 miles of trails. A great spot for bird watching. Opens $\frac{1}{2}$ hour before sunrise and closes $\frac{1}{2}$ hour after sunset.

Take a Concord Tea Party Walking Tour. This two-mile walking tour is a great way to learn firsthand about the town's important place in early American history and literature. The tour meets in front of the Colonial Inn, and lasts two hours. It ends with tea and Concord teacakes on the porch of the leader's Victorian home. Offered mid April through October on Saturday and Sunday afternoon at 2:00 P.M. and Saturday and Monday morning at 9:30 P.M. Other times can be arranged by appointment. For information call Paula Robbins at 508/369-1430. Tickets: $15.

Visit the Thoreau Lyceum, 156 Belknap St., Concord, 508/369-5912. Located in a run-down house on a quiet residential street, the Lyceum is in no way a spiffy tourist attraction, but rather a resource center for real Thoreau lovers. It contains a research library, permanent collection of memorabilia, and a large supply of books by and about Thoreau. In back of the Lyceum is a replica of Thoreau's cabin in Walden Woods. Hours: Open March through December and weekends in February. Call for specific times.

Have Tea at the Colonial Inn, 48 Monument Square, Concord, 508/369-9200. Take a step back in time and enjoy high tea, complete with watercress sandwiches, scones, and marmalade. It's served Monday through Saturday 2:30 P.M. - 4:30 P.M. Reservations are recommended.

Visit the Gropius House, 68 Baker Bridge Rd., Lincoln, 617/259-8843. Walter Gropius, the founder of the Bauhaus movement and the leading proponent of modern architecture, built this as his family home in 1938. Furnishings and memorabilia are arranged as they were during the last decade of Gropius's life. Hours: 12:00 P.M. - 5:00 P.M. Friday through Sunday, from June 1 through mid October; 12:00 P.M. - 5:00 P.M. Saturday and Sunday, from November through May. Admission: $3.

Visit the DeCordova Museum, Sandy Pond Road, Lincoln, 617/259-8355. This is a small museum for contemporary art that has changing exhibitions and a sculpture park. Hours: 10:00 A.M. - 5:00 P.M. Tuesday through Friday; 12:00 P.M. - 5:00 P.M. Saturday and Sunday. Admission: $4.

GETTING THERE

BY AIR: All major carriers fly into Boston's Logan International Airport. From the airport, you can rent a car, or take a Massport bus (Logan's ground transportation service 800/235-6426) to the subway. Take it to North Station. From there, you can catch a train to Concord.

On Boston's subway, take the blue line to the orange line. Get off at the North Station stop to take the train.

BY CAR: From the south, take I-95 to Route 128 north, to Route 2 west to

Concord. From the north, take I-95 or I-93 to Route 128 south, to Route 2 west to Concord. Route 2 also intersects I-91. From there, travel east to Concord.

BY TRAIN: From North Station in Boston, take the Fitchburg/Gardner commuter rail. On weekdays, the first train to Concord leaves at 7:35 A.M. and the last 12:10 A.M. On Saturdays, trains leave North Station from 8:30 A.M. to 11:00 P.M., and on Sundays, from 9:30 A.M. to 11:00 P.M.

BY BUS: No bus service is available.

CAR RENTAL: Budget (617/787-8200), Sears (800/527-0770 or 617/787-8220), Avis (800/331-1212), Hertz (800/654-3131 or 617/569-7272), American International (800/527-0202 or 617/569-3550) all have offices at Logan International Airport. In Lexington, SSK Leasing (617/862-7603).

TAXI/LIMOUSINE SERVICE: In Concord call Colonial Taxi (508/369-3433) or Bill's Taxi (508/369-3433).

INFORMATION: The Concord Chamber of Commerce, ½ Main St., Concord 01842, 508/369-3120. Hours: 10:00 A.M. - 2:30 P.M. daily. An information booth is located on Heywood Avenue just outside the center. Hours: 9:30 A.M. - 4:30 P.M. late spring through fall. Also, the Lexington Visitors Center, 1875 Massachusetts Ave., Lexington 02173, 617/862-1450.

Mystic & Stonington, Connecticut

ike so many seaside resorts, Mystic and its surrounding southeastern Connecticut towns, are clogged with tourists throughout the summer. Yet the area has far more than sandy beaches to recommend it.

One of the most historically significant places in New England, Mystic (an anglicized version of its Indian name, "misatuck," meaning "big tidal basin") came into prominence during the 19th century as a shipbuilding center. Its shipyards built some of the finest vessels in the world, including whalers, steamers, and large clipper ships.

Today, these century-old shipyards still play a vital role, as the home of the Mystic Seaport Museum, the nation's most well-respected living-history museum. People come to this 17-acre exhibit from all over the world to learn about U.S. maritime history. The museum offers a re-created 19th century village, as well as tall ships, whaling vessels, historic buildings, exhibits, and a planetarium. Real maritime enthusiasts could spend the entire weekend at the museum and still not see everything.

Mystic is also home to an aquarium, a seaport filled with dazzling pleasure boats, and a quaint downtown reminiscent of those from the pre-mall era. Yet Mystic isn't just a tourist town, living off the greatness of its past. It is a real community with drugstores, dry cleaners, and the occasional fast food restaurant.

Nearby, the far quieter and tonier Stonington is known for its grandly restored sea captains homes, restaurants, and fine antique shops. Unlike Mystic, which has built a village to resemble the past, Stonington seems virtually unchanged from the turn of the century.

Similarly unchanged is Noank, a sleepy village which flanks Mystic's west side. Situated on the tip of a peninsula, it has a slightly vulnerable appearance, at the mercy of the sea that quite literally rolls to its doorsteps.

Both Noank and Stonington provide stunning visual contrasts to Mystic, which has been built up and modernized to accommodate the many tourists it attracts. They offer visitors a chance to get a visceral sense of the past, outside the textbook context of the museum.

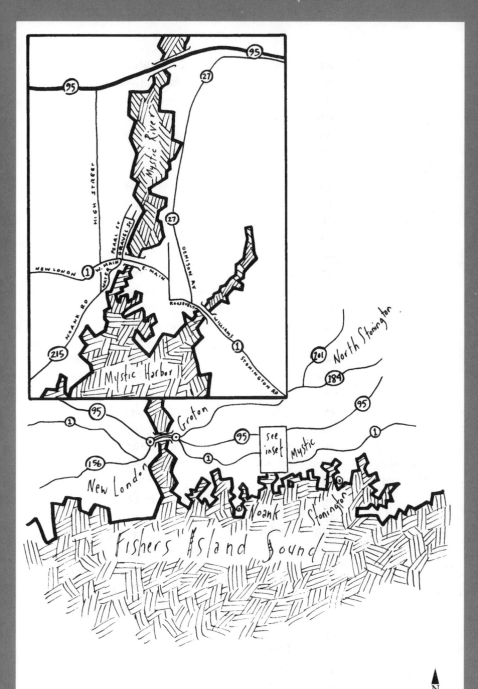

95 95 27

Mystic River

HIGH STREET

27

WATER ST

GRAVEL ST

PEARL ST

NEW LONDON 1 W. MAIN E. MAIN

DENISON AV

ROOSEVELT

NOANK RD

215

Mystic Harbor

WILLIAMS

1 STONINGTON RD

North Stonington

201

184

95

Groton 95 95 1

1 see inset Mystic

156

New London

Noank Stonington

Fishers Island Sound

N

MYSTIC & STONINGTON

Spring is a particularly pleasant time to visit. The onslaught of summer tourists has yet to arrive, magnolias have just begun to bloom, and the bite of cold sea air has turned refreshingly crisp.

Where To Stay

Steamboat Inn, ♡ ♡ ♡ ♡, $$-$$$$, 73 Steamboat Wharf, Mystic 06355, 203/536-8300. With only two small signs pointing to a yellow clapboard structure huddled next to a refurbished ship building plant, the Steamboat Inn is easy to miss. But this B&B is a little gem, elegant and truly unique.

Located right on Steamboat Wharf in downtown Mystic, all six rooms have birdseye views of the yachts and schooners cruising along the Mystic River, and of those docked beside the inn. It would be easy to spend a morning gazing out your window and observing the boats' comings and goings.

Guest rooms have a mixture of fine antiques and high-quality reproductions. Beds are dressed with dramatic designer fabrics and coordinating headboards or canopies. Amenities include wood-burning fireplaces, telephones, televisions, and toiletries.

All rooms are stately, but the Mystic, with views straight down the river, is Steamboat's most popular. The queen-size bed has a burnt-orange Oriental design cover with matching drapes and canopy. A gilt-framed mirror hangs above the fireplace that is flanked by stocked bookshelves. If you're looking for a softer decor, consider the Summer Girls, outfitted in shades of yellow with coordinating florals. (All rooms are named after boats made in Mystic.)

What you won't find at Steamboat is a typical B&B experience. Although it's meticulously run by the innkeeper, Kitty Saletnik, she is not the owner nor does she live here. Yet Kitty has a warm manner, and chats with guests during the complimentary continental breakfast that she prepares herself. Items include homemade muffins, cereal, juice, and coffee. In the afternoon Kitty sets out hot cider, tea, and snacks in Steamboat's only common room, a dining area with peach walls, black and white linoleum floor, and café tables and chairs.

Steamboat doesn't serve dinner, but Kitty will work with local caterers to arrange a candlelight meal for two served fireside in your room.

RATES PER NIGHT: $145-$165 weekends, $125-$150 weekdays in spring; $165-$185 weekends, $140-$160 weekdays in summer; $155-$175 weekends, $130-$150 weekdays in fall; $120-$145 weekends, $95-$120 weekdays in winter.

ACCOMMODATIONS: 6 rooms with private baths.

AMENITIES: Air conditioning. Fireplaces, telephones, and televisions in all rooms.

RESTRICTIONS: No smoking.

Antiques and Accommodations, ♡♡-♡♡♡, $$-$$$$, 32 Main St., North Stonington 06359, 203/535-1736. Located in a quiet country setting just 10 minutes from downtown Mystic, this Victorian B&B is a must visit for anyone with an appreciation for formal antiques. Dealers by trade, innkeepers Ann and Thomas Gray have filled three rooms, two suites, and common areas with fine English and American period furniture. Even the dining table is set with antique silver and china.

Although large enough for a family, consider the suites in the garden cottage. They are both secluded and charming, and have kitchens and sitting areas. Decor includes hand-painted walls, cotton rugs, and ficus plants. The baths are modern, but the Grays have infused them with an old world look. Among their clever touches is a free-standing sink enclosed in an antique wooden chest.

Rooms in the main house are more formal. The Bridal Room, the inn's most popular, has a canopy bed with an embossed white cotton coverlet, peach and green floral walls with coordinating peach carpeting. Thoughtful touches include a silver hairbrush and mirror placed on the dresser, and cream sherry in an antique glass decanter to refresh guests after their arrival.

Breakfast is served by candlelight; the candlesticks are of course old English silver. A typical menu might include banana nut waffles, lemon bread, warm apple and plum sauce, juice, and coffee.

RATES PER NIGHT: $135-$145 for rooms and $185 for suites weekends, $85-$110 for rooms and $125 for suites weekdays.

ACCOMMODATIONS: 3 rooms with private baths, 2 rooms with shared bath, and 2 suites with kitchens and baths.

AMENITIES: Air conditioning. Virtually all antiques that furnish the inn are for sale.

RESTRICTIONS: Smoking on porch only. No pets.

Randall's Ordinary, ♡♡, $$-$$$, Route 2, North Stonington 06359, 203/599-4540. Set at the end of a long, narrow dirt road, this austere brown, clapboard inn isn't for everyone. But if you appreciate authentic colonial architecture and furniture, and have always wanted to step back in time – without sacrificing electricity and indoor plumbing – Randall's Ordinary is a treat.

Innkeepers Bill and Cindy Clark have done an amazing job refurbishing and outfitting this inn, originally built more than 300 years ago. (Ordinary is an old name for a tavern with sleeping quarters.) In fact, Randall's is as much live theater as it is inn. The Clarks greet guest in colonial garb, Bill in britches, stockings, and square-toed shoes and Cindy in a long flowing skirt. Rooms have bare wide pine floors, working open fireplaces (they didn't use screens in the 1600s), and spindle post beds covered with fine wool blankets. Few adornments are found – no pictures on the walls or lacy pillows on the beds. Yet all 12 rooms have an elegant simplicity. And fortunately, all baths are modern and include heat lamps and whirlpool tubs.

Antique aficionados should choose one of the three rooms in the main inn, all of which have working fireplaces and a historically authentic ambiance. A converted milking shed and silo hold an additional 10 rooms; all of these have phones and televisions, but no fireplaces. If you want to splurge, consider Randall's newly completed luxury suite located in the silo. (It can sleep up to five, but you can still rent it for two.) It boasts a four-person Jacuzzi that's located on the top floor of the silo and offers panoramic views of the fields and woodlands.

Set on 27 bucolic acres, a large part of Randall's appeal is its location. The Clarks keep vegetable, herb, and flower gardens, and many animals. They raise their own pigs for the restaurant, and keep a team of oxen for hauling wood (and for show).

Guests are treated to a complimentary continental breakfast of homemade muffins, juice, seasonal fruit, and coffee.

If you really get into colonial living, you can request a "hearth" breakfast ($4-$10). All food is cooked in the fire and is from period recipes, such as codfish cakes with baked beans and biscuits, and maple toast with fried apples and Shaker apple salad.

The Clarks also serve lunch and dinner to guests and the public. Like their breakfasts, only authentic colonial recipes are used, and all food is cooked in the fireplace. Guests are welcome to watch. They even offer period drinks, such as a cherry bounce, which is crushed cherries aged in rum with a splash of sparkling water.

RATES PER NIGHT: $90-$140, $175 for the suite.

ACCOMMODATIONS: 12 rooms with private baths, 1 suite.

AMENITIES: Air conditioning. Some rooms have fireplaces. Others have televisions and telephones. The suite has a four-person Jacuzzi, television, and telephone.

RESTRICTIONS: No pets.

FRIDAY EVENING
Dinner

Harborview Restaurant, ♡ ♡ ♡, $$$, 60 Water Street, Stonington, 203/535-2720. In transit: From downtown Mystic, head east on Main Street to Route 1. Follow Route 1 north to Stonington, then follow signs to downtown Stonington. Water Street is Stonington's commercial thoroughfare. The Harborview is on the right. From North Stonington, follow Route 2 south to Route 1 south to Stonington.

When New Yorkers travel to the Mystic area, they don't leave the city without securing a dinner reservation at the Harborview. It is both the most popular and one of the best restaurants in the area. That said, the region isn't known as a gourmet enclave. The Harborview has garnered its reputation for serving honestly good French-oriented cuisine and for being one of the few local quality restaurants that actually has a good view of the water.

Friday evening for most weekend travelers is usually a casual affair. The Harborview's bar, with its wood floors and tables, flickering candles, and wine barrels strung from the ceiling, is a great spot. The place only has about a dozen tables, but be sure to wait for one by the window.

A particularly nice aspect of the bar is that you can order from the dining room's menu. There is something romantic – almost clandestine–about eating escargot in a scruffy lounge. Other appetizers include bouillabaisse (outstanding) and brie en croute. Entrees range from Chateaubriand to escalopes (scallops) Normande, served with Calvados, cream, and fresh apples.

If you're longing for a formal setting, consider the main dining rooms. Decor is country club-esque with subdued wood paneling and pink tablecloths. Hours: 5:00 P.M. - 10:00 P.M.

Skipper's Dock, ♥, $$, 66 Water Street, Stonington, 203/535-2000. In transit: Skipper's Dock is right behind the Harborview restaurant and is owned by the same people. Follow directions to Harborview.

If the weather is warm and you're in the mood for dockside dining, Skipper's is a good bet. Located right on Long Island Sound, Skipper's has outdoor picnic benches, and a casual indoor restaurant. The menu is strictly fish–baked haddock to bouillabaisse. Although the fish is excellent, the accompaniments – salad, bread, and potatoes–are pedestrian. But then again, a goat cheese and arugula salad would seem out of place in this spot.

Skipper's bar is popular with locals. Not a bad place to find yourself if you have to wait for a table, or if you want an after-dinner brandy.

SATURDAY MORNING

Visit the Mystic Seaport Museum, Route 27, 50 Greenmanville Ave., Mystic, 06355, 203/572-5317. In transit: The Seaport Museum is right outside downtown Mystic. From the town center, head east on Main Street. Turn right onto Broadway, which leads to Route 27. The Seaport is about a mile down on the left. Look for the free parking signs on the right. From North Stonington, take Route 2 south, to Route 184 west, to Route 27 south. From this direction, the Seaport will be on your right. The Seaport is the most popular attraction in the Mystic area. You'll see signs for it everywhere.

"Museum" is really a misnomer for this 17-acre exhibit of artifacts, ships, and skills related to maritime history. "Working village" would be a far better description. Once the site of ship and boat building yards, the oceanside park contains more than a dozen replicas of 19th century seaside businesses, including a tavern, apothecary, dry goods store, and bank. All buildings are open to visitors and furnished with period details. Guides, stationed at each locale, give talks, and answer questions about seaport life. As hokey as this notion might sound, the Mystic Seaport Museum is nothing short of fascinating, even for people with just a marginal interest in American history.

One reason for its success is that it exhibits both replicas and the real thing. The museum's plum is the Charles W. Morgan, an 1841 whaling ship, the only such surviving vessel of its time. During her 80 years of whaling, the Morgan cruised the length and breadth of the Pacific, Indian, and Atlantic oceans, surviving storms, ice, and even a cannibal attack in the South Pacific. In all, the Morgan brought home more than 54,000 barrels of oil and 152,000 pounds of whalebone. Today visitors can tour all three levels of the ship and view the captain's stateroom, the pantry, the "blubber" room, and the steerage, which housed all non-officers aboard the vessel.

In addition to the Morgan, the museum has two additional vessel exhibits, an 1882 training ship and a 1921 fishing schooner, as well as a steam-powered passenger ferry that offers short tours along the river.

Of the eight gallery exhibits, by far the most interesting is Figureheads. This mini museum houses actual decorative ship carvings – typically likenesses of busty women built into the bow of a ship – from nearly two dozen 19th century American vessels.

Real maritime history nuts could spend a whole day here. But a full morning should give you plenty of time to leisurely tour the museum's high points without giving you an information-overload headache. Hours: 9:00 A.M. - 5:00 P.M. (grounds close at 6:00 P.M.) spring and fall, 9:00 A.M. - 8:00 P.M. (grounds close at 9:00 P.M.) from the third weekend in June through Labor Day, 9:00 A.M. - 4:00 P.M. (grounds close at 5:00 P.M.) from after Labor Day to January, 10:00 A.M. - 4:00 P.M. (grounds close at 5:00 P.M.) from January to April. Admission: $14.

Bicycle Ride to Noank.

In transit: You could try leaving your car at the museum and bike from there. But you're better off driving to Main Street in Mystic and parking. Take a left onto Route 27 from the parking lot, then right on Broadway, and left on East Main. You'll see signs for downtown. There are no meters. Signs suggest street parking is limited to two hours. Your trip shouldn't take much longer than that. Once you're on your bike, head west on Main Street. You'll see signs directing you to Noank (Route 215). It's just 2½ miles from Mystic.

The village of Noank, on the west side of the Mystic River, is a tiny peninsula that is home to only 200 year-round residents. (Local myth has it that Noank's wharves harbor 10 times that many boats.) What makes the village interesting is not just its grand water views, but also its architecture. During the 19th century, Noank prospered as a shipbuilding and fisheries center. The affluence of that period is reflected in the many grand homes that still stand today. A sleepy Yankee community, Noank is a distinct contrast to the far more commercial and bustling Mystic.

From Route 215, you'll see a sign pointing to downtown Noank. At that sign, turn left. Mosher Street will take you to Main Street. Turn right on Pearl Street to Abbott's Lobster in the Rough. (If you're not hungry, you could plan your afternoon bike ride before lunch. But after a long morning at the Seaport Museum, you might enjoy your ride more if you eat first.)

Lunch

Abbott's Lobster in the Rough, $-$$, 117 Pearl St., Noank, 203/536-7719. In transit: Pearl Street runs off Main Street. Coming from Main, Abbott's is on the left.

If you're a fan of traditional Maine lobster shacks, you'll love Abbott's. This bright, red, wooden, seaside restaurant has been serving these venerable crustaceans for more than 50 years. It has been garnering praise from food pundits for nearly as long. According to *Gourmet* magazine, Abbott's lobsters are "the epitome of how lobster should taste."

Other seafood includes steamers, stuffed clams, mussels, shrimp, crab, and chowder. Abbott's has seafood rolls too. If you still have room for dessert, try some cheesecake or carrot cake.

Dine at picnic tables on the dock, underneath Abbott's tent, or in its enclosed dining room. It's the perfect spot to relax and take in some fresh salt air before your ride back into Mystic.

Note: If you're not a bicycle maven, follow the same directions and drive to Noank. You can have just as much fun touring the streets by car. If you feel the need to stretch your legs, park on Main Street and walk down Pearl to Abbott's.

Saturday Afternoon

Bicycling around Noank. From Abbott's, head back up Pearl Street, then turn right onto Chester Street to River View Avenue, which affords great views of Mystic Harbor. Continue along River View to Front Street, then turn left onto Ward Avenue.

From this point, you can turn right on Mosher and head back toward Mystic, or continue on Ward back to the center of Noank. You can take Sylvan Street to High Street, which leads back towards Pearl. Noank is such a small area (the village is really part of Groton), you won't get lost. You don't even really need these directions to get around, but they will help you get your bearings. Don't be afraid to duck down a few side streets and explore.

Visit Shops on Mystic's Main Street.

In transit: Retrace the same path you took on your way to Noank. From Main Street, turn right onto Mosher Street, then right onto Route 215 into downtown Mystic.

Although Mystic attracts its share of tourists, unlike Nantucket or Newport it is not a fantasy community. People really live and work here. There are fast food shops and motels, lawyers' and dentists' offices. But its Main Street, located right on the Mystic River, has a magical quality, reminiscent of a charming small-town downtown. Dotted with many quality clothing, craft, and antique stores, it's a great place to poke around for an hour or two. Following are a few stores you should visit. They are all on Main Street and all within a few blocks of each other, so only their phone numbers are given:

The Company of Craftsmen, 203/ 536-4189. The most interesting shop in town, the Company of Craftsmen carries high-quality handmade pottery, quilts, furniture, jewelry, and rugs. Heaven for the folk art and crafts aficionado.

Trade Winds Gallery, 203/536-0119. Extensive selection of antique maps and prints. Of course, most have a nautical theme. Even if you're not in the market to buy, this is a fun spot for browsing.

Labyrinth, 203/536-6020. Arguably the hippest clothing store in town, Labyrinth offers a nice selection of casual apparel for both men and women. Look for lots of wild prints and slouchy cuts.

Susan Casey Ltd., 203/572-1909. If you're a woman and looking for something a bit more conservative, you'll enjoy Susan Casey. It's Talbots-like, but with flair.

Framers of the Lost Art and The Finer Line Gallery, 203/536-8339. Although you'll find lots of seascape posters, this shop also carries works by local artists, including original etchings and lithographs. If you'd like, the store will even frame your piece and ship it home.

Kane's Fudge Dock, 203/536-4516. A great old-fashioned candy shop. If you have a sweet tooth you won't be able to pass up the homemade fudge. Kane's also has ice cream, frozen yogurt, and popcorn.

SATURDAY EVENING

Sunset Cruise Aboard the Argia, Voyager Cruises, Steamboat Wharf, Mystic, 203/536-0416. In transit: Steamboat Wharf is right off Main Street, just west of the bridge.

Sailing on the Argia–which is an authentic replica of a 19th-century gaff-rigged schooner, complete with varnished mahogany interiors and brass lamps–will make you feel as if you're among the elite. The sunset trip, which lasts about two hours, travels down the Mystic and into Fishers Island Sound. If you want, just lounge topside and sip iced tea and nibble hors d'oeuvres. Both are complimentary. (Voyager supplies coolers for guests who want to bring their own wine and beer.) Or offer to help the captain steer and hoist the ship's sails.

The Argia is 81-feet long and holds a maximum of 49 passengers. But the schooner is usually only filled to capacity on Saturday evenings in summer. Open water temperatures are usually 10 degrees cooler than land, so don't forget to bring a sweater, windbreaker, and rubber-soled shoes. Hours: departs 6:00 P.M., returns 8:00 P.M. Tickets $26. Voyager also offers half and full day sails, as well as two-hour morning and afternoon sails.

Dinner

Captain Daniel Packer Inne, ♡ ♡ ♡, $$$, 32 Water St., Mystic, 203/536-3555. In transit: Although you'll probably choose to go back to your hotel to change for dinner, Captain Daniel Packer is just down the street from Steamboat Wharf. From downtown Mystic, head west on Main Street. Turn left onto Route 215/Water Street. The Inne (it's really only a restaurant) is ²⁄₁₀ of a mile on the left.

For old world colonial charm, you can't beat the Captain Daniel Packer Inne. On the National Register of Historic Places, the inn, which was built in 1754, has retained its wide, pine floorboards, wood beams, and fireplaces.

In fact, most of the light in the main dining room is thrown by its two blazing fires, set without screens as they would have been when Captain Daniel Packer operated the inn in the 1700s. Candles glow on tables, which are set with white cloths and small fresh flower arrangements. Walls and mantles are decorated with nautical art, replicas and paintings.

The food is satisfying and well prepared. A complimentary basket of crackers (unfortunately wrapped in cellophane) and cheese spread are served while you peruse the menu. This old-fashioned touch might lead you to believe that the menu is humdrum, but the food is fairly adventurous, particularly the nightly specials. On our visit, the specials included braised caribou roast with spring vegetables, onion gravy, and wild rice, or Norwegian salmon with sun-dried tomatoes and sweet basil buerre blanc over pasta. The regular menu is a bit more simple and includes such items as tenderloin and scallops with bread crumbs, wine, and butter.

If you're a lover of rich desserts, save room. You won't be able to pass up the white chocolate raspberry cheesecake or the double chocolate mousse pie. Hours: 5:00 P.M. - 10:00 P.M.

Flood Tide, ♡ ♡, $$$-$$$$, Routes 1 and 27, Mystic, 203/536-8140. In transit: From downtown Mystic head east on Main Street. Turn right onto Broadway, then follow signs to Route 1. The Inn at Mystic is on a hill onto your left. Flood Tide is in the inn's complex.

The Flood Tide is considered the Mystic area's most elegant restaurant. Positioned on the town's highest hill, it offers magnificent views of Mystic Harbor and Long Island Sound. In clear weather, you can even see Montauk at the tip of Long Island. If you want to dress up for an evening, the Flood Tide will make you feel at home. (A jacket and tie, however, are not required.) The interior is formal, with wall-to-wall carpeting, salmon-colored floral wallpaper, and a long panel of windows that overlooks the harbor. Tables are set with crystal and starched white cloths and napkins.

Although the restaurant offers a few standards—such as the Mystic cocktail appetizer, which is clams, shrimp, and oysters, served with horseradish and cocktail sauce—most items are inventive. Appetizers include smoked salmon rosettes with a Dijon sauce, and smoked carpaccio with peppercorn and herb dressing. If you're a lobster bisque fan, try the Flood Tide's version, which is laced with brandy and sherry.

Many dishes are prepared or served tableside. While some people find this bit of dining drama annoying, but the food is excellent. One such tableside dish for which Flood Tide is famous, is beef Wellington, flavored with Flood Tide's own paté, wrapped in pastry, and served with a Madeira sauce. Most fish dishes, (including shrimp and artichoke Provençale and fillet of salmon with

Galliano buerre blanc) are prepared (mercifully) in the kitchen.

Desserts, decadent and dangerously caloric, include Grand Marnier cheesecake, chocolate hazelnut torte, and crêpes praline. Hours: 5:00 P.M. - 9:00 P.M.

After Dinner Drinks

Both restaurants have pleasant bars. Flood-Tide's is quiet and formal and a perfect spot for conversation before retiring. Or if you're looking to rub elbows with the natives and hear some live (usually rock) music, head to the tavern at the Daniel Packer Inne.

SUNDAY MORNING

Brunch at Randall's Ordinary, ♡ ♡, $, Route 2, North Stonington, 203/599-4540. In transit: From Route 27 in Mystic, head north toward Old Mystic. Take Route 184 east to Route 2. Follow Route 2 west to North Stonington. Randall's Ordinary is on the right. Or from Route 27 north, take I-95 north to exit 92. Randall's is $\frac{1}{3}$ of a mile north on Route 2.

Even if you're not staying at Randall's, you really should make a point of having a meal here. It's an experience you won't forget. In addition to outfitting their inn in period decor, Cindy and Bill Clark have gone to extraordinary lengths to insure that Randall's dining experience is consistent with what an inn-goer would find in the late 1600s.

Only historic recipes are used. And virtually everything that can be is cooked over an open fire in the main dining room.

Staples include Johnny cakes, griddle cakes, and codfish cakes served with baked beans and biscuits. Eggs are also served any style, with fried apples, potatoes, and corn bread. Randall's makes all its own venison and pork sausage, and even raises the pigs it uses for the sausage. Thankfully Randall's has made at least one modern concession – orange juice!

After breakfast you can digest by walking Randall's 27 pastoral acres. Hours: 7:00 A.M. - 11:00 A.M.

Visit the U.S.S. Nautilus Submarine and Museum, U.S. Naval Submarine Base, Route 12, Groton, 203/449-3174 or 800/343-0079. In transit: From Randall's, follow Route 12 south to I-95 south. Take exit 86 and follow signs to the memorial.

Even if you have no interest in naval history, you're probably fascinated by submarines. And while the reality of life 20,000 leagues under the sea might be frightening, the chance to visit a submarine is a thrill. At the U.S.S. Nautilus Submarine and Museum you'll be able to take an informative self-guided tour through the world's first nuclear sub. Launched in 1952, the Nautilus served the Navy for 23 years before it was decommissioned in 1980.

Upon boarding, visitors receive a tape player that provides an overview of submarine life. Among the areas you'll be guided through are the officers' and enlisted men's quarters, galley, dining room, and various control areas. The efficient use of space is awe-inspiring, and the minuscule bunks claustrophobia-producing. As corny as it might sound, the Nautilus tour will give you a new appreciation of our men in uniform.

The adjoining submarine museum will interest history buffs. Exhibits detail the beginnings of the United States Submarine Force in the modern Navy. Other features include working periscopes, an authentic submarine control room, and two five-minute movies. On the museum's grounds are several model submarines from Japan, Germany, and Italy. Hours: 9:00 A.M. - 5:00 P.M. mid April through mid October, 9:00 A.M. - 3:30 P.M. mid October through mid April. During peak season the line to see the Nautilus closes at 3:30 P.M. All those in line at that time will be able to visit the submarine. Admission free.

Tour Stonington's Antique Shops. In transit: Follow Route 12 south back to I-95 north. Take exit 89 to Mystic, then follow Route 27 south to Route 1 toward Westerly, Rhode Island. Follow signs to Water Street and downtown Stonington.

Stonington is a small community that combines the commerce of Mystic with the quaintness of Noank. As its name suggests, Water Street, Stonington's main thoroughfare, overlooks the harbor. The salt air and parade of lobster boats add to the pleasure of perusing the town's antique shops, most of which are housed in old, white clapboard buildings. Following are a selection of the more interesting stores:

Déjà Vu, 68 Water St., 203/536-3520. Specializing in antiques, as well as reproductions and interior design, this shop has the largest selection of merchandise in town. Much is of the grand Newport mansion variety – gilt-framed mirrors and Louis XIV parlor chairs.

Ornkey & Yost Antiques, 148 Water St., 203/535-4402. If you're looking for an antique Oriental rug, this is the place to come. Other specialties include decorative accessories – lace, silver, china – from all periods, as well as 18th and 19th century American furniture.

Grand & Water, 135 Water St., 203/535-2624. A great spot for finding an elegant dining room set. Most merchandise is 19th or 20th century formal mahogany furniture.

Samper D. Janssens, 141 Water St., 203/535-1712. This isn't an antique shop, but is a must visit for anyone who appreciates Quimper faïence, the famous colorful French country china. The selection is great and Janssens will ship anywhere.

Lunch

Noah's, $, 113 Water St., Stonington, 203/535-3925. In transit: Noah's is on the left side of the street, away from the water.

Noah's is the kind of funky, storefront café you might stumble upon in Cambridge, Massachusetts. With a pressed-tin ceiling, large windows, and small wooden tables, the place has a casual ambiance. The menu is varied and includes quiche, steamers, clam chowder, large salads, and sandwiches. Be sure to save room for dessert; Noah's serves some great cookies and cakes. Hours: 11:30 A.M. - 2:30 P.M.

SUNDAY AFTERNOON

Tour Stonington Vineyards, Taugwonk Road, Stonington, 203/535-1222. In transit: From Water Street, head north back over the bridge. After the bridge, take the first left. Take a right at the stop sign. You will be on North Main Street. At the light, continue straight. At the next stop sign, turn right onto Taugwonk Road. Travel about three miles, under I-95, and you'll see the Stonington Vineyards sign on the left.

If you're a wine connoisseur, you'll enjoy touring one of New England's growing number of vineyards. Stonington Vineyards, under Nick and Happy Smith's supervision since 1986, is best known for producing a good Chardonnay and Pinot Noir. Both have won several regional competitions. It also makes Riesling and French hybrids.

Only producing about 6,500 cases a year, Stonington is one of the region's smaller vineyards. Yet they offer an educational tour of their operations, in which guests visit the area where grapes are crushed and then stored (some in French oak barrels) to age. Stonington grows most of its own grapes. The setting is truly pastoral. Visitors are free to walk the fields surrounding the grapes, but discouraged from touring the actual vineyard.

Afterward, you'll be treated to a wine tasting in Stonington's shop. Don't leave without taking home a bottle. If you like red, the 1987 Pinot Noir is a good choice. Hours: 11:00 A.M.-5:00 P.M. Tours are given daily year-round. Call ahead for specific times.

Scenic Drive to Watch Hill, Rhode Island.

In transit: Retrace your steps back down Taugwonk Road and under I-95. Turn left onto North Main Street. This intersects with Route 1. Follow Route 1 north toward Westerly, Rhode Island. Continue on Route 1, to Route 1A and Watch Hill. The drive should take no more than 40 minutes.

Even if you're traveling home in the opposite direction, you should make a point of visiting Watch Hill, an unimaginably posh and exclusive seaside community. It appears little changed from the Victorian era, when many of these homes were built. Its most famous landmark, the hand-carved Flying Horse Carousel located in the center of town, is among the oldest carousels in the nation.

Route 1A will take you right to Bay Street, the main thoroughfare. Park your car and tour the local shops, or get back to Route 1A and travel down any of the side streets to get a glimpse of these mini mansions.

If you want a snack before you head home, visit the **Olympia Tea Room** (Bay Street, 401/348-8210).

Additional Activities

Visit Mystic Marinelife Aquarium, 55 Coogan Blvd., Mystic, 203/536-3323. Examine more than 6,000 sea life specimens in 49 living exhibits. Outdoor attractions include Seal Island, a 2.5-acre outdoor exhibit with seals and sea lions, and the Penguin Pavilion. Hours: 9:00 A.M. - 4:30 P.M., open until 5:30 P.M. from July 1 through Labor Day. Admission $8

Visit Monte Cristo Cottage, 325 Pequot Ave., New London, 203/443-0051. Tour the boyhood home of playwright Eugene O'Neill. The house was the basis for the sets of *Ah, Wilderness* and *Long Days Journey into Night*. Hours: 1:00 P.M. - 4:00 P.M. Monday through Friday. Closed December 21 through April 1. Admission $3.

Visit the U.S. Coast Guard Academy, Mohegan Avenue, New London, 203/536-4941. One of the nation's four service academies, this school has a visitor's center with a multi-media show on cadet life. Military reviews and U.S. Coast Guard Band concerts are held in spring and fall. Tours of the tall ship Eagle are available when in port. Hours: 9:00 A.M. - 5:00 P.M. Eagle tour hours: 1:00 P.M. - 5:00 P.M. Friday through Sunday. Admission free.

Visit the Connecticut Early Music Festival, P.O. Box 329, New London 06320, 203/444-2419. If you're a classical music lover, you'll enjoy this annual festival. Held every June in the Mystic-Stonington area, the festival organizes about 10 concerts. Most are held on weekends. Call for details.

GETTING THERE

BY AIR: The Groton-New London Airport (203/445-8549) and Westerly (Rhode Island) Airport (401/596-2357), provide full commuter service from most New England cities and all major New England "hub" cities.

BY CAR: From I-95, take exit 90 to Route 27. For Mystic, head south on 27 and for North Stonington (Randall's and Antiques & Accommodations) head north.

BY TRAIN: Amtrak (800/USA-RAIL) has daily service from Boston and New York to Mystic.

BY BUS: No major bus service is available.

BY FERRY: Cross Sound Ferry (203/443-5281) provides service from Orient Point, Long Island, to New London, Connecticut. New London is about 15 minutes south of Mystic. The ferries accommodate cars. Or you can call for a taxi from the terminal.

BY BOAT: Full service marine facilities for small and large pleasure boats are available at several marinas. Contact Seaport Marina (203/536-9681).

CAR RENTAL: Avis (203/446-4200), Hertz (203/445-8585), and National (203/445-7435) have offices at the Groton-New London Airport. In Westerly, call Thrifty (401/596-3441). In Mystic, call Valenti's (203/572-0501).

TAXI/LIMOUSINE SERVICE: Yellow Cab (203/536-8888) offers 24-hour service.

INFORMATION: Mystic Chamber of Commerce, P.O. Box 143, 16 Cottrell St., Mystic, CT 06355, 203/572-9578. Hours: 9:00 A.M. - 5:00 P.M. Monday through Friday. Also check the Mystic and Shoreline Visitor Information Center at Mystic Village, Route 27/Coogan Boulevard, Mystic, CT 06355, 203/536-1641. Hours: 9:00 A.M. - 4:30 P.M. Sunday through Friday, 9:00 A.M. - 5:30 P.M. Saturday. There's also a good Connecticut information center just off I-95, near exit 90.

Newport, Rhode Island

ewport, Rhode Island. The very name connotes money and privilege. Few other places enjoy the cachet associated with this seaside community located on a small island wedged between Narragansett Bay and the Atlantic Ocean.

Famous for its wildly extravagant gilded-age mansions, world-class yachting events, and social high life, Newport ironically had a far more humble beginning. Founded in 1639 by Massachusetts Bay Colony dissidents seeking religious freedom, it was established as a safe haven for persecuted minorities, among them, Quakers, Baptists, and Jews. In fact, it is home to the nation's first synagogue, which is still in operation today.

But since the early 1700s, Newport has been known as a seat of affluence. It was first a commercial center for silver and furniture manufacturing, then a vital port in the illegal "triangle trade"– exchanging rum, molasses, and slaves, between New England and Africa and the West Indies – and later a tourist destination for southern plantation owners.

It wasn't until after the Civil War, which put a crimp in Newport's tourist trade, that the New York elite began flocking to its shores. It is here where turn of the century industrialists, who made their fortunes prior to the imposition of state and federal income taxes, built their summer palaces and ushered in the "Gilded Age of Newport." This period exemplifies the most unbridled and obscene conspicuous consumption that this country has ever known.

Each new mansion was designed to outdo the others built before it. The ne plus ultra of these "cottages," as their owners were wont to call them, was The Breakers built by Cornelius Vanderbilt II. Designed to resemble an Italian palace, construction required more than 2,000 craftsmen; its ornamentation rivals some of the world's greatest museums.

Not surprisingly, life during Newport's Gilded Age was similarly excessive. The "season," the eight weeks of July and August, was a blur of dinner parties and balls. The most notorious of these events was a dinner party held at Belcourt Castle in which guests were presented with sterling silver shovels to search for party favors of rubies and sapphires that were buried in sand on the dining room table!

The Point

238

SCHREDDEN

THIRD

FAREWELL

BROADWAY

ELM

AMERICA'S CUP

Goat Island

Fort Adams

Newport Harbor

Down Town

ST ADAMS RD

WELLINGTON AV

MARKET

STONE

MEMORIAL BLVD

Cliff Walk

The Breakers

LIGHTHOUSE RD

HARRISON AV

NARRAGANSETT

RIDGE RD

BRIDGE

BELLEVUE AV

CASTLE HILL AV

Brenton Point State Park

OCEAN AV

Brenton Point

Atlantic Ocean

N

NEWPORT

The first World War brought this age to an abrupt and irrevocable halt. Yet Newport's appeal remains. The wealthy still summer here. Visitors still come to glimpse its magnificent shoreline. And thanks to some rigorous preservation societies, you can tour the mansions that once housed the Vanderbilt's, Astors, and Belmonts.

It would be a mistake, however, to concentrate on Newport's more notorious history. Equally interesting, albeit far less glamorous, are the Touro Synagogue, the White Horse (the nation's first tavern), and the many restored Colonial homes in Newport's Point section.

Newport's primary tourist season is still summer, and the town gets overrun. The crush of cars and wandering pedestrians can ruin even the most patient traveler's visit. Mid march through mid June is a far more civilized time to visit. All the mansions, and most of the sights are open, yet the town is far more peaceful.

WHERE TO STAY

Elm Tree Cottage, ♡ ♡ ♡, $$$-$$$$, 336 Gibbs St., Newport 02840, 401/849-1610. Set on a quiet street overlooking Easton Pond, the Elm Tree Cottage is the perfect retreat from bustling downtown Newport, just 5 minutes away. Once the summer cottage of Mrs. Crawford Hill, the Pennsylvania Railroad heiress, innkeepers Priscilla and Tom Malone have gone to great lengths to restore the Queen Ann Victorian to its former grandeur.

The Malones purchased the house in 1990, and spent more than six months painting, rewiring, and refurbishing. They replaced several of the windows with their owned stained glass creations. (It was their trade before becoming innkeepers and something they still do for special clients.) The end product is an elegant yet comfortable inn, thoughtfully furnished with estate sale treasures. In fact, all five guest rooms have grand antique Louis XV bed frames.

Common rooms include a spacious dining room, sun room, lounge, and living room with two pianos, a six-foot gilt-framed mirror, and five bay windows facing the pond. The lounge, refurbished in the early 1930s to look like a yacht's stateroom, is completely paneled with wood. It is here Priscilla sets out snacks each afternoon (baked Brie and fresh fruit are typical) and keeps a small refrigerator and glasses, so guests can store their own food and fix drinks.

Although the Malones have done an admirable job decorating these common areas with wicker, chintz, and antiques, mixed with more pedestrian furnishings, they pale in comparison to the guest rooms.

The 40 x 20 Windsor Suite, with seafoam green carpeting, peach and tan floral wallpaper, and a beige damask couch near the wood-burning fireplace, is soft-looking without being fussy. The king-size bed with crown canopy, French headboard, and peach and green linens is the room's showpiece. The bath is huge, and includes a mirrored vanity table, crystal chandelier, and sink with crystal legs, all original to the house. (At this writing another oversized room was being completed on the first floor. Known as the Library Suite, it will have a more masculine flavor.)

Not quite as large, but equally well appointed, are four other guest rooms. Three have fireplaces. The Mary Channing Eustis Room, though beautifully done in soft yellows, greens, and deep rose, is the only room without one.

Priscilla takes pride in Elm Tree's full breakfasts, which include a buffet of fruits, juices, cereals, and homemade muffins, as well as an elaborate entree. Guests' favorites include Portuguese sweet bread French toast and seafood crêpes.

But what really sets Elm Tree apart is the couple's concern for their guests. Guests are greeted with a bowl of fruit in their rooms. Two of their most thoughtful extras are fresh fruit provided in all guest rooms and complimentary morning newspapers in the dining room.

RATES PER NIGHT: $75-$125 January through early May, $90-$250 early May through mid June, $125-$250 mid June through mid October, and $90-$200 mid October through January.

ACCOMMODATIONS: 6 rooms with bath.

AMENITIES: Air conditioning. Some rooms have fireplaces, one has a television.

RESTRICTIONS: No smoking. No pets.

Ivy Lodge, ♡ ♡ ♡, $$-$$$, 12 Clay St., Newport 02840, 401/849-6865. Terry and Maggie Moy aren't your typical innkeepers. Prior to taking over the Ivy Lodge in 1991, Maggie worked with recovering cocaine addicts, and Terry, a former Navy Seal, was on a police bomb squad! Yet their enthusiasm and attention to detail make them innkeeping naturals and the Ivy Lodge one of Newport's most pleasant inns.

Located just off "Mansion Row," the Ivy Lodge is grand in its own right. The 33-foot high entrance hall to this restored Victorian is outfitted entirely in carved oak and boasts a three-story spiral staircase. The constantly roaring fire in the hall fireplace and glowing mantle candles add to the elegance.

Despite the Gothic, almost mysterious, feel of the hallway, the rest of the house is light and airy. All eight guest rooms have been recently refurbished and redecorated with lively florals and stripes, and interesting antiques and reproductions. The effect is refreshing and feminine, but not overdone (i.e., you won't be visually assaulted with dried flower arrangements or wooden ducks and bunnies).

Among the most sought after guest rooms is the Turret Room, not surprisingly in the house's turret. The king-size carved oak bed lends an air of grandeur. (Arnold Schwarzenegger and Maria Shriver stayed in this room when they were in town for her brother's wedding.) Similarly impressive is room 1, which boasts an 8-foot carved bed frame, 7-foot mirror, and pine-paneled ornamental fireplace. The color theme is similarly dramatic, with shades of deep pink. On the first floor, the Library Room has a Jacuzzi, sleigh bed, and ornamental fireplace with original Delft tile.

The Moys serve a candlelight breakfast on the dining room's 20-foot mahogany table. In addition to homemade granola and muffins, Maggie whips up treats like French toast and eggs Benedict. In good weather, guests sometimes take their meal on the wraparound porch.

Common rooms include a sun room furnished with wicker, and a large living room outfitted with dhurries and a pink and white striped couch.

Like all good innkeepers, Maggie and Terry enjoy providing guests with special touches, not the least of which are the 300-thread count cotton bed linens or the afternoon lemonade and snacks.

RATES PER NIGHT: $126-$165 May through November, $100 December through April.

ACCOMMODATIONS: 8 rooms with private baths.

AMENITIES: Air conditioning. Some rooms have fireplaces, one has a Jacuzzi.

RESTRICTIONS: No smoking. No pets.

The Cliffside Inn, ♥ ♥ ♥, $$$-$$$$, 2 Seaview Ave., Newport 02840, 401/847-1811. Situated on a residential, tree-lined street, just one block from the Cliff Walk and two blocks from the beach, The Cliffside Inn is the perfect spot for couples who want to sniff the salt air.

Perhaps the most authentically and regally appointed of Newport's small inns, the Cliff Walk has had many incarnations. Built in 1880 as the summer home of Maryland's governor, by the turn of the century it housed the prestigious boy's preparatory school, St. George's. More recently, it was home to eccentric artist Beatrice Turner, who painted herself almost exclusively. One of Turner's few exceptions was her father. When he died, she embalmed the body, propped him up in the parlor, and spent two weeks painting his figure!

Today, the sun-drenched parlor, with freshly upholstered, flowery Victorian settees and large bay windows draped in voluminous peach curtains, bears no trace of Turner's macabre undertaking. The walls, however, are graced with a few of her paintings.

Although all of Cliff Walk's rooms are well appointed with antiques, needlepoint rugs, and Laura Ashley fabrics, the most sought after room is the Governor's Suite. It includes a dramatic deep green sleeping alcove with matching bedspread, and a large sitting area complete with television, VCR, and refrigerator. If you're looking for something with a more old-world feel, consider Miss Adele's room with a seven-piece matching antique bedroom set. Miss Beatrice's room, which has an extra large bath with bay windows and a Jacuzzi, as well as a hand-carved queen-size bed and ornamental fireplace, is another good choice.

Innkeepers Annette and Norbert Mede make breakfast each morning. In addition to homemade granola, muffins, and coffeecake, they prepare one hot entree such as French toast or crêpes. Although the Medes are not the Cliffside's owners, they live on the property and take a keen interest in their guests.

If the weather is right, relax on the expansive front porch, which is outfitted with wicker furniture. It's a great spot to unwind after a long day of touring.

RATES PER NIGHT: $95-$165 November through April, $115-$195 May through October.

ACCOMMODATIONS: 12 rooms with private baths.

AMENITIES: Some rooms have air conditioning and/or television and/or whirlpool baths. One suite has a television, VCR, and refrigerator. Television in common room.

RESTRICTIONS: No pets. No smoking. No children under 13.

The Inn at Castle Hill, ♡-♡ ♡, $-$$$$, Ocean Drive, Newport 02840, 401/849-3800. If you want to stay right on the ocean, the Inn at Castle Hill is your only choice in Newport. From the famous Ocean Drive, you'll enter a long narrow driveway surrounded by small, gnarly trees. At its end sits Castle Hill, a rambling gray shingled summer cottage that is quite a bit less impressive looking than the length of the driveway would indicate.

The inn's overall appearance is a bit world weary. Some might turn their noses up at the remnant shag rugs found in a few rooms, and the sparse furnishings. However, the Inn at Castle Hill has many things to recommend it, not the least of which is its private beach, incomparable ocean views, and rich and colorful history.

Originally constructed for the renowned 19th century scientist Alexander Agassiz, it was built to resemble the chalets of his native Switzerland. After making his fortune in some copper mines in Michigan, Agassiz was not only able to devote his life to marine biology, he was also able outfit his home with impressive art. His favorite was Chinese and Japanese porcelains and bronzes. In fact, many of the home's original works remain in the inn.

The lounge, essentially the only common area besides the three dining rooms, is graced with several of Agassiz's pieces. They are complemented by a deep red Oriental rug, intricate inlaid woodwork walls, and a hand-carved fireplace.

Despite the ocean view, the inn has a dark, Gothic aura, enhanced by the doleful sound of distant bell bouys. Agassiz's wife reportedly never felt comfortable in this house. And rumor has it, that her ghost remains. No one has actually seen her spirit, but once or twice a year guests report inexplicable loud crying, usually during a storm!

Rooms vary greatly in size, so it's important to be specific when making reservations. Of the 10 rooms in the main house, 8,6, and 9 are the top choices. In fact, Thornton Wilder, who was a frequent guest, wrote much of Theophilus North in room 9. It is unusually large, has pink and peach floral wallpaper, an ornamental fireplace, and bay windows that look directly onto the sea.

If taking a long hot soak is one of your favorite romantic activities, opt for room 8. Its oversized bath has a deep clawfoot tub that is right by a large ocean side window.

Continental breakfast includes juice, coffee, homemade muffins, cheeses, fruits, meats, and yogurt. In the afternoon, tea and snacks are served in the lounge. The inn also has a bar with a full liquor license, and a full-service restaurant that's open April through October.

Although the spring weather may not be quite warm enough for tanning, you'll enjoy Castle Hill's three small pebbly beaches and 40 acres along the Atlantic's rocky shoreline. Rates per night: $90-$180 (rooms with shared baths $50-$65) April through November; $180-$225 ($65-$80) June through October; $90-$130 ($40-$50) January, February, March and December.

ACCOMMODATIONS: 9 rooms in main inn, 6 with private baths, 3 with shared bath, and 1 suite with bath. In the chalet (a separate building 50 yards from the inn) are 2 rooms with shared bath, 1 room with private bath, and 1 suite with private bath. Harbor House has 6 rooms with baths. Efficiencies have kitchens and baths. Note: In summer and fall Castle Hill also opens the Harbor House, a one-story structure with 6 rooms all with knotty pine paneling and private baths. Also, 18 one-room efficiencies are available by the week in summer, and by the night in spring and fall.

AMENITIES: Full service restaurant. Small private beach.

RESTRICTIONS: No pets.

Friday Evening
Dinner

La Petite Auberge, ♡ ♡ ♡, $$$, 19 Charles St., 401/849-6669. In transit: Charles Street is small and narrow and runs between Marlborough Street and Washington Square. You might find parking on Charles, but if you're traveling on a weekend it could be difficult. To be safe, park at the Gateway Visitors Center on America's Cup Avenue just three minutes away. America's Cup is the main street that runs along the harbor. Head south on Memorial Boulevard and right on America's Cup. Gateway is on the left, just past the Marriott. To continue to Charles Street, turn right onto Marlboro and right onto Charles.

If you're a francophile, you'll love La Petite Auberge, an authentic French restaurant–the kind you'd expect to find nestled in the hills of Provence. During the course of our meal, the chef, replete with tall white cap, came to pour himself a little red wine from the bar and puff on a cigarette, all the while chatting up his patrons, several of whom spoke French exclusively.

Although the main restaurant has several lovely quasi-formal dining rooms with lace curtains and tablecloths, head to the small café. It has a blazing fireplace and dark wood paneling and wooden bar lit with small lamps on either side.

Food preparation is simple but delicious. Appetizers include assorted patés and escargot in garlic butter. A few staples on the entree list are roasted quail with walnut and grape compote, and grilled lobster in herbs. Fish and chicken are offered daily, but with different preparations and vegetables. On our visit, roast chicken, which was wonderfully tender, was served in light butter and wine sauce with roasted garlic, carrots, and green beans.

Although the appetizers and entrees are where La Petite Auberge shines, you might consider finishing with some chocolate mousse or a slice of pie.

The dining room offers a slightly more formal menu that includes lobster bisque, frog legs in garlic butter, and trout with hazelnuts. Hours: 6:00 - 10:00 P.M. Monday through Saturday, 5:00 - 9:00 P.M. Sunday.

Puerini's, ♡ - ♡ ♡, $$-$$$, 24 Memorial Blvd., 401/847-5506. In transit: Memorial is one of the main streets in Newport. It runs perpendicular to Bellevue and Spring. If you're traveling north from the wharf area and Thames Street, Puerini's is just south of Bellevue Avenue.

Puerini's is a simple storefront with small tables covered with white butcher paper, which doesn't take reservations or serve liquor. (You can bring your own though.) But in season, the wait is sometimes more than two hours. Why? This family run operation serves stupendous pasta that's made fresh daily.

Start off with some roasted peppers in oil and garlic, prosciutto and provolone, or perhaps some pesto bread. Entrees rely heavily on pasta and include linguine (al burro e formaggio), served with herb butter, pecorino cheese, and spices, and cavatelli (ai quattro formaggio) served with gorgonzola, ricotta, fontinella, and mozzarella. If you like chicken, consider the pollo a fontinella, which is a cutlet breaded and stuffed with fontinella cheese, pine nuts, and marinated artichoke hearts. As with most authentic Italian trattorias, meals come with hearty crusty bread, and the bottled water served is San Pelligrino.

Peurini's atmosphere is boisterous and jovial, and the crowd, although mixed, is typically young. Noise, however, never gets so loud that you can't conduct a quiet conversation. If you consider yourself a connoisseur of real Italian cuisine, this restaurant is a must visit.

Saturday Morning

Visit Newport's Mansions.

In transit: Virtually all of Newport's eight mansions that are open to the public are located on, or directly off, Bellevue Avenue. Also known as "Mansion Row," Bellevue runs parallel to Thames and Spring streets. It is the next major avenue north of Spring. If you're traveling north on Memorial Boulevard, turn right onto Bellevue. All the mansions are located east of the Newport Casino.

While some visitors come to see all Newport's mansions, most people are satisfied visiting just a few. Deciding which mansions to visit isn't easy, and depends on individual interest.

It would be a mistake, however, to forego **The Breakers** (Ochre Point Avenue, 401/847-1000). This, Newport's most lavish palace, is resplendent in marble, stone, and alabaster imported from Italy, France, and Africa. Constructed in only two years, it best exemplifies the unbelievable excess the Industrial Revolution spawned.

Of the 70 rooms, the dining room is the most astounding. The ceiling painting, Aurora at Dawn, hovers over the grand space ornamentally supported by massive red marble columns. Similarly impressive is the Grand Salon, with gold inlay ceilings and walls. The room was completely constructed in France, dismantled, then rebuilt by the same French artisans in Newport.

Among The Breakers' more interesting features is its water system. All baths have four spigots, for hot and cold fresh water and for hot and cold sea water, which was pumped in from the ocean and stored in giant tanks in the basement. Hours: 10:00 A.M. - 5:00 P.M. daily May through

September, Friday through Sunday year-round. Admission: $7.50

Romantic New England Getaway's choice for a second mansion visit is **Rosecliff** (Bellevue and Marine avenues, 401/847-1000). Built by Mrs. Herman Oelrichs, whose father made a fortune striking the largest vein in the Comstock Lode, it resembles Louis XIV's Grand Trianon Palace at Versailles. The 40-room French chateau features a garden terrace, a replica of the 18th-century French Court of Love designed for Marie Antoinette.

For movie buffs, **Belcourt** is a must visit. Much of *The Great Gatsby* was filmed here. Its ballroom, the largest of all the Newport mansions, features a ceiling painted to resemble a lightly clouded sky from which hang massive gold chandeliers. Hours: 10:00 A.M. - 5:00 P.M. daily from March 30 through November 1. Admission: $6.

Six of Newport's mansions are operated by the Preservation Society of Newport County (401/847-1000.) They are: The Breakers, Rosecliff, Marble House, Kingscote, The Elms, and Chateau Sur Mer. Combination tickets can be purchased at all of these mansions. If you plan on visiting two or more operated by the Preservation, it's best to buy a combination ticket; one that admits to any two mansions is $11. Or tickets can be purchased for all mansions at the Gateway Visitors Center.

Plan on spending about 1 ½ hours at each mansion. Although the tours don't take much more than an hour, you'll want to explore the grounds and gift shops.

Following are short descriptions of Newport's other mansions, should you be interested in visiting them as well.

Kingscote, Bellevue Avenue, 401/847-1000. The smallest mansion in Newport, it was built around 1840 prior to the Gilded Age. The Gothic Revival home was originally built by a Savannah plantation owner; in the 1860s, it was sold to China trade merchant William King for $35,000. Among the manse's more interesting features are its Tiffany glass windows and original furnishings. Hours: 10:00 A.M. - 5:00 P.M. weekends April, October, and November; daily May through September. Admission: $6.

The Elms, Bellevue Avenue, 401/847-1000. Built in 1901 for coal magnate Julius Berwind, The Elms resembles a French chateau. The interior features authentic Louis XIV and XV furniture. The grounds boast the only sunken gardens in Newport. Hours: 10:00 A.M. - 5:00 P.M. weekends in April, daily through November. Admission: $6.

Marble House, Bellevue Avenue, 401/847-1000. So named for the many kinds of marble used in construction, it was built for William K. Vanderbilt by Breakers architect Richard Morris

Hunt. The house, known for its ornamentation with scenes and figures of Greek and Roman mythology, was closed by Vanderbilt after he and his wife divorced. She subsequently married O.H.P. Belmont and moved into his Newport mansion, Belcourt. Hours: 10:00 A.M. - 5:00 P.M. daily March 30 through November 1.

Belcourt Castle, Bellevue Avenue, 401/846-0669. Patterned after Louis XIII's hunting lodge at Versailles, Belcourt houses the nation's largest collection of 13th century stained glass. Belmont, who made his fortune in banking, built the 60-room mansion for $3 million. (That's in 1890 dollars!) He and the ex Mrs. Vanderbilt loved entertaining. They orchestrated Newport's infamous "silver shovel" dinner party. Hours: 9:00 A.M. - 4:00 P.M. daily February through April, 10:00 A.M. - 5:00 P.M. daily April and May, 9:00 A.M. - 5:00 P.M. daily June through September, 10:00 A.M. - 4:00 P.M. weekends October through December. Closed January. Admission: $6.

Chateau-Sur-Mer, Bellevue Avenue at Shepard Street, 401/847-1000. A granite Victorian castle, the Chateau was built in 1852 and is thus less ornate than the mansions built at the end of the century. Architect Richard Morris Hunt made significant restorations in 1872. Hours: 10:00 A.M. - 5:00 P.M. weekends April and October, 10:00 A.M. - 5:00 P.M. daily May through September.

Beechwood, Bellevue Avenue, 401/846-3772. Known more for its inhabitants than its architectural details, Beechwood was the summer home of Caroline Astor, the queen of American high society in the 1890s. Proud of her position, Caroline insisted on being called "The" Mrs. Astor. Today Beechwood is Newport's only living museum; actors inhabit the house and bring to life Beechwood as it was in Astor's day. Hours: 10:00 A.M. - 4:00 P.M. weekends mid February to mid May and November through mid December; 10:00 A.M. - 5:00 P.M. daily mid May through October.

Lunch

Picnic Lunch at Brenton Point State Park, Ocean Drive. In transit: Head east on Bellevue Avenue to Ocean Drive. This 10-mile drive, along the rocky, jagged Atlantic coast, is considered to be among the most scenic roads in the nation. The panorama includes mansions poised at the ocean's edge, open seas, and peaceful inlets surrounded by fields of sea grass. After lunch, continue along Ocean Drive; it winds back into Newport center.

Brenton Point, situated about half way along Ocean Drive, was once a family sheep farm. But during World War II the government took over the land to install radar stations. Although animals no longer graze here, its current incarnation is equally bucolic. The park includes hiking trails, grassy banks, and a stone fishing pier. A great spot for exploring tidal pools. Enjoy your lunch on the rocks right at the foot of the sea, or set your blanket on the lawn across the street. Free parking and rest rooms.

Top Spots For Procuring a Picnic:

Ocean Coffee Roasters, $, 22 Washington Square, 401/846-6060 In transit: Head west on Bellevue, then turn left onto Memorial Boulevard, then right onto Spring Street and left onto Washington Square.

This is the best spot for picking up a sandwich, coffee, or sweets and pastry in Newport. No mayo-laden deli style sandwiches here. How about Tuscan tuna with olive oil and lemon, or imported Genoa salami and provolone, all on homemade bread? Finish with a mouth-watering chocolate brownie and cappuccino. Ocean roasts its own coffee and bakes their breads and sweets daily. It's all outstanding. Hours: 7:00 A.M. - 11:00 P.M. Tuesday through Saturday; 8:00 A.M. - 11:00 P.M. Sunday.

Cappuccino's, $, 92 Williams St., 401/846-7145. In transit: Williams is west of Narragansett Avenue, just off Bellevue. It's just after the municipal parking lot, across from the casino, on the left.

Although Cappuccino's doesn't have the same wide selection as Ocean Coffee

Roasters, it serves quality food. Different sandwich specials are offered daily. Selections might include chicken cutlet or grilled tuna. Don't leave without picking up some of Cappuccino's chocolate walnut biscotti. Hours: 8:00 A.M. - 6:30 P.M. Tuesday through Saturday; 8:00 A.M. - 2:00 P.M. Sunday.

SATURDAY AFTERNOON

Explore Newport on Foot.

In transit: Park at the Gateway Visitors Center. From the end of Ocean Drive, simply follow signs back to Newport center.

They will lead you onto Ridge Road, to Harrison Avenue, past Hammersmith Farm. Then you'll turn left onto Halidon Avenue, then right onto Wellington. This leads right to Thames Street, which leads to America's Cup Avenue and the Gateway Visitors Center.

Newport is a picturesque town. With brick sidewalks, cobblestone streets, and refurbished waterfront factory buildings filled with restaurants and shops, it's perfect for strolling. Yet as is often the case with many tourist towns, the shops, chockablock with T-shirts, mass produced pottery, and sweet-smelling bath products, can be mind-numbingly dull.

Enjoy the scenery. Stroll the waterfront. But for the more interesting collection of stores, make your way to lower

Thames Street, then walk back toward the Gateway along Spring Street. These areas provide a far funkier and more interesting version of Newport.

Following are some shops that you should make a point of visiting:

The Erica Zapp Collection, 477 Thames St., 401/849-4117. Undoubtedly the best collectible store in Newport, Zapp offers an eclectic mix of African masks and wooden sculptures, Italian-inspired sprays of dried wheat and flowers, post modern pottery, and mod jewelry.

Full Swing Textile, 474 Thames St., 401/849-9494 It's not quite fair to list this spot as a store. Michele Mancini, a hip fabric merchant whose merchandise was featured on the cover of *Metropolitan Home*, recently closed her retail operation. But she still purveys her 1920s through 1950s inspired designs to the trade from this storefront. You can get a good look at some of the fabric she works with through the windows. Retro addicts will flip. If you're serious, call for information.

Antiques Etc., 516 Thames St., 401/849-7330 You won't find extraordinarily high-end pieces, but this shop does have a quirky collection of quilts, silver, estate jewelry, furniture, and American Indian artifacts.

The Liberty Tree, 104 Spring St., 401/847-5925. A decidedly upscale shop stocked with contemporary American folk art, weather vanes, and hand-painted pine furniture, as well as American Indian jewelry and pottery.

Handmaids, 128 Spring St., 401/849-0732. This is heaven for a craft lover. Look for all manner of handmade "art," including toys, clothing, and furniture. If you've a hat fetish, Handmaid has a wacky selection of floppy straw ones adorned with giant flowers and fake fruit.

SATURDAY EVENING
Drinks

Sunset Cocktail at the Mooring, Sayer's Wharf (indoors ♥) ♥ ♥, $$, 401/846-2260. In transit: If you go back to your room to change, just drive back to the Gateway and park for the evening. There's also parking at the Mooring, but it's more expensive. From Gateways walk past the Marriott on America's Cup Avenue. The Mooring is a large white building set right on the water, plainly visible from the street.

Once the home of the New York Yacht Club Station #6, the Mooring is a casual and popular spot that's known more for its view than its food. The harborside outdoor terrace is an ideal perch for yacht watching. If you're visiting in cooler weather, the indoor bar still offers glimpses of the harbor, as well as an oversized fireplace.

Dinner

The White Horse Tavern, ♡ ♡ ♡, $$$$, Marlborough and Farewell streets, 401/849-3600. In transit: Walk up to Thames Street, which runs parallel to America's Cup. Turn left onto Thames, then right onto Marlborough. The White Horse is on the left.

The White Horse may be famous because it's the oldest tavern in America, but it also just happens to serve the best food in Newport. It's the kind of institution you'd suspect couldn't live up to its reputation, but The White Horse is as good as everyone says it is.

Built in 1673, the exterior's wooden clapboards are painted deep maroon. Inside, the low-beamed ceilings, dark, wide floorboards, and massive fireplaces give the place an unmistakable authenticity. The pristine white table clothes, soft candlelight, and fresh flowers provide a stark and pleasant contrast to the rough-hewn wood.

The menu consists primarily of traditional continental items, such as grilled breast of duck, chateaubriand, and rack of lamb. Nightly specials might include grilled tuna with salmon mousse, For oenophiles, the White Horse has an extensive French and California wine list, which has won an award of excellence from the *Wine Spectator*. Hours: 6:00 P.M. - 10:00 P.M. daily. (Lunch and Sunday brunch are also served.)

The Commodore Room, ♡ ♡ ♡, $$$, Bannister's Wharf, 401/846-5264. In transit: From The Mooring, with your back to the sea, Bannister's Wharf is directly to the left of Sayer's Wharf. Just walk through one of the porticos, or turn left on America's Cup Avenue. The Black Pearl is at the end of the wharf.

The name sounds auspicious, as if it might be the formal dining room at an exclusive club. In reality, The Commodore Room – part of the The Black Pearl, a casual waterfront café and bar – is just a small dining room tucked behind the Pearl's kitchen. However, its harborside perch and excellent food make it one of Newport's best-loved restaurants.

Although the Commodore Room has some of the same dark varnished wood as the Black Pearl, the white tablecloths and candlelight (not to mention the water view) give the place a far more elegant feel.

Begin with a cup of the Black Pearl's famous chowder, which is spiced with a bit of dill. Or if you'd prefer something more exotic, consider oysters warmed with truffles and cream, or black and blue tuna in a red pepper sauce. Entrees are best described as adventurous continental. They include veal chops with green peppercorn sauce, medallions of veal with morels and champagne sauce, and shrimps, scallops, and lobster with a thermador sauce.

When making reservations, ask for a table by the window in the front. Reservations are a good idea, The Commodore draws crowds even in the off season. Hours: 5:30 P.M. - 10:30 P.M. daily.

Sunday Morning

Stroll along The Cliff Walk.

In transit: This public walk has several access points, but the best place to begin is at the tip of Narragansett Avenue. You can park for free by the side of the road. Narragansett is accessible from all the major thoroughfares: Thames Street, Spring Street, Bellevue Avenue, and Annandale Road. From any of these streets, head west on Narrangansett (away from the harbor). It dead-ends at the Cliff Walk.

This three-mile public path, that separates the majestic blue Atlantic from the great lawns of Newport's finest mansions, is magically, almost surreally, picturesque. Carved out of the craggy rocks that line the shore, it wends its way past Belcourt Castle, Marble House, Beechwood, Rosecliff, Chateau Sur Mer, The Elms, and The Breakers.

If you begin at Narragansett Avenue, you'll be about 10 minutes past the official beginning of the Walk, which starts at Cliff Walk Manor, near Memorial Boulevard. Besides the street parking, Narrangansett is a nice place to start because it is also the site of The Forty Steps. Originally built in 1839, the steps descend nearly 50 feet for a close-up

ocean view. At the end of the 1980s, the old wooden steps were replaced with 48 granite ones.

From the steps (with your back to the street) turn right on the Cliff Walk. This will take you past the mansions. Most of the path is hard-packed gravel, however, outer portions are seriously eroded. It's best to wear sneakers or hiking shoes.

Cliff Walk ends at Bellevue Avenue. You can return via the Walk or on the street. From Bellevue turn right on Narragansett. This will take you back to the Forty Steps.

NOTE: Don't forget your camera.

Visit Hammersmith Farm, Ocean Drive, 401/846-0420. In transit: Drive east on Narragansett Avenue. Then turn left onto Thames Street, and left onto Wellington Avenue. Follow signs for Ocean Drive and Fort Adams State Park. Hammersmith is adjacent to Fort Adams.

Hammersmith Farm holds a special place in American mythology. Here Jacqueline Bouvier and (then Senator) John Kennedy held their wedding reception. This grand weathered shingle 28-room seaside cottage looks every inch Camelot.

Originally built in 1887 by John Auchincloss, the house was used by four generations of the family. Jackie's mother was married to John Auchincloss's son, Hugh. Not only did Jackie summer here during her youth, Kennedy used the home as a summer White House. He had his own office at the house and signed many bills into law here.

Now open to the public, the house is maintained as it existed when the Auchincloss and Kennedy families enjoyed it during the late fifties and early sixties. A pleasant respite from the imposing Bellevue mansions, Hammersmith is at once grand and comfortable. The tour takes visitors through most of the house, including Jackie and Jack's bedroom. (It chastely houses twin beds.)

But perhaps the most interesting area is the dining room. Its floor-to-ceiling windows, revealing a wonderful ocean view, can electronically drop into the basement at the press of a button. Kennedy used to enjoy landing an Air Force I helicopter right on the lawn and walking directly into dinner through the open windows. Tours are held daily from April through October, but weekends only in March and November. Hours: 10:00 A.M. - 5:00 P.M. spring and fall, 10:00 A.M. - 7:00 P.M. summer. Admission: $6.

Lunch

The Black Pearl, $$, Banister's Wharf, 401/846-5264. In transit: Retrace your steps from Hammersmith Farm. At Thames Street, turn left, then turn onto America's Cup Avenue. Park either at the municipal parking lot in front of the Mooring, or continue on to the Gateway Visitors Center. The Black Pearl is at the end of Banister's Wharf, which is right off America's Cup Avenue.

Even if you've already eaten dinner at the Commodore Room, you may want to return to its downscale sister café, the Black Pearl. Several innkeepers report that guests often visit the Pearl more than once on a weekend visit. The reason? Simply, the chowder. And while aficionados differ on exactly what qualities comprise an award winning concoction, most will agree that the Pearl's version – creamy, dill-flavored and thick with clams–is first rate. In addition, the restaurant serves omelets, salads, and sandwiches. Don't expect anything too exotic, most are along the lines of tuna melts and ruebens. If you've really worked up an appetite, try one of the Black Pearl's daily specials.

Decor is nautical, with varnished dark wood walls decorated with maps. Unfortunately, though, the water view is reserved for Commodore Room patrons. Hours: from 11:30 A.M. daily.

Le Bistro, $$-$$$, Bowen's Wharf, 401/849-7778. In transit: Follow the same directions and parking instructions back from Hammersmith Farm. Bowen's Wharf is just north of Bannister's Wharf.

If you're looking for an elegant yet casual repast, consider Le Bistro. Lunch items might include grilled pizza with asparagus and ham, crab cakes with radicchio, and littlenecks on the half shell with creole remoulade. If you'd like a nice harbor view, ask for a seat by the window. Hours: 11:30 A.M. - 5:30 P.M. daily.

La Forge Casino, $$, 186 Bellevue Ave., 401/847-0418. In transit: From Hammersmith, retrace your way back toward Newport. Turn right onto Thames Street, then left onto Narragansett Avenue. Turn left onto Bellevue. La Forge is located at the International Tennis Hall of Fame. A parking lot is directly across the street.

Although La Forge isn't numbered among the best restaurants in Newport, it does serve good food and is a perfect spot for tennis buffs. Enjoy a seafood salad sandwich on the porch that overlooks the grass courts on which the first national tennis championship was played. These courts, still used for professional play, host the annual Volvo Grand Prix and Virginia Slims tournaments. Hours: 11:00 A.M. - 3:00 P.M. (Although lunch is only served on the porch until 3:00, food is served throughout the day and evening in the main dining room.)

SUNDAY AFTERNOON

Short Walking Tour of the Historic Point Section:

In transit: If you've parked by the Mooring or at the Gateway Visitors Center, leave your car. From La Forge, you can either walk directly or drive back to the Gateway and park there. Head north onto Bellevue, then turn left onto Memorial Boulevard, then left on America's Cup Avenue to the Gateway.

After doing the Cliff Walk this morning, you may not be interested in another long walk. But a short, self-guided tour of Newport's Point section will help balance your image of this historic town.

The oldest section of Newport, the Point encompasses the land north of Long Wharf (the Gateways) to the Newport Bridge. The streets are narrow and filled, end-to-end, with neatly restored Colonial houses, most of which are still private residences. Once home to merchants and sea captains, the neighborhood is a sharp contrast to the lavish Bellevue mansions. Despite Newport's past and present fame as a summer mecca for high society, the Point retains a staid Yankee flavor.

Although it will be enjoyable just strolling the streets, you're better off getting a brochure from the Gateway Visitors Center. They have several booklets that provide detailed information on colonial Point homes. Among the more interesting streets are Washington, Bridge, and Elm.

To reach this area, turn left on America's Cup Avenue outside the Gateway. Then turn left onto Bridge.

Elm runs parallel to Bridge, and Washington is perpendicular.

Hunter House (54 Washington St.) is one of the few Point homes open to the public. Operated by the Preservation Society of Newport County, it's considered one of the nation's 10 best examples of residential colonial architecture. The building served as a home to two Rhode Island governors, and also was the headquarters of Admiral de Ternay, commander of the French naval forces during the American Revolution. Now completely restored, it is furnished with fine, authentic 18th century furniture. A National Historic Landmark, Hunter House is open weekends April and October, and daily May through September. Hours: 10:00 A.M. - 5:00 P.M. Admission $6.

Visit Touro Synagogue, 72 Touro St., 401/847-4794. In transit: From the Gateway, walk straight up Marlborough Street, then turn right onto Thames Street, then left onto Touro. The synagogue is right behind the Colony House, which is on the corner of Spring and Touro streets.

Opened in 1759, the Touro Synagogue is the oldest Jewish house of worship in the United States. Moreover, its existence represents the premise on which the original Newport colonists based their lives – religious tolerance. Named after Rabbi Isaac De Touro, who emigrated from Holland and encouraged the synagogue's construction, the build-

ing's tan stucco exterior is simple save the classically inspired columned portico. The building sits diagonally on its lot so that it faces Jerusalem.

Although the Touro Synagogue is still active, it is open to the public and informal tours are given. Hours: 1:00 P.M. - 3:00 P.M. Sundays September through May; 10:00 A.M. - 5:00 P.M. Sunday through Thursday, 10:00 A.M. - 3:00 P.M. Friday, June through August. Closed Saturday. Worship services follow the Sephardic Orthodox ritual. Call for schedule.

Additional Activities

Visit the Museum of Yachting, Fort Adams State Park, Ocean Drive, 401/847-1018. Located in a waterfront 19th century brick building, the museum has an extensive collection of photographs, artifacts, memorabilia, and even small crafts. Among the more interesting exhibits are the America's Cup Gallery and the "mansions and the yachts." The latter tells of the great yachts owned by the gilded age mansion set. Hours: 10:00 A.M. - 5:00 P.M. daily, mid May through October 31. The museum welcomes visitors throughout the year, but by appointment only. (If you plan to visit in winter, be warned that the gallery has no heat.) Admission $3, $2 for seniors.

Visit St. Mary's Church, Spring Street at Memorial Boulevard, 401/847-0475. If you're one of the many Americans with an insatiable interest in all things Kennedy, you'll want to visit St. Mary's. The late President Kennedy married Jacqueline Bouvier here in 1953.

Visit Redwood Library and Athenaeum, 50 Bellevue Ave., 401/847-0292. Built in the late 1740s, this is the oldest library in the United States. As hard as it might be to imagine, Redwood was in operation even before George Washington became president. This National Historic Landmark also houses paintings from several famous Newport artists. Hours: 9:30 A.M. - 5:30 P.M. Monday through Saturday, 9:30 - 5:00 P.M. Monday through Saturday, July and August.

GETTING THERE

BY AIR: The T.F. Green State Airport (401/331-4520) in Providence is about one hour away from Newport. Direct flights are available from several major cities including New York, Philadelphia, Orlando, and Chicago.

BY CAR: Newport is not off a major highway. However, it is easily accessible. From the north, take I-93 south to Route 24 south to either Route 138 south or Route 114 south. Both will take you directly into downtown Newport. From the west, take I-495 east to Route 24 south. From the southeast, take I-195 west to Route 24 south. And from the south, take I-95 to Route 138 east.

BY TRAIN: No train service is available to Newport. However, it is possible to take Amtrak (800/USA-RAIL) to Providence or Kingston, then take a bus into Newport. The Rhode Island Public Transit Authority (401/647-0209) provides daily service from both stations.

BY BUS: Bonanza Bus Lines (401/846-1820, 800/876-2429) offers daily service to Newport from points all around New England.

CAR RENTAL: Thrifty (401/646-4371) at 763 West Main Rd. Other nearby companies include Avis (401/846-1843) at Marina Plaza, Goat Island, and Budget (401/849-5910) at 2199 Post Rd., Warwick.

TAXI/LIMOUSINES SERVICE: Cozy Cab (401/846-2500) at 129 Connell Highway offers shuttle service to and from T.F. Green Airport, as well as regular taxi service.

INFORMATION: The Gateway Visitors Center, America's Cup Avenue (401/849-8098) is a great resource. Hours: 9:00 A.M. - 5:00 P.M. daily. Be sure you pick up a map here. Many streets in downtown Newport are one way, which makes getting around a bit difficult.

Summer

Down East – Blue Hill & Deer Isle, Maine

Lake Champlain Islands, Vermont

Litchfield Hills, Connecticut

Martha's Vineyard, Massachusetts

Wellfleet, Massachusetts

Down East – Blue Hill & Deer Isle
Maine

With little more than 70 hotel and inn rooms available, Blue Hill and Deer Isle are hardly the sort of places that get overrun with tourists. (They leave that to nearby Bar Harbor, which is crowded by visitors from Acadia National Park.) Yet these spits of land, connected by a suspension bridge and known collectively as the East Penobscot Peninsula, have devoted fans.

While its seclusion is appealing to many visitors, the peninsula's quiet beauty is the real key to its allure. Almost surreally peaceful, verdant, blue-berry-bush covered hills surround its small villages, and moss-covered pine forests hug rocky harbor coves the color of midnight.

Yet natural beauty isn't the region's only attraction. For a combined population of just under 4,000, Blue Hill and Deer Isle are amazingly urbane, and are meccas for artists and crafts people. Together the towns boast nearly a dozen galleries, and many artists have well-publicized home studios open to visitors. Among them is Ronald Hayes Pearson, whose work is on permanent collection at New York's Museum of Modern Art. Blue Hill also has two potteries, two book stores, two gourmet restaurants, and its own eclectic radio station (89.6 FM), which is owned by Paul Stookey of Peter, Paul, & Mary fame. And Deer Isle is home to the internationally famous Haystack Mountain School of Crafts.

Interesting too is the region's architecture. Shipbuilding and sea trading brought prosperity to the area in the 19th century. Stately Federal-style homes from that era, meticulously maintained, still line the streets.

While this portion of the Maine seacoast is a popular summer destination, it's not the sort of place people come to flop in the sun. Despite its ocean-side location, it has a surprising dearth of beaches; its shoreline is far more rock than sand. This factor, combined with its remote location and surprising sophistication, makes the Penobscot Peninsula delightfully peaceful – the perfect respite for people who crave a bit of quiet and culture along with their sunshine.

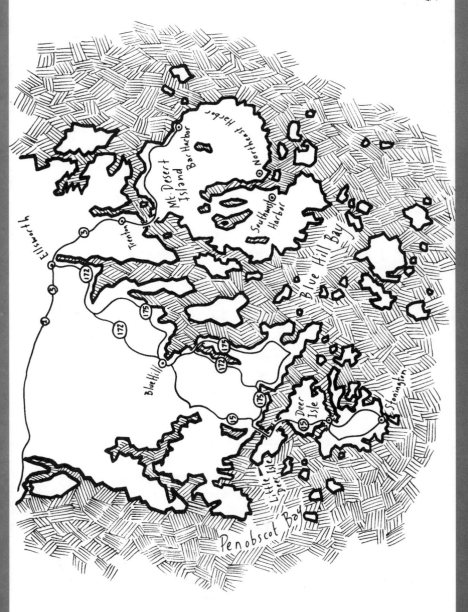

N

Mt. Desert Island

Bar Harbor

Northeast Harbor

Southwest Harbor

Ellsworth

Trenton

3

172

175

172

Blue Hill

172

175

172

Blue Hill Bay

173

Deer Isle

15

15

Stonington

Little Deer Isle

Penobscot Bay

BLUE HILL & DEER ISLAND

Where To Stay

The Blue Hill Inn, ♥ ♥ ♥, $$-$$$, Union Street, Blue Hill 04614, 207/374-2844. The Blue Hill Inn is one of those spots that makes you relax as soon as you walk through the door. It could be the classical music wafting through the rooms, the roaring fire in the living room, or the savory smells emanating from the kitchen where gourmet dinners are prepared.

The Blue Hill Inn doesn't look extraordinary. Like so many other fine inns, it's outfitted with hand-hooked rugs, antiques, and quilts. What makes Blue Hill outstanding is the attention innkeepers Mary and Don Hartley pay to their guests. Mary is always somewhere to be found, ready to offer suggestions on what to do, or just to chat. She genuinely enjoys innkeeping—and it shows.

Common areas include a comfortable living room with blue pineapple stenciled wallpaper, maroon wing chairs, a deep, red Oriental, and some interesting antiques, including a bank safe, now a table. A game room has stocked bookcases, set-up games of chess and checkers, and a long wooden table filled with information on the area.

Of the 11 guest rooms, three have working fireplaces. If you don't mind being on the ground floor (these rooms tend to be the noisiest), one of the most pleasant rooms is number 10. It has a queen-size bed, wine-colored wallpaper, crewel drapes, and a pale gray wood floor covered by an Oriental rug.

Room 5 has a much lighter look, but is equally pleasant with mauve-flowered wallpaper, a needlepoint rug, queen-size cannonball bed, working fireplace, and an an antique writing desk.

Even if you can't get a room with a fireplace, you won't be disappointed, for all of Blue Hill's rooms are decorated with equal style and taste. However, they do vary a bit in size.

Known as much for its food as its rooms, the inn serves an elegant full breakfast that includes coffee, fresh-squeezed orange juice, homemade muffins and granola, yogurt, and a selection of entrees that range from blueberry pancakes to fresh herb omelets with smoked salmon.

Every evening at 6:00, hors d'oeuvres are set out in the living room, where Mary and Don mingle with guests. Dinner starts promptly at 7:00 P.M., and is served in the dining room, which is elegantly set with lace-covered tables and candles. (See Friday Dinner.)

The Blue Hill Inn is located in the heart of town. Galleries and shops, as well as the town's harborside park, is within easy walking distance.

RATES PER NIGHT: $120-$160 including breakfast and dinner. B&B rates are $90-$130.

ACCOMMODATIONS: 11 rooms with private baths.

AMENITIES: Some rooms have working fireplaces.

RESTRICTIONS: No children under 13. No smoking. No pets.

(The Blue Hill Inn also offers overnight schooner sails on Penobscot and Blue Hill bays. The three-night package includes two nights at the inn and one on the schooner. We didn't have the chance to take the trip ourselves, but it sounds exciting.)

John Peters Inn, ♡ ♡ ♡, $$-$$$, Peters Point, Blue Hill 04614, 207/374-2116. Set on a hill overlooking Blue Hill Harbor, this Federal-style brick mansion, with four massive Doric columns supporting a front porch, looks like something from Gone With the Wind. Indeed, the John Peters is the area's most elegant inn. It sits on 25 waterside acres, just one mile outside of town.

Innkeepers Barbara and Rick Seeger, who've owned the John Peters since 1985, have done a nice job giving the inn a sophisticated feel. Furnishings are restrained and stately. The living room runs the full length of the house and boasts twin fireplaces (only one is actually used), a grand piano, and three Oriental rugs. Walls are painted off white, and the furniture is similarly neutral.

Of the inn's 14 rooms, the most sought after is the Blue Hill room. Its king-size four-poster bed is covered with a fluffy down comforter and the wood floors are covered with pale blue Orientals. Other features include a working fireplace, sitting area, and private deck – where Barbara is happy to serve a private breakfast. (For couples celebrating a special occasion, she's been known to throw in a bottle of champagne.)

Seven additional rooms are located in the main inn. The Surry Room is another top choice. It has a soft look – cream walls with a rose border, king-size bed with a rose-patterned comforter, fireplace, sitting area, and harbor views.

A carriage house holds five rooms. These accommodations are more casual but equally pleasant. Both the Searsport and Westport rooms have fireplaces, kitchens, and private decks.

The John Peters offers full breakfasts, complete with a wait staff. It's usually served on the sun porch, which has French doors that frame magnificent views of the harbor. The porch is furnished with antique wooden chairs covered with needlepoint cushions and small tables dressed in pale blue cloths. The menu has extensive selections that include fresh-squeezed orange juice, poached eggs with asparagus, cinnamon French toast, and pecan waffles.

RATES PER NIGHT: $85-$135. Open only through the end of October.

ACCOMMODATIONS: 14 rooms with private baths. Some rooms have fireplaces and/or decks, and kitchens.

AMENITIES: Swimming pool, canoe, and sailboat.

RESTRICTIONS: No children under 12. No smoking. No pets.

Pilgrim's Inn, ♥ ♥ ♥, $$$, The Sunset Road, Deer Isle 04627, 207/348-6615. Built 200 years ago by a groom for his bride, the brick-red clapboard house was considered the island's finest residence in 1793. Today, the Pilgrim's Inn is still among the nicest places to live on Deer Isle–even if only for a weekend. Innkeepers Dud and Jean Hendrick, who bought the inn in 1982, have done a fine job of preserving its historic flavor.

The main sitting area, with a remarkably large wood-burning fireplace, low-beamed ceilings, and polished wood floors, has an unmistakable authenticity. The room is casually outfitted with country antiques, comfortable furniture, and has lovely views of the millpond behind the inn.

Upstairs, off the main entrance, are two more formal public rooms. The library has built-in bookshelves (exceedingly well-stocked), a large blue and mauve Oriental, and green wing chairs–perfect for reading. Opposite is the parlor in which the Hendricks display works from many local artists, including sculpture, paintings, and herbal and flower wreaths.

Of the 12 guest rooms, number 8 is the most pleasant. Antique lovers will appreciate the elaborately hand-carved pine bed frame. (Unfortunately, it's only a double.) The comforter and curtains are done in a cheery blue, yellow, and green flowered print. And the wood floor is covered with a pale yellow and blue checked rug. Room 5 is another winner, with burgundy walls, cherry furniture, and a blue paisley bed quilt, all of which provide a masculine aura.

For those looking for complete seclusion, Pilgrim's also has a one-bedroom cottage in the heart of Deer Isle Village, just a two-minute walk from the inn. It includes a full kitchen, dining area, bedroom, bath, and living room with beamed ceilings and a fireplace.

Full breakfast is served in the inn's dining room, which derives its funky appeal from its barn-board walls, straw mat floor, and wood stove. However, the most popular meal of the day at Pilgrim's is dinner. (It has won rave reviews from *Bon Appetit!* And Julia Child has even dined here.)

The evening begins at 6:00 with an elaborate selection of hors d'oeuvres set out in the Tavern Room, which has a full liquor license. Dinner is served at 7:00 and features one nightly entree.

RATES PER NIGHT: $72-$120. MAP rates which include dinner are $135-$160.

ACCOMMODATIONS: 12 rooms, 8 with private baths.

AMENITIES: Restaurant serving breakfast and dinner. Tavern with full bar. Bicycles available for guests.

RESTRICTIONS: No smoking in guest rooms or dining room. No pets.

Goose Cove Lodge, ♡♡-♡♡♡, $$-$$$, Goose Cove Road (P.O. Box 40), Sunset 04683, 207/348-2508. The Goose Cove Lodge is not for everyone. Accommodations are in individual rustic cabins that have no Oriental rugs or fine antiques. Yet its location in a secluded pine grove directly on Goose Cove, a quiet bay inlet, is spectacular.

That said, it should also be noted that Goose Cove is known primarily as a family resort — it's swarming with young children in July and August, precisely because the lodge makes every effort to accommodate them. However, it's included here for couples who may choose to visit in the early fall, when the galleries and lobster shacks are still open. By then, when the children have finally gone back to school, the Lodge takes on a quiet, peaceful demeanor. It's the perfect escape for couples who appreciate the wilderness and have always dreamed of that little cabin in the woods.

All told, Goose Cove has 11 individual cottages. The most desirable of these are Linea and Elm, both of which are located directly on the water. Linea is perhaps the more romantic of the two. It features a kitchenette, stone fireplace, pine-paneled walls, and pale green wood floors covered with a hand-hooked rug. A double bed is located off the sitting area, and a small bedroom has two twin beds and a bath. A deck that raps around the entire cabin affords perfect water views.

An additional 10 cabin-style rooms are located in two lodge annexes. Although less desirable than the cabins, most have fireplaces and some have ocean views.

Breakfast is served in the main lodge, a great log cabin with a grand stone fireplace, piano, comfortable green plaid upholstered furniture, and kilm rugs. The buffet offers juice, fruit, homemade breads and muffins, hot and cold cereals, and some hot entrees.

Dinner is served at the lodge through mid September. It is included in the room rate. Although guests are free to dine elsewhere, the rate is not reduced. (Free box lunches are given as compensation.) From mid September to late October, when the lodge closes, only bed and breakfast accommodations are available.

RATES PER NIGHT: $90-$130. Rates for July and August are per person and include dinner; they are $78-$98.

ACCOMMODATIONS: 10 suites and rooms in 2 annexes, and 10 cottages that sleep between 2 and 6.

AMENITIES: Restaurant that serves breakfast and dinner. (Dinner is BYOB.) Hiking trails adjacent to property.

RESTRICTIONS: No pets during July and August.

FRIDAY EVENING
Dinner

The Blue Hill Inn, ♡ ♡ ♡, $$$, Union Street, Blue Hill, 207/374-2844. In transit: If you're just coming into Blue Hill on Route 15 south, follow it until you reach the center of town. Turn right on Main Street. At the town hall, bear right onto Union Street. The Blue Hill Inn is just a few doors down on the left. If you're coming on Route 15 north from Deer Isle, the town hall will be on your left, as will Union Street.

Even if you're not staying at the Blue Hill Inn, you should try it for dinner. Innkeeper Mary Hartley no longer does the cooking herself, but she still orchestrates the evening, greeting both inn and dinner guests at the 6:00 P.M. cocktail hour. Enjoy a glass of wine and an assortment of cheeses while you mingle with other diners, or just relax by the living room fireplace.

At 7:00 o'clock you'll move into the dining room, a simple room that appears to be a converted porch, made magical by a spectacular French brass chandelier lit with real candles. Dinner is a fixed-price affair ($30 per person at this writing) consisting of an appetizer, fruit ice (as a palate refresher), a choice of two entrees, salad, and dessert. When we visited, the meal began with a wild mushroom and chevre tart, followed by grapefruit orange ice. Entrees included honey bourbon glazed quail or poached trout with lemon butter. Salad was served with the meal, which ended with chocolate and hazelnut torte.

Real gourmets might consider visiting the Blue Hill during one of its "tasting" weekends. Four times a year the inn holds a spectacular wine dinner that consists of seven courses served with five different wines. A recent wine dinner included caviar crêpes, venison carpaccio, Calvados-cider ice, roast duck with cassis, green salad, assorted cheeses, and Babas au rhum with marrons glacé. Hours: 7:00 P.M., one seating only. Reservations are required.

Pilgrim's Inn, ♡ ♡, $$$, The Sunset Road, Deer Isle, 207/348-6615. In transit: Follow Route 15 south into Deer Isle. At the village center, you'll see signs for Pilgrim's Inn. Bear right on the Sunset Road. The Pilgim's Inn is a few building's down on the left. It's barn red—impossible to miss.

Like the Blue Hill Inn, Pilgrim's Inn is known for its gourmet dinners. One of the reasons both these places have gone to such lengths to make fine dining part of their business is that the

East Penobscot Peninsula is so remote. While that's precisely what attracts visitors to the area, there isn't a myriad of dining opportunities. (That said there are two other excellent restaurants in Blue Hill. But they are the only real, non-inn restaurants in the area.)

Innkeepers Dud and Jean Hendrick have a great interest in food and put just as much effort into creating their menus as they do into decorating the inn. (On the day we visited, Jean was taste testing smoked oysters at 9:00 A.M. for possible inclusion in a dish.) Jean cooked dinner herself for seven years and won accolades, and while she now has two full-time chefs, she still holds a firm reign on the kitchen.

Cocktails begin at 6:00 P.M. in the Tavern Room, the Pilgrim Inn's full-service bar. Hors d'oeuvres might include cheese fondue served with freshly baked bread, paté, goat cheese, and savory tarts.

Dinner is served in a converted goat barn, which is given a spot of sophistication with starched green and white cloths and candlelight. The fixed-price menu ($27.50 at this writing) includes only one entree offering, but diners with dietary restrictions can be accommodated. Meals are accompanied by soups or appetizers, salads, homegrown vegetables, breads, and desserts. Offerings might include grilled lamb with fresh herbs, roast pork with fruit, or a Maine favorite, boiled lobster. Hours: 7:00 P.M., one seating only. Reservations are required.

SATURDAY MORNING

Explore the Galleries of Blue Hill.

In transit: If you're staying in Deer Isle, simply follow Route 15 north. It will take you right into Main Street. Most galleries and stores are within walking distance of each other. Start your tour at the furthest point and work your way in. Travel down Main Street through the center of Blue Hill. Veer left onto Route 172 (Ellsworth Road). Your first stop, Rackliffe Pottery, is about a mile down on the left. After visiting this shop and Peninsula Weavers, head back to Main Street. Park your car and walk to the rest of the galleries.

Rackliffe Pottery, Ellsworth Road, 207/374-2297. Phyllis and Phil Rackliffe worked at Blue Hill's venerable Rowantrees Pottery for 22 years before breaking out on their own. They offer a similar but more limited selection of products – dinner sets, serving bowls, canisters, and jelly sets. They use local clay and earth colors: sea blue, moss green, and a daffodil yellow. Among Rackliffe's most famous products are its dishes, which are hand painted in a blueberry pattern.

One nice aspect of Rackliffe's is that its work area is right off the showroom, and they're happy to have visitors watch.

Peninsula Weavers, Ellsworth Road, 207/374-2760. This shop is tiny, but carries an interesting selection of woven rugs, blankets, table linens, and scarves, all made in the upstairs studio. It also carries some Swedish imports, including yarns and hand-painted clogs.

Handworks, Main Street (above Blue Hill Department Store), 207/374-5613. With its wonderful collection of contemporary crafts, all done by local artists,this shop is a don't miss. Merchandise includes hand-painted floor cloths, lamps, furniture, clothing, and jewelry. It's almost impossible to visit and not buy something.

S.L. Kinney Studio & Gallery, Main Street, 207/374-5894. One of Blue Hill's newer galleries, S.L. Kinney offers a fascinating selection of contemporary American, Native American, and Shamanic art. (Shamans are honored people in tribal communities who are an intermediaries between the natural and supernatural worlds.) Works include paintings, sculpture, Mayan medicine carvings, and Southwestern Pueblo jewelry.

North Country Textiles, Main Street, 207/374-5894. Merchandise includes a large selection of nubby blankets, sweaters, scarves, and baby items in silks and cottons.

Liros Gallery, Main Street, 207/347-5370. This is a good spot for people with traditional taste in art. Liros specializes in old maps and prints, and American School works. Liros also has an extensive selection of 18th and 19th century Russian and Greek icons.

Sweet Myrtle, Main Street, 207/374-2101. Although this shop doesn't deal in art per se, it does have some lovely dried flower arrangements, including wreaths and topiaries. Other items include birch bark picture frames and birdhouses.

The Leighton Gallery, Parker Point Road, 207/374-5001. Voted the best gallery in Maine in 1991, it enjoys a cachet usually awarded to urban haunts. Artist Judy Leighton features not only her own work, but that of about 40 other contemporary artists. Among the gallery's most popular artists is local wood-carver Eliot Sweet. Sweet, now an octogenarian, is famous for his hand-carved whimsically painted animals. After you've perused the art inside, don't forget to check out Leighton's outdoor sculpture garden.

Rowantrees Pottery, Union Street, 207/374-5535. The story goes that it was Mahatma Ghandi who convinced Adelaide Pearson, a wealthy matron who dabbled in pottery, to devote herself to the craft. (He told her it was one of man's basic arts dating back to the dawn of civilization, and should be approached seriously.) And thus, in 1939, one of the country's most famous potteries was born. Today, Sheila Varnum, one of Pearson's protégés, runs Rowantrees. She still churns out the same products that first brought the studio attention:

simple earthy bowls, mugs, and plates, made with local clay and granite. (The glazes are made with ground granite from Bar Harbor and Blue Hill.)

Lunch

The Left Bank Café, $, Ellsworth Road/Route 172, Blue Hill, 207/374-2201. In transit: From Main Street, head north on Route 15, back toward Rackliffe's. Turn left onto Route 172. The Left Bank is on the left.

Groovy is the best way to describe the Left Bank Café, the closest thing Blue Hill has to a restaurant "institution." The sound of folk music wafts through Left Bank's two rooms. And on the day we visited, patrons and restaurant workers were debating the benefits of libertarianism.

The front room houses the "bar," where locally made wines and ciders are served, as well as a take-out bakery counter, a few wooden booths, and a wood stove. The back room has many windows that overlook a large vegetable garden. Cream walls are decorated with works by local artists.

The menu, while leaning toward the healthful, is in no way "crunchy." Lunch items include homemade soups, pizzas, salads, and hearty sandwiches, all served on dense, freshly baked bread. Selections include ham and Jarlsberg, and turkey with cheddar, bacon, avocado, and Swiss cheese. If you're a coffee lover, know that Left Bank brags that it grinds beans for every cup! Hours: 7:00 A.M. - 10:00 P.M. Breakfast, lunch, and dinner are served.

Partridge Drug, $, Main Street, 207/374-2864. In transit: Partridge Drug Store is in the center of Blue Hill. If you're heading south on Main Street, it's on the left, diagonally across from the town hall.

If you're not hungry for a real lunch, consider heading over to Partridge Drug. This place is an old-fashioned drug store that looks as if it hasn't changed since the '40s. Its soda fountain is still the place where locals congregate to discuss the day's news. Order a dish of vanilla ice cream and a cup of coffee and join in the fun.

SATURDAY AFTERNOON

Scout Out Individual Artists' Studios and Galleries Throughout Blue Hill and Deer Isle. In transit: Fortunately for tourists, the towns allow artists and galleries to post roadside signs. It's easy to find these studios without specific directions because they are so well marked. And virtually all have their signs along Route 15. All a traveler has to do is follow the arrows. Starting in Blue Hill, just drive along Route 15 south and enjoy. Following is a list of some of the more interesting studios and galleries. Directions are provided when appropriate. (Although most artists have their studios open full time through mid October, it's a good idea to call ahead.)

Janet Redfield, Cape Rosier Road, Harborside, 207/326-4778. In transit: From Route 15, you'll see signs pointing to Janet Redfield's. Turn right on Route 176 and pass through the town of South Brooksville. Cape Rosier Road is on the left. Redfield's studio is a few miles down on the left.

If you enjoy stained glass, Janet Redfield's studio is worth a trip. She produces colorful, representational work – vegetables, birds, and flowers. Most of her pieces are hanging panels, but she also does light fixtures and planters. Redfield does work on commission, and has been known to recreate a painting in stained glass.

Kathy Woell, 156 Old Ferry Road, Deer Isle, 207/348-6141. Woell hand weaves some great, funky clothing using wool, mohair, rayon, and chenille. Ready-made work is available, or choose your own material and colors and Woell will design to order.

Ronald Hayes Pearson, Old Ferry Road, 207/348-2535. Pearson is among the most famous artists on the Penobscot Peninsula. His work is on permanent exhibit at New York's Museum of Modern Art, the Smithsonian Institution in Washington D.C., and the American Craft Museum in New York. Although an accomplished sculptor, he is best known as a jewelry maker. His many silver and gold creations – which include pins, earrings, bracelets, and wedding bands – are on sale in a second-floor gallery.

William Mor Stoneware & Oriental Rugs, Reach Road, Deer Isle, 207/347-2822. In transit: Mor's studio isn't hard to find, but just keep in mind that it's a "country" 3 ½ miles down Reach Road. Don't give up, you'll get there eventually. It's on the right.

Mor produces simple, functional, handthrown pottery. Most pieces are glazed in earthy shades of brown. He also sells wonderful tribal and village rugs from Turkey and Afghanistan, both new and antique. (Prices are excellent.) All merchandise is housed in a new post and beam barn.

The Blue Heron Gallery, Church Street, Deer Isle, 207/348-6051. Located in an old barn, this gallery carries American contemporary crafts primarily from faculty at the Haystack Mountain School of Crafts. Works include pottery and sculpture.

Visit the Sow's Ear Winery, Route 176, Brooksville, 207/326-4649. In transit: From Route 15 south, turn right on Route 176. Sow's Ear is on the right. You pass it on the way to Janet Redfield's. So you may want to stop here on your way.

This quirky little place, which appears to be more of a shack than a winery, is a fun detour. Proprietor Tom Hoey always made cider for himself and friends, but is now making it commercially. He produces a dry, English-style hard cider from organically grown apples. Most apples come from wild trees on the Penobscot Peninsula. However, a few come from the young orchard Hoey has planted; he's growing 60 different varieties, primarily historical types that farmers pressed some 200 years ago.

Hoey is happy to explain the cider process, and give a tour and free tastings. (The copper bar used for the tastings alone is worth the visit.)

An added bonus: Hoey's wife Gail Disney is a hand weaver who makes custom wool and cotton rag rugs. Her studio is above the winery, and guests are free to visit.

Saturday Evening
Dinner

Jonathan's, ♥-♥ ♥, $$$, Main Street, Blue Hill, 207/3374-5226. In transit: Jonathan's is in the center of Blue Hill village. If you're traveling north on Route 15 from Deer Isle, it's on the left.

Jonathan's is a lifesaver for locals with discerning palates. It's the only gourmet restaurant open year-round, and thus has a devoted following. To visitors it offers uncomplicated but pleasant surroundings and inventive food.

The el-shaped dining room has oyster colored walls adorned with a few small pieces of art, and tables dressed with blue cloths and crystal candle holders. It's nothing fancy, but the lights

are soft, and the general feeling is comfortable.

Emphasis is on local produce. Appetizers include a warm green salad with smoked mussels, chevre, and pine nuts; spanakopita (a savory Greek pastry filled with spinach and feta cheese); and homemade soups. On the night we visited, the selection was a delicious apple and turnip soup.

Although the chef makes several specials every night, a typical menu might include grilled swordfish with pesto mayonnaise; Maine crab cakes with red peppers, garlic, and cilantro cream; and locally-raised rabbit braised with honey, mustard, garlic, and tarragon.

Wine aficionados will appreciate the extensive list – a *Wine Spectator* award winner – which includes some locally-produced fruit wines. They are balanced with selections from California, Italy, France, and Australia.

Desserts are a little less sophisticated. A favorite is Jonathan's sweet potato pie. Hours: 5:00 P.M. - 9:00 P.M. Friday and Saturday, 5:00 P.M. - 8:30 P.M. Tuesday through Thursday. Closed Monday.

Firepond, ♥ ♥ ♥, $$$, Main Street, Blue Hill, 207/374-2135. In transit: Firepond is in the heart of Blue Hill village, just a few doors down from Johnathan's. If you're traveling north on Route 15 from Deer Isle, it's on the left.

The Firepond has enjoyed a reputation as *the* gourmet restaurant on the East Penobscot Peninsula since it opened more than 17 years ago. However, it has changed hands and chefs several times over the past few years, causing great consternation among its fans. The restaurant seems to have steadied its course recently, and locals are garnering it with praise again.

Appetizers include lobster ravioli in a roasted pepper cream sauce; warm greens with bacon vinaigrette; and a selection of pâtés and terrines. Entrees are similarly well conceived. Lobster Firepond is an elaborate preparation of Maine's most popular crustacean: It's served in a cream sauce of Boursin, fontina, and Romano cheese, over a bed of pasta. Other entrees include scallops with fresh leeks, which are simmered in vermouth and served with a mushroom cream sauce, and lamb with fresh basil, roasted garlic, and wild mushrooms in a brandy sauce.

Although top-notch food has always been Firepond's claim to fame, it also has a great location—perched on the edge of an old mill stream. The porch, which sits almost on top of the water, is a perfect spot for summer dining. If the weather is cool, the rustically elegant interior with soft candlelight, Oriental rugs, and barn-board walls is also pleasant. Hours: 5:00 P.M. - 9:30 P.M. Open Memorial Day through Columbus Day. (Some years it has been open longer.)

SUNDAY MORNING

Hike To the Top of Blue Hill.

In transit: Head north on Route 15 to Blue Hill center. Follow Main Street north, then turn left on Route 172. Across from the Blue Hill Fair Grounds is Mountain Road. Turn left, and travel about 1.5 miles. On the right you'll see a rocky gravel path and to the left a shoulder in the road where you can park your car. There are no signs, but the path is fairly easy to identify.

This pleasant, short hike winds its way up to the top of Blue Hill and affords spectacular views of the town, harbor, and surrounding mountains. It should take no more than 45 minutes to reach the summit. And although obviously uphill, it is not too strenuous. The trail is gravel, rock, and mud. You can easily walk the path in sneakers, but it's not a bad idea to wear hiking boots if you have them.

Early Snack

Merrill & Hinckley, $, Union Street, Blue Hill, 207/374-2821. In transit: This grocery store and deli is on the corner of Main and Union Streets, across from the town hall.

Rather than have a full lunch, get a light snack and relax after your hike. Merrill & Hinckley carries fruit, juice, yogurt, muffins, cookies, and deli snacks. The reasoning behind this suggestion is that you can't leave the area without eating at Eaton's Lobster Pool, which is only open from 5:00 P.M. - 9:00 P.M. Perfect for an early dinner before you go home.

Relax at Blue Hill Town Park. In transit: From the Blue Hill path, continue along Mountain Road to the end. Then turn left onto Pleasant Street. Turn left onto Main Street. Then turn left at the drugstore. This road dead-ends at the Blue Hill Town Park.

Although little, this park sits right on Blue Hill Harbor and is a wonderfully peaceful spot. It's the perfect place to catch your breath after a brisk hike. (Bring along your snacks.) Relax on the small rocky beach. If the tide is low, you may be able to walk out to one of the large rock formations near the shore.

Sunday Afternoon

Visit the Haystack Mountain School of Crafts, Sunshine Road, Deer Isle, 207/348-2306. In transit: Follow Route 15 south to Deer Isle. Turn right on Sunshine Road. Follow it all the way to the end. The road dead ends at Haystack.

This internationally famous craft school holds courses throughout the summer. And for several hours each week (call for specific hours), it offers free visitor tours. Guests not only learn about the school's history, but also have a chance to visit the artists in their studios. (Don't expect in-depth discussions, most of the artists are hard at work.)

Even if you don't make the scheduled tour, Haystack's grounds are always open to the public and are alone worth a visit. The school's low-rise natural wood structures are built into a hill that rises up from the bay. A long descent of wooden stairs leads to the water. Several walking trails surround the school, and visitors are free to use them.

Walk Around Goose Cove and out to the Barred Island Nature Preserve. In transit: From Haystack, follow Route 15 north back to Deer Isle Village. Turn left onto the Sunset Road. (You'll see signs pointing to the Goose Cove Lodge.) Follow it to Goose Cove Road. It dead-ends at the Lodge, which offers parking and trail maps to visitors who want to hike.

This 70-acre preserve offers absolutely magical walking trails through pine forests, along rocky beaches, and through an island nature conservancy. It's possible to spend the entire afternoon walking among the seven marked trails.

One of the most popular is the Shore Trail. It meanders through a moss-covered pine forest and offers glimpses of Goose Cove all along the way. It dead-ends at a small beach. During low tide, hikers can walk across the sand bar to Barred Island. There, a hiking trail runs around the island's perimeter. (The sandbar is a great spot for finding interesting shells and driftwood.)

EARLY DINNER

Eaton's Lobster Pool, ♡, $$, Blastow's Cove, Little Deer Isle, 2207/348-2383. In transit: Follow Route 15 north back toward Blue Hill. A sign for Blastow's Cove and Eaton's will be on your left.

Having eaten my first lobster here at the age of 5, Eaton's has always held a special place in this lobster lover's heart. Since 1960, it has been considered the area's premier lobster pound. Considering its reputation, the setting is surprisingly simple (but therein lies its charm) – a cluster of white clapboard buildings hugging a quiet cove.

Sit outside on picnic benches right by the water. Or, if it's cold and drizzly, get an inside table near the stone fireplace. (The indoor dining room has grown considerably over the years and now seats 125.)

Eaton's is famous for its shore dinners, which include steamers, lobster, salad, chips, and a roll. Other selections include fried scallops, clams, and haddock, as well as steamed clams and oysters, and a variety of seafood sandwiches. For carnivores, Eaton's also offers steak. Hours: 5:00 P.M. - 9:00 P.M.

Open through Columbus Day. Eaton's is BYOB.

Additional Activities

Visit the Crockett Cove Woods Preserve, Whitman Road, Stonington. This 100-acre coastal forest was donated to the Nature Conservancy in 1975 by a local architect. The self-guided nature trail winds through dense spruce woods and crosses a miniature bog covered with a thick mat of sphagnum moss. A brochure at the preserve's entrance describes the various walks and points of interest.

Mail Boat Trip to, and Hiking on, Isle Au Haut. Catch the mail boat in Stonington and visit this quiet island. Only six miles long and three miles wide, it has a year-round population of 46. A section of Acadia National Park covers much of the island and offers many trails for walking and hiking. A map of these trails is available at the Isle Au Haut boat dock. Call 207/367-5193 for boat information.

Visit the Big Chicken Barn, Route 3, Ellsworth, 207/667-7308. Billed as the largest antiquarian book shop and antique dealer in Maine, this 21,000-square-foot store offers a huge array of merchandise. It's a great spot for browsing, and is filled with junk and treasures alike. Prices are excellent. On our visit, hand-carved antique pine dressers were selling for about $250. (It's about a half hour from Blue Hill.)

Go Sea Kayaking. Explorers at Sea, P.O. Box 469, East Main St., Stonington, 207/367-2356. It offers supervised sea kayaking adventures from May through September. Half day and full day trips are available.

Visit the Maine Crafts Association, 6 Dow Rd., Deer Isle, 207/348-9943. Check out the portfolio slides of more than 100 Maine artists. This is a great spot for those serious about craft collecting. However, it's only open 9:00 A.M. - 5:00 P.M. Monday through Friday.

GETTING THERE

BY AIR: Hancock County-Bar Harbor Airport in Trenton, Maine, is the closest airport to the East Penobscot Peninsula. It is serviced by Colgan Air (800/272-5488), which flies from Boston's Logan Airport. Bangor International Airport is about 90 minutes from Blue Hill and Deer Isle. It is serviced by Delta (800/638-7333), Continental (800/231-0856), and United (800/241-6522).

BY CAR: The East Penobscot Peninsula is about a five-hour ride (250 miles) from Boston. Take I-95 north to Augusta. Then take Route 201, to Route 202 east. Follow Route 202 to Route 3

east, past Bucksport. Then take Route 15 south to Blue Hill and Deer Isle. Route 202 is also accessible from the Maine Turnpike. From northern New Hampshire or Vermont, follow Route 2 east to Bangor. Then take Route 395 to Route 15 south.

BY TRAIN: No train service is available.

BY BUS: No direct service is available. However, Greyhound/Trailways (617/423-5810) has daily service to Bangor from New York, Boston, and other eastern seaboard cities.

CAR RENTAL: Hertz (800/654-3131), Avis (800/331-1212), and Budget (800/787-8200) have offices at the Hancock County-Bar Harbor Airport. Avis, Hertz, Budget, National (800/227-7368), and Dollar (207/947-0188) all have offices at the Bangor International Airport.

TAXI/LIMOUSINE SERVICE: A-Z Taxi & Tours, P.O. Box 184, Stonington 04681, 207/348-6186. This company also rents cars.

INFORMATION: Write the Blue Hill Chamber of Commerce, P.O. Box 520, Blue Hill, ME 04514. For information on Deer Isle, call the Stonington Chamber of Commerce, 207/348-6124.

Lake Champlain Islands, Vermont

When you're driving to northern Vermont, and you happen upon a recipe-swap talk show while scanning the car radio dial, you'll know you're close to the Lake Champlain islands. Quietly tucked in the state's northwest corner, and surrounded by the nation's largest body of fresh water next to the Great Lakes, these islands are amazingly anachronistic. Beat-up, boat-sized Chevys and Oldsmobiles roam winding roads flanked by cornfields and cow pastures. Unmanned vegetable stands rely on the honor system for payment. And the nightlife doesn't get much wilder than an occasional church supper.

Thirty miles long and four miles wide, the Lake Champlain Islands comprise five communities that are linked via a set of bridges. They are North Hero, South Hero, Grand Isle, Isle La Motte, and Alburg (the latter is really a peninsula bordering Canada). Virtually uninhabited until the late 1770s, the islands were settled in 1779 as part of a charter granted to Ethan and Ira Allen and their Green Mountain Boys. (The area is named after the brothers, both of whom were "heroes" in the American Revolution.)

The islands have certainly developed since the Allens inhabited them, but they remain sleepy communities with a total year-round population of 5,000. And although the southern tip is less than 20 minutes from Burlington, and the northern end only an hour from Montreal, the Lake Champlain islands have remained largely undiscovered by tourists. As such, they lack the high-priced shops, gourmet restaurants, and lavish accommodations that tourism so often encourages. Yet they offer great beauty—placid, crystal blue water with views of the Green Mountains to the east and the Adirondacks to the west. They are the perfect respite for those looking to escape the traffic and trappings of modern life.

The islands offer leisurely outdoor activities. Their main attractions are, of course, the lake, as well as their little-traveled shoreside roads which are a treat for bicyclists. If you're content to loll in a canoe, bicycle through farmlands, and enjoy a homemade cider donut at a roadside stand, you'll fall in love with this little corner of New England.

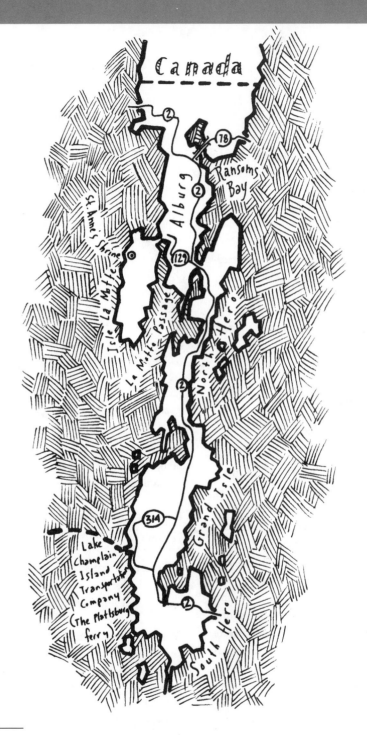

Canada

2

78

St. Anne's Shrine

Alburg

Ransoms Bay

2

129

Isle La Motte

La Motte Passage

North Hero

2

Grand Isle

314

Lake Champlain Island Transportation Company (The Plattsburg ferry)

2

South Hero

N

LAKE CHAMPLAIN ISLANDS

Where To Stay

North Hero House, ♡-♡♡, $-$$, Route 2, North Hero 05474, 802/372-8237. (From mid September to mid June, call 908/439-2837.) Serving travelers to the Lake Champlain islands for more than 100 years, the North Hero House is a venerable establishment and the islands' only true country inn.

The main building, a small mustard-colored clapboard structure, looks every inch the old-guard lakeside retreat. An American flag flies over the door. The front porch is lined with cherry-red rockers that face the lake and the distant Green Mountains. And the reception area has an old-fashioned wooden check-in counter, as well as a sitting area with wicker chairs and a small brick fireplace.

Seven rooms are located in the main inn. However, the most sought-after accommodations are across the street in the three lakeside cottages. Of these, among the most desirable is The Cobbler's Room (room 3) in The Homestead, which was originally built as a private home more than a century ago. The room boasts a separate sitting area with a fireplace and a private screened porch that overlooks the beach and lake. Another top spot is the Cove House's room 1. Although it doesn't have a sitting area, its porch juts right over the lake.

All told, 17 of North Hero House's rooms have private porches, and an additional seven have semi-private porches. Rooms are unfussy and pleasant; many have chenille spreads and wood paneling. Old-home aficionados will enjoy the Cove House's exposed brick walls and ambiance.

One of the nicest things about North Hero is its amenities. Besides a small beach, guests may lounge on wooden deck chairs set up along what was once a steamboat dock, but is now a lovely green lawn. Also on hand are a clay tennis court, shuffle board court, sauna, and bicycles. The inn also has sunfish, paddle and motor boats, all available for a small fee.

Guests are treated to a continental breakfast, served in North Hero's dining room, that includes juice, coffee, tea, and homemade muffins. Lunch and dinner are also available, but for an extra charge.

Rates per night: $41-$95. The inn is open mid June through mid September.

Accommodations: 23 rooms with private baths; 13 rooms have private porches, and 7 have semi-private porches.

Amenities: Restaurant serving breakfast, lunch, and dinner. Tennis court, sauna, small private beach, and shuffleboard. Boat rentals available. Fans in rooms.

Restrictions: No pets.

Thomas Mott Homstead, ♥, $$, Blue Rock Road, Alburg 05440, 802/796-3736, outside Vermont 800/ 348-0843, ex 12. Pat Schallert, a retired wine dealer from Los Angeles turned innkeeper, runs his B&B with unflagging enthusiasm and genuine concern for his guests.

Pat has converted a 170-year-old lakeside farmhouse into a cozy inn with four guest rooms. Many of the heavy beamed original walls remain, as well as some ceiling beams and wooden floors. Yet all guest rooms enjoy such modern amenities as private baths and carpeting. They are simply and pleasantly decorated with wooden furniture and handmade quilts that Schallert either uses as a bedspread or wall displays. The choice room is Ransom's Rest, a truly rustic romantic retreat with a low, sloping ceiling, angled fireplace, and a balcony with views of Ransom's Bay and Mt. Mansfield.

Pat takes great pride in his breakfasts, which are served family style at an antique Canadian tailor's table. In addition to grinding coffee beans each day, he has a repertoire that includes green tomato omelets and raspberry pancakes. In fact, Pat is willing to prepare virtually anything that strikes a guest's fancy.

Common rooms include a living room with stunning lake views, a fireplace, television, and some good-for-flopping furniture, as well as an enclosed porch, and three outdoor porches.

This B&B is a bit off the beaten path. And Pat makes it easy for guests to lounge around the inn all day, rather than venturing out to the islands. Guests are free to use Pat's canoe. He also has bocci ball, croquet, and other games, which guests can set up in the expansive yard. For those interested in more sedentary – and gastronomic – pursuits, he keeps 10 pints of Ben & Jerry's ice cream in the freezer (along with iced glass bowls) so people can help themselves.

Although Thomas Mott doesn't serve dinner, Pat will arrange for gourmet chefs to come to the inn and prepare a private meal. In summer, it's served on the enclosed porch.

RATES PER NIGHT: $50-$65.

ACCOMMODATIONS: 4 rooms with private baths

AMENITIES: Television in common room. Canoe. Private dinners canbe arranged.

RESTRICTIONS: No smoking. No pets. No children under 6.

Shore Acres Inn, ♥-♥ ♥, $$, Route 2, North Hero 05474, 802/372-8722. The name is a misnomer of sorts. Shore Acres is really a motel. And while a motel hardly seems the ideal place for a romantic holiday, Shore Acres is no ordinary motel. Dedicated owners Susan and Mike Tranby have put their hearts into giving this place the feel of a true country inn. And they have succeeded.

Recently refurbished, all rooms have modern, quasi-Mission style bleached wood furniture and white walls enlivened with original prints from famous Vermont artist Sabra Field (Field designed a 29-cent U.S. stamp depicting Vermont cornfields.) The rooms are immaculately clean and a have fresh summery feel. Nineteen of Shore Acres twenty three rooms have lake views and communal porches with lounge chairs. The remaining four are in the Garden House located in the middle of the property. While the motel unit is closed in winter, the Garden House serves as the inn's wintertime bed and breakfast.

Equally impressive are Shore Acres' grounds – set off the road and directly on the lake, the hotel sits amidst 50 acres of perfectly manicured rolling hills, and enjoys a half mile of private lake shore. This is a great spot for swimming – Shore Acres has a diving platform set out in the lake, as well as a 90-foot floating dock.

Meals are not included in the room charge. But breakfast, lunch, and dinner are served in the pine paneled dining room, which has a grand stone fireplace and dramatic lake and mountain views. The Shore Acres kitchen is the best on the islands.

RATES PER NIGHT: $70.50-$91.50 from early June through October, $60.50-$91.50 November through early June.

ACCOMMODATIONS: 23 rooms with private baths; 19 rooms have lake views.

Amenities: Air conditioning or ceiling fans and televisions in rooms. Restaurant and bar.

RESTRICTIONS: None.

FRIDAY EVENING
Dinner

The North Hero House, ♡, $$, Route 2, North Hero, 802/372-8237. In transit: Directly on Route 2, the main road that runs the length of the islands, in North Hero. It's impossible to miss unless you have your eyes closed.

If it's a pleasant warm evening, you'll want to head straight to the North Hero House for its Friday night lobster boil. Served outside on the old steamship dock, which is now a nicely manicured grass jetty that juts out into the lake, patrons sit family style at engine red picnic tables. Food is served buffet style. Everything is homemade at the inn; selections include soup; Caesar, potato, and pasta salads; fresh fruit salads; and pies. For those who don't like lobster, roasted chicken with honey mustard sauce is also available. Hours: 6:00 P.M. - 8:00 P.M.

Déjà Vu Café, ♡ ♡, $$-$$$, 185 Pearl St., Burlington, 802/864-7917. In transit: From I-89, take the downtown Burlington exit (there's only one). This will put you on Route 7, which goes straight into Burlington. Turn left onto Main Street/Route 2. Park at any of the downtown lots. The walk is short. Pearl Street runs parallel to Main. The restaurant is four blocks north.

Although you might be eager to head straight to the islands, most area restaurants close by 9:00 P.M. If you're traveling any distance, you might find it difficult to make it that early. A nice alternative, particularly if you're traveling from the south, is to stop for dinner in Burlington.

Long considered among Burlington's best restaurants, the Déjà Vu has at once a funky and upscale atmosphere. It boasts soaring ceilings, exposed brick, scattered Orientals, modern oil paintings, and a lively piano player. The food is a mix of continental cuisines and covers a broad spectrum. Entrees include West Indies grilled chicken rubbed with herbs and served with grilled bananas and vegetables, grilled flatbread pizza topped with smoked salmon, artichoke hearts, and Parmesan and cheddar cheeses, and Rain Forest catfish served with pasta in a Brazil nut pesto. If you're not feeling quite so adventurous, Déjà Vu also serves a good burger.

If you don't have reservations, you may have to wait for 20 minutes or so. The bar, however, is pleasant, and some great beers are on tap—Whitbread and John Courage! Hours: 5:30 P.M. - 10:00 P.M.

SATURDAY MORNING

Bicycle around Isle La Motte to Alburg.

In transit: If you're staying at the Thomas Mott Homestead you may want to start in Alburg, rather than driving down to Isle La Motte. From North Hero, follow Route 2 north. Then turn left on Route 129. You'll see signs to Isle La Motte. Once on the island, you'll see signs for St. Anne's Shrine, a perfect starting point for your trip. If you need to rent bikes, contact Champlain Island Cycling, 32 Old Quarry Road, Isle La Motte, 802/928-3202.

The following bicycle tour totals about 28 miles. Terrain is relatively flat and can be easily completed by recreational riders. If you don't want to bicycle that far, you can choose to take the 12-mile loop around Isle La Motte, then drive to Alburg for lunch.

Begin your tour at St. Anne's Shrine, perhaps the islands' most well known tourist attraction. The site is that of Vermont's oldest white settlement; Fort St. Anne was constructed here in 1666. Although the fort no longer exists, in its place stands St. Anne's shrine. This small chapel with open-air seating and outdoor stations of the cross is a popular Catholic pilgrimage site. It is mantained by the Society of St. Edmund (an order of priests) who also operate St. Michael's College in Winooski, Vermont.

St. Anne's, however, is popular with tourists of all faiths because of its lovely lakeside setting and small sandy beach and picnic area. The Edmundites allow tourists to use the beach, parking lot, and picnic area free of charge. But they do appreciate any donations, which you can make at the information booth on the property. The information booth also has a good bike map of Isle La Motte.

From the parking area, follow the road along the lake, past the shrine's snack area. It meanders around to almost the tip of the island, then meets Route 129. This road cuts down the middle of Isle La Motte and offers beautiful views of pastoral farmland.

If you appreciate fine Shaker furniture, be sure to make a stop at the McGuire Family Collection. If you're traveling back toward the shrine it will be in a small brick house on your right. These furniture makers produce fine Shaker pieces, from small clocks to large cupboards. Merchandise is expensive – up to $5,500 for the largest cupboard – but extraordinarily beautiful. Even if you're not in the market, it's great to browse.

Continue along Route 129 to West Shore Road. This road hugs the lake all the way in to Alburg. It eventually ends at Route 2: turn left on to Route 2 into Alburg center. (Route 2 is Alburg's main street.)

Lunch

The Alburg Country Store, $, Route 2, Alburg, 802/796-3417. In transit: On Route 2, a few miles north of the intersection with Route 78. If you're traveling north, it's on the left.

The Alburg Country Store is just the sort of place you'd hope to find in a tiny northern Vermont town. Entirely unfussy, it purveys penny candy, locally hand-made quilts, antiques, and Vermont products from soap to maple syrup. Order a sandwich from the small deli counter in the back of the store (consider maple cured ham with Vermont cheddar bread). Don't forget to try the Champ potato chips (named after the fabled Lake Champlain Lochness-like monster). They're even better than New England's favorite, Cape Cod chips.

The store has a wooden table up front where you may eat, as well as picnic benches on a porch outside. If you have room, check out the country store's soda fountain. It's one of a dying breed that serves up such old time treats as root beer floats and butterscotch sundaes.

SATURDAY AFTERNOON

Bicycle back to Isle La Motte. Retrace your path back down West Shore Road to Isle La Motte. If you want a change of pace, follow Route 2 south to Summit Road. Turn right on Summit.

It leads to Route 129 and Isle La Motte. Be warned however, Route 2 is less scenic and has more traffic.

Note: Even though the ride is fairly straightforward, it's always a good idea to carry a map. Charlie's Northland on Route 2 in North Hero, just beyond the North Hero House, carries a good map book called the *Champlain Voyager*.

Relax and Swim in the Lake.

In transit: Each of the suggested inns has a lovely lakefront property and offers a beautiful spot for basking in the sun or swimming. If you want to check out one of the islands' sand beaches, head to Knight Point State Park. From Isle La Motte, head south on Route 2. The park is on Route 2, at the southern end of North Hero.

Like many lakes, Lake Champlain, has few sandy beaches and a mostly rocky bottom. For those accustomed to ocean swimming, those facts may be disappointing. However Lake Champlain is a real treat. The water is sparkling clean – some people even drink it – and relatively warm.

Saturday Evening
Dinner

The Shore Acres Inn, ♡ ♡, $$, Route 2, North Hero, 802/372-8722. In transit: Shore Acres is right on Route 2 in North

Hero. If you're traveling north, it's on the right.

Quite simply, you won't find a more pleasant or better restaurant on the Lake Champlain islands. Located right on the lake, the restaurant's large picture windows run the length of the dining room affording wonderful views. The walls are pine paneled and decorated with antique maps and prints from popular Vermont artists. A huge stone fireplace dominates the back wall. Tables are adorned with fresh flowers (each table has a different arrangement) and candles.

Shore Acres' menu is short and simple. But everything is prepared and served well. As soon as you're seated, a waitperson delivers a plate of cheese and crackers. Dinner is accompanied by a small homebaked loaf of bread, and a salad. Appetizers include shrimp cocktail and mushrooms stuffed with smoked bacon, cheese, and onions. Entrees emphasize simply prepared meat, chicken, and fish. Shore Acres uses top grade meat and both the New York sirloin and tenderloin filet are delicious. Other choices include fresh fish (the type changes daily), grilled chicken, and lamb chops served with a yogurt mint sauce. All meals are served with potatoes and fresh seasonal vegetables.

Desserts feature Ben & Jerry's ice cream and frozen yogurt, as well as a selection of homemade pies and cakes. Hours: 4:30 P.M. - 9:00 P.M.

Note: A few other restaurants are located on the islands, but they're not particularly pleasant or enjoyable. Shore Acres is really head and shoulders above the rest. If for some reason you can't or don't want to go to Shore Acres, take the 25 minute drive into Burlington. If you follow the itinerary, you should end the evening in Burlington anyway.

The Daily Planet, ♥ ♥, $$, 15 Center St., Burlington, 802/862-9647. In transit: Follow Route 2 south all the way into downtown Burlington. Then turn left on Church Street, then right on Bank Street, then right on Center Street. There's a parking lot diagonally across from the Daily Planet.

The Daily Planet could just as well be in Cambridge or Berkeley as Burlington. This bohemian café is one of the city's most popular restaurants. (City is a relative term for Burlington, its population is only 35,000.) The Planet has a bar and two dining rooms. The solarium in the front of the restaurant is a bit noisier and tends to attract college students. The back room, with exposed brick walls and low ceilings, is far quieter. The small tables, dim lights, and clientele (many of whom look like they went to Woodstock) give the place the feel of a coffeehouse.

Food isn't gourmet, but for the most part it's innovative and interesting. The menu offers a wide range of cuisines, but emphasizes Asian, Mediterranean, and New American. You might consid-

er mixing things up a bit yourself. Try starting off with the Planet's crab cakes, followed by a Vietnamese-inspired dish of squid and monkfish with cellophane noodles. Hours: 5:00 P.M. - 10:00 P.M.

After Dinner

Moonlight Cruise on the Spirit of Ethan Allen, Perkins Pier, Burlington, 802/862-9685. In transit: If you're in North Hero, follow Route 2 south all the way into Burlington. Once in the center of town, Route 2 becomes Main Street. Follow Main Street to the lake. Turn left on Battery Street, then left on Maple Street to Perkins Pier. If you're at The Planet, turn right on Bank Street, then right on South Winooski Street, then right on Main Street.

Surprisingly, the only tourist boat that plies the waters of Lake Champlain is the Spirit of Ethan Allen. Ferries cross over to New York from Essex, Grand Isle, and Burlington, but the trips aren't that long or that pleasant. The Spirit of Ethan Allen, however, is a great little excursion boat. A replica of an old-fashioned paddle wheeler, it holds no more than 149 passengers. The moonlight cruise lasts 1½ hours and tours the Champlain shoreline. In addition to an open-air deck, The Spirit also has an enclosed and heated deck should the breezes be too brisk.

Be sure to keep your eyes peeled for "Champ," the legendary Lake

Champlain monster. Although, like the Loch Ness, many people claim to have seen it, Champ's actual existence has never been documented. In July 1984, however, 70 passengers on the Spirit of Ethan Allen made the largest group sighting ever recorded.

Food and drinks are served on board; carry-on beverages aren't permitted. Hours: departs 9:00 P.M. Friday and Saturday evenings from late June through Labor Day. The Spirit of Ethan Allen also has narrated daytime cruises, as well as dinner cruises.

Sunday Morning

Rent a boat and tour Lake Champlain.

You can't fully appreciate the beauty of Lake Champlain until you actually get out into the middle of it. Whether you want to zoom around in a 9-horsepower motor boat or lazily paddle a canoe, you can find a boat to rent on the islands.

For canoes and motorboats head to **Charlie's Northland Inc.,** Route 2, North Hero, 802/372-5683. Canoes are $36 a day. Prices for motorboats range from $28-$58, depending on length.

Even if you've never used a motorboat, Charley Clark (Charlie's owner – and yes the name's are spelled differently) says it's pretty simple. And he's happy to give some quick pointers. "We

get people who've never been in a motorboat before," he says. "And so far, every one has come back at the end of the day."

If you prefer sailing, head to **Tudhope's Sailing Center and Marina,** Route 2, North Hero, 802/372-5320. Half-day rental for a 14-foot day sailor is $45-$55. Tudhope's also has sunfishes, and sleepers up to 30 feet. Day and weekly rates are also available.

Unlike canoes and motorboats, sailboats require a certain amount of skill. It's not something you can just "get the hang of." For that reason, Tudhope's only rents to qualified sailors.

Lunch

Picnic at Knight Point State Park, Route 2, North Hero, 802/372-8389. In transit: Head south on Route 2. Knight Point is at the end of North Hero, on the right.

Sit at one of the picnic tables in the pine grove near the beach and watch the boats sail under the bridge that connects North Hero and Grand Isle.

For picnic supplies, head to Grand Isle Store and Deli, $, Route 2, Grand Isle, 802/372-4771. This store has been supplying islanders with food and other life staples for more than 150 years. It's a great place to pick up a sandwich and some local color.

SUNDAY AFTERNOON

Visit the Royal Lipizzan Stallions, Route 2, North Hero. In transit: Head North on Route 2. The stallions' ring is on the right. Large signs make it impossible to miss.

The Lipizzan Stallions, who now call North Hero home during the summer, are the biggest thing to hit the Lake Champlain Islands ever. Made famous in the Walt Disney movie Miracle of the White Stallions, these horses are descendants of Austrian war horses who led the Hapsburg armies. They were prized because they had the ability to learn to leap high in the air. As used in war, they were trained to jump more than five feet high, over an assailant's head. They're also trained to kick their legs, a ballerina like move, yet deadly to those who stand in their way.

The advent of gun powder made the use for the stallions obsolete. Yet they were—and still are—considered prized animals. In fact, Ottomar Herrmann, director of the Lipizzans, with the help of his father and General George Patton, smuggled the horses away from the Russian Army at the end of World War II.

Today Herrmann and his family keep and train the 14-horse fleet. They offer four 90-minute performances every week, held in an outdoor arena. The event has the jovial atmosphere of a local fair. Vendors sell popcorn, hot dogs, and sodas. And a woman, dressed in traditional Austrian garb, hawks programs. Hours: 2:30 P.M. Sunday, 6:00 P.M. Thursday through Saturday.

EARLY EVENING SNACK

Apple Farm Market, $, Route 2, South Hero, 802/372-6611. In transit: Head south on Route 2 into South Hero. The market is on the right.

You can't leave the islands without splurging on one of Apple Farm's famous homemade cider donuts. (They are made in the back of the stand every morning.) They also sell homemade muffins and cookies, as well as apples, apple cider, and other Vermont made food and products. A snack bar sells ice cream and frozen yogurt. Sit outside on a picnic bench and enjoy the comings and goings, or get a travel bag and enjoy your snacks on the ride home.

Additional Activitied

Visit the Missiquoi Wildlife Refuge, Route 78, Swanton, 802/868-4781. This 5,800-acre wildlife refuge encompasses the Missiquoi River delta's marshes, as well as open water, old fields, and wooded swamps. More than 200 species of birds use the area for nesting, resting, and feeding. A three-mile (roundtrip) nature trail follows along the delta.

Visit the Hyde Log Cabin, Route 2, Grand Isle, no phone. This log cabin is suspected to be the oldest such structure in the eastern United States. Built in 1783, the 20 x 25-foot cabin was once home to Jedediah Hyde, his wife, and their 10 children. The house is now filled with clothing and artifacts from the period.

Shop at Island Antique Shops. Although not an antique haven, the Lake Champlain islands do have a few stores of interest, including The Back Chamber, Route 2, North Hero, 802/372-5544; Vallees Den of Antiquity, Route 2, Grand Isle, 802/372-8324; and Apple Country Antiques, Route 2, South Hero, 802/372-5837.

Charter a Fishing Boat. Contact Gary Frazier at Pirate Charters, Grand Isle, 802/372-8357.

GETTING THERE

BY AIR: Burlington International Airport is just 25 minutes from the southern tip of the Lake Champlain Islands and is served by most major airlines. US Air (800/428-4322) has direct flights from New York, Philadelphia, and Chicago.

BY CAR: From the southeast, take I-95 north, to I-93 north, to I-89 north. Take exit 17 to Route 2 north. Route 2 is the main road that goes through the middle of the islands. I-89 is also accessible from I-91. Or, from I-87 in New York, take Route 373 to Port Kent. Then take a ferry from Port Kent to Grand Isle. It takes about 20 minutes.

BY TRAIN: Amtrak offers daily service to Burlington/Essex Junction from Boston, New York, and other regional cities. For information call 1 /800-USA-RAIL. Burlington is about 25 minutes from the southern tip of the islands.

BY BUS: Greyhound (617/423-5810) has daily service to Burlington from New York, Hartford, and Boston.

CAR RENTAL: No car rental companies are located on the Lake Champlain islands. Four car-rental companies have offices at the Burlington International airport: Hertz (800/654-3131), Budget (800/787-8200), Avis (800/331-1212), and National (800/227-7368).

TAXIS/LIMOUSINE SERVICE: No taxi or limousine services are available.

INFORMATION: Lake Champlain Islands Chamber of Commerce, P.O. Box 213, North Hero, Vermont 05474, 802/372-5683. The chamber operates an information office right on Main Street (Route 2) in Grand Isle. It's on the north side of the road. Hours are roughly 9:00 A.M. - 5:00 P.M., but are not entirely dependable.

Litchfield Hills, Connecticut

The Litchfield Hills in Connecticut are, in the simplest terms, a rural Vermont for New Yorkers. As snide as that remark might sound, it is meant as a compliment. The area has all the charm of a Vermont village – white steepled churches, stately 18th century farmhouses, and verdant hills. Yet tucked within the folds of its narrow, winding roads are gourmet restaurants, upscale home accessory stores, and word-class antique shops.

Moreover, the Litchfield Hills are a haven for flower lovers. They boast more than a half dozen garden and herb centers, two of which are nationally renowned: White Flower Farm in Litchfield, and Hillside Farm in Norfolk. Traveling around this extended cluster of genteel communities, roughly bounded by routes 8, 22, 44, and I-84, one is never unaware that it's a retreat favored by the rich. (Weekend residents include Diane Sawyer and Mike Nichols, and Tom Brokaw.)

Never showy, this northwest corner of Connecticut exudes a quiet wealth.

And while Vermont derives much of its beauty from its austerity, the Litchfield Hills are overwhelmingly quaint. It is the perfect spot for couples who want to escape the urban (or even suburban) hustle and bustle, without sacrificing sophistication.

Although there are many activities and no less than 14 state parks and forests, many visitors are attracted to the area solely for its antique shops. It has more than 40, and a large percentage offer collector-quality merchandise. Yet even for the amateur antique browser, these stores offer a wealth of decorating ideas.

Despite the fact it attracts a moneyed crowd, it's not essential to have rich blood to enjoy the Litchfield Hills. Overall, the area has a quiet demeanor— a remarkable accomplishment since it has attracted Manhattanites since the turn of the century. Yet New Yorkers who come to this part of Connecticut come precisely to leave the city behind. Unlike another famous New York escape hatch, the Hamptons on Long Island, it has not succumbed to brash trappings of urban life.

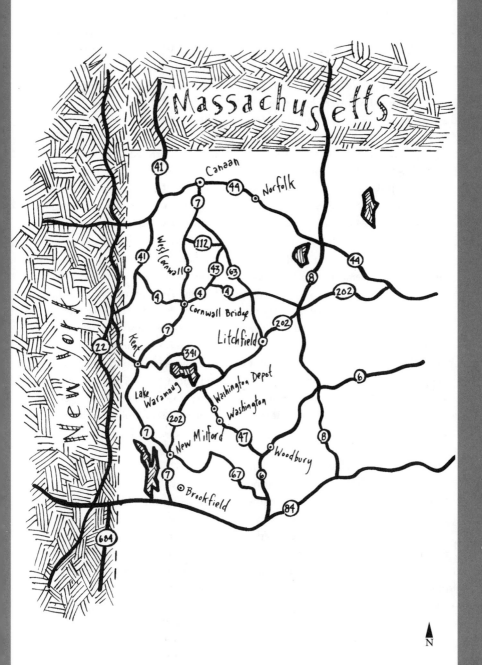

Massachusetts

New York

Canaan

Norfolk

41

44

7

West Cornwall

112

41

43 63

44

4 4

202

4

Cornwall Bridge

8

7

202

Kent

Litchfield

202

341

6

Lake Waramaug

Washington Depot

202

Washington

7

New Milford

47

8

Woodbury

7

67

6

Brookfield

84

684

N

LITCHFIELD HILLS

Where To Stay

The Mayflower Inn, ♡ ♡ ♡ ♡,
$$$$, Route 47, Washington 06793,
203/868-9466. Since its opening in May
1992, The Mayflower has received
extraordinary publicity from the New
York press. And for good reason.
Although firmly set on New England
soil, it effuses the brand of "rustic"
charm the Park Avenue set craves: that is,
a mahogany-paneled library filled with
antique leather chairs, walls hung with
collector-quality oils of someone's
long-dead relatives, and a garden that
bears a triking resemblance to Versailles.

On the morning we arrived, an army of
groundskeepers were dispersed over the
property, and three Jaguars and two
Mercedes were parked by the front
door. If you have a craving to spend
a weekend in what you imagine to be
Ralph Lauren's leather slippers, this is
the perfect inn.

Owners Adriana and Robert Mnuchin
(he–a retired Wall Street investment
banker; she - founder of the Tennis
Lady and Cashmere Cashmere store
chains) have gone to extreme lengths
to renovate this one-time boys school
into a country oasis. Its 28-acres are
impeccably landscaped; interspersed
with 100-year-old rhododendrons are
rare specimen trees, encouraged to grow
by underground heating coils.

The inn's common rooms are impressively
outfitted with Oriental rugs, finely
upholstered furniture, and carefully placed
china and silver decorative accessories.
The look alludes to the finely-worn,
but most pieces – even the mahogany
paneling in the library – are new.

Fifteen rooms are located within the
main inn. Like the common rooms,
they are outfitted with fine rugs, overstuffed furniture, and highly polished
antiques. The beds are magnificent-
king-size four-posters, plumped with
featherbeds and down comforters, and
covered with Frette Italian linens. Baths
are outfitted in mahogany and marble,
with brass and Limoges porcelain
fittings. Each room has a gas fireplace
(hokey, but they're good for effect),
well-stocked mini bar, television, and
telephone. Virtually no detail has
been overlooked. It's impossible to get a
bad room. However, some rooms are
larger than others, the biggest being
a three-room suite with a dining
area (there's no kitchen), living room,
and bedroom.

An additional eight rooms are located in
two separate buildings. Appointments
are identical to those in the main inn.

The dining rooms serves three meals a
day, as well as Sunday brunch. But
meals are not included in the price of
the room. Other services include a
health club with massage services, a
hiking trail, an outdoor swimming pool,
and a tennis court.

RATES PER NIGHT: $190-$475

ACCOMMODATIONS: 23 rooms with private baths.

AMENITIES: Televisions, telephones, and mini bars in rooms. Full-service restaurant and bar. Health club, as well as outdoor swimming pool, hiking trail, and tennis court. Fax service. Gift shop. Many rooms have fireplaces and/or private balconies.

RESTRICTIONS: No smoking in bedrooms. No pipe or cigar smoking in buildings. No children under 12. No pets.

Greenwoods Gate, ♥ ♥ ♥ ♥, $$$, 105 Greenwoods Road East, Norfolk 06058, 203/542-5439. Many innkeepers cater to couples, but Deanne Raymond, owner of Greenwoods Gate, goes one step further. She has imbued this little gem with a sense of romance, evident in virtually every corner. Bedrooms are soothing, decorated with just enough lace and scented with only a hint of potpourri. Small bottles of Courvoisier and sherry and dishes of chocolate kisses are set bedside. Even the pancakes Raymond serves for breakfast are heart-shaped. Some cynics may find this touch a bit overblown, but Raymond is a bona fide romantic and has a genuine interest in making Greenwoods Gate a place where couples have a chance to reconnect.

Although all three guest rooms are lovely, the most sought after is the Levi Thompson Suite. Set on three small floors, it feels like a doll house. Off the entrance hall is a large bath with a two-person Jacuzzi and shelves stocked with perfumes, powders and colognes. Walk up a few steps to a small sitting area with polished cherry floors, pale blue-flowered wallpaper, and pink and white upholstered chairs. Walk up four steps to the loft, which features a queen-size bed with a white eyelet lace cover and lace curtains draped above.

Also charming is the E.J. Trescott suite, done in shades of china blue and white. It features a white iron antique bed, a cozy sitting area, and bath with a claw foot tub.

Raymond has a laid-back breakfast policy, and will serve guests whenever they decide to eat. The feast starts out with coffee, tea, and muffins delivered to t he rooms. Once guests are downstairs, Raymond whips up a full breakfast that includes juice, coffee, fruit, and entrees like Grand Marnier French toast, herb omelets, or apple puff pancakes. Although she serves in the dining room, many guests enjoy eating in Raymond's kitchen. Its long wooden table is positioned right next to a two-sided fireplace.

Other common rooms include: a sitting room, located on the other side of the open fireplace, with a television and shelves stocked with books and games; the living room; and a formal dining room, which features Raymond's collection of antique china tea pots. All rooms are carefully decorated with a mixture of country furniture and fine antiques, and they are immaculately clean.

In the afternoon, Raymond offers guests wine, cider, tea, and an array or hors d'oeuvres. She also has a small but well-stocked bar to which guests may help themselves.

RATES PER NIGHT: $150-$195, a fourth small bedroom that is only sold with the Captain Phelps Suite is $35. Off season (November through June) mid week rates are $135-$175.

ACCOMMODATIONS: 3 rooms with private baths and private entrances.

AMENITIES: Television in common room. Massage therapist available.

RESTRICTIONS: No children under 12. No smoking. No pets.

The Manor House, ♥♥-♥♥♥, $$-$$$, 447 Maple Ave., Norfolk 06058, 203/542-5690. If you appreciate Tudor architecture, you owe yourself a visit to the Manor House. Built in 1898 by Charles Spofford, architect of London's subway system, it boasts magnificent stained glass windows that were a gift from Louis Comfort Tiffany to the original owners.

Sold in the 1940s, the house has gone through several incarnations, including serving as a rooming house. Since Diane and Hank Tremblay purchased the place in 1984, they've gone to great lengths to restore it to its former grandeur. And while the inn is still plagued with a few pieces of dated wall-to-wall carpeting, The Manor House indeed lives up to its name.

The most luxurious space is the oversized living room, which has cherry paneled walls, a stone fireplace with a Grecian relief above the mantle, and several Tiffany windows. Exuding a lived-in elegance, it's decorated with two Orientals, Victorian antiques, some modern upholstered furniture, a grand piano, and artwork from the Tremblay's travels around the world.

Adjacent is the dining room, with a green tile fireplace, and more Tiffany windows. Other public rooms include a small sun porch, library, and bar, where the Tremblays keep a guest refrigerator, glasses for setups, and fixings for tea and hot cocoa.

Of the eight guest rooms, the Spofford Room is the most amenity laden, with a large sitting area, wood-burning fireplace, and private porch that faces west and is ideal for sunset viewing. It offers a king-size bed with a lace canopy, and has an overwhelming Victorian feel with floral wallpaper and velvet cushioned furniture.

The English room is another good choice. Also oversized, it features a large bath with a two-person Jacuzzi. Lincoln's Room, although smaller, is the inn's coziest and features a beautiful hand-carved sleigh bed.

The Tremblays pride themselves on their breakfasts, which feature herbs and berries from their garden as well as fresh honey from their three beehives. The menu changes daily and might feature orange waffles, French toast with raspberries, or poached eggs with a lemon-butter chive sauce. Coffee, tea, juice, and fresh fruit are always available.

RATES PER NIGHT: $90-$150

ACCOMMODATIONS: 8 rooms with private baths. One of these rooms can be set up as a suite, with a private bath and an adjoining sitting room/bedroom. (This adjoining room, however, is not sold separately.)

AMENITIES: Television in common room. Some rooms have working fireplaces and/or private decks. One room has a private elevator.

RESTRICTIONS: No smoking in guest rooms or dining area. No children under 12. No pets.

Hilltop Haven, ♥-♥♥, $$, Dibble Hill Road, West Cornwall 06796, 203/672-6871. If Norman Bates had been a nice guy, and had run a B&B instead of a motel, it might have looked something like Hilltop Haven. This isolated inn, a natural fieldstone house set among 64 acres of woods at the end of a long dirt road, isn't for everyone. But Hilltop and its innkeeper, Everett Van Dorn, have a quirky charm. The house is decorated with a mishmash of furniture – from lovely antiques that Van Dorn inherited from his mother, to just old furniture that looks a bit shabby around the edges.

What makes Hilltop Haven worth a visit is the absolutely spectacular views it offers of the surrounding hills and the Housatonic River that flows through the valley 800 feet below. Nothing is more peaceful than sitting on the open air stone deck, surrounded by trees, and listening to the rushing water.

Hilltop's library is also an impressive sight, with its stone walls, floors, fireplace, and a high ceiling with heavy wood beams. It is the inn's most elegantly furnished room, decorated with a large red and brown Oriental rug and a few antiques, including a round oak table with four hand-carved chairs. Other public rooms include a small sun room, which has floor-to-ceiling windows, and a living room with a grand piano, television, and (oddly) a black velvet Victorian settee that's roped off to prevent guests from using it.

The two guest rooms both have wood-paneled walls, tan carpeting, and 1950's style baths, plus some very nice furniture. One room has an antique brass bed, and the other a hand-carved sleigh bed with matching dresser.

Van Dorn, who lives in a cabin next door to give guests complete privacy, serves a full breakfast, either in the library or on the deck. It includes fresh-ground coffee, fresh-squeezed orange juice, and a hot entree, such as apple pancakes, Grand Marnier French toast, or shrimp cheese strada.

RATES PER NIGHT: $95

ACCOMMODATIONS: 2 rooms with private baths.

AMENITIES: Television in common room. Air conditioning.

RESTRICTIONS: Smoking on terrace or screened porch only. No pets. No children under 14.

The Boulders, ♡ ♡ ♡ ♡, $$$$, Route 45, New Preston, CT 06777, 203/868-0541. The Boulders has the look of a grand old country inn. The building has a fieldstone porch, natural brown shingles, green-striped awnings, and is perched on a sloping hill above Lake Waramaug. And the pine-paneled living room, with floral couches, Oriental rugs, a wood-burning fireplace, and views of the lake is, without exaggeration, the epitome of cozy. The dining room too, with stone walls and French windows, has a rustic elegance.

Innkeepers Kees and Ulla Adema operate The Boulders with their daughter Vanessa and her husband Tony Daou. And despite the fact that the inn has 17 rooms, the Ademas and Daous infuse The Boulders with homespun charm. Homemade cookies greet guests in their rooms upon arrival, and tea is typically served in the late afternoon.

Six rooms are located in the main house. While all are quaintly appointed and have a country flavor, the South-west room is considered The Boulders' best. It features a queen-size four poster bed with a rose, tan, and blue floral canopy, marble-top end tables, lamps with hand-pierced shades, and a small private deck with lake views.

The three rooms in the Boulders' new carriage house are the inn's most sophisticated and elegant offerings. Room 2 is outfitted with a magnificent sleigh bed, stone fireplace, and skylight. It features cream walls, beige carpeting, a sitting area with a black and rose floral couch and lounge chair, and an old sea captain's chest that serves as a coffee table.

For those interested in seclusion, The Boulders also has eight private cottages, all of which have fireplaces and their own decks. They, however, are more rustically appointed than the rooms in the main inn or carriage house.

Full breakfast is served in the dining room or on the patio. Selections include strawberry pancakes, farmer's omelets, and steel-cut oatmeal. In addition, a buffet table offers fresh-squeezed orange juice, fruits, and muffins.

After breakfast you might decide to head down to Boulders' boat house and take out a sailboat or paddle boat. (All equipment is complimentary.) Or you might choose a hike up to Pinnacle Mountain: it rises behind the inn and The Boulders has a private hiking trail.

Lest you think you've found inn perfection, The Boulders has a drawback: it offers only limited B&B rates. Guests are usually required to pay for a modified American plan, which includes breakfast and dinner. The Boulders has a good dining room, but because the Litchfield Hills area has so many fine restaurants, why limit yourself? The Boulders accepts B&B guests only on Monday through Thursday; they only accept B&B-rate weekend guests if they have a vacancy. Unfortunately, they usually don't.

RATES PER NIGHT: $225 MAP, $175 B&B from May 1 through November 1; $175 MAP, $125 B&B from November 1 through May 1. B&B rates aren't available during Christmas week.

ACCOMMODATIONS: 18 rooms with private baths; 6 rooms in the main house, 3 in the carriage house, and 8 private cottages.

AMENITIES: Fireplaces in carriage house and cottages. All cottages, and some rooms, have private decks. Some rooms have air conditioning. Tennis court. Beach front with boat house that has paddle boats and sailboats. Private hiking trail. Full-service restaurant that serves breakfast and dinner.

RESTRICTIONS: Children allowed by special arrangement only. No pets.

FRIDAY EVENING
Dinner

The Hopkins Inn, (♥ indoor dining) ♥ ♥ ♥, $$-$$$, 22 Hopkins Rd., New Preston, 203/868-7295. In transit: The Hopkins Inn is off Route 45 next to Lake Waramaug. Route 45 is directly accessible from Route 7 and Route 202. Once on Route 45, turn down Lake Shore Road. You'll see a sign pointing to the Inn on Lake Waramaug. If you're traveling north on Route 45, it will be on your left. Turn right at the sign for Hopkins Vineyard. There are no signs for the road or the inn, but the vineyard's sign is clearly visible.

On a warm summer evening there is no more enjoyable place to dine than on the Hopkins Inn's terrace. Perched on a hill right above Lake Waramaug, the towering chestnut trees surrounding the stone patio and the magnificent iron chandelier that hangs from a tree limb give the place a truly magical feel.

The food is tasty and well presented, but not gourmet. Emphasis is on German dishes. Appetizers include marinated herring, avocado in vinaigrette dressing, onion soup, and shrimp cocktail. Among the entree selections are weinershnitzel, backhendle (breaded chicken) with lingonberries, sweet breads Milanese, and grilled salmon with herb butter. Desserts are typically traditional and gooey. On our visit, the nightly selection included mint parfait, cheesecake, and meringue glacé. Hours: 6:00 P.M. - 9:00 P.M. Tuesday through Thursday, 6:00 P.M. - 10:00 P.M. Friday, 5:30 P.M. - 10:00 P.M. Saturday, and 12:30 P.M. - 8:30 P.M. Sunday.

West Street Grill, ♡ ♡ ♡, $$$, 43 West St., Litchfield, 203/567-3885. In transit: The West Street Grill is right in Litchfield center, off Route 202. If you're traveling south on Route 202 into Litchfield, West Street is on your right. It runs parallel to Route 202 and is separated from it by a small grassy green. Street parking is available.

Discerning palates will be thrilled at their good fortune, for the West Street Grill, though unassuming from its exterior, is one of Connecticut's best restaurants. Inside, West Street is every inch a spare, sophisticated bistro. The long narrow room has simple white walls decorated with large black-framed mirrors and some colorful original art done in pastel crayon. A small bar at the front of the restaurant displays vintage wines.

Appetizers include cilantro marinated tuna tartare with seaweed salad, leek and potato soup, and pumpkin tortellini filled with wild mushrooms. Both appetizers and entrees change regularly. On the night we visited, the entree selection included pan-seared cod with mashed potatoes and carmelized onions, roasted loin of pork, and grilled salmon with saffron aioli served on a bed of lentils.

Desserts are equally impressive. Among the line-up were creme brûlée, fresh banana ice cream, mango sorbet, and chocolate tart. Hours: 5:30 P.M.-9:00 P.M. Sunday through Thursday, 5:30 P.M. - 10:30 P.M. Friday and Saturday.

SATURDAY MORNING

Antique Shopping in Woodbury.

In transit: From Norfolk, follow Route 44 east to Route 8 south to Route 6 south. Route 6 leads straight into Woodbury. From West Cornwall, follow Route 7 south to Route 4 east, which intersects with Route 8. And from Washington, follow Route 47 south to Route 6.

With nearly 30 shops on its Main Street, Woodbury reigns as the undisputed antiques capital of Connecticut. Unlike many towns known as antique centers, Woodbury is not the kind of place where you're likely to find attic treasures. Most stores are geared to serious collectors. Its proximity to New York enables most shopkeepers to get top dollar for their merchandise. That said, Woodbury is still a wonderful place to hunt for antiques.

Stores are spread out along a four-mile stretch of road. Some shops are close enough together so you can walk from one to the other. But for the most part, you'll have to drive. Following are a selection of Woodbury's better antique stores:

Country Loft Antiques, 88 Main St. North, 203/266-4500. A perfect spot for those who admire the French country look of Pierre Deux. Country Loft specializes in 18th and 19th century French armories, tables, chairs, commodes, and desks, as well as faïence china.

British Country Antiques, 50 Main St. North, 203/263-5100. With 11 rooms of fine English antiques and accessories, you could spend well more than an hour here. Great stop if you're trying to give your home the feel of a country manor. Also a selection of French fruitwood furniture, paint-decorated antiques, and reproduction chairs.

Tucker Frey Antiques, 451 Main Street St., 203/263-5404 If you're looking for the simpler look of 18th and early 19th century American antiques, be sure to stop at Tucker Frey. Merchandise includes paintings, decorative accessories, and furniture. The showroom is small, but everything is extraordinarily high quality. We found a magnificent walnut dresser. Too bad it was $21,500!

Monique Shay, 920 Main St. South, 203/263-3186. Huge selection of Canadian country furniture. Most of the stuff is hand-painted and has the "distressed" look that is so popular today. Great spot if you're looking for storage cabinets, butcher blocks, or big dining tables.

Grass Roots Antiques, 12 Main St., 203/263-3983. Lots of decorative accessories—lamps, porcelain bowls, small tables—from the 18th, 19th, and 20th centuries. Also antique books, maps, and estate jewelry.

Lunch

The Café, $-$$, Route 45, New Preston, 203/868-7333. In transit: Follow Route 6 south to Route 47 north to Route 202. Head south on Route 202 to Route 45 north. The trip should take about a half hour.

The Café is a miniature oasis—not just a place to eat, but also a place to relax. This tiny restaurant has loads of atmosphere —stone floors, stone and pine paneled walls, a raised wood-burning fireplace, and overstuffed couches mixed with wooden chairs. Cheery green and white checked cloths cover the tables. The food is top-notch and just a little bit different.

Selections change frequently, but might include eggplant, pepper, and goat cheese sandwiches, pizza with caramelized onions and tomatoes, chicken pot pie, and tuna salad niçoise.

Hours: from 11:30 A.M. Closed Tuesday. Also serves breakfast and dinner.

The Olive Tree, $-$$, Barclay Square, Woodbury, 203/263-45555. In transit: Follow Route 6 south. You'll come to a set of lights and a cluster of shopping malls. Turn left. The Olive Tree is in a small building straight ahead.

The Olive Tree serves a perfectly good lunch–hamburgers and sandwiches (from open-faced hot turkey to cold tuna), as well as salads and a few Greek specialties. And the atmosphere is pleasant–lots of windows, plants, and wooden Windsor chairs. However, compared to the Café, it is strikingly ordinary. The Olive Tree is included here because it's one of the few places in Woodbury to get a decent lunch. If you're too famished to withstand the ride to New Preston, it's an acceptable spot. Hours: 11:00 A.M. - 2:30 P.M. Tuesday through Saturday.

SATURDAY AFTERNOON

Shopping around New Preston.

In transit: Follow Route 6 south to Route 47 north to Route 202. Head south on Route 202 to Route 45 north. The trip should take about a half hour. If you're at The Café, you're already there. You can park anywhere along the main street.

This small cluster of shops tucked into a shoulder of Route 45 is deceiving. It's not much of an exaggeration to say that if you

blinked twice, you'd pass them by. However, New Preston offers some of the best and most interesting shopping in the area with its mixture of antique, clothing, and home accessory stores. Following are some of the more noteworthy stores:

Rigamarole, Route 45/Main Street, 203/868-9914. You'll find a wonderful selection of garden accessories, decorative housewares, and French and American informal antiques. Look for lots of one-of-a-kind items. Be warned, merchandise is very expensive. Even if you can't afford a $2,500 pair of porcelain vases, you'll have a great time browsing.

Timothy Mawson, Route 45/Main Street, 203/868-0732. This shop is heaven for gardeners. It has a large selection of fine edition out-of-print garden books, as well as botanical prints, and exquisite topiaries.

J. Seitz & Co., Route 45/Main Street, 203/868-0119. Proprietor Joanne Seitz brings the style of the Southwest to Connecticut with her antiques and folk art from Santa Fe and Taos. There's also a nice selection of southwestern style clothing (beaded belts, suede vests, and hand-knit sweaters), home accessories, and trinkets.

Black Swan Antiques, Route 45/Main Street, 203/868-2788. One of the most well-respected antique shops in New Preston, the Black Swan carries lots of

17th and 18th century English country furniture. Perfect stuff for giving your home a "clubby" look. Also a selection of antique prints and period accessories.

ESPY, Route 45/Main St., 203/868-1338. Although small, this store packs lots of style. Emphasis is on decorative accessories, linens, teapots, candles, and soaps. Good stop if you're looking for some interesting antique china.

Jonathan Peters, Route 45/Main Street (at the fork in the road), 203/868-9017. Gorgeous selection of dried flowers – roses, hydrangeas, and more. Also lots of antique lace, linens, and pillows.

SATURDAY EVENING

Champagne Carriage Ride through Norfolk with Horse & Carriage Livery, Loon Meadow Drive, Norfolk, 203/542-6085. In transit: From New Preston, follow Route 45 south to Route 202 north. Follow 202 to Route 8 north to Route 44 and the Norfolk Common.

If you're in the mood for pulling out all the stops, take a champagne carriage ride through picturesque Norfolk. Horse & Carriage Livery will pick you up at the Hawk's Nest Pub (right on the main common). A bottle of chilled bubbly will await you inside your antique carriage. If the weather is cool, you can cuddle up under a buffalo fur throw. (Owner Beth Denis collects antique carriage blankets for her guests' use.)

When the sun goes down, the carriage is lit with an antique kerosene lamp. The 50-minute ride follows Norfolk's main streets past its many historic homes, then goes off the beaten path to tour the countryside.

For an extra fee, guests staying at either the Manor House or Greenwoods Gate can arrange to be picked up right at their B&B. Rates: $50 for 2. Custom rides can also be arranged. Champagne is an additional charge. Carriage & Livery operates only by appointment.

Dinner

Note: The Mayflower Inn is a good 45 minutes from Washington. If you're staying in Norfolk, or if the ride just seems too long, consider dinner at Freshfields. Or, flower lovers may opt to forgo the carriage ride altogether. An hour spent strolling through the Mayflower's poetic gardens could be just as romantic.

Freshfields, ♡ ♡, $$-$$$, Route 128, West Cornwall, 203/672-6601. In transit: From Norfolk, follow Route 44 north to Route 7 south to Route 128. Go through the covered bridge; Freshfields is in the center of tiny West Cornwall on the left.

One of the region's most popular restaurants, Freshfields enjoys a picture perfect location – just down the street from an old, red covered bridge, and poised at the edge of a babbling brook. If you visit while the weather is warm, you might be able to snag a table on the enclosed porch that faces the water.

As its name suggests, Freshfields focuses on simple foods that are well prepared. Start off with a cup of vegetarian chili or a Tuscan salad with roasted garlic, black olives, polenta croutons, sun-dried tomatoes, and fresh mozzarella. Pasta entrees include rotelli with black olives, cannellini beans, and spinach in a garlic sauce, and penne served with eggplant, red pepper, ricotta, and mozzarella.

Those interested in a bit more protein should consider Freshfields' Long Island duck served with a plum wine sauce, or broiled salmon fillet with ginger- lime and roasted red pepper sauce.

Desserts, like the rest of the menu, change regularly. But Freshfields usually offers a mix of sinful chocolate desserts and lighter fruit-based options. Hours: 5:30 P.M. - 9:00 P.M. Thursday through Sunday. Also open for lunch and Sunday brunch.

Mayflower Inn, ♡ ♡ ♡, $$$$, Route 47, Washington, 203/868-9466. In transit: From New Preston, take Route 45 south to Route 202 north to Route 47. Follow Route 47 south into Washington. From Norfolk, take Route 272 south to Route 4 east to Route 202. Follow Route 202 south to Route 47 to Washington.

If you're in the mood to be pampered, and have a whim to eat in a royally elegant setting, consider the Mayflower. Whether you eat in the main dining room – decorated in soothing shades of cream and tan – or on the patio that affords sweeping views of the Mayflower's gardens, you'll feel, at least for the night, that the world is your oyster.

Tables are set with sterling, crystal, and Limoges china. Service is friendly, but not smarmy. As you would expect from the surroundings, the food is excellent. The Mayflower's chef has received accolades from both *Food & Wine* and *Gourmet,* which probably explains why so many Manhattanites drive out just for a meal.

The menu changes daily, but some appetizers you might expect are roasted beet salad with baby mustard greens and foie gras terrine; seared Nantucket scallops with country bacon, wheatberry, and spinach stew; and Mayflower smoked salmon. When we visited, entrees included roasted haddock with lobster and lima bean stew, grilled pheasant breast with carrot Daupinois and steamed kale, and tagliatelle with borlotti beans, arugula, and baby artichokes.

Wine connoisseurs will admire the extensive range of prices and varieties. The Mayflower has a sommelier on hand, as well as a list of suggested wines for each menu.

If you can, save room for dessert. It's hard to pass up sweets like double chocolate mousse cake with vanilla cream and cream anglaise, warm raspberry tart with raspberry ice, or a strawberry rhubarb sundae. Hours: 6:00 P.M. - 9:30 P.M. Also open for breakfast and lunch.

SUNDAY MORNING

Visit Hillside Gardens, 515 Litchfield Rd./Route 272, Norfolk, 203/542-5345. In transit: From West Cornwall, follow Route 7 north to Route 44 east to Route 272. Follow 272 south. The sign for Hillside is hard to see, but it's right near the Dennis Hill State Park. Both are on the left. From Washington, follow Route 47 north to Route 202 north to Route 272 north.

To flower lovers, the Hillside Gardens are famous. Although relatively small– just six acres – it is considered one of the finest perennial gardens in the country. In fact, some patrons make yearly pilgrimages from as far away as California to visit, get ideas, and buy plants. Owners Mary Ann and Frederick McGourty are authors of several well-respected books on perennial gardens. Among the more famous is the aptly titled, *The Perennial Gardener.* Hours: 9:00 A.M. - 5:00 P.M. daily May through September.

Visit Nobody Eats Parsley, Route 272, Norfolk, 203/542-5479. In transit: From

Hillside, continue north on Route 272 toward Norfolk center. Nobody Eats Parsley is about two miles up on the left.

A nice contrast to Hillside, this shop carries dried flowers, herb plants, and beautiful rosemary and myrtle topiaries. It also has a selection of dried herbs, pot pourri, and specialty jellies and vinegars that locals rave about.

Hiking at Campbell Falls, Route 272, Norfolk. In transit: Follow Route 272 north. Campbell Falls is exactly 4.6 miles past the yellow blinking light in Norfolk center. This is noted because there is no sign, except for a long thin white vertical road stake that marks Campbell Falls Road, which is on the left. There is a narrow open area where you can park. Campbell Falls is an undeveloped preserve owned by the Connecticut Parks and Recreation Department. It has no amenities per se, not even a real parking area, but locals consider it one of the most beautiful wilderness areas around.

As soon as you step out of your car, you can hear the water breaking over the rocky falls. A trail leads through woodlands and to the splashing cascades that comprise Campbell Falls. The entire hike is only about a mile long. But if offers a nice break from your shopping expedition.

Visit White Flower Farm, Route 63, Litchfield, 203/567-8789. In transit:

From Norfolk, follow Route 272 south past Norfolk center to Route 4 west. Follow Route 4 to Route 63. Follow Route 63 toward Litchfield center. White Flower Farm is on the left.

Most catalog mavens know White Flower Farm. It is the Bloomingdale's of flower catalogs. At its grounds in Litchfield, you can peruse White Flower's fabulous perennials in person. White Flower also specializes in shrubs and specimen plants. With more than five acres of display gardens and forty acres of perennial production fields, all open to the public, you could spend hours admiring these natural works of art.

White Flower also has a retail store where you can buy plants, flowers, clay pots, and garden accessories. Hours: 10:00 A.M. - 5:00 P.M. Monday through Friday, 9:00 A.M. - 5:30 P.M. weekends and holidays.

Lunch

Doc's, $$-$$$, Route 45, New Preston, 203/868-9415. In transit: From White Flower Farm, follow Route 63 south to Route 202 south to Route 45. Follow Route 45 north past New Preston center to Lake Waramaug. Doc's is a small, one-story mustard colored building on the right side of the road opposite the lake.

Since it opened a few years ago, people have been in a constant clamor to get one of the nine tables at Doc's. Just call up the restaurant and listen to the taped message listing those precious times still open for seatings.

Interestingly, Doc's isn't particularly chic – the tables are covered with white butcher paper and have mismatched green wooden chairs. The place doesn't even have a liquor license. (But you can bring your own.) What it does have is some of the best Tuscan food you're likely to eat this side of Florence. It would be a great spot for dinner, except it can get extremely noisy – the only complaint ever heard about the place. Things tend to be much quieter at lunch, so you can leisurely savor your meal.

The pizzas are phenomenal, with thin crispy crusts and served in a wooden Brie wheel. Try the verde with sautéed spinach and onions, pecans, and goat cheese, or the Joanna with fresh red and yellow peppers, walnuts, pesto, and mozzarella. Hours: 12:00 P.M. - 2:30 P.M. Friday through Sunday. Dinner is also served Wednesday through Sunday.

SUNDAY AFTERNOON

Drive around Lake Waramaug, and Relax at the State Park. In transit: From Doc's continue north on Route 45 which goes along the lake. Turn left on North Shore Road, which is right at the sign for the Inn on Lake Waramaug. This road bears left and becomes Lake Waramaug Road. You'll drive right into the park.

Lake Waramaug is the second largest body of fresh water in the state, and is generally regarded as Connecticut's most beautiful lake. The six-mile drive around the perimeter is lovely. But to really enjoy the lake you should stop at Lake Waramaug State Park. It has picnic tables among a pine grove, a small beach, and boat rentals. Paddle out to the middle of the lake in a canoe, lie back, and soak up the sun. Admission: $5 per car for Connecticut residents, $8 for nonresidents. Rates apply on weekends and holidays only. Paddle boats are $6 per half hour, $10 per hour. Canoes are $7 per hour, or $25 per day.

Additional Activities

Visit the American Indian Archaeological Institute, Curtis Road, Washington, 203/868-0518. This small museum was designed to help visitors understand the history of New England's Indian population. Exhibits include modern Indian art, as well as historic artifacts. Among the most interesting exhibits is the authentically constructed Alongkian settlement with three wigwams, a meeting "house," a rock shelter, and a garden planted with corn, beans, and squash.

Go Shopping in Kent. In the past decade, this small town has emerged as a center for fine art galleries and craft and clothing stores. It has more than a dozen galleries and antique stores on its main street. Among the most notable are the Paris New York Kent Gallery, Rose Gallery, Kent Antiques Center, and Tiglieto, a women's clothing and accessories store.

Visit the Norfolk Chamber Music Festival. This annual, six-week summer festival has developed an excellent reputation among music lovers. Recent performers have included the Tokyo String Quartet, New York Woodwind Quintet, and Janos Starker and friends. For information call 203/432-1966, after June 1 call 203/542-5537.

Go for a Balloon Ride with Watershed Balloons, 179 Gilbert Rd., Watertown, 203/274-2010. Not a bad place to pop "the" question. Watershed has two flights a day, one at sunrise and another two hours before sunset. The flights last about an hour and are followed by a champagne reception. Cost is $175 per person.

GETTING THERE

BY AIR: Bradley International Airport in Windsor Locks, Connecticut, is about 75 minutes from the Litchfield area. All major airlines service the airport.

BY CAR: The Litchfield area is about 130 miles from Boston and 100 from New York City. From the north, take I-91. To get to the Norfolk area, take Route 44 west. Or take I-84 to Route 8 north to Route 44 west. To get to the southern part of the hills, take I-84 south to exit

15. Then take Route 67 to Route 199 for Washington.

From New York, take the Henry Hudson Parkway to the Saw Mill River Parkway to I-684 to I-84 east. To get to the Norfolk area, follow Route 202 north to Route 272.

BY TRAIN: No direct service is available, but Amtrak (800/872-7245) has daily service to Hartford, Connecticut, from Boston, New York, and other east coast cities.

By Bus: Bonanza (800/556-3815) has daily service from New York City to Canaan, Connecticut (near Norfolk). However, no direct service is available from Boston. The closest connection is Peter Pan (800/322-0364) from Boston. Then take Bonanza (800/556-3815) to Kent, Connecticut (near Washington).

CAR RENTAL: Avis (800/331-1212), Dollar (800/800-4000), and Hertz (800/654-3131) are located at Bradley International Airport. Dollar also has an office in downtown Hartford. Ugly Duckling Rent-A-Car (203/824-5204) is one block from the Bonanza bus stop in Canaan.

TAXI/LIMOUSINE Service: I'll Drive (203/354-1712) in New Milford. From Hartford, contact Airport Taxi (800/242-TAXI) or Yellow Cab (203/666-6666). Most inns and B&Bs are also equipped to arrange limo service.

INFORMATION: Litchfield Hills Travel Council, P.O. Box 1776U2-3, Marbledale, CT 06777, 203/868-2214. Call or write for information. The council also operates an information booth at Route 202 On-the-Green in Litchfield. Hours: 9:30 A.M. - 4:30 P.M. daily from June through October. It's also open the last two weekends in May and the third weekend in October.

Martha's Vineyard, Massachusetts

a summer enclave for Hollywood celebrities, business moguls, and the idle rich, Martha's Vineyard enjoys the cache typically reserved for such elitist retreats as the Hamptons and Malibu. Yet despite its sprinkling of trendy restaurants and high-priced stores, this island has a distinctly Yankee personality. Flash, in all its forms, is considered bad taste. People here live in unprepossessing weathered shingle houses, wear rubber thongs and baggy cotton clothes, and would rather discuss their wysteria bushes than Washington politics.

Year-round residents who include fishermen, artists, farmers, and tradesmen number more than 13,000. In summer, however, more than 80,000 people call Martha's Vineyard home. While that may seem staggering for an island, the Vineyard (as residents commonly call it) is 24 miles long and 10 miles wide. And unlike Nantucket or Block Island, it's not the sort of place that you can scoot around exclusively on a bike.

In fact, Martha's Vineyard seems to be many islands, not just because of its size, but because each of its communities has its own distinctive personality and terrain. Vineyard Haven (also known as Tisbury), the commercial center, is busy year-round. It's the place where most islanders come off-season to do their grocery shopping, buy a hammer, or see a movie. Home to much of the island's working class, it is also considered liberal and tends to attract the erudite urban set. Edgartown, with its abundance of quaint shops, inns, and side streets lined with whaling captains' homes, is the Vineyard's tourist center. Its classic architecture attracts conservative, low-key summer residents. Oak Bluffs, on the other hand, is full of whimsical Victorians and has a honky tonk, cotton candy atmosphere. In fact, it is the only town on the island that was founded as a summer vacation spot.

These communities, known collectively as down island, comprise Martha's Vineyard's residential and commercial centers. Up island are the sparsely populated communities of West Tisbury, Chilmark and Gay Head. Atmospheric light-years away from the down-island hustle, they offer visitors tranquil and and intensely beautiful scenery —verdant pasture and farmland, fresh-water ponds, tiny fishing villages, and soaring oceanside cliffs.

Another part of the Vineyard, Chappiquidick, regrettably best known as the site of the Kennedy-Kopechne tragedy, is a tiny island just beyond Edgartown, and is accessible via the On Time ferry. Virtually uninhabited until the 1970s, it is home to peaceful wildlife sanctuaries and long, wide sandy beaches.

To truly enjoy a weekend on the Vineyard, it's best not to try to see everything. Although many people think they can "do" the island in one weekend, the Vineyard is simply too big and diverse. You'll only exhaust yourself if you try. Rather, relax. Adjust to the island pace. Believe that you are far removed from your workaday world. For as one innkeeper opined, Martha's Vineyard isn't just a place, it's a state of mind.

WHERE TO STAY

The Charlotte Inn, ♥ ♥ ♥ ♥, $$$$, South Summer St., Edgartown 02539, 508/627-4751. The grand dame of Martha's Vineyard's inns, The Charlotte deserves every superlative accorded it over the past 20 years. It is undoubtedly one of the most elegantly appointed small inns in all New England, if not the country.

Its three buildings comprised of two meticulously restored sea captains' homes and a carriage house – gracefully

sit among manicured lawns with winding brick pathways, latticework fences, and a profusion of flowers and carefully tended shrubs. Although it is in the heart of Edgartown, its atmosphere is quiet and restful.

Three common rooms in the main house serve as The Charlotte's art gallery. The 100 plus original works that hang on the walls are all for sale. These rooms, with rich, dark wallpaper, white ceilings, overstuffed club chairs, and well-placed pieces of china and silver, reflect the feel of the entire inn – that of a 19th century English country manor. Innkeepers Gery and Paula Conover are exuberant anglophiles who make yearly pilgrimages to London in search of antiques.

Paula, who decorated the entire inn herself, has made sure that no two rooms are alike and no detail is left unattended. Perhaps the most awe-inspiring of the inn's 24 room's is the suite above the carriage house. Walk in your private entrance and glimpse the gleaming forest green, 1939 "woody" station wagon, housed on the bottom floor. Upstairs you'll enter a sitting room with 12-foot ceilings, deep green walls, and green velvet drapes surrounding palladian windows that look out on a garden. Relax in a high-back red leather chair. Enjoy the warmth of the fireplace. In the bedroom – outfitted with antique lace linens – vintage leather suitcases (including a Louis Vuitton) casually sit in the corner of the room. Other touches

MARTHA'S VINEYARD

include a shoe rack and shoe-shining machine, discreetly kept in the closet.

Another large room in the Summer House has a white grand piano (always graced with a profusion of flowers), fireplace, and black and white tiled bath with an antique tub.

Complimentary continental breakfast is served every morning in L'etoile, the Charlotte's restaurant cum greenhouse. Full breakfast is also served, but for an additional charge. In warm weather, afternoon snacks are served on the wrap-around porch.

RATES PER NIGHT: $175-$350 early June through mid October, $125-$350 late spring, $85-$350 off season.

ACCOMMODATIONS: 22 rooms with private baths, 2 suites with private baths.

AMENITIES: Air conditioning. Television and telephones in some rooms. Television in common room. Fireplaces in some rooms. Restaurant.

RESTRICTIONS: No children under 14. No pets. Light cigarette smoking only.

The Outermost Inn, ♡ ♡ ♡, $$$-$$$$, Lighthouse Road, Gay Head 02535, 508/645-3511. Singly perched at the very tip of Martha's Vineyard on the Gay Head cliffs, the Outermost Inn boldly faces the Atlantic. Its remote location (20 miles from the Vineyard Haven ferry) and magnificently stark setting is perfect for couples who truly want to get away from it all.

In 1990, with their children grown, Hugh and Jeanne Taylor decided to convert their family home into a bed and breakfast. Set on about 30 acres of moors and a few hundred yards from the Gay Head light house, this rambling clapboard gem with its ocean-view wrap-around porch, has a funky flavor that perfectly suits the remote locale.

Walk past the small garden, through the front door, and hear the sounds of Ella Fitzgerald waft through the house. The living room is casually but pleasantly outfitted with a few country antiques, a pastel dhurrie, as well as a piano, electric keyboard, guitar, maracas, and various other instruments. Hugh is James Taylor's youngest brother, and has inherited the family's musical inclination. (Although Hugh typically doesn't play for guests, he has a regular gig at David's Island House, a local watering hole.)

The Outermost's dining room, where fully country breakfasts are served, is dominated on one side by ocean views, and on the other by a great brick fireplace which blazes on all but the warmest days. Small wooden tables, each with a bouquet of flowers, are covered with a mix of lace cloths and India prints. The inn's decor would fit as well in Vermont as it does here.

The seven guest rooms are all new additions to the house, which Hugh and Jean designed and built themselves. Floors are all glossy blond woods, such as beech, ash, and cherry. Walls are stark white and accented with original oils by local artists.

Furnishings are similarly simple yet elegant. Even the bath towels are unbleached white. The plainness is a perfect complement to the dramatic ocean views, which every room enjoys.

In the afternoon, complimentary drinks and set-ups (Gay Head is dry) are provided on the front porch, arguably the most picturesque spot on all of Martha's Vineyard. And dinner is served Thursday through Sunday. The evening meal, however, isn't included in the room rate.

The Outermost has access to the private beach reserved for town residents. And if you have an itch to get on the open waters, Hugh charters day trips to Cuttyhunk.

RATES PER NIGHT: $195-$220 mid June through mid September, $125-$140 spring and fall, $90-$110 December through March.

ACCOMMODATIONS: 6 rooms with private baths, 1 suite with private bath and deck.

AMENITIES: Telephones. Television in living room. Television in rooms upon request. One room with whirlpool.

RESTRICTIONS: No pets.

The Thorncroft Inn, ♡ ♡ ♡, $$-$$$$, Main Street, Vineyard Haven 02568, 508/693-3333. The small electric candles in the first floor windows give the Thorncroft a cozy glow, a hint to the nature of this classic, traditional country inn. Owners Karl and Lynn Buder, a former narcotics officer and an insurance executive respectively, are not Vineyard natives. But they fell in love with the island when they first visited more than 16 years ago. Their enthusiasm about island life, and relaxed attitude, is infectious.

The Buders purchased the house along with its 3 1/2 acres in 1981, four years after they visited the island for the first time as tourists. However, Thorncroft has been an inn since the 1940s, and in fact was originally built as a guest house for the oceanside estate across the street.

Common rooms – living, dining, and sun rooms – are decorated with soothing, muted mauves and dusty blues. Thick, soft wall-to-wall carpets cover the floors. (The Buders are meticulous and change carpets every three or four years.) Lace curtains and wicker furniture abound.

All of Thorncroft's bedrooms are similarly well-appointed with antiques, plush carpeting, and private baths; most have working fireplaces. Room one is particularly pleasant, with an 1855 carved walnut bed frame and matching dresser, an authentic Victorian love seat, and antique tub. And if you're interested in catching some sun in private, room 6 has its own deck. For complete seclusion, opt for one of the two rooms in the carriage house. They have their own entrances, as well as cable television. One boasts a two-person Jacuzzi and the other a hot tub.

Full country breakfasts are served every morning. Guest favorites include buttermilk pancakes with blueberry honey sauce, and scrambled eggs with sausage and biscuits. Homemade granola, juice, and coffee are also available. Afternoon tea, which the Buders always attend, is served every day between 4:00 and 5:00 P.M.

Although it's not part of the room rate, dinner is served every evening for guests only. The Thorncroft's chef comes from The Four Seasons in Boston, so you can be assured an elegant meal. The Thorncroft has a lovely private dining room where you can arrange a candle-lit meal just for the two of you.

Other impressive amenities include nightly turn down service and a daily Boston Globe.

RATES PER NIGHT: $99-$219 Labor Day through late June, $129-$299 late June to through Labor Day.

ACCOMMODATIONS: 13 rooms in 2 buildings, all with private baths. One room with two-person Jacuzzi, one with hot tub, one with deck, and six with fireplaces.

AMENITIES: Central air conditioning. Television in common room.

RESTRICTIONS: No smoking. No pets.

The Shiverick Inn, ♡ ♡, $$-$$$$, Pent Lane, Edgartown 02539, 508/627-3797. Poised at the edge of downtown Edgartown, The Shiverick could only have a better location if it were right on the ocean. Originally built in 1840 for the town's first full-time physician, the inn, with polished oak double doors, imposing mansard roof, and soaring cupola, has maintained the house's original stately ambiance.

First time innkeepers and new owners Marty and Denny Turmelle are working hard to maintain the inn's fine reputation built by the original owners. The first clue to their attentiveness is the well-tended English garden next to the private parking lot. Its adjacent to a garden room with white wicker furniture, marble fireplace, and clusters of cushioned iron chairs and tables. The living room has a mix of 18th and 19th century American and English antiques and reproductions. (At at this writing, it was not entirely furnished because the Turmelles had only been innkeepers for a month.)

All 10 of Shiverick's guest rooms have a refined, understated elegance—no heart wreaths or mounds of lacy throw pillows. Room 4, which has a working fireplace, is outfitted in shades of tan, from walls to linens to carpeting. Crystal lamps sit on twin bedside tables, and plush terry robes hang in the closet. Room 6 is more dramatic, with a king-size carved wood four-poster with delicate lace curtains. All rooms are graced with impressive Orientals and starched crisp linens (Denny irons them herself). Although none of the rooms has a television, a second-floor library has one; it also has a terrace that overlooks downtown Edgartown.

Breakfast is served in the garden room with proper silver, china, crystal, and a spray of fresh flowers on the sideboard. Selections include homemade granola, muffins, pastries, fruit, juice, and coffee. Tea and snacks are also served in the afternoons.

RATES PER NIGHT: $150-$225 June through mid October, $75-$165 mid October through May.

ACCOMMODATIONS: 10 rooms with private baths. One room can be made into a suite.

AMENITIES: Some rooms have fireplaces. One room has a terrace. Central air conditioning, except for two guest rooms. Common room with television.

RESTRICTIONS: No children under 12. No pets. No smoking.

Breakfast at Tiasquam, ♡ ♡, $$-$$$, Off Middle Road, Chilmark 02535, 508/645-3685. In transit: Set about ½ mile down a dirt road in the middle of rural Chilmark, Breakfast at Tiasquam isn't your typical B&B. Built, owned, and operated by bachelor Ron Crowe, this extraordinarily well-built new cape has 20 skylights that flood the interior with light and provide the feeling of being outdoors.

Crowe has a serious appreciation of fine craftsmanship. All the inn's doors are solid, carved cherry, sinks are hand-thrown ceramic, and the dining room table and chairs (at which Crowe serves his famous breakfast) are hand-made.

That said, Breakfast at Tiasquam isn't for everyone. The eight guest rooms are simply furnished, yet are clean and pleasant nonetheless. The Master room is the B&B's most impressive offering, with 16-foot ceilings, two skylights, wood stove, and two-person Jacuzzi.

One unusual amenity is a secluded outdoor shower that is open to the air but for one side. Many couples enjoy taking showers in the nude, he says. "You haven't taken a shower until you have taken one outside with the sun warming your skin."

After your wash, you might decide to lounge in the hammock, or relax on one of several decks that overlook woodlands and wildflower fields.

Another of Crowe's prides, and after which he named the B&B, is his copious breakfasts. Served from 7:00 A.M. - 9:30 A.M., Crowe cooks whatever guests, or any other islanders who happen to drop by, want (provided he has the ingredients in his kitchen). Among the guests' favorites is Crowe's own invention of fresh corn and blueberry pancakes served with Vermont maple syrup.

RATES PER NIGHT: $90-$150 early September through October, $70-$115 November through early April, $100-$175 early June through early September.

ACCOMMODATIONS: Unlike most spots listed in Romantic New England Getaways, not all rooms have private baths. Two rooms with private baths; six rooms share three and a half baths.

AMENITIES: Television and stereo in common area.

RESTRICTIONS: No children. No pets.

Note: For couples interested in nude sunbathing, Chilmark is the only town on Martha's Vineyard that has designated clothing optional beaches. If you stay at Breakfast at Tiasquam, you'll have the benefit of a beach pass to Lucy Vincent Beach, open only to Chilmark residents. Bluff climbing isn't allowed.

But do feel free to doff your swim suit. Nudies typically sit to the left, clothed bathers to the right. Lucy Vincent is essentially a family beach, however, so proper behavior is expected.

FRIDAY EVENING
Dinner

Home Port, ♥, $$$, North Road, Menemsha, 508/645-2679. In transit: From the Outermost, follow the Lighthouse Road to West Basin Road, and follow signs to Menemsha and Chilmark. From Main Street in Vineyard Haven, take State Road. It leads to North Road and signs for Menemsha. From Edgartown, follow the Edgartown/West Tisbury Road, to South Road, to Menemsha Cross Road. As with the other routes, this too will have signs for Menemsha.

This old-fashioned, fish dining hall, set right on Vineyard Sound, is an island landmark. Although it may not have linen tablecloths and candlelight, Home Port has the kind of casual, elbows-on-the-table atmosphere that fits so well with island living. You won't mind the acoustic tiling or the taxidermied fish on the walls, because the views, not to mention the seafood, is spectacular.

You might start with some quahog chowder, then maybe some baked stuff Vineyard scallops, or Menemsha swordfish. Lobster lovers should try the Home Port Shore Dinner, which includes one lobster, corn on the cob, a stuffed quahog, steamed mussels, and broth.

All entrees include soup, salad, beverage, and dessert. And although all the seafood is tempting, you will want to save room for a slice of home-baked berry pie.

Home Port is BYOB, but it does offer set-ups of tonic water, club soda, and ginger ale.

For couples who really want to be by themselves, a nice option is to order take-out from the Home Port. Walk down to the Menemsha town beach by Dutcher's Dock and spread out a blanket. The sunsets are magnificent. (You'll see the sign for Dutcher's Dock right before the fork for Home Port.) Hours: 5:00 P.M. - 9:30 P.M., off season hours are reduced.

The Black Dog, ♥, $$-$$$, Beach Street Extension, Vineyard Haven, 508/693-9233. In transit: Assuming you're going to dinner straight from the ferry, the Black Dog is just beyond the ferry terminal. You'll see the Black Dog Bakery on the left. Then turn left on the beach street extension. Or you can park in the lot directly across from the terminal and walk over. From the Oak Bluffs ferry terminal, take the Beach Road into Vineyard Haven, then turn right onto the Beach Street extension, which is right at the five corners. From the airport, take the Airport Road (a.k.a.

Barnes Road) north, then follow signs to Vineyard Haven.

To some people, natives and tourists alike, The Black Dog *is* Martha's Vineyard. It's not that it's the only place to go on the island, or that it serves the best food, or is the most interesting. But its position and atmosphere embody all that is Martha's Vineyard. Perched smack on the edge of the harbor, The Black Dog has a funky no-nonsense flavor whose heavy varnished wood tables are as pleasing to fishermen as they are to artists. (Fishermen, however, are more likely to come for breakfast because it is far more reasonably priced than dinner.)

And despite the notoriety, and the T shirts and mugs sold in The Black Dog annex, and the occasional flies that buzz about the tables, it would be a mistake to visit Martha's Vineyard without stopping here. If you can, sit on the screened porch so you'll have a clear harbor view. Because of its size, long and narrow, it's far more intimate than the large, main dining room.

Not surprisingly, the Dog's best and most popular offerings are its fish dishes. They include grilled yellowfin tuna with spicy ginger sauce, bluefish with mustard soufflé sauce, and baked cod with small shrimp and leeks. However, meat lovers won't be disappointed with the roasted prime rib or the New York sirloin.

If your appetite isn't quite so hearty, you may order from a selection of appetizers, salads, and light meals. Among the offerings are Brie and Saga blue cheese with French bread; cheese tortellini with proscuitto, peas, and cream; smoked bluefish with yogurt and dill sauce; and quahog chowder.

If you opt for a light meal, you might still have room for dessert. Offerings include ricotta cake with raspberries, fudge bottom pie, carrot cake, and blueberry pie. Hours: 5:00 P.M. - 10:00 P.M. (If you come in late fall, call ahead, off-season the Dog only serves dinner until 9:00 P.M.)

SATURDAY MORNING

Bicycle From Vineyard Haven to Edgartown.

In transit: If you're staying at the Thorncroft, you won't have to do any traveling. From Gay Head and Chilmark, follow either Middle, North, or South Roads to State Road, which leads to downtown Vineyard Haven. If you're traveling east on Middle, you'll dead end. Turn left on Panhandle Road, then right on Scotchmans Bridge, and left onto State Road. Although streets are poorly marked, getting around is easy. Thankfully signs posted at most forks point to the various towns. Simply head east and follow signs to Vineyard Haven. From Edgartown, follow Main Street north to

the Vineyard Haven road, which leads right to Main Street. Your best bet for all-day parking is at Owen Park on the harbor and next to the Steamship Authority. If that's filled, you can try the west side of Franklin Street, which runs parallel and west of Main Street. Also, some side streets around Franklin have all-day parking. Don't get lazy and park in the two-hour spots. The Vineyard Haven meter attendants are notorious ticketers.

Note: If you're staying in Edgartown, you might be tempted to start your bike trip here. Although this is feasible, the day is planned so that you can enjoy the afternoon in Edgartown. Since everyone has to make the round-trip bike ride anyway, simply bike directly to Vineyard Haven first thing. The shortest route is down the Vineyard Haven road. You can access it from Main Street and it goes right down the center of the island.

If you're unfamiliar with the Vineyard, one of the best ways to experience it is by bike. It gives you the opportunity to slowly savor the scenery – pounding surf, swaying sea grass, brightly-colored Victorian cottages, and stately colonials. Virtually all of Martha's Vineyard's most scenic roads have separate paved bike paths, which makes pedaling a true pleasure.

This tour will give you a glimpse of the Vineyard's three town centers. Each has its own distinct personality, and you'll want to spend time wandering the streets, soaking in their unique flavors. Every town center has racks so you can lock your bike.

Although the commercial center, Vineyard Haven will still appeal to visitors. Its main street offers an eclectic, off-beat mix of shops, and is a refreshing alternative to the relentless perfection of Edgartown. Conversely, it is crammed with stores selling items that appeal to travelers with money to burn – gourmet vinegar, handmade quilts, antiques, silk lingerie. This might be off-putting to well-traveled tourists if it weren't for the magnificently preserved 18th century homes, surrounded by split rail fences and flowering bushes, that sit primly on the town's side streets.

Oak Bluff's has a far different flavor. Music emanating from the wooden carousel in the town center, adds to the carnival atmosphere. Tiny shops in the center of town hawk cheap trinkets. Pizza is sold by the slice. And teenagers walk up and down the streets cautiously checking each other out.

The entire bike ride is about 20 miles round trip, and is on paved flat surfaces. Most people in reasonably good shape can make the ride without a problem. Another option, however, is to rent mopeds.

From the steamship terminal on Union Street in Vineyard Haven, turn left on Water Street (assuming your back is facing the ocean), then left on Beach Road to Oak Bluffs. The bike path runs right along the side of the road.

From Oak Bluffs, continue along the Beach Road to Edgartown. It flows right into Main Street. This ride is particularly breathtaking. For much of it, you'll be surrounded by water on both sides of the road. Once you get into Edgartown, you'll be ready for lunch.

Following are a few spots in Vineyard Haven and Oak Bluffs you won't want to miss:

Brahman & Dunn, Main Street, Vineyard Haven, 508/693-6437. The best women's clothing and housewares store on the island. It's no wonder Carly Simon (an island resident) is a patron. Downstairs look for silk sweaters, whimsical straw hats, and billowy yet elegant island-style clothes. Upstairs houses an eclectic array of linens, small lamps, frames, and other home accouterments. Beware, everything is expensive.

Bunch of Grapes, Main Street, Vineyard Haven, 508/693-2291. The best book shop to visit if you're looking for a wide selection of books about the island. A great spot to browse for bibliophiles.

Crispin's Landing, Main Street, Vineyard Haven, 508/693-6758. If you're looking for an island memento, don't miss this spot. It features a wide selection of the locally made Chilmark Pottery, handmade jewelry, leather goods, rugs, and a limited supply of clothing (mostly "groovy" wear).

Rainy Day, Main Street, Vineyard Haven, 508/693-1830. Cotton rag rugs have made a huge comeback in recent years, and they're particularly big in island homes. This housewares stores has an excellent selection of cheerily-colored rugs that you may not be able to resist.

Flying Horses Carousel, off Oak Bluffs Avenue, Oak Bluffs. Considered one of the oldest carousels in the nation, don't miss a ride on this covered gem. Thrill seekers might be disappointed that the horses only go round and not up and down. But it will still bring you back to your childhood.

Ocean Park, along Beach Road, Oak Bluffs. This grand, ocean-side park is surrounded by some of the best examples of Victorian architecture in the nation. Most houses are painted bright colors with their intricate swirling trim perfectly restored. They almost appear as if they've come to life from the pages of a child's storybook.

Lunch

Among the Flowers Café, $, Mayhew Street, Edgartown, 508/627-3233. In transit: Mayhew is a short street that runs parallel to Main and is right in the center of town.

This casual spot, with a small outdoor patio, is famous for its espresso shakes. But you'll also find some good sandwiches, tuna to lobster, as well as soups and salads. Nothing too fancy but perfectly satisfying. Save room for a slice of carrot cake or a peanut butter chip brownie. Hours: 11:30-A.M. - 3:30 P.M. Desserts only are served from 3:30 P.M. - 4:00 P.M.

The Wharf, $-$$, Main Street, Lower Main Street, Edgartown, 508/627-9966. In transit: If you're walking toward the water, the Wharf is on the left, just about a block up from the water.

A popular pub with locals, the Wharf is your basic dim and narrow watering hole, with pewter tankards hanging over the wooden bar. If you're hot and sweaty and looking to get out of the sun, its cool darkness is refreshing. A perfect spot if you're feeling carnivorous. The Wharf serves great, juicy burgers. Also good chowder, sandwiches, and lobster salad. Hours: 11:30 A.M. - 10:00 P.M., service is available straight through.

Saturday Afternoon

Visit the Dukes County Historical Society, Museums and Library, Cooke and School streets, Edgartown, 508/627-4441. In transit: From Lower Main Street, near the Wharf, walk up

Main away from the water. Turn left on School Street.

This isn't the best or the biggest of historical museums, nor will it provide you with a whole history of Martha's Vineyard. But it's an interesting spot for those taken with historic remains. The Francis Foster Museum (it's actually just one room), which is attached to the library, contains photographs and artifacts, including personal diaries, from the whaling era. Also on the property is the Carriage Shed, which contains authentic vehicles and vessels; among them are a 30-foot whaleboat, an 1856 fire engine, and a hearse. Other points of interest are the original Gay Head Light, the First Order Fresnel Lens operated from 1856 to 1952, and the Captain Francis Pease House, which has changing exhibits.

The most interesting Historical Society operation, is the Thomas Cooke House. Built in 1765, this restored home houses 18th and 19th century Vineyard tools, furnishings, and clothing, all viewed with the help of a museum guide. (The Cooke House is closed off season)

Shopping in Edgartown.

In transit: You could retrace your steps back toward Main Street, but Edgartown's side streets are so picturesque, it will be more fun to get a close-up view of some of its cottages and restored captain's houses.

Walk down Cooke Street toward the water, turn left on South Summer Street. This will take you back to Main Street.

All of Edgartown's shops are either on or just around Main Street. You won't get lost just ambling around. Following are some of the more interesting shops:

Augusta Coleman, South Water Street, 508/693-6880. Unusual array of southwestern memorabilia, from small frames to beaded leather vests. Merchandise is artfully arranged and is interesting to just look at, even if you don't buy.

Traditions, Antiques & Fine Furnishings, 43 Main St., 508/693-4500. An interesting and relatively affordable selection of merchandise, including quilts, mirrors, china, occasional furniture, and some wild tulle-swathed straw hats.

Le Roux, Nevin Square on Winter Street, 508/627-6463. Among the more interesting clothing shops for men and women, it has a nice supply of casually hip apparel, including men's linen shirts, mysterious-looking English sunglasses, shoes, and Patagonia sportswear.

Island Pursuits, Main Street, 508/627-8185. If you're looking for an island memento in the form of a high quality T-shirt or sweatshirt, this is the place. Also a healthy supply of conservative but colorful sportswear and outerwear.

Tashtego, Main Street, 508/627-4300. Good spot if you're looking for fine housewares—linens, glasses, placemats. Lots of hand-painted dishes, fine porcelain, and other European imports.

Late Afternoon Snack At Mad Martha's, $, North Water Street,

508/627-9768. In transit: North Water is the first major cross street if you're walking away from the water. If you're walking up from the bottom of Main, turn right.

This ice cream shop with three locations on the Vineyard is famous with locals and tourists alike. Their homemade ice cream is tops, and so are their creative concoctions. You might throw calorie caution to the wind when you spy their offerings, which include: orange creams, shakes made with vanilla ice cream and fresh squeezed orange juice; Peter Paul Mounds sundaes, made with coconut ice cream, Mounds bars, hot fudge, and whipped cream; and ice cream flavors from maple walnut to Snickers. Go ahead, you'll work off the calories riding back to Vineyard Haven. Maybe.

Bicycling Back to Vineyard Haven.

You could retrace your path back through Oak Bluffs. This ride is indeed the most pleasant. But you could save time on your return trip if you went out Main Street and followed the Vineyard Haven Road back. You'll see the sign. It

cuts straight through the middle of the island. It too has a paved bike path.

SATURDAY EVENING
Dinner

L'etoile, ♡ ♡ ♡, $$$$, at the Charlotte Inn, South Summer Street, Edgartown. In transit: From Vineyard Haven, follow the Edgartown Road back into Edgartown to Main Street. Turn right off Main Street onto South Summer. From Gay Head take the State Road to South Road. Then follow the West Tisbury/Edgartown Road to the center. From Chilmark, take Middle Road east until it dead ends. Turn right on Music Street to South Road to the West Tisbury/ Edgartown Road.

Although their are many fine and romantic restaurants on Martha's Vineyard, none can compare to L'etoile when you're looking for a sophisticated atmosphere. Pleasantly, it is without the stuffiness or affectations of so many fine restaurants.

The dining room is really a solarium, filled with greenery and a working fountain, that overlooks one of the Charlotte's well-tended gardens. White linens and candlelight warm the brick and stone floors. Although you are not actually eating outdoors, you almost feel as if you are.

Self-taught chef Michael Brisson, gained much of his considerable expertise at

L'espalier in Boston. It's no surprise then that the menu features adventurous New England-oriented cuisine. Appetizers include curried lobster and shrimp bisque with fried sweet potato bread, and cider glazed quail on grilled corn bread with sautéed apples and calavados vinaigrette. A half dozen entrees are offered, among them roast rack of lamb with a goat cheese and spinach custard, and roasted Norwegian salmon fillet with a horseradish and ginger crust and spiced tomato coulis. Desserts change nightly, but always include an extravagant selection of tarts, cakes, and ice cream. Hours: 6:30-9:30 Thursday through Sunday. (Although the dining room is open weekends throughout the year, the number of weeknights it's open changes with the season. If you're planning to visit during the week in the off season, be sure to call ahead.)

Savoir Fare, ♡ ♡, $$-$$$, Old Post Office Square, Edgartown, 508/627-9864. In transit. Follow directions to downtown Edgartown from above (L'etoile). Old Post Office Square is behind the town hall off Main Street.

Urbanites looking for a hip downtown haven in Martha's Vineyard will feel at home at Savoir Fare. Although small and quiet, it's hand-painted floors, stark white walls, and partially open kitchen revealing dangling copper pots, bespeaks a city sophistication.

Thankfully, the menu delivers the goods. In fact, gastronomically speaking, Savoir Fare is perhaps the best restaurant on the Vineyard. The menu is broken out into small plates, mid courses, and large plates. It's possible to order a small plate and mid course and have a perfectly satisfying (and also not particularly expensive) meal.

Although the restaurant's name is French, the food has a decidedly Italian flair. After you're seated, a basket of warm crusty bread arrives at your table accompanied with a plate of olive oil. Small plate selections include crisp match sticks of zucchini with toasted almonds and pecorino, warm vegetable cake with sweet pepper dressing, and roast portobello mushrooms with arugula sherry vinegar and Parmesan shards. Most of the mid courses rely on pasta. Among the best are penne with duck confit, eggplant, tomato, and chevre;and cheese ravioli with fava beans and ham hocks in a tomato broth.

Usually a half dozen large plates appear on the menu, which changes monthly, as well as a few nightly specials. Selections might include crispy salmon with garlic mashed potatoes and endive, and grilled squab with smokehouse bacon, parsnip and sweet potato.

Like savory offerings, sweets all have a down-home twist. Chocolate banana marscapone cream pie, and butterscotch pudding with chocolate sauce are two favorites. Hours: 6:00 P.M. - 10:00 P.M.

SUNDAY MORNING

Cruise on the Laissez Faire.

Meet at the Lothrop Merry House, Owen Park, Vineyard Haven, 508/693-1646. In transit. From the five corners in Vineyard Haven (where so many roads converge just beyond the Black Dog Bakery) follow Main Street past the Steamship Authority to Owen Park. You'll see signs for the Lothrop Merry House, a small B&B. The Laissez Faire is moored at the town dock.

John and Mary Clarke have been offering charters on Martha's Vineyard for more than a dozen years. Also owners of the Lothrop Merry House, the Clarkes enjoy the Laissez-Faire, a classic wooden 54-foot Alden ketch, so much that they live on it. (In winter they migrate to the Caribbean and conduct charters there as well.)

The boat only takes up to six passengers so you can be assured a quiet and intimate experience. Depending on the wind and tide, the morning cruise takes passengers toward the Elizabeth Islands or Woods Hole. John and Mary offer snacks of ice tea, lemonade, cookies, and vegetables. The trip lasts four hours, from 9:00 A.M. TO 1:00 P.M.

Note: If you didn't have the time or inclination to take breakfast at your inn, consider having your morning meal on board. The Black Dog Bakery serves some delicious fat, juicy muffins and good coffee, and it's right on the way to the boat. Hours: 6:00 A.M. - 6:00 P.M.

Lunch

Take-Out at The Martha's Vineyard Deli, $, Main Street, Vineyard Haven, 508/693-1943. In transit: From the Lothrop Merry House, turn left onto Main Street. The deli will be on the right.

Good delis aren't always easy to find in resort communities, but the Martha's Vineyard is a find for luncheon meat addicts. Liverwurst, Genoa salami, corned beef—they've got all the essentials. Or you might prefer one of their own concoctions, named after stars who either visit or live on island. Among the more interesting are the Patricia Neal, peanut butter with bacon on toasted whole wheat, and the Carly Simon, cheddar, red onion, sprouts, and chutney, served hot in a toasted pita. Hours: 9:00 A.M. - 7:00 P.M.

SUNDAY AFTERNOON

Picnic and Beach Lounging at Wasque Reservation, (pronounced Way squee), Chappiquidick. In transit: Head south on Main Street and follow the Edgartown Road to downtown Edgartown. From there, you'll see signs pointing to the Chappiquidick ferry. This ferry, known as the "On Time," because it only leaves where there are people to take, holds only three cars and makes its crossing in about one minute. A round-trip ticket for a car and two passengers is $5.50. When you get off the ferry, there will be only one road. Follow it. When you come to a fork, bear right. This is Litchefield Road, which will lead to Wasque Road (dirt) and the Wasque Reservation.

The Wasque Reservation, along with the adjacent Cape Pogue Wildlife Refuge, is a 689-acre peaceful and starkly beautiful stretch of beach that's a maze of low dunes, cedar thickets, salt marshes, brackish ponds, tidal flats, and scrubby upland. If you visit in summer, you'll have a chance to see the reservation in full bloom with blueberry and bayberry bushes and wild asters. A winding wooden walkway leads to the beach, which is a favorite spot with bluefish fishermen. Enjoy your picnic, relax at the beach, stroll the shore line. Energetic visitors can also hike one of the many marked trails on the reservation.

If you're serious about hiking, consider stopping by the Land Bank, 167 Main St. in Edgartown (508/627-7141) for a map of the walking trails.

EARLY SUPPER

Le Grenier, ♡ ♡, $$$-$$$$, Main Street, Vineyard Haven, 508/693-3037. In transit: From Edgartown, follow Main Street to the Vineyard Haven Road. Traveling north on Main Street in Vineyard Haven, Le Grenier is on the left.

Both the name ("attic" in French) and the casual atmosphere, belie the fact that Le Grenier is one the Vineyard's best and most well established restaurants. It's the perfect spot—and not coincidentally near the ferry—if you're looking for one last great meal to end your weekend.

From your second story perch you can gaze out at Vineyard Haven harbor, just a block away, while you enjoy authentic French cuisine. Begin with vichyssoise or escargot bourguignon. Cleanse your palate with a demi Caesar salad. Then move onto calf's brains grenobloise (served with black butter and capers), quail with a cognac and red and white grape sauce, or venison with a red currant game sauce.

For the less adventurous, Le Grenier also offers more familiar fare, such as veal Oscar, Dover sole almandine, and steak au poivre, served with cognac, black pepper cream sauce.

If you've no interest in showering and making yourselves presentable before dinner, you could opt for La Patisserie, Le Grenier's downstairs casual café. It serves light meals for both breakfast, lunch, and dinner. Hours: Le Grenier accepts reservations from 6:00 P.M.; La Patisserie's hours are from 7:00 A.M. to 10:00 P.M. Both are open from May through October.

Additional Activities

Visit Chicama Vineyards, Stoney Hill Road, West Tisbury, 508/693-0309. This 30-acre vineyard produces 17,000 gallons annually. Varieties include Chardonnay, Cabernet Sauvignon, Riesling, Merlot, and Pinot Noir. Chicama also produces vinegars, mustards, and other gourmet food products. A tour of its processing plant takes about 20 minutes. The shop is a great spot for picking up mementos for friends and family. Hours: 11:00 A.M. - 5:00 P.M. Monday through Saturday through October.

Horseback Riding. Several farms offer horseback riding. Among them are Pond View Farms, New Lane, West Tisbury (508/693-2949) and Misty Meadow Farm, Old County Road (508/693-1870).

Visit Chilmark Pottery, State Road, 508/693-6476. An old barn at the end of a long dirt road houses the best pottery you'll find on the Vineyard. Even if you decide not to buy anything it's fun to browse and chat with the potter himself who's happy to take you back to his studio and show you around. Both clay and porcelain are available. Hours: 9:30 - 5:30 P.M.

Dinner at the Oyster Bar, 162 Circuit Ave., Oak Bluffs, 508/693-3300. This hip noisy bistro is very Manhattan and one of the most popular restaurants on the island. In addition to a great raw bar, you'll find such eclectic items as duck sausage pizza and oven-roasted citrus infused cod served with tangerine lime butter. Diners are not here just to eat, but to see and be seen. Hours: 6:30 P.M. - 11:00 P.M.

Dancing at the Hot Tin Roof, Airport Road, Oak Bluffs, 508/693-1137. If you're looking for serious live rock n' roll, this is *the* place on the island.

GETTING THERE

BY AIR: No major airlines fly directly to the Vineyard. However, Cape Air (800/352-0714) has daily direct flights from Boston. It has joint ticket and baggage handling agreements with US Air, Delta, Continental, and United. It also has service from New Bedford and Nantucket, MA. Charter service is available from Direct Flight (508/693-6688).

BY CAR: You can't drive directly to Martha's Vineyard. It is after all an island. You must drive to Woods Hole, then take a 45-minute ferry to Vineyard Haven or Oak Bluffs. (It doesn't matter where you land. The docks are just 10-minutes away from each other.) Even though some people may like the immediacy of flying, the ferry ride is truly a thrill and makes getting to the island as much fun as being on it. Sit on deck and enjoy the ocean breeze.

From the north, take I-93 south to Route 3 south to the Sagamore Bridge.

Don't cross the bridge. At the traffic circle, just before the bridge, follow signs to Route 6 west and Buzzards Bay (Bourne). Cross the Bourne Bridge and follow Route 28 south to Woods Hole. Follow signs to the ferry. Or take I-95 to Route 24 to I-495 to Buzzards Bay. Cross the Bourne Bridge and follow Route 28 south into Woods Hole.

You can park your car in Woods Hole, walk on the ferry, then rent a car on the Vineyard. But it's cheaper to bring your own car over. However, you must decide to do this well in advance. The ferry has limited space for cars and it fills up fast. To make reservations, call the Nantucket Steamship Authority (508/540-2022). You can take your chances and go stand-by, but that's advisable only in the off season. The ferry does have a guarantee however. If you get into the stand-by line by 2:00 P.M., you're assured of getting on a ferry sometime that day. Round-trip for a car and two passengers is $90. Passenger tickets are $9 round-trip, and an extra $5.50 for a bicycle.

Passenger-only ferries are available from Hyannis (Hy-Line, 508/775-7185) and New Bedford (Cape Island Express, 508/997-1688).

BY TRAIN: No train service is available.

BY BUS: Bonanza Bus Line (800/556-3815), or outside New England (401/331-7500), daily service from Boston, Providence, and New York. All buses stop right at the Woods Hole ferry terminal.

From mid May through mid October, Martha's Vineyard Transportation Services (508/693-1589) has regularly scheduled bus served among Vineyard Haven, Oak Bluffs, and Edgartown. Also, the Martha's Vineyard Transit Authority (508/627-7448) runs seasonal trolley service (through mid September) from parking lots outside Edgartown to the town center, and also to Katama, South Beach.

CAR RENTAL: Some people will tell you that you don't need a car on the island. Don't believe them. It is possible to enjoy the Vineyard without a car—taxis and public buses are in abundance—but it's far more convenient to have one. The entire island is 100 square miles.

Six rental companies have offices on Martha's Vineyard: Adventure Rentals of Martha's Vineyard/Thrifty Rent-A-Car (508/693-1959 or 508/693-1053), All-Island Rent-A-Car (508/693-6868), Atlantic Rent-A-Car (508/693-0480 or 693-0698), Budget Rent-A-Car (800/848-8005 or 508/693-1911), Hertz Rent-A-Car (508/627-4727), and Holmes Hole Car Rental/Rent A Wreck (508/693-8838).

TAXI/LIMOUSINE SERVICE: Taxis are typically waiting at the ferry dock and the airport. Martha's Vineyard has many taxi services precisely because lots of people don't bring their cars. Following is a list of the larger companies: Martha's Vineyard Taxi Co. (508/6693-8660), Muzik's Limousine Service (508/693-2212), Marlene's Taxi (5508/693-0037), and Hathaway's Taxi (508/627-4462).

BIKE/MOPED RENTAL: Ride-On Mopeds and Bikes, Oak Bluffs (508/693-2076), Adventure Rentals, Vineyard Haven (508/693-1959), DeBettencourt's Bike Shop, Oak Bluffs (508/693-0011), and R.W. Cutler Bike Shop, Edgartown (508/627-4052).

INFORMATION: Martha's Vineyard Chamber of Commerce, Beach Road, Vineyard Haven 02568, 508/693-0085. Hours: 9:00 A.M. - 5:00 P.M., 10:00 A.M. - 2:00 P.M. on Saturday in summer. This chamber has a wealth of brochures. It's just up the street from the Black Dog Bakery.

Wellfleet, Massachusetts

For those who have never visited Cape Cod, the very word symbolizes a seaside haven of towering dunes, long sandy beaches, and salt-worn shingle houses surrounded by split-rail fences and wild rose bushes. Unfortunately, most of the Cape has succumbed to commerce and today bears a far stronger resemblance to Coney Island.

Just a few pockets of its past unspoiled beauty remain, and among the most well-preserved of these is Wellfleet. Intensely peaceful, the town is located at the beginning of the Cape's thread-thin hook that juts out to sea. Half the town's acreage is under National Seashore jurisdiction. Yet if offers a surprising amount of urban sophistication. Next to Provincetown, Wellfleet is the Cape's artistic center, with nearly 20 fine art galleries. It also boasts some of the region's best dining, from gourmet restaurants to clam shacks.

Wellfleet's combination of art, natural beauty, and relative seclusion draws a high-brow tourist crowd. It's a favorite vacation spot of New York psychiatrists, college professors, and lawyers, all of whom come not "to be seen," but to savor Wellfleet's small town flavor.

Its center, an eclectic mix of dime stores, boutiques, galleries, and restaurants, is anchored by a stately white Congregational church. (Its belfry clock is the only one in the world that strikes ship's time.) Just behind this commercial cluster is Wellfleet harbor, where sailboats, trawlers, and fishing vessels alike bob serenely from their moorings.

The town's beaches are similarly picturesque, but with a decidedly more solitary flavor. Ocean side beaches are marked by long stretches of smooth sand, flanked by mountainous dunes and pounding surf. The less dramatic bay side offers warmer, calmer waters.

Although less than two miles wide, Wellfleet is known for its numerous glacier kettle holes. These "ponds," created by glaciers that melted several hundred thousand years ago, offer a pleasant alternative for fresh water bathers.

WHERE TO STAY

Cahoun Hollow Bed & Breakfast, ♡♡, $$, Cahoun Hollow Road, P.O. Box 383, Wellfleet 02667, 508/349-6372. Cahoun Hollow is a gem of a B&B. Proprietor Bailey Ruckert, a local fiber artist, has transformed a 19th century sea captain's home into an elegant respite for the world weary.

The house has two bedrooms, each with private bath. (If you can, opt for the room on the second floor—it's a bit more spacious and private.) Common rooms include two living rooms and a kitchen, all of which are at guests' disposal. (Massachusetts law prohibits guests from making meals. But Bailey welcomes them to keep snacks and picnic supplies in the kitchen, and brew a cup of tea.)

Throughout the house you'll find wide pine board floors and an eclectic mix of antique and elegant modern furniture. Many of Bailey's own baskets and rugs are artfully displayed.

Bailey cooks breakfast every morning and serves it on the patio. Staples include granola, pancakes, muffins, and bacon and eggs. Ever cheerful, Bailey loves to chat while she serves. She and her husband live right next door and are full of suggestions about what to do on the outer Cape.

Although Cahoun Hollow's grounds are lovely—the yard has a great hammock and flower garden—it is not on the ocean. But then again, few of Wellfleet's accommodations are. But the beach, ponds, and downtown are just a 10-minute bike ride away.

RATES PER NIGHT: $85 Memorial Day to Columbus Day, $80 off season. (Those interested in real seclusion might consider renting the whole house.)

ACCOMMODATIONS: 2 rooms with private baths.

AMENITIES: Televisions. Bicycles available for guests.

RESTRICTIONS: No children under 5. No smoking. No pets.

Sea Cliff, ♡♡♡, $$$$, P.O. Box 889, Ocean View Drive, Wellfleet 02667, 508/349-3753 (from mid June through September), 212/741-1832 (balance of year). Sea Cliff is the only public accommodation in Wellfleet that sits directly on the Atlantic Ocean. Views are unforgettable.

Sea Cliff isn't so much a B&B as a private oceanside room. Several years ago, Marla and Betram Perkel decided to share their home's magnificent vantage point with Wellfleet visitors and built a spacious room with a private bath, pantry, and expansive deck onto their home. The original house has been in

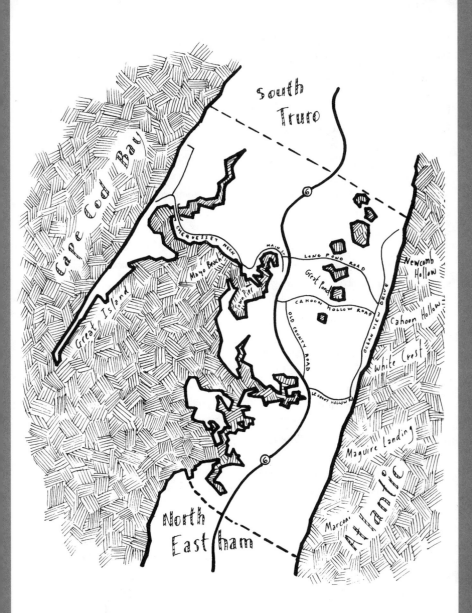

South
Truro

Cape Cod Bay

Great Island

CHEQUESSET NECK

MAIN ST.

Mayo Beach

Duck River

LONG POND ROAD

Great Pond

CAHOON HOLLOW ROAD

OLD COUNTY ROAD

OCEAN VIEW DRIVE

LE COUNT HOLLOW RD.

Newcomb
Hollow

Cahoon Hollow

White Crest

Maguire Landing

Marconi

Atlantic

North
Eastham

N

WELLFLEET

Marla's family for many years and was built before the surrounding property was claimed as National Seashore in 1961. Because so much of Wellfleet's beachfront is earmarked for preservation, very few homes enjoy similar positions.

Although not quaint, like many B&Bs, Sea Cliff is clean and well appointed with a king-size bed, refrigerator, and microwave. The view from the bay window is ambiance enough.

Marla gets great pleasure from making visitors feel comfortable. Guests are greeted with a basket of homemade cookies and chocolates in their room. And although she doesn't present an elaborate breakfast, it is substantial. Juice, coffee, a variety of homemade muffins, and Marla's famous dried fruit and champagne compote are served on the patio.

A true romantic, Marla keeps the guest room supplied with candles, and has installed a secluded wooden bench amidst overgrown beach grass at the top of a dune. It is these touches, along with the idyllic location, that make Sea Cliff a top-notch getaway.

RATES PER NIGHT: $195 with two night minimum, $95 each additional night.

ACCOMMODATIONS: 1 room with private bath.

AMENITIES: Phone, television, and pantry with refrigerator, microwave, and hot pot.

RESTRICTIONS: No children. No pets.

Brehmer Graphics Bed & Breakfast, ♥, $$, Commercial Street, Wellfleet 02667, 508/349-9565. Located in the very heart of Wellfleet in a Victorian sea captain's home, Brehmer is at once an art gallery and bed and breakfast.

Artist and owner Bethia (Beth) Brehmer has a casual and friendly style. She opened the B&B above her gallery several years ago to help augment her income. And she appears to do both jobs with relative ease.

The B&B shares the gallery entrance. Guests are greeted in the dining room opposite the main showroom. It too is graced with Beth's work, mostly ethereal pastel etchings.

Upstairs are two simple but tasteful guest rooms, which share a private bath. Under most circumstances, this wouldn't be optimum for a romantic getaway. Yet this B&B is so reasonably priced, it's possible to rent both rooms and have the entire upstairs to yourself.

Brehmer's choice room is number 1. Decorated with family heirlooms, it boasts a fishnet canopy bed covered with an antique pink and blue wedding ring quilt, and several small Oriental rugs. The common bath has a great old clawfoot tub, which is perfect for soaking.

A full breakfast is served in the peaceful backyard garden, complete with brick paths and a miniature lily pond. Beth fixes breakfast herself, and in addition to juice and coffee usually serves homemade muffins and a hot entree. One of the guests' favorites is her French crêpes.

RATES PER NIGHT: $60.

ACCOMMODATIONS: 2 rooms with shared bath.

AMENITIES: None

RESTRICTIONS: None

FRIDAY EVENING
Drinks

Captain Higgins Seafood Restaurant, ♡ ♡ ♡, $$, Wellfleet Harbor, 508/349-6055. In transit: From the Sea Cliff and Cahoun Hallow, follow Route 6 south to the intersection for Wellfleet center. Turn left at intersection–you'll see the arrow. At the fork, bear left for Wellfleet Harbor. The restaurant is on the right. You can walk from Brehmer Graphics. Just follow Commercial Street south, past the town pier. It will only take you a few minutes.

Forget the hokey name, Captain Higgins has the best outside deck in Wellfleet. The atmosphere is relaxed; you can go in shorts and a t-shirt. Lounging harborside is the perfect way to begin a beach weekend. Try to get there in time to enjoy a magnificent sunset.

If you need to take the bite out of your appetite, try Higgins' steamers. Dipped

in steaming hot butter, they're a true delicacy. Hours: 12:00 P.M. - 9:30 P.M.

Dinner

The Bayside Lobster Hutt, ♡, $$, Commercial Street, Wellfleet 508/349-6333. In transit: From Captain Higgins, follow Commercial street north. It's on the right, and will only take you a couple of minutes to walk.

Bayside's ambiance is strictly "early trawler"–buoys and fishnets adorn the walls. Tables are picnic-style, and service extends no further than the cook screaming out an order number. But any lobster aficionado knows the only way to enjoy this fine crustacean is to eat it in surroundings where you don't mind getting your fingers sticky.

Surprisingly, Bayside only has indoor seating. But the fish shanty ambiance is a treat. The menu includes all types of seafood–baked, fried, broiled, and in chowder and rolls. There's also a salad and raw bar. The restaurant has no liquor license, but patrons may bring beer or wine.

Why not celebrate the beginning of your getaway weekend with a bottle of champagne. (Even beer doesn't go as well with lobster.) Wellfleet has three liquor stores: Seaside Liquors, Route 6, (508/349-2728), Brady's Liquor Locker, Route 6, (508/349-6880), and Wellfleet Spirits Shoppe, Main Street (508/349-3731). Hours: 4:00 P.M. - 10:00 P.M.

Adrian's, ♥ ♥, $$$, Route 6A, North Truro, 508/487-4360. In transit: Head toward Provincetown along Route 6. In North Truro, you'll see the intersection for 6A. Follow 6A for a few miles. The restaurant is on the left.

If you don't need a water view with your meal, Adrian's is a great spot to have a casual meal. A favorite with locals, the place has an eclectic clientele and a decidedly beachy feel. Walk through the old screen door and you'll find a simple A-frame room with rough-hewn pine paneling, and varnished wood tables set with candles set in heavy crystal holders. Adrian's only decorations are a few paintings done by local artists.

The menu is strictly pasta, pizza, and appetizers. Old-time Italian standbys are nicely balanced with new cuisine. For starters, consider the pappa al pomodoro. This hot bread and tomato soup is popular in Florence, and Adrian's version is amazingly credible. Other good choices include bruschetta, which is grilled bread topped with olive oil, garlic, and hot red pepper, and polenta served with a sausage and hot pepper ragu, garnished with romano and fresh basil.

Pasta dishes range from the basic spaghetti with tomato sauce and sausage to cappelletti (little caps of pasta) filled with gorgonzola, and served with a sage butter and parmesan cheese sauce. Pizzas

similarly run the gamut from New York style topped with pepperoni, peppers, mushrooms, and olives, to a grilled pizza that's brushed with olive oil, tomatoes, goat cheese, and fresh rosemary. Hours: 5:30 P.M. - 10:00 P.M. daily. (As *Romantic New England Getaways* was going to press, Adrian's was about to move to a new location on Route 6 in Truro, which has ocean views.)

Dessert

Just Desserts, $, Commercial Street, Wellfleet, no phone. In transit: This tiny spot is just behind The Bayside Lobster in Wellfleet Harbor.

Finish off your meal with espresso and a sweet or some ice cream from Just Desserts. Don't forget to bring a blanket. You can head down to the beach across the street from Captain Higgins and savor your treats. Hours: 5:00 P.M. - 10:00 P.M. daily.

SATURDAY MORNING

Bike Ride Along Ocean View Drive.

In transit: Begin your bike ride at the First Congregational Church in Wellfleet center. Head down Main Street toward Route 6. Cross Route 6 and then turn left. You'll ride just a short distance to Long Pond Road. Turn right on Long Pond Road and follow it to the end. Turn left on Ocean View Drive, and ride to Newcomb Hollow Beach. Retrace your steps and go back toward Long Pond Road. Pass Long Pond and continue along Ocean View Drive. Follow Ocean View to the end, then turn right on Le Count Hollow Road. Turn right on Route 6 and head back to the center of town. Or if you want, you can retrace your path along Ocean View Drive. The entire trip is about 12 miles.

This scenic road will take you by Wellfleet's most dramatic beaches: Newcomb Hollow, Cahoun Hollow, White Crest, and Maguire Landing. As lovely as this ride is, the dunes sometimes obstruct the water views. You'll probably feel the urge to hop off your bikes and hit the sand. All beaches charge for car parking, but there is no charge for bicycles.

Lunch

Flying Fish Café, $, Briar Lane, Wellfleet, 508/349-3100. In transit: Follow Main Street through Wellfleet center. Turn right on Briar Lane. The restaurant is on the left.

Flying Fish is a great little bohemian café that could just as easily be located in Harvard Square. Although not on the ocean, the place has character and is a favorite with locals. Decor is simple – wooden tables adorned with small bouquets of flowers, and a driftwood counter for those who want to eat on the run. The menu ranges from bluefish sandwiches to burgers.

It's pleasant to eat lunch inside the restaurant, sitting by a large window overlooking a salt marsh. However, if you're in a hurry, you might consider heading into the bakery and getting a slab of paté and a brownie to go. The Flying Fish is famous for its home-baked goods. You should take a peek in, even if you don't plan to take out. Hours: 12:00 P.M. - 3:00 P.M. daily. (Breakfast is also served.)

The Bookstore & Restaurant, $$, Kendrick Avenue, Wellfleet, 508/349-3154. In transit: From the First Congregational Church in Wellfleet center, turn down Banks Street. (It's on the left if you're facing into the center.) Then turn right on Commercial Street. At the town pier, Commercial Street veers to the right and becomes Kendrick Avenue. The Bookstore is on the right.

The second story deck of the Bookstore's lounge (known as the Bomb Shelter) is the perfect place for enjoying quick lunch and a spectacular harbor view. The deck isn't big or fancy, so you won't feel out of place in biking shorts and a t-shirt.

Naturally the emphasis is on seafood. The Bookstore serves all the standards – lobster rolls, fried clams, fish and chips, and boiled lobster. For those looking for beef, there's also hot pastrami, burgers, and French dip. Other items include salads, chowders, and omelets. Hours: 11:30 P.M. - 4:00 P.M.

Saturday Afternoon

Hit the Beach. In transit: All of Wellfleet's ocean beaches are along Ocean View Drive. From the town center, follow Main Street to Route 6. Turn right on Route 6, then turn left on Cahoun Hollow Road. Follow it to the end, where it intersects with Ocean View Drive.

With some of the breathtaking beaches on the Cape, most people come to Wellfleet to do one thing – soak up the sun. None of the beaches charge for bicycles. However, if you're into sunning paraphernalia, such as chairs, sodas, and a library of books and magazines, you'll want to take your car.

Because of the influx of summer tourists, Wellfleet has a beach sticker permit program. Parking permits are required at most town beaches. Visitors can purchase a one week permit for $25 at the Town Pier. To purchase a permit, you must have a permit form signed by your landlord. These permits are also required at all the town pond beaches.

Exceptions include Mayo Beach, which is on the harbor side just beyond the Town Pier. Here parking is free. Also, White Crest and Cahoun Hollow offer daily parking for $10.

Although picking the best Wellfleet Beach is a matter of personal preference, many locals consider White Crest to be the town's best offering. Its pyramid-like sand dunes dotted with seagrass are as beautiful as the forceful cobalt water. If you walk down a few hundred feet to the right, you can have the place all to yourselves. Lifeguards are on duty. A snack bar and restrooms are near the parking lot.

Saturday Evening
Dinner

Cielo Gallery Café, ♡ ♡ ♡ ♡, $$$, East Main Street, Wellfleet, 508/349-2108. In transit: From the center of town, head down Main Street, toward Route 6. Cielo Gallery is on the right, across from The Inn at Duck Creek. Look carefully for the dirt path next to the building. It leads to the small lot.

Cielo is unquestionably the most romantic restaurant in Wellfleet. This tiny place, located in the back of the Cielo art gallery, feels like an exclusive hideaway. With only seven tables and one seating, it offers a wonderfully relaxed and quiet alternative to Wellfleet's busy restaurants.

Guests enter the restaurant through the art gallery, and are free to peruse its offerings. Works include pottery, paintings, and jewelry. You can also bring a bottle of wine and relax in the sitting room before dinner. (Cielo doesn't have a liquor license. But guests are free to bring their own libations.)

The dining area is simple. White walls are adorned with paintings by local artists, and picture windows afford a sweeping view of one of the town's most beautiful salt marshes. Tables are small, and covered with pink floral cloths and tiny candles.

Dinner is a five-course affair. There is no menu or choice. Guests eat whatever is served. And while that may frighten less experimental diners, rest assured that Cielo serves delicious and inventive cuisine: it's considered one of the best restaurants in the area.

On one visit, its menu consisted of wild mushroom ravioli, followed by artichoke herb soup. The main course was chicken roulade served with grilled shrimp in lemon and parsley sauce, followed by a salad of summer peppers and feta cheese with mixed greens. Dessert was a luscious plum almond tart.

Cielo posts its menu on the front door of the gallery every week. If you're particularly fussy, you can always make your reservations based on what is being served on a particular night. Hours: one seating at 8:00 P.M. Wednesday through Sunday. Reservations are a must.

Aesop's Table, ♥ ♥, $$$, Main Street, Wellfleet, 508/349-6450. In transit: Aesop's Table is right in Wellfleet center, next door to the First Congregational Church.

The grand dame of Wellfleet's restaurants, Aesop's Table is a darling with food critics and has been reviewed in several national magazines. Naturally the publicity has created a huge demand for tables. And on summer nights, lines wend out the door and onto the brick garden path.

Aesop's popularity, however, is understandable. It's got a winning combination–a gourmet menu and a casual atmosphere. Located in a 19th century sea captain's home, the restaurant has six intimate dining rooms, and a great upstairs bar with overstuffed couches and chairs.

Each of the dining rooms has a slightly different feel—some have deck chairs, and wooden tables, others, cloth covered tables and wooden chairs. Yet all are candle-lit and have pale walls, dotted with local art.

The menu is new American, so the chefs make the most of native foods. Aesop's even has its own vegetable and herb garden. Although menus change frequently, they all mix old favorites with more inventive dishes.

Appetizers might include clam chowder, corn and shrimp fritters with Cajun remoulade, and Aesop's oysters, which are wrapped in spinach, baked in roasted garlic pine nut butter, and topped with sun-dried tomato pesto.

Some typical entrees are steamed Kennebunkport lobster, served with a potato pancake; pan roasted lamb chops with a garlic rosemary demi-glace, served with linguini; and fennel crusted tuna with orange vinaigrette.

As appetizing as the savory foods may be, Aesop's is best known for its desserts. One is even trademarked. Death By Chocolate™ is a dense chocolate mousse in a deep brownie crust. Other popular sweets include La Petite Isadora, which is a delicate cheesecake with raspberry-blueberry sauce, and a cranberry pecan tart served with vanilla ice cream. Hours: 5:30 P.M. - 10:00 P.M. daily.

Sunday Morning

Hike around Great Island in Wellfleet.

In transit: From the town center, follow Commercial Street to the Town Pier. Commercial veers right and becomes Kendrick Avenue. Continue straight along Kendrick. It eventually becomes Chequesset Neck Road and leads to Great Island. The National Seashore maintains a parking lot here.

Great Island, which juts out into Cape Cod Bay, offers some of the most pleasant hiking on the Cape. The entire trail is known as the Great Island Trail. However, at the start of the trail, three separate walks are identified. The Smith Tavern Trail (1.8 miles one way) is a large loop. If you continue straight rather than walking the loop, you'll arrive at Great Beach Hill (2.9 miles). Or, continue along the path to the island's tip. However, this destination, Jeremy Point (4.1 miles), is only accessible at low tide.

Although most of the trail is relatively flat, it's considered to be moderately difficult because much of it is along soft sand. It follows along the National Seashore's protected dunes. It's a good idea to take along drinking water and wear comfortable sneakers.

About ½ mile into the trail, a boardwalk goes over the dunes and leads to an ocean beach. It's the perfect spot for a picnic.

Lunch

Picnic at Great Island, from Box Lunch $, Briar Lane, Wellfleet, 508/349-2178. In transit: From the center of Wellfleet, continue along Main Street, away from Route 6. Turn right on Briar Lane. Box Lunch is on the right

It's not easy to think about lunch right after breakfast. But if you want to have a beach picnic, you'll have to stop by Box Lunch before your morning hike.

This popular take-out spot specializes in rolled pita sandwiches. (That's all they offer.) The menu ranges from peanut butter and jelly to Porky's

Nightmare, which is melted cheese, ham, tomatoes, and onions with a mustard vinaigrette sauce. All told, Boxed Lunch offers 33 different kinds of sandwiches. If none of those temp you, Box Lunch will customize a sandwich for you. Hours: 6:00 A.M. - 8:00 P.M.

SUNDAY AFTERNOON

Visit Wellfleet's art galleries.

In transit: From the National Seashore parking lot, head back down Chequesset Neck Road, onto Kendrick Avenue to Commercial Street. Turn left on Banks Street. Then turn left onto Main Street. A municipal parking lot is right behind the First Congregational Church. You can also park at a lot by the Town Pier.

Wellfleet enjoys a reputation as an artists' haven – it boasts nearly 20 galleries. While some show pedestrian "seagull and salt marsh" water colors, many offer contemporary art. To make your own decisions, stroll by them all.

Virtually all galleries are located on Main, Commercial, East Commercial, and Banks streets. Most are open until 6:00 P.M. Following are some of Wellfleet's more interesting spots:

Hopkins Gallery, corner of Main Street and Holbrook Avenue, 508/349-7246. This contemporary art gallery is arguably the best in Wellfleet. It features established and emerging local and regional artists. Works include paintings, photography, sculpture, ceramics, art glass, woodworks, and jewelry.

Chandler Gallery, East Main and School Streets, 508/349-1620. Modern sculpture, glass, paintings, drawings, and original prints are the emphasis at Chandler. Both local and nationally recognized artists are featured. The gallery features "big" work. But with five floors and an outdoor sculpture gallery, they certainly have the space.

The Cove Gallery, Commercial Street, 508/349-2530. Cove features local and regional emerging and established artists. Works are primarily oils and watercolors, as well as sculptures. The Cover has an outdoor sculpture gallery overlooking Duck Pond. Regularly shown artists include John Grillo and Carla Golembe.

The Left Bank Gallery, Commercial Street, 508/349-7939. One of the largest galleries in Wellfleet, Left Bank has a wide range of art and crafts including pottery, clocks, sculpture, and paintings. Although it does have serious art, it's a good place to shop if you're looking for a simple Wellfleet memento.

Late Afternoon Swim at Great Pond, Cahoun Hollow Road, Wellfleet. In transit: From the First Congregational Church, follow Main Street back to Route 6. Turn right onto Route 6, then left onto Cahoun Hollow Road. The pond is on the left. To park, you'll need a Wellfleet permit.

Wellfleet's three kettle holes, or fresh water ponds, offer warm placid water surrounded by tall evergreens. They are a wonderfully peaceful alternative to the beaches and its pounding surf.

These kettles were formed hundreds of thousands of years ago during the Ice Age. When glaciers began to melt, huge chunks that separated from the receding ice became surrounded by accumulating sand. When the glaciers melted, they left holes in the earth; holes that were deep enough to intersect ground water became ponds.

Be sure to make arrangements with your inn so that you might leave your luggage and return to change clothing in the late afternoon. Most places are accommodating.

Dinner

Note: Most visitors head home by late Sunday afternoon; chances are if you join them, you'll end up cursing your way through hours of standstill traffic. Instead, enjoy the last vestiges of your weekend and have dinner in Wellfleet. If you hang around to catch a movie at the drive-in, you won't be on the road until well after 9:00 P.M. This may seem late, but the traffic is just too unbearable if you leave any earlier.

The South Wellfleet Clam Shack, ♥, $, Route 6 and Le Count Hollow Road, South Wellfleet, 508/349-2265. In transit: Follow Route 6 south, back toward Hyannis. The Clam Shack is on the left.

You can't spend a weekend at the beach without going to a clam shack. Yes, it's a little run down. Yes the food is greasy. And yes, you have to eat at picnic tables. But that's the whole point. It's just fun. The South Wellfleet Clam Shack is the area's most popular and for good reason. They serve great clams for a great price.

Sit outside and munch away.

See a movie at The Wellfleet Drive-In, Route 6, 508/349-2520 or 255-9619. In transit: The drive-in is on the north side of Route 6. You'll pass it on the way to the Clam Shack.

When was the last time you went to the drive-in movies? It's hard to do these days with multiplex cinemas replacing small theaters and drive-ins. What could be more nostalgically romantic than catching a movie snuggled in the back seat of your car. Movies start at dusk. Call ahead to check what's playing.

Additional Activities

Sunset Dune-Buggy Ride in Provincetown, Art's Sand Dune Tours, 508/487-1950 or 1050. This tour takes you along Provincetown's narrow streets, through a pine grove, then onto the dunes and beach. The guide points out beach houses of Provincetown's famous artists and writers, as well as the spot the inspired Eugene O'Neil to write many plays.

Whale Watching Dolphin Fleet, Box 162, Eastham, 800/826-9300. Considered one of the top whale watching fleets in the nation, it has been featured in The New York Times and 20/20. Scientists are on board every ship. Meals and drinks are served. All boats leave from Provincetown.

Antique Shopping in Brewster. God forbid your weekend contain a rainy day. But if it does, a pleasant option is snooping through the antique shops in Brewster. This town is known as the antique capital of the Cape. More than two dozen such stores dot Route 6A. From Wellfleet, head down Route 6 toward Hyannis to 6A north to Brewster.

See a Play at the Wellfleet Harbor Actors Theater, Commercial Street, Wellfleet, 508/349-6835. The theater produces primarily Broadway-proven plays, e.g., Sam Shepard's Fool for Love and The Kathy and Mo Show. Occasionally big names zoom in for benefit performances. (On our visit, Julie Harris was in a production of "Love Letters.") Curtain time is 8:00 P.M. If you plan to visit, be sure to make dinner reservations early.

Visit the Provincetown Museum, at the Pilgrim Monument, Provincetown, 508/487-1310. This museum can be crowded, but if you're interested in pirates, it shouldn't be missed. On display are gold and silver ingots, cannons, cannonballs, jewelry, clothing, and other personal effects from the Whydah, the only pirate shipwreck ever found. Captained by the legendary "Black Sam" Bellamy, that ship sank off Wellfleet's coast in 1717.

GETTING THERE

BY AIR: Cape Air (800/352-0714) has daily service from Boston to Provincetown. Small plane phobics take note: Cape Air flies nine-seater Cessna 402s.

From New York (Newark and LaGuardia), Business Express an arm of Delta has service to Hyannis on a 34-passenger, turbo propeller plane. The planes typically make stops in Providence, and passengers are then required to change planes in Boston. An easier, but more expensive, option is to take a shuttle to Boston then switch to a Cape Air flight.

Wellfleet is about 15 minutes from Provincetown and about 40 minutes from Hyannis (in light traffic). Cab service is available from both airports.

BY TRAIN: No rail service is available to Cape Cod.

BY CAR: Route 6 is the main road that travels the length of Cape Cod. From the north it can be reached via Route 3 south or I-495 south. From the south, access is via I-95 north. Follow Route 6 south to Wellfleet. Signs will point the way to Wellfleet Center. (It's a left off Route 6.)

Cape traffic can be brutal in season. Travel from the Bourne Bridge to Wellfleet can take two to three hours. (It should take no more than an hour in regular traffic.) To avoid automotive hell, it's imperative to avoid traveling Friday between 3:00 P.M. and 10:00 P.M. and Sunday between 2:00 P.M. and 9:00 P.M. Of course the best alternative is to take a long weekend. Or try for a half day Friday and return late Sunday night. (The traffic is lighter than early Monday morning.)

BY BUS: From Boston, Peter Pan (800/322-0364) offers daily service to Provincetown. Buses leave from South Station. Peter Pan also operates service from Worcester and Spring-field, Massachusetts, via a transfer in Hyannis.

From New York, Bonanza (508/556-3815) operates daily service to Provincetown. Buses depart from New York Port Authority.

Cab service is available from the bus terminal.

BY BOAT: Bay State Cruises (617/ 723-7800) has daily seasonal service to Provincetown from Boston. The boat leaves from Long Wharf and Commonwealth Pier. The trip takes three hours. Daily service is available from Memorial Day through Labor Day, then on weekends through Columbus Day.

CAR RENTAL: Should you travel by plane or bus, you may want to rent a car. Although you could use rental bikes for transportation, a car is really essential to getting the most from your stay in Wellfleet.

In Provincetown, Budget (508/487-1539) or Thrifty (508/487-9418). And in Hyannis, Budget (508/775-3833), Trek (508/771-2459), or Avis (508/775-2888.)

TAXI/LIMOUSINE Service: Call Schatzi's Taxi in Provincetown, 508/487-1827.

INFORMATION: Wellfleet Chamber of Commerce, P.O. Box 571, Wellfleet 02667, 508/349-2510. The chamber has a great book on Wellfleet that you should send for before you visit. An information booth is located just off Route 6 in South Wellfleet. Hours: 9:00 A.M. - 6:00 P.M. daily, weekends only in spring and fall.

Fall

Block Island, Rhode Island

Grafton & Weston, Vermont

Jay & Montgomery, Vermont

Lenox & The Berkshires

Portsmouth, New Hampshire

Block Island, Rhode Island

Carved 400 centuries ago by the same glacier that made Martha's Vineyard and Nantucket, Block Island is the smallest and least populated of New England's famous trilogy of tourist islands. Unlike the Vineyard or Nantucket (both featured in *Romantic New England Getaways*), Block Island is not an international tourist destination studded with fashionable shops and gourmet restaurants. Yet this 10-square-mile chunk of land, 12 miles off the Rhode Island coast, is a paradise for nature lovers. Its beaches are among the most beautiful and dramatic in New England. Its moors are a migratory way station for hundreds of species of birds. And its pastoral interior of rolling hills, old stone walls, and pristine farm houses is often shrouded in a steamy ocean mist, reminiscent of Scotland.

With only 800 year-round residents and a 2,000 plus summer population, Block Island maintains a quiet civility that the other islands just can't match. Of course it does have a few T-shirt and trinket stores, but for the most part Block Island is in every sense a place for people to escape the modern world. There are no billboards, neon signs, or traffic lights. Car activity is minimal. Tourists are encouraged to bike or use mopeds. (Because of this, it's often been called the Bermuda of the north.) And although a car does come in handy, you don't really need one.

Besides, people who come to Block Island aren't the sort who take their vacation sitting down. It is more a destination for those interested in hiking (nothing too strenuous, mostly lowlands), bicycling, and simply being out of doors. In fact, the Nature Conservancy, the world's largest nonprofit organization dedicated to protecting rare plants, animals, and natural communities, recently named Block Island one of the 12 Last Great Places.

Although a popular summer vacation spot, tourism virtually grinds to a halt in September. Yet most stores and restaurants remain open at least through Columbus Day to catch the stragglers. This is the perfect time to visit. You have the benefits of summer, without the crowds. The weather and water are still pleasant. And in the

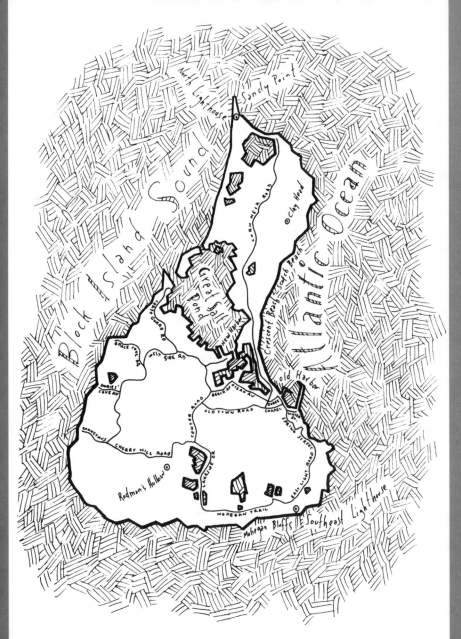

North Lighthouse • Sandy Point

Block Island Sound

Atlantic Ocean

Corn Neck Road

Clay Head

Great Salt Pond

Crescent Beach • Scotch Beach

New Harbor

Grace Cove

West Side Rd

Coast Guard Rd

Dorie's Cove

Beacon Hill

Old Harbor

Ocean Av

Dodge

Center Road

Cooneymus

Cherry Hill Road

Clay Town Road

Chapel

Water St

Spring Street

Lakeside Dr

Rodman's Hollow

East Light Road

Mohegan Trail

Mohegan Bluffs • Southeast Lighthouse

N

BLOCK ISLAND

autumn quiet, the island's bucolic character can be fully appreciated.

WHERE TO STAY

The Sea Breeze, ♡ ♡ ♡ ♡, $$-$$$$, Spring Street, Block Island 02807, 401/466-2275. This collection of small, weathered shingled cottages, wedged between the island's two most prestigious inns, is easy to overlook. However, the Sea Breeze, is a gem of a B&B, offering the most sophisticated accommodations on Block Island.

Owners Mary and Bob Newhouse also operate the eclectic Sea Breeze Gallery in the center of town. They bring to their B&B an artistic flair that makes any visit an out-of-the ordinary pleasure. The five individual cottages – the Sea Breeze's prizes – are all outfitted with French and English linens, antiques, and modern art, and have cathedral ceilings and plenty of windows, flanked by wooden shutters. Walls are a creamy white accented with rich pastel moldings and beams. Each room has a small table, set with hand-painted ceramic cups (on sale at the gallery).

Although all of the new rooms are wonderful, the most sought after is number 10. In addition to a small sitting area and a bedroom with clear ocean views, it has a private porch that faces the sea. The setting is nothing short of magnificent. From the porch, a grassy hill, dotted with wildflowers, leads down to a salt pond that skirts the beach.

Although most rooms have some ocean views and side porches, chairs are scattered near the wildflower meadow so that guests can enjoy a clear panorama.

In addition to the premium rooms, there are five rooms with two shared baths in a refurbished 200-year-old rooming house. These rooms are also pleasingly decorated, but are a bit more rustic. If you're looking to save some money, you might consider requesting the room on the top floor. It's located right next to the bath, and has a small sitting area and ocean views.

Breakfast is brought in a large wicker basket to each guest's room. It consists of Viennese coffee, croissants, homemade muffins and breads, fruit, juice, and coffee.

RATES PER NIGHT: $130-$160, $80-$100 for shared bath.

ACCOMMODATIONS: 10 rooms, 5 with private bath, another 5 share 2 baths.

AMENITIES: Guest refrigerator. Outdoor shower.

RESTRICTIONS: Smoking on grounds only. No pets.

The 1661 Inn, ♡ ♡ ♡, $$-$$$$, Spring Street, Block Island 02807, 401/466-2421 or 401/466-2063. Known for more than two decades as the place to stay on Block Island, the 1661 is an amenity laden retreat with traditional charm. Set on a hill facing the ocean, nine guest rooms are housed in this stately white clapboard colonial, and an additional three rooms are located in the recently opened Nicholas Ball Cottage.

For those who want to indulge, consider the Edwards room (all rooms are named after Block Island settlers). It's regally decorated with dusty blue carpeting, beige wallpaper, a four-poster canopy bed, antiques, and seascape oil paintings. A decanter of brandy and dish of hard candy are set out on a small wooden table (an amenity all rooms enjoy). In addition to a private wraparound deck with views of gardens and ocean, the room boasts a loft with a four-person Jacuzzi. The Staples room is similarly appointed; however, its Jacuzzi is located in the corner of the bedroom.

In the process of final completion at this writing, the Nicholas Ball Cottage –a replica of the St. Anne's Church that was destroyed by a hurricane in 1938–is equally, if not more, luxurious. Its three rooms all have wood-burning fireplaces, Jacuzzis, and marble baths. Of these, only the Nicholas room has its own private deck. However, the Cassius room has a two-story cathedral ceiling, a downstairs bedroom and a loft with a Jacuzzi, fireplace, and sitting area. As with the main inn, guest rooms are furnished with a mixture of antiques, reproductions, and wicker.

A grand buffet breakfast, that's open to the public, is complimentary for inn guests. It includes scrambled eggs,

smoked b⟨ other calori⟨ a cozy, albei⟨ curtains and ⟨ room with o⟨ weather, breakfa⟨ outside deck, whi⟨ ⟨⟩ean.

The Abramses, who own the 1661, are perhaps the most well-known family on the island. With their restoration of the 1661, and subsequent purchase and restoration of The Manisses, a quaint Victorian Hotel directly across the street, they are the prime movers in bringing tourism back to Block Island.

Another one of their endeavors, which guests are free to enjoy, is an animal farm, located right next door to The Manisses. The farm is not stocked with usual fare, but with Sicilian donkeys, llama, ostriches, and Pygmy goats. Watching these creatures roam over an oceanside hill amidst rolling fog is truly a sight.

RATES PER NIGHT: $90-$275 from Labor Day through Columbus Day, $88-$180 until the first week in November. Rates are lower in spring and higher in summer. The 1661 closes after the third week in November. However, The Manisses and the Nicholas Ball Cottage are open year-round.

ACCOMMODATIONS: 9 rooms with private baths. Nicholas Ball Cottage has 3 rooms with private baths. The 1661 also has a guest house (not recommended here) that has an additional 10 rooms, 5

...baths and another 5 with ...hs.

AMENITIES: Telephones and refrigerators in rooms. Some rooms have fireplaces and private decks. Three rooms have kitchenettes. Restaurant and bar. (The Manisses across the street has a full service restaurant and bar that serves dinner nightly until the third week in November, and on weekends from December to Memorial Day.)

RESTRICTIONS: No pets.

Note: Though not included here, The Manisses, might be a good choice for Victorian-era aficionados. Although well furnished, rooms are generally smaller, darker, and less lush than those at the 1661. Interestingly, however, the Manisses' common rooms have far more charm.

Bayberry Heath, ♡ ♡ ♡, $$, Black Rock Road, Block Island 02807, 401/466-2838. Located well outside of town on a secluded dirt road, Bayberry Heath is a charming hideaway, for couples seeking real privacy. (Guests should take a car.) Innkeepers Marion and Bill Blake offer a two-story suite that's attached to their home, but is completely private and has a separate entrance. Downstairs is an airy sitting room with plenty of windows, including sliding glass doors that open onto a private porch that faces the ocean. (The house is really about a ¼ mile from the beach, but because it sits up on a hill the ocean is clearly visible.)

Marion is a photographer who works at the Rugged Sailor Gallery downtown, and her artistic flair shows through in Bayberry Heath's decoration. The sitting room is graced with a blue and white Oriental rug, antiques, and works by local artists, including a beautiful green stained-glass window.

Upstairs are the bath and bedroom. The latter has a queen-size brass bed and Palladian windows that flood the room with light. This sunshine, combined with the white walls and wood floors, gives the place an earthy, natural, charm.

Marion serves continental breakfast to guests in their room or on the porch. The meal includes coffee, juice, fruit, and homemade breads and muffins.

RATES PER NIGHT: $100, $120 in summer.

ACCOMMODATIONS: Suite with private bath.

AMENITIES: Television in room.

RESTRICTIONS: No pets.

FRIDAY EVENING
Dinner

Winfield's, ♡ ♡ ♡, $$-$$$, Corn Neck Road, Block Island, 401/466-5856. In transit: From the ferry docks, continue west on Water Street. (With your back facing the water, go right.) Water Street veers left and becomes Dodge Street. At the intersection, bear right on Corn Neck Road. Winfield's is on the right.

Winfield's offers one of the best and most pleasant dining experiences on Block Island. Located in an unassuming clapboard building (right next door to Yellow Kittens, the island's rowdiest nightclub), Winfield's is an oasis of casual elegance. The interior has an English Tudor look with dark beamed ceilings, rough-hewn wainscoting, cream-colored walls, and soft lights.

The menu isn't extensive, but offers varied cuisine. Appetizers include foccacia (a great Italian herb and olive oil bread), as well as the more locally-inspired steamed mussels. Winfield's preparation of this common mollusk is inspired: They're served in white wine with whole tomatoes, onions, and fennel seed. Nightly dinner specials might include grilled salmon with mustard hollandaise, or pan-fried flounder with peach beurre blanc. Entrees lean toward the Italian. They include tortellini filled with chicken shrimp and spinach, served in a spicy marinara sauce with Saga blue cheese; and veal saltimbocca, which is sautéed veal topped with prosciutto, sage, and fresh mozzarella with a Marsala demi-glace. Although some of Winfield's dishes might sound "heavy," all are prepared with a light hand.

Desserts change regularly, but include such girth-enhancers as double chocolate torte and raspberry cheesecake. And Winfield's espresso and coffee are excellent. Hours: 6:00 P.M. -10:00 P.M.

Mohegan Café, ♥, $$, Water Street, Block Island, 401/466-5911. In transit: Directly across from the ferry dock on Water Street. It's impossible to miss.

If you're looking for a relaxed meal in a pub-style atmosphere, the Mohegan Café is a good choice. Located in the heart of Block Island's main thoroughfare, it's a popular watering hole for locals that features nightly entertainment in summer. In fall, things quiet down a bit, yet it remains one of the island's livelier spots.

Decor is basic – dark wood paneling and wooden tables covered with maroon cloths. Yet the soft lights and location, directly across the street from the harbor, provide a cozy ambiance. The menu offers a good supply of pub standards—nachos, potato skins, and chicken fingers. And while the selections may not be gourmet, the Mohegan prepares them well.

Entrees include crab-and lobster-stuffed shrimp in a lemon dill cream sauce, charbroiled New York sirloin, and Black Forest chicken, which is sautéed with shallots, bing cherries, and brandy, and served with crème fraîche. A catch of the day is featured nightly, and is typically simply broiled with lemon juice and olive oil. Hours: 5:30 P.M. – 10:00 P.M.

Coffee and Dessert

Juice & Java, Dodge Street, Block Island, 401/466-5220. In transit: From Winfield's, follow Corn Neck road back into town. It turns into Dodge Street. Juice & Java is a few buildings down on the left. It's located in the Sea Breeze Gallery. From Water Street, walk to the Surf Hotel. (When you walk out the door, turn left.) Water Street veers left and becomes Dodge Street. Juice & Java is on the right. You can walk from both restaurants. It will take less than five minutes from either location.

This tiny spot–which is just a counter and a few white plastic tables and chairs–seems like a little slice of San Francisco. In addition to freshly squeezed juice, and fresh ground coffee, espresso, and cappuccino, Juice & Java serves fabulously decadent desserts— all homemade. For white chocolate fans, consider a slice of white satin sin. Other treats include creamsicle cheesecake, cappuccino mousse cake, and banana mocha praline cake. This is also a great choice for a light breakfast. Juice & Java makes coffeecakes, and has fresh bagels, scones, and muffins. Hours: 8:00 A.M. – 2:00 P.M. and 6:00 P.M. – 10:00 P.M. daily. Hours are extended in summer.

SATURDAY MORNING

Bicycle or Moped around Block Island.

In transit: Block Island has many bike and moped rental shops. Two that are particularly convenient are Esta's (401/466-2651), which is just behind Esta's store on Water Street, and Aldo's (401/466-5018) on Chapel Street. Chapel is a side street right off the center of Water Street. It almost looks like an alley.

Unquestionably, the most enjoyable way to see Block Island is on two wheels. With its gently rolling hills and nearly car-less roads, it's a bicyclist's dream. A complete loop of the island, taken at a leisurely pace, shouldn't take more than two or three hours, depending on how many dirt paths you meander down or how many times you stop to take in the magnificent vistas. If you're in moderately good shape, you should have no trouble with the ride.

For those interested in something less strenuous, a moped is a great option. You'll still get a birds-eye view of the island, albeit somewhat noisier. If you've never ridden a moped before, don't be afraid. They're simple to use, even for the uncoordinated.

The Chamber of Commerce, located across from the statue of Rebecca at the Well at the head of Water Street, has good maps of the island. (The Women's Christian

Temperance Union erected the statue of the famous Biblical figure in 1896.)

From the Chamber of Commerce, follow Water Street back toward the center of town. Turn left on Dodge Street. Continue straight to Ocean Avenue, rather than bearing right on Corn Neck Road. Then turn left on West Side Road. Once on West Side, you'll find several small dirt roads that lead to the beach. Don't miss a chance to travel down at least some of them. They lead to magnificent stretches of beach, more often than not deserted. The primary dirt roads, all marked, are Grace Cove Road, Dorie's Cove Road, and Cooneymus Road.

At Cooneymus Road, West Side veers to the left and becomes Cherry Hill Road. Follow it, then turn right on Lakeside Drive, which eventually veers to the left and becomes Mohegan Trail.

At Southeast Lighthouse, you may want to get off your bikes to explore. At this writing, the lighthouse, built in 1873, was closed to the public. Because of coastal erosion – three feet disappear annually – the lighthouse has recently been moved 220 feet from the edge of the bluff where it originally stood.

At the lighthouse, Mohegan Trail becomes Southeast Light Road. It leads to Spring Street, which will take you back to the statue of Rebecca and the tip of Water Street.

Other bicycle and moped rental shops include: Seacrest Inn & Bicycle Rentals, (401/466-2882), High Street; Old Harbor Bike Shop (401/466-2029), Ferry Landing; Cyr's Cycles (401/466-2147), Dodge Street; Island Sport Shop (401/466-5001), Weldon's Way.

Lunch

Take-out from the Corn Neck Country Kitchen, Corn Neck Road, Block Island, 401/466-5059. In transit: Stay on your bike/moped and continue down Water Street. Turn left on Dodge Street. Then at the intersection, bear right onto Corn Neck Road. The Country Kitchen is a few buildings down on the left.

This funky spot, a favorite with locals, may not be much to look at, but you will get a good sandwich. Selections are straightforward – smoked ham and cheese, tuna salad, and turkey. If you want to get cookies and other snacks, walk down to Dodge Street to Block Island Depot (mostly natural food) or Juice & Java. Seaside Market also serves sandwiches and snacks, and is right across the ferry on Water Street. Hours: 5:30 A.M. – 2:30 P.M. Saturday and Sunday, 5:30 A.M. – 1:30 P.M. Monday through Friday.

SATURDAY AFTERNOON

Picnic and Hike through "The Maze."

In transit: Continue along Corn Neck Road for about 2½ miles. Look for a sign for the Clayhead Nature Trail on the right side of the road. It's thin, gray, and vertical (and so, easily missed). Turn down the dirt path. You'll come to a clearing where you can lock your bikes or mopeds.

This meandering conglomeration of trails, once appropriately called "The Maze," is now known as the Clayhead Nature Trail. Sponsored by the Rhode Island Department of Environmental Management, the trails are privately owned, yet the public is welcome to enjoy them. There are no specific maps or signs for the individual trails, although some are marked on the chamber's map. Yet you won't get lost.

The interior trails traverse pine groves, fields, and meadows, and offer glimpses of ponds and the ocean. The entire Maze covers approximately nine miles. If you follow the main trail dead east (it's shown on the chamber map), it will lead to a secluded beach known as Sugar Loaf Cove. This is the perfect spot for a quiet picnic. Set up camp by a smooth, old piece of driftwood and enjoy the beauty.

After lunch, you may want to walk north along the beach toward the North Lighthouse and Sandy Point. (It's about a mile.) Built in 1867 of granite imported from Connecticut and hauled by ox cart to the site, the lighthouse is now undergoing restoration. It houses a small but interesting maritime museum.

If you don't want to walk the entire way, you could hike back to your bike or moped. Then, continue along Corn Neck to the end. You will reach Settler's Rock, a memorial to those who first colonized Block Island in 1661. The North Lighthouse is straight ahead.

SATURDAY EVENING
Drinks

The Atlantic Inn, ♥ ♥, $ $, High Street, Block Island, 401/466-5883. In transit: From the Sea Breeze or the 1661, travel down Spring Street back toward the center of town. At the statue, make a sharp left on Atlantic. (At the beginning, it almost runs parallel to Spring Street.) The Atlantic is easily visibly. It's set up on a hill and is on the right. From Heather Heath, follow Black Rock Road toward the beach, you'll have to make a left onto a dirt road. It leads to Mohegan Trail. Turn right on Mohegan. It eventually leads to Spring Street. From there follow directions to the Atlantic.

Its location on one of Block Island's highest hills and its magnificent views of the sea and village make the Atlantic's verandah the perfect place to enjoy a sunset. A grand, old, white clapboard building, the inn has all the gentility of a turn-of-the-century hotel. Its front porch and lawn are dotted with comfortable chairs made for relaxing. Full bar service is available here, as well as in the cozy Victorian-style lounge. Hours: from 4:00 P.M.

Dinner

The Manisses, ♥ ♥ ♥ ♥, $$$, Spring Street, Block Island, 401/466-2421 or 401/466-2063. From the Atlantic Inn, travel down High Street back toward the center of town. At the statue, make a sharp right on to Spring Street. The Manisses is on the right.

While most chapters in *Romantic New England Getaways* feature several suggestions for a Saturday night meal, this chapter includes only one. The reason? The Manisses is simply the best place to go on Block Island if you want to share a candlelit dinner and a good bottle of wine by a glowing fire. No other place can compare in ambiance. And the food rivals Winfield's as the best on the island.

The dining room has several compartments. The library, which has stone walls and a low ceiling, houses a raw bar. The seating area off the lounge also has stone walls, as well as a fireplace located in a dark nook. This is the spot to get a table if you can. A third section is off an outdoor deck and has plenty of windows and plants. Tables are covered with deep burgundy cloths and lit with candles.

Although the menu changes regularly, some fall appetizers might include baked herb polenta, citrus salmon mousse, and grilled venison and andouille sausage with garlic and Dijon mustard. Entrees feature a nice selection of fresh fish. The Portuguese fish stew with swordfish, monkfish, linguica, red onions, peppers, tomatoes, kale, and kidney beans, served over rice, is outstanding. Other selections include baked bluefish with a Dijon herb crust, grilled swordfish with pineapple salsa, and roast chicken with orange sage glaze.

Desserts too change nightly, but always include a healthy selection of cakes, tarts, and pastries. Hours: 6:00 P.M.–9:00 P.M.

After Dinner Drinks and Coffee

The Top Shelf Bar at The Manisses, Spring Street, Block Island, 401/466-2421 or 401/466-2063. In transit: Nothing could be simpler, just walk upstairs to The Manisses lobby. The bar is directly off the lobby.

One of the most pleasant experiences of this writer's many New England getaways was wiling away several evening hours in the Top Shelf, sipping Opal Nera sambuca over crushed ice and playing Scrabble. Resplendent in Victorian charm, the two sitting rooms are outfitted in wicker furniture and velvet settees. Walls are covered with pale blue flowered paper; a fireplace's blazing light plays off the stained-glass windows.

Besides offering all manner of liqueurs, you can get some great spiked coffees, many of which arrive at your table flaming. Games like Scrabble, checkers, and chess are set out, encouraging guests to play. What could be more civilized?

Hours: 6:00 P.M. – 10:00 P.M. (It often stays open later on weekend evenings.)

SUNDAY MORNING

Early Morning Coffee and Sroll along the Mohegan Cliffs

In transit: Pick up coffee to go at either the Corn Neck Country Kitchen or Juice & Java (Corn Neck opens at 5:30 A.M. and Juice at 8:00 A.M). From there, head down Water Street back toward the center of town. Then turn left onto Spring Street, which eventually becomes Southeast Light Road, then Mohegan Trail. If you're driving, you can park your car on the side of the road. If you travel down the dirt path, you'll find a metal rack to lock your bikes or mopeds.

The short trail that leads to the top of Mohegan Bluffs offers the most dramatic view of the island. Here, 150 feet up from the beach, you can look over the expanse of deep blue ocean and the red, rocky cliffs that rise from the sandy beach. It is truly breathtaking. A long descent of wooden stairs leads to the beach.

Before you test the water, however, you may want to sit, sip your coffee, and savor the sight. The best spot for doing this is a large, secluded, rocky crevice just down the road that seems made for contemplation. To get there, walk back out to the road and turn left. A few hundred feet down you'll notice a semi-circle dirt patch. It leads to the rocky ledge.

Sea Kayaking at Crescent Beach.

In transit: Go to Ocean & Ponds, the Orvis Store, Ocean Avenue, 401/466-5131. Head back down toward Water Street. Turn left onto Dodge Street. At the Corn Neck intersection, stay straight to Ocean Avenue. Ocean & Ponds is on the corner of Ocean and Connecticut Avenue.

Sea kayaking may sound like a hair-raising adventure, but even novices can enjoy a few hours cruising along the shoreline. It's relatively easy to get the hang of, and it's a wonderful way to get a good view of the island.

Ocean & Ponds makes the whole expedition simple. They take the kayak (you can get one built for two) to the beach of your choosing, and pick it up when you're finished. One of the easiest beaches for novices to kayak from, and among the simplest to get to, is Crescent Beach. It starts at the tip of Water Street and continues north.

In addition to sea kayaks, Oceans and Ponds also rents canoes, and offers charter sail and fishing boats. Open from Memorial Day to mid October. Rental rates for surf kayaks: $30 for a half day, $45 for a whole day.

Lunch

Finn's, $-$$, Water Street, Block Island, 401/466-2473. In transit: Head up Water Street, toward the statue of

Rebecca. Finn's is behind Ernie's restaurant and faces Old Harbor and the ferry parking lot.

Finn's may not win any awards for quaintness, but this little spot is one of the most popular restaurants on the island. One of the reasons is its top-notch clam chowder, a favorite with locals.

Decor is simple – slate floors, wood-look Formica tables, and lots of plants. The most pleasant place to sit is in the bar area, which is smaller and more quiet than the main dining room. The menu is similarly straightforward. Selections include fish and chips, lobster rolls, broiled fish sandwiches, and bacon cheeseburgers. Finn's also has a raw bar. If you can, save room for a slice of Finn's pecan rhubarb pie. Hours: 11:30 A.M. – 11:00 P.M. Friday and Saturday, 11:30 A.M. – 10:00 P.M. Sunday through Thursday.

Shopping around Water Street.

In transit: From Finn's Walk up to the statue of Rebecca to start you tour.

Block Island isn't known as a shopping mecca. And you'll be disappointed if you come expecting a plethora of nautical boutiques. However, it does have several interesting shops and galleries. Following is a list of our favorites. On Sunday, most shops are open 12:00 P.M. to 5:00 P.M.

The Red Herring, Water Street, 401/466-2540. One of Block Island's

newest additions, and its most interesting store. Chockablock with locally made hand-painted furniture, pottery, hand-blown glass, and other crafts, the Red Herring is a visual feast. It also sells a nice selection of jewelry. Prices aren't cheap, but fair. Be sure to keep your eyes peeled for the sign; the store is on the second floor above The Shoreline.

The Shoreline, Water Street, 401/ 466-2541. This is a good spot for casual clothes, for both men and women. The selection is small, but pleasing. Lots of Esprit and baggy cotton merchandise.

Esta's at Old Harbor, Water Street, 401/466-2925. If you're looking for kitschy mementos, this is the place. Toothpick holders, shot glasses, mugs, and T-shirts are all emblazoned with various versions of a Block Island logo.

Scarlet Begonia, Dodge Street, 401/466-5024. A great little housewares store. It has lots of small cotton rugs, pillows, and tablecloths. Just the spot for picking up a few summery accents for your home.

Sea Breeze Gallery, Dodge Street, 401/466-5870. One of the most interesting galleries on the island. Small but exciting collection of local, modern paintings, as well as some pottery and hand-blown glass.

Été, Dodge Street, 401/466-2925. This is the funkiest clothing store on the island, with casual wear for both men and women. Lots of wild-print shirts and big pants.

The Ragged Sailor, Chapel Street, 401/466-7704. Block Island's most well-established gallery, the Ragged Sailor carries a nice selection of traditional "seascape" watercolors and photographs.

Additional Activities

Hike around Rodman's Hollow. This low-lying cleft of land is home to hawks, wild deer, and several species of rare wildflowers. The heart of the hollow is reached by a series of paths known as the Greenway. Maps are available at the Chamber of Commerce.

Visit the Block Island Historical Society, Dodge Street, 401/466-2481. The museum has an interesting exhibit called Manisses, Prehistoric Block Island. Hours: 10:00 A.M. – 4:00 P.M.

Rent a Canoe and Paddle around the Great Salt Pond. Canoes are available at Oceans & Ponds, Ocean Avenue, 401/466-5131.

Play a Set of tennis. Three spots on the island have tennis courts open to the public, and available by reservation: They are the Atlantic Inn (401/466-5883), Champlin's Marina (401/466-2641), and The Block Island Club (401/466-5939).

Go Bluefishing. Charter one of Block Island's most popular fishing boats, the G. Willie Makit, a 28-foot Custom Harris Cuttyhunk. Call Captain Bill Gould (401/466-5151 or 203/245-7831). He welcomes beginners and experts alike. Hourly, half-day, and full-day expeditions are available.

Go Horseback Riding. The only trail ride service on the island is at Rustic Rides Farm (401/466-5060). They even have gentle horses for novices. Rustic also offers carriage rides, if you'd prefer to put some distance between you and the horse.

Note: If you're unlucky enough to have a rainy day, you're pretty much stuck. Block Island doesn't offer a lot of indoor activity. The best tack is to chalk it up to "weather happens." Head over to the Book Nook on Water Street and stock up on all the magazines you've been wanting to read. Then hit the Seaside Market, get some Pepperidge Farm cookies and hot tea, and go back to bed for reading and munching.

GETTING THERE

BY AIR: New England Airways (401/466-5959 or 800/243-2460) has service from Westerly, Rhode Island. Flights run almost hourly Friday through Sunday, 6:30 A.M. – 8:30 P.M. and until 10:30 P.M. on Friday evening. Regularly scheduled flights are also available throughout the week.

Action Airlines (800/243-8623 and 203/448-1646) has charter flights from Groton/New London (CT) Airport. And Capital Airlines (203/264-3727 and 800/255-3727) offers on-demand charters from any airport throughout the Northeast and Canada.

BY CAR and FERRY: Block Island is 12 miles off Rhode Island's mainland. It is therefore only directly accessible via ferry. The only year-round ferry service is from Galilee State Pier at Point Judith, Rhode Island, via Interstate Navigation Company (401/783-7328 or 401/783-4613.) From Labor Day through the end of October, Interstate runs four ferries to Block Island daily. The trip takes about an hour.

If you're planning on taking your car, be sure to call ahead for reservations. Round-trip for cars is $40.50, and $12.20 for passengers.

From mid June through mid September, Interstate also operates a ferry from New London. The trip takes two hours and leaves daily at 10:00A.M. (A 7:15A.M. ferry is also available on Friday.) Boats leave from Block Island at 4:00 P.M. Monday through Friday and 4:30 P.M. Saturday and Sunday. Round-trip for cars is $50, and $27 for passengers.

Passenger-only service is available from mid June through Columbus Day on the Montauk (Long Island, New York) Ferry (516/668-2214.) Round-trip

tickets are $26 for the same day and $28 different days.

BY TRAIN: Amtrak (800/USA-RAIL) has service to Westerly, Rhode Island. From there, you can take a cab to New England Air in Westerly for a flight to Block Island. Or, you can take Amtrak to Kingston, Rhode Island, and take a cab to the Point Judith ferry.

BY BUS: No bus service is available.

CAR RENTAL: Although they sometimes come in handy, cars really aren't necessary on Block Island. However, if you choose to rent one, call Block Island Bike & Car Rental (401/466-2297), Boat Basin Rentals (401/466-2631), Coastline Rental & Leasing (401/596-3441), or the Old Harbor Bike Shop (401/466-2029).

TAXI/LIMOUSINE SERVICE: On Block Island, call OJ's (401/782-5826 or 466-2872). OJ's also offers private island tours. For service from Amtrak to Westerly or Point Judith, call Wright's Oceanview Taxi (401/789-0400).

INFORMATION: Block Island Chamber of Commerce, Water Street, 401/466-2982. The mailing address is Drawer D, Block Island 02807. Hours: 9:00 A.M. – 4:00 P.M. Monday through Thursday, 9:00 A.M. – 5:00 P.M. Friday and Saturday, from Memorial Day through Labor Day. Other times of the year the office is open 10:00 A.M. – 4:00 P.M. Monday through Saturday.

Grafton & Weston, Vermont

The Green Mountain towns of southern Vermont are among the most picturesque places in the nation. They give form to the quintessential country village – a common green dominated by a white steepled church and a red clapboard general store where people congregate to discuss the day's news.

Unquestionably, the most well known and frequently visited of these towns is Manchester. Now an outlet shopping mecca, it has been a famous summer resort for more than a century, once attracting the likes of Mary Todd Lincoln (Abraham's wife) and her son Robert Todd. The town is also home to the state's most lavish resort, The Equinox. This 224-year-old hotel – favorite overnight stop for several U.S. presidents – has recently undergone a multimillion dollar restoration.

While Manchester is attractive and interesting, it doesn't have the stuff of which bucolic dreams are made. To experience the beauty and peacefulness of a real, rural Vermont town, you must leave Route 7 (Vermont's equivalent of a major thoroughfare) and venture down some of the state's winding back roads.

Among the most archetypal Vermont villages are Grafton and Weston.

A postcard-perfect community, Grafton is the embodiment of charm – grand, white antique clapboard houses, spiraling church steeples, a bright red country store, and a Federal-style inn. Its pristine appearance is due in part to the Windham Foundation, a nonprofit organization founded to maintain Vermont's rural heritage: It owns many of Grafton's buildings. Windham isn't just concerned with retaining the town's patina, but also with the industries that helped build the state in its early years. To that end, it established the Grafton Cheese Company as well as The Blacksmith Shop, which has a full-time "smithy" who hand-forges fireplace tools and cooking utensils using traditional methods.

Weston, while not maintained by a benevolent and well-endowed organization, has its own beauty. Established in 1799, it is every inch classic Vermont. The Old Parish Church bell and clock tower rises above the main street.

GRAFTON & WESTON

The perfectly manicured town green sports a Victorian bandstand. And The Vermont Country Store, with its rickety front porch, is perhaps the nation's most well-known purveyor of American nostalgia. It carries thousands of old-fashioned products, including such days-gone-by essentials as manual typewriters, vinyl rain booties, and porous peppermint puffs.

Yet Weston has many cultural attractions as well, not the least of which is the Weston Playhouse, Vermont's oldest theater company. The Weston Priory, home to a group of Benedictine monks, is located just two miles outside the town center. People of all faiths attend their services to hear their spiritually uplifting music.

Also, the first weekend in October brings the Weston Antiques Show, which attracts dealers from all over the eastern United States, and buyers from as far away as California. This weekend is the perfect time to visit. The antiques show is a treat. And while it does draw visitors to the town, the streets are in no way clogged—or for that matter, even busy (unlike Columbus Day weekend). In addition, foliage in the beginning of October is at or near peak.

For those unfamiliar with rural Vermont, keep in mind that it's necessary to drive to get just about anywhere. Towns are often separated by mountain passes and accessible only via gravel roads. Weston and Grafton, though considered just "next door" by Vermont standards, are actually about 30 minutes apart. No matter what you do, whether it's going out to dinner or visiting a museum, you'll be taking a drive. But then again, driving leisurely is part of the Vermont experience—it's the perfect way to take in the region's natural beauty.

WHERE TO STAY

The Old Tavern at Grafton, ♡ ♡, $$$, The Townsend Road, Grafton 05146, 802/843-2231. The Old Tavern is the quintessence of a Vermont country inn. In continuous operation since 1888, the gracious white-washed brick Federal style building is the focal point of Grafton's main street.

Step onto the porch, through the front door, and you'll enter a living room that exudes colonial simplicity and elegance. This very same living room has welcomed such prestigious guests as Ulysses S. Grant, Ralph Waldo Emerson, and Rudyard Kipling.

All 35 rooms in the main tavern building, and the Windham and Homestead cottages across the street, have a colonial flavor. They are understated—well-appointed but not fancy, and simple but not plain. Many have hand-hooked rugs, fishnet canopy beds, antiques, and ornamental fireplaces.

Among the nicest rooms is the Deerfield Room. It boasts an arched fishnet canopy bed with an ornate chenille spread, a hooked rug, wing chair, and mahogany dresser. Although the Grant Room isn't quite as sunny as the Deerfield, it's a treat for history buffs. In addition to a hand-carved wooden bed frame and pineapple stenciled walls, it has several photographs and paintings of Grant, the U.S. Army general who broke the back of the confederate forces during the Civil War. (Southern visitors have been known to cover up the pictures, or take them down, while sleeping there.)

The Old Tavern also has a private cottage, known as the Hillside, and five guest houses that sleep between seven and nine people. These guest houses all come with full kitchens and can be rented out entirely or by the room.

If you're looking for real seclusion, the Hillside, also known as the "honeymoon cottage," is a good choice. It's located off a quiet gravel road, about a half-mile outside of town. A knubbly tan rug covers the floor in both the sitting room and bedroom, both done in shades of peach and green. Unlike most rooms at the Old Tavern, the Hillside is outfitted with a television and telephone. Although the bedroom, with a chenille-covered double bed, is relatively small, the views of the Green Mountains are wonderful.

The Old Tavern has a good restaurant that serves breakfast, lunch, and dinner. An elaborate buffet breakfast, as well as afternoon tea, is included in room rates. Full breakfasts are also available, but for an additional charge.

In addition to the restaurant, an adjacent barn houses a rustic lounge. The soaring rough-hewn paneled walls are hung with antique quilts. And a small sitting area features a wood-burning stone fireplace. The place is wonderfully cozy, perfect for relaxing at the end of the day.

RATES PER NIGHT: $98-$155 during foliage season and Christmas season, $450 to rent an entire house. Other times of the year, rates are $95-$135, and $410 for houses. When you call to make a reservation, be sure to describe the type of accommodation you want. Although rooms in the main inn have a similar flavor, the houses do vary in decor.

ACCOMMODATIONS: 35 rooms in the main inn, and the Windham and Homestead cottages across the street. All have private baths. Five guest houses, each equipped with full kitchens, sleep between seven and nine; each bedroom has a private bath. The Hillside cottage has a bedroom, sitting room, and private bath.

AMENITIES: Full-service restaurant and bar. Televisions in common rooms. Natural swimming pond. Stable that includes six box stalls and carriage shed. (Guests can bring their own horses.) Tennis and platform tennis courts. Bicycles available for rent.

RESTRICTIONS: None, however pets and children are welcome only in certain rooms.

Eaglebrook at Grafton, ♥ ♥, $$, Main Street, Grafton 05146, 802/843-2654. Visiting Eaglebrook is like staying with old friends. With only three rooms, innkeepers Marge and Eli Prouty are able to give guests plenty of personal attention. A warm, friendly couple, the Proutys do their best to make guests feel comfortable. But then, it's not hard to feel comfortable at Eaglebrook. The Proutys have a good sense of style and have done a wonderful job retaining their home's Federal flavor – it's on the National Register of Historic Places – while infusing it with some modern art and architecture. (They've added a solarium to the back of the house, which is a perfect spot to take breakfast.)

Unfortunately, only one room has a private bath. This, the Southeast Room, has a sunny, French country flavor. It boasts blue and white check curtains, a king-size bed with a chenille spread, and a side table also covered in chenille.

Although the other two rooms are equally interesting, they do have a shared bath. And while *Romantic New England Getaways* doesn't typically rec-

ommend shared bath accommodations, Eaglebrook's bath is plush and immaculate. The Southwest Room is outfitted in deep red tones and has American country antiques. For those preferring a Victorian flavor, consider the Northwest Room, with its soft, yellow prints.

Stencil aficionados should take note of the downstairs hallway. It was originally done in the 1840s by Moses Eaton, one of New England's most famous and prolific itinerant stencilers. (Eaton's original stencil box is on display at the Museum of the Society for the Preservation of New England Antiquities.)

The front parlor is formally and attractively furnished and has a Colonial flavor – white walls with mustard yellow trim, formal upholstered furniture around a soapstone fireplace. Yet guests seem to gravitate toward the garden room, a former woodshed turned sitting room. Its cathedral ceilings, towering brick fireplace, and many plants give it a comfortable look.

Continental breakfast – which includes juice, fruit, coffee, and homemade muffins and breads – is served in the dining room. This, perhaps the most authentic looking room in the house, still has its original dry sink and brick beehive oven and ash pit. Original cooking hardware is displayed throughout the room.

In addition to the inn, the Proutys operate one of Grafton's nicest gift shops featuring imported Scottish and English sweaters and woolens, special soaps, jewelry, and Vermont-made products.

RATES PER NIGHT: $70-$75.

ACCOMMODATIONS: 3 rooms, one with private bath.

AMENITIES: None.

RESTRICTIONS: Smoking only in the garden room. No children. No pets.

The Wilder Family Homestead Inn, ♥ ♥, $$, off Route 100 (RR 1, Box 106-D), Weston 05161, 802/824-8172. Before opening the Wilder Family Homestead in 1986, innkeepers Roy and Peggy Varner ran a farm in Pennsylvania. Their down-home sensibilities fit Vermont, and help make them top-notch innkeepers. On the day we visited, a couple had returned to the Wilder for a third stay, this time bringing relatives.

The brick, Federal-style home, illuminated to passersby with electric window candles, sits on a small hill just above the town common. Inside, the Wilder has a less regal, yet entirely pleasant appeal. Downstairs there are four common rooms, including a small library, living room, music room, and dining room. Each is decorated with a different flavor. The library is dark and usually glows with a roaring fire. Furniture includes an antique leather rocker. In contrast, the living room is made for flopping, with large cushy (albeit not particularly stylish) beige couches and chairs. It also houses the inn's television. Far more formal is the music room, which has a large Oriental rug, an ornamental fireplace, and an old-fashioned player piano.

The inn's focal point, however, is the dining room. It features a large fireplace with a soapstone hearth, wet bar (where cheese and crackers are set out in the afternoon), hand-stenciled walls, and a long wooden table where the Varner's serve their famous farm-style breakfasts. The spread usually includes coffee, juice, biscuits and jam, home fries, country sausage, as well as a selection of eggs, pancakes, waffles, and French toast.

All seven guest rooms feature Pennsylvania Amish bed quilts. The most requested room is the Moses Eaton. Its walls are decorated with dainty, stenciled flowers, done by Eaton in the 1840s. (See the Eaglebrook listing for more on Moses Eaton.) It also features a queen-size fishnet canopy bed, as well as a day bed, country antiques, and an ornamental fireplace flanked by Doric columns. Another winner is the Tuttle Room, which features wooden floorboards painted pale blue, pink and blue floral wallpaper, and an ornamental fireplace.

RATES PER NIGHT: $60-$90.

ACCOMMODATIONS: 7 rooms, 5 with private bath.

AMENITIES: Television in common room.

RESTRICTIONS: No smoking. No pets. No children under 6.

Rowell's Inn, ♡ ♡ ♡, $$$, Route 11 /30, Simonsville 05143, 802/875-3658. If you can get over the fact that Rowell's Inn is in the middle of nowhere, you're in for a real treat. (Simonsville is between Weston and Grafton, but it has no real "town" to speak of.) Built in 1820 as a stagecoach stop, the inn remains a stylish respite for weary travelers. And although it only has five guest rooms, Rowell's is not just a B&B, but a full service small hotel, complete with a bar and restaurant that serves breakfast and dinner.

Despite the inn's decidedly Federal-style exterior – a brick front with three wooden veranda's–the interior has a Victorian flavor. When F.A. Rowell bought the inn in 1900, he undertook a major renovation that included adding elaborate tin ceilings, new wood floors, and central heating and indoor plumbing.

Innkeepers Lee and Beth Davis have put their souls into the inn, decorating with the goal to make guests feel as if they're stepping back in time. Walk into the front parlor and you'll be directed to a wooden check-in desk to sign the guest register. The room is done in shades of deep maroon, and features a highly polished wood floor

with alternate planks of cherry and maple. Walk down the hall to the library, which has a large Oriental rug, fireplace, leather chairs, shelves filled with books, and tables set with games of checkers and chess.

The tavern room, located in the back of the inn, is perhaps the area of which the Davises are most proud. The epitome of cozy – it has low ceilings, a wood stove, brick walls, long wooden benches, and a working antique Coke machine and cash register. Beer (including a large variety of stouts and ales), wine, and sodas are available, as well as a ready supply of pretzels and peanuts.

All guest rooms are equally pleasant, although none have anything larger than a double bed. The most grand, however, are the two third floor rooms because they were carved out of what was once a ballroom. Room 5 boasts an arched ceiling, huge deep red Oriental rugs, and a dramatic bed that features a 7-foot moiré drape headboard. The bath has black and white tile, an antique tub, and a heated towel rack. Other rooms, similarly deco-rated, have Victorian settees, antique bureaus, brass beds, and large baths outfitted with pedestal sinks and claw-foot tubs. Room 1 has a working fireplace.

Beyond their concern about decor, the Davises are tireless in their efforts to keep guests well fed. Beth is up at 5:00 A.M. to prepare the morning meal; coffee is ready by 6:00 A.M. for early risers. She serves a full breakfast between 8:00 and 9:00 A.M. Selections include eggs (Beth will cook whatever kind you want), hash browns, sticky buns, waffles, baked apples, and cereal.

Tea is served every afternoon, and the cookie jar is kept brimming with Beth's homemade treats. In early evening, cheese and crackers are set out in the library. And at 7:00 P.M., dinner is served. On the day we visited, the five-course meal included herb cheese pie, fiddlehead fern soup, Caesar salad, Cornish hen with carrots, and apple pie. (Although only one menu is offered nightly, the Davises will make alternative meals for guests who request it.)

RATES PER NIGHT: $140-$160 including breakfast and dinner. If you arrive late on Friday, they will deduct the missed meal from your bill.

ACCOMMODATIONS: 5 rooms with private baths.

AMENITIES: Tavern serving beer and wine. Restaurant serving breakfast and dinner.

RESTRICTIONS: No children under 12. No pets.

FRIDAY EVENING
Dinner

The Old Tavern at Grafton, ♡ ♡ ♡, $$-$$$, Main Street, Grafton, 802/843-2231. In transit: Traveling from Weston, follow Route 100 south to the intersection of routes 11 and 30. Head east on Route 11 to Route 121. Follow Route 121 (a gravel road) into Grafton Center. Turn right at the center. The Old Tavern is on the right. From Simonsville, head east on Route 11/30 to Chester, then follow Route 35 south to Grafton. This will take you right into Grafton center.

This is the perfect place to start your weekend in the country. Before dinner, have a drink in the Old Tavern's barn. Sit in the overstuffed couch by the blazing fire and admire the antique quilts hung on the walls.

The dining room, located just off the lobby in the main part of the inn, has three distinct seating areas. The front rooms are formal – dressed in subtle wallpaper and oil paintings of someone's long dead relatives. The back room – a solarium with lots of plants, white tablecloths, and soft candlelight – is more casual, but also much more cozy.

As soon as you sit down, a waitperson brings a small plate of crackers and cheese, just enough to take the edge off your hunger. Appetizers include lobster ravioli in cream sauce, clam fritters, and a variety of soups. Entrees are straightforward, but elegant: steamed salmon in herbs and wine broth, medallions of venison with caramelized red onions in port wine sauce, and, for vegetarians, acorn squash stuffed with wild rice and dried cranberries.

To give your meal a real country finish, don't miss the Old Tavern's Indian pudding. This simple, warm molasses treat, topped with vanilla ice cream, will make you forget more elaborate modern confections. Hours: 6:00 P.M. – 8:45 P.M.

The Blue Coyote, ♡, $$, 92 Rockingham St., Bellows Falls, 802/463-3300. In transit: If you're traveling on I-91, stopping at The Blue Coyote along your way is a nice option. Bellows Falls is about a half hour from Grafton and 50 minutes from Weston. From I-91 north, take the Rockingham/ Bellows Falls Route 5 exit. Take a left into Bellows Falls on Route 5. Travel about three miles, bear left at the fork. The restaurant is about a mile ahead on the right. If you pass the Miss Bellows Falls Diner, you've gone too far.

The Blue Coyote is among the hippest restaurants in southern Vermont. It's not the place to go if you want to jump right into the "Vermont" experience, but it serves great, inventive food. (Rumor has it that it's a favorite dining spot of Ken Burns, local folk hero who produced *The Civil War* series for PBS.)

Atmosphere is casual. The entrance area contains a take-out lunch counter and a view into the wide open kitchen. Upstairs, the dining room is a bit more quiet. Walls are painted a pale, salmon

pink, and colorful cactuses in the windows give the place a Southwestern flavor. Long wooden benches, set against the wall, are mixed with wooden chairs and tables to accommodate dinners.

The Blue Coyote mixes things up with a menu that reflects a variety of ethnic areas, including Mexico, Italy, and Japan. Appetizers include orange ginger root linguine with smoked mussels and tomatoes, smoked trout with gazpacho salsa and stone ground wheat crackers, and puff pastry filled with seasoned spinach and Jarlsberg cheese.

Entrees are similarly inventive: Among them are Maryland lump blue crab cakes with orange mint butter, grilled organic chicken served with roasted corn salsa, and cheese tortellini with sun-dried tomatoes, artichoke hearts, black olives, fresh basil, and grilled eggplant.

Sorbet, served between courses to refresh your palate, and homemade bread are included with meals. Desserts change regularly and include a wide array of high-calorie treats. Hours: 5:30 P.M. – 9:00 P.M. Thursday through Saturday.

SATURDAY MORNING

Explore Grafton.

In transit: Traveling from Weston, follow Route 100 south to the intersection of routes 11 and 30. Head east on Route 11 to Route 121. Follow Route 121, a gravel road, into Grafton Center. Turn right at the center. The Old Tavern is on the right. From Simonsville, head east on Route 11/30 to Chester, then follow Route 35 south to Grafton. This will take you right into Grafton center.

If ever a town looked like a Hollywood movie set, it is Grafton, Vermont. Pristine, white colonial homes, fenced with brilliant red maples, line Main Street. A luminous white steepled church stands sentry at the town's entrance, and the Old Tavern, a grand Federal brick building, holds court in the center. As gushing as this description sounds, it is not overstated.

One of the reasons for this apparent perfection is the Windham Foundation. This nonprofit organization, founded by Dean Mathey in 1963, is devoted to restoring both buildings and economic vitality in Grafton. When Mathey died in 1973, he left his residual estate to the Foundation. Today Windham not only operates the Old Tavern, but also the Grafton Village Cheese Company, Grafton Village Nursery, Grafton Village Garage, Gallery North Star, Grafton Village Store, and Idyll Acres Farm. In addition, it owns and has refurbished many of the residential homes in town.

While this organization's arm may seem long to some, it employs more than 100 people, and has imbued Grafton with the kind of energy it hasn't seen since

its heyday in the 1800s when it was an important stop on the post road from Boston to Albany.

Start your tour by strolling Main Street. Some of the shops you might want to poke into include:

Grafton Village Store, 802/843-2348. This red clapboard building houses the town grocery store, and includes a section of Vermont-made products—cheese, maple syrup, herbal vinegars, and other treats.

Jud Hartmann Gallery, 207/359-2544. This Blue Hill, Maine, artist moves his gallery to Grafton every fall. The store carries Hartmann's majestic bronze Indian sculptures, as well as watercolors, oils, and pastels by Neil and Jan Drevitson and William Bracken.

Eaglebrook of Grafton, 802/843-2564. Attached to the B&B of the same name, this is a small but interesting store carrying crafts by local artists, imported sweaters and textiles, and folk art.

Vermont Artisan Designs, (located a few hundred feet behind the Village Store), 802/843-2614. The store isn't particularly attractive, but it has a nice selection of crafts, including pottery, blown glass, wood, jewelry, and toys.

Gallery North Star, Townsend Road, 802/843-2276. (Townsend runs perpendicular to Main Street, right on the side of the Old Tavern. Perhaps the most elegant gallery in town, it features work by some of Vermont's best artists. Although most of the work is traditional (representational), you can find a few modern pieces.

The Blacksmith Shop, 802/843-2211. In this shop, which is owned and operated by the Windham Foundation, you can watch the resident blacksmith use traditional methods and forging tools to create old-fashioned fireplace and hearth-cooking utensils, as well as brackets, hooks, hinges, and decorative items. Goods can be purchased and made to order.

Stroll to the Grafton Village Cheese Shop, 802/843-2221. In transit: If you're on Main Street, turn down Townsend Road. Then turn left on Pleasant Street, and then right on Water Street. Walk under the old-fashioned covered bridge, known as the Kidder Bridge. From there, follow any one of three marked footpaths through a large field. They all lead to the Grafton Village Cheese Company on Townsend Road. You will be able to see it from any of the paths. The entire walk should take you no more than a half hour.

The Grafton Village Cheese Shop is just a small store, but it's significant because the Windham Foundation has revived a business that once thrived here in the early 1800s, before New England farmers pulled up stakes to find their fortunes in the west. No guided tours are given. But if you visit in the morning – that's usually when the cheese is made – you can watch the cheese maker at work. Don't forget to try the free samples in the gift shop.

Lunch

Harry's Country Picnic, $, Route 100 at the Millyard, Weston, no phone. In transit: From Grafton, take Route 121 west to Route 11 west. Then take Route 100 north into Weston.

This is a tiny, unassuming spot, with just a few tables, but it's one of two lunch spots in Weston. (The other is the Bryant House, attached to the Vermont Country Store.) And besides, it serves delicious homemade soups and gourmet sandwiches. Start with a bowl of split pea with ham (that was the soup of the day when we visited). And if you're still hungry, you can go for a baked ham and cheese, or perhaps another one of Harry's hearty selections.

Sugar addicts should head next door to the Weston Fudge Shop. All the fudge is made in the kitchen right behind the candy counter, so you can be assured of fresh merchandise. In addition to fudge, the shop sells caramel corn, lollipops, and other sweets. One word of warning about the fudge: Take small bites. The stuff is a real tooth acher. Hours: 11:30 A.M. – 4:00 P.M. (roughly).

Saturday Afternoon

Visit the Weston Antiques Show, held at the Weston Playhouse, Route 100, Weston, 802/824-3967 or 802/824-4186. Leave your car at the Millyard, and walk down to the show. The playhouse is directly on the Weston Green.

For more than 30 years the Weston Antiques Show has been attracting a discerning group of dealers and buyers. While it may have started out considerably smaller, today the show has more than 30 exhibitors, all of whom cram their wares into the playhouse's three floors. If you're a real browser, it's possible to spend the entire day.

Merchandise is extraordinarily varied—you can find Italian marble lamps, sterling silver, Oriental rugs, early American folk art, even antique beaded Indian jewelry, vests, and purses.

As pleasing as the show is to peruse, the prices are daunting. That's not to say you won't find some magnificent pieces, but you'll have to pay for them. If you're looking for a "trinket" for under $100, or maybe even $200, you'll probably be disappointed. If, on the other hand, you're in the market for a rug, or an important piece of furniture, you'll have plenty of choices. Hours: 5:00 P.M. – 7:30 P.M. on Thursday for preview, 10:00 A.M. – 6:00 P.M. Friday and Saturday, 10:00 A.M. – 4:00 P.M. Sunday. Admission: $4 per day. Preview evening costs $25.

Visit the Vermont Country Store, Route 100, Weston, 802/824-3184. In transit: From the Green, walk south on Main Street. The store is on the left, just beyond the Green.

The first revived country store in the United States, the Vermont Country Store sells feel-good nostalgia by way of hard-to-find products that you'd like to think your granny wore, cooked with, or kept in her cupboards. Opened in 1946 by Vrest Horton, it is operated today by his son, Lyman, who maintains his father's philosophy of offering old-time merchandise of high quality and everyday function.

Cotton broadcloth garter belts, plaid flannel nightshirts, pine-tar shampoo, chenille bedspreads, hurricane lamps, white enamel bread boxes – the Vermont Country Store has two floors packed with thousands of items. Among its most popular products, however, are its penny candies. Large glass jars are filled with such old favorites as Mary Janes, White Rock candy, sour balls, and chocolate babies.

Decor is predictably unfussy – wood plank floors, wooden bins, and glass cases. Even cynics will find it charmingly un-hokey. Hours: 9:00 A.M. – 5:00 P.M. Monday through Saturday.

Peruse Downtown Weston.

In transit: From the Vermont Country Store, walk south on Main Street and begin your tour at the Weston House.

Weston isn't a shopping mecca by any stretch of the imagination, but it does have a few spots worth a browse. They include:

Weston House, Route 100, 802/824-3636. If you're in the market for a quilt, you should stop here. Although new quilts, no matter how attractive, don't have the charm of antiques, they are easier to come by – and aren't as musty. Weston House carries a large selection of primarily traditional quilts handmade by local artisans. Also a selection of quilted pillows, throw rugs, and woven baskets.

Freight Wagon Antiques, Route 100 at the Millyard, 802/824-6909. After the antique show, you may not be in the mood for more. But at the Freight Wagon you can find a few affordable items – baskets, bowls, and silver pieces – as well as some fine country furniture.

West River Jewelry Company, Route 100, 802/824-3618. This shop has an eclectic selection of gold and silver jewelry, handcrafts, and Christmas ornaments.

Visit the Weston Priory, Route 155, Weston, 802/824-5409. In transit: From Weston, head north on Route 100 for 3½ miles. Route 100 will take a sharp right. Continue straight ahead to Route 155. The Priory is about a half mile down on the left. You'll see a small brown sign.

If your image of a monk is a joyless man shuffling about in a brown hair-cloth gown performing his daily activities in silence, you owe it to yourself to visit the Weston Priory. Even for non-Catholics, the Priory, set on the edge of the National Forest, is a spiritually uplifting experience. It was founded in 1953 by Brother Leo Abbot from the Dormition Abbey in Jerusalem as a home to a community of Benedictine monks.

Grounds are simply, yet perfectly, manicured and feature a large man-made pond. Guests are free to walk around the property. And while some come just to contemplate the natural beauty of the land, most visitors are also drawn to the monks' daily services, in which virtually all prayers are sung. Their voices are beautiful and harmonious – the brothers believe that no voice should be more dominant than another.

A gift shop houses Benedictine art and tapes of the monks' music. Hours: 10:30 A.M. 5:15 P.M. Tuesday, Thursday, Friday, and Saturday. Masses are held at 5:15 P.M. Monday, Wednesday, and Friday, and at 11:30 A.M. Saturday and Sunday.

SATURDAY EVENING
Drinks

The Marsh Tavern at the Equinox, ♥, $$, Route 7A, Manchester Village, 802/362-4700. In transit: From Grafton, take Route 121 west to Route 11 west. Follow that into Manchester to the intersection with Route 7A. Follow 7A south into Manchester Village. The

Equinox is on the left. From Simonsville, continue west on Route 11, then follow directions above. From Weston, follow Route 100 south to Route 11 west.

While Manchester and the Equinox may not exemplify "country" Vermont, the hotel itself is so architecturally interesting that it would be a shame to be so close and not visit. This grand four-story Federal building with two front porches, each supported by four two-story Doric columns, is, in a word, magnificent. Marble sidewalks that lead to the entrance, only add to the majesty.

Although the Equinox hardly looks its 224 years, the Marsh Tavern, located to the right of the lobby, was a gathering spot for colonials during the American Revolution. The tavern, however, was expanded in the latest renovation. The original room is located at the far end of the building and is somewhat set off from the rest of the lounge. It has deep red walls, original wood floors, and a working fireplace. A great place for relaxing and soaking in a little history. Hours: from 11:00 A.M.

Dinner

The Chantecleer, ♡ ♡, $$$, Route 7, East Dorset, 802/362-1616. In transit: From Manchester Village, follow Route 7A back toward Manchester. At the intersection of routes 11 and 30, you'll continue straight ahead, through the center of town to Route 7. The Chantecleer is on the left, about 3.5 miles past this intersection.

Long considered one of southern Vermont's best restaurants, the Chantecleer lives up to its reputation as a fine French restaurant. Yet despite its traditional continental cuisine, the atmosphere is rustic and relaxed. (Proper attire is suggested. But in Vermont that just means no jeans. You don't really have to wear a suitcoat or tie.) Housed in an old dairy barn, the dining room has plaster and barn board walls. Tables are covered with blue cloths and lit with modern glass oil lamps. The prime seating area is next to the soaring field-stone fireplace. If you want a table here, it's a good idea to make reservations.

Appetizers include seafood gumbo, liver pâté, and shrimp mousse served with dill crème fraîche. Among the entrees are sautéed frogs legs with garlic and lemon butter, veal sweetbreads with morels and shallots served with Madeira demi-glaze, and chicken framboise, which is boneless breast in a hazelnut crust served with fried plaintains and a raspberry sauce. All meals come with an assortment of vegetables and a choice of potato, rice, and spatzle.

A selection of primarily chocolate desserts is usually available – from fondue to flourless chocolate cake. The wine list is good, ranging from Clos Du Bois to Chateau Margeux. Hours: 6:00 P.M. – 10:00 P.M. Closed Tuesday.

Sunday Morning

Hiking around Grafton.

In transit: From Weston, follow Route 100 south to the intersection of routes 11 and 30. Head east on Route 11 to Route 121. Follow Route 121, a gravel road that leads into Grafton Center. Turn right at the center. Park anywhere along Main Street. From Simonsville, head east on Route 11/30 to Chester, then follow Route 35 south to Grafton. This will take you right into Grafton center.

The Grafton Historical Society produces an excellent guide to nine walks around Grafton. They range in length from one to eight miles. If the Society, located on Main Street diagonally across from the Old Tavern, is closed, you can pick up a map at the Old Tavern's front desk.

One of the more interesting walks is up Kidder Hill to Grafton's old soapstone quarries, which were once the two largest in the United States. This walk, which is about 4½ miles long, will take you down an ox path, along which animals hauled huge blocks of soapstone to the mill.

If you're interested in a shorter hike (the truly vigorous could complete both hikes in a morning), consider a trip up to Point Lookout. This trail, also marked on the Grafton Historical Society's map, starts at the brick church in Grafton center and enters the Village Park, 70 acres of semi-woodland, trails, seats, and shelters, as well as a picnic table and grill. This two-mile (round-trip) trail, to the top of Point Lookout, affords sweeping views of Townsend Valley.

Lunch

Take-out from the Grafton Village Store, $, Main Street, Grafton, 802/843-2348. In transit: Right on Main Street next to the Old Tavern.

Pick up some deli sandwiches, sweets or fruit, and if you're feeling really relaxed, maybe even a bottle of wine. The Village Store doesn't have any indoor seating. But the outdoors is so picturesque, you'll want to enjoy the view. Good picnic spots can be found near either of the two covered bridges in town. Hours: 8:30 A.M. – 6:00 P.M. Monday through Saturday, 9:00 A.M. – 6:00 P.M. Sunday.

Sunday Afternoon

Bicycle Ride to Plummer's Sugar House, Townsend Road, Grafton, 802/843-2207. In transit: Bike rentals are available at the Old Tavern. The inn's bike rental shop is across the street from the Tavern on Townsend Road.

Plummer's is only about three miles from Grafton center. You could drive here, but two wheels will provide the leisurely pace most appropriate for taking in the countryside. The road is relatively flat and should be easy enough for even rusty bicyclists.

If you visit in the fall, you won't have the chance to see maple syrup actually being made, but a visit to Plummer's is still worth a trip. The family is friendly and more than happy to give you a tour of their sugar house. Unlike many Vermonters who make syrup for fun (and, if they're lucky, profit), the Plummers have a successful and sophisticated operation. Each year they tap more than 4,500 maple trees. Rather than gather sap in buckets, they utilize an elaborate series of rubber hoses. A combination of gravity and vacuum suction helps the syrup travel through the hoses and into a vat in the sugar house.

Once inside, the sap is boiled down; it takes 45 gallons of sap to make just one gallon of maple syrup. (Now you know why it's so expensive.) In addition to syrup, the Plummers sell maple cream and candy. Hours: The sugar house is open for tours most any time. Just call ahead to make sure someone's around. Admission is free.

Go Apple Picking at Hidden Orchard Farms, Route 121, Grafton, 802/843-2499. In transit: Continue to Hidden Orchard on your bikes. It's only a mile west of Grafton center and just four miles from the Plummers. Follow Townsend Road back into Grafton center. Turn left on Main Street past the Old Tavern. Then turn left on Route 121. Hidden Orchard is about a mile down on the left.

A fall trip to Vermont isn't complete without an apple picking expedition. Hidden Orchard is in a great location, on a quiet gravel road where the only sound you'll hear is the apples falling from the trees. No matter what variety of apple you fancy, Hidden Orchard is likely to grow it – Macintosh, Cortland, Empire, as well as at least a dozen other varieties.

Stop by the farm stand to let them know you want to pick. They'll supply you with bags and directions to the orchard, which is just down the road from the stand. When you're finished, you may want to stop back for some cider donuts. Donuts and fresh cider will make a good snack for the ride home.

Hidden Orchard also sells its own preserves, as well as pumpkins, syrup, and other Vermont-made products. Hours: 8:30 A.M. – 5:00 P.M. daily through late October.

Additional Activities

Ride on the Green Mountain Flyer, Bellows Falls Station, 8 Depot St., Bellows Falls, 802/463-3069 or 463-9531. If you're an old train aficionado, consider a trip on the Green Mountain Flyer. Although this 26-mile train ride is billed as a foliage excursion, the scenery is relatively humdrum. The real treat is the classic wooden coaches (available for an extra fee). The Osgood Bradley Car was built in 1913, and the Wagner Car in 1891. The latter is possibly the oldest passenger car still active on New England railroads. Round-trip tickets for the classic coaches are $13. Trains depart at 11:00 A.M. and 2:00 P.M. and run through late October.

Visit Hildene, Route 7A, Manchester Village, 802/362-1788. This 24-room Georgian Revival mansion was built by Robert Todd Lincoln, Abraham Lincoln's son. Lincoln, in fact, died in this house in 1926. It remains authentically furnished with original family effects. The tour includes a slide show about Robert Todd Lincoln, and a visit to the restored formal gardens. Carriage and sleigh rides are often available. Hours 10:00 A.M. – 4:00 P.M. through late October. Admission: $6.

Visit the Vermont State Craft Center, Route 7A, Manchester Village, 802/362-3321. Although the main gallery resides in Middlebury, this new outpost has an extensive collection of works by Vermont's finest crafts people. Look for everything from hand-carved furniture to woven scarves. This shop is a "don't miss" if you appreciate fine crafts.

Grafton Historical Society Museum, Main Street, Grafton, 802/843-2211. Interesting collection of local antiques. Incredibly knowledgeable workers. Hours: 2:30 P.M. – 4:30 P.M. Saturday. Admission is free.

Go hiking along the Appalachian/ Long Trail. These two trails follow the same route from the state's southern border to the Shelburne Pass. For details on good hiking routes, consult the Green Mountain National Forest Ranger Station, Route 11/30, Manchester, 802/362-2307. The station is only open from 8:00 A.M. – 4:30 P.M. Monday through Friday. If you want maps, call ahead and have them sent to you.

GETTING THERE

BY AIR: Albany County (New York) Airport is the closest major airport to southern Vermont. Most major carriers fly into Albany, including American (800/433-7300), Continental (800/231-0856), Delta (800/638-7333), Northwest (800/441-1818), United (800/241-65223), and US Air (800/468-7247). From there, you can rent a car and drive to the area. It's less than 50 miles and should take you no more than 75 minutes.

Some visitors choose to fly into the Bradley International Airport in Windsor Locks, Connecticut. It's about two hours from the Grafton/Weston area. Two limousine services offer transportation from the airport. They are Thomas Transportation (800/526-8143) and Ambassador Limo (203/727-8561).

Also, SKYmaster (800/553-9021), a small airline based in Keene, New Hampshire, has daily scheduled flights to Rutland, Vermont, from Boston and Newark, New Jersey. Both flights, however, have stops in Keene. Rutland is about 45 minutes north of Manchester.

BY CAR: Unless you're coming from a great distance, driving makes the most sense. A car is a a prerequisite for enjoying this weekend.

From the south, take I-91 north into Vermont. Then take the Route 30 exit. To Grafton, follow Route 30 to 35. For Weston, follow Route 30 to Route 100. Southern Vermont is also accessible via the Massachusetts Turnpike. Follow the Pike west into Stockbridge. Then take Route 7 north into Vermont. For Weston, follow Route 7 to Route 11, to Route 100 north. For Grafton, follow Route 7 to Route 11, to Route 35 south.

BY TRAIN: Amtrak (800/USA-RAIL) has daily service to Bellows Falls, Vermont, from Boston and New York. Bellows Falls is about a half hour from Grafton and 50 minutes from Weston.

BY BUS: No direct bus service is available. But if you must, get yourself to Albany. (Greyhound has service from New York City and other eastern seaboard areas.) From there, Vermont Transit (802/864-6811) has daily service to Manchester.

CAR RENTAL: Several car rental companies are located at the Albany County Airport. They are: National (800/227-7368), Avis (800/331-1212), Hertz (800/654-3131), Budget (800/527-0700), Alamo (800/327-9633), Thrifty (800/367-2277), and Dollar (518/869-1201 or 869-1202). National, Hertz, and Avis also have offices at the Rutland Airport. Hertz, Budget, Avis, and National have offices at Bradley International Airport.

If you want to rent a car once in the area, you'll have to go to Manchester. Call Hand Chevrolet (802/362-1754), routes 7 and 11/30, Manchester Center, or Manchester Motors (802/362-1808), Route 11/30, Manchester Center.

TAXI/LIMOUSINE SERVICE: Matteson's Taxi (802/375-6549) based in Arlington, makes trips to local airports and the train stations. Phillip's Taxi (802/362-1800) is located in Manchester Center.

Information: The Windham Foundation, Townsend Road, Grafton 05146, 802/843-2211. Hours: 8:30 A.M.- 4:30 P.M. Monday through Friday. The Windham Foundation owns the Grafton Inn and it keeps all its brochures and information in a small area just off the lobby. Also, the Manchester and Mountains Chamber of Commerce, Route 7A, Adams Park Green, Manchester Center 05255, 802/362-2100. Hours: 9:00 A.M.– 5:00 P.M. Monday through Friday, 10:00 A.M.– 5:00 P.M. Saturday, and 10:00 A.M. – 2:00 P.M. Sunday.

Jay & Montgomery, Vermont

*I*n Vermont, there is an invisible geographic barrier that lies just north of St. Johnsbury and Stowe beyond which only the most adventurous traveler will cross. While most of the state is considered an outdoor playground, for many, the Northeast Kingdom is just a barren tundra separating civilization from Montreal.

And while it's true that this northernmost quadrant is the least populated region of the nation's third least populated state, it has much to recommend it. Not the least of which is its hardscrabble beauty. Surrounded by white-capped mountains, the landscape resembles a sepia watercolor of undulating brown hills punctuated with sturdy old farmhouses that have settled somewhat crookedly into their fieldstone foundations. It's the kind of place where farmers, out doing their daily chores, wave to every passing car. Travelers, of course, aren't a common sight.

Yet people do visit the Northeast Kingdom. It attracts outdoor types who prefer to spend their leisure time hiking, fishing, mountain biking, or, in winter, skiing. In fact, skiing is the Northeast Kingdom's biggest claim to fame. Jay Peak, located in Jay, just a few miles from the Canadian border, is one of Vermont's best ski resorts. It boasts the biggest average snowfall of any ski area in the Northeast: In the past 10 years, Jay's annual snowfall has exceeded 295 inches, compared to Killington, which only gets an average 166 inches. (Also by comparison, Waterville Valley in New Hampshire gets about 140 inches.)

All this snow, combined with Jay's uncrowded slopes and European flavor (about 50 percent of its patrons are Canadian), make it a near perfect ski destination for those who don't mind forsaking the glamour of its southern relations.

Although Jay does have a slopeside hotel, most visitors prefer to stay off the mountain where there is more activity. One of the most popular spots is Montgomery, about eight miles south. Considered to be the most cosmopolitan of the Northeast Kingdom's towns (a very relative statement), it boasts several B&Bs, good restaurants, a general store, and a few interesting shops.

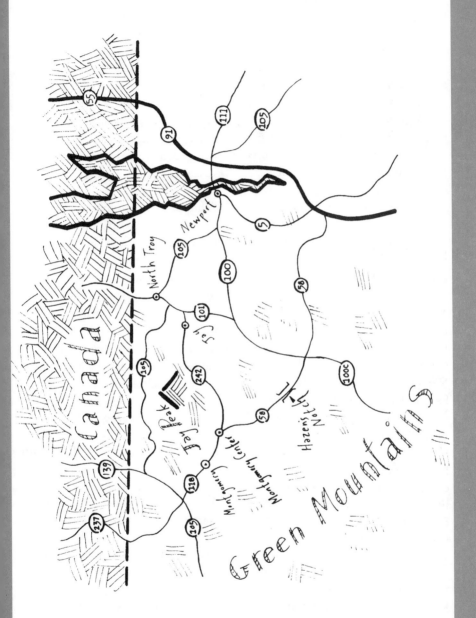

JAY & MONYGOMERY

A perfect time to visit the area is between Thanksgiving and Christmas. (Remember, it's officially "fall" until December 21.) Not only will it provide a much needed break from the season's attendant frenzy (you wouldn't be able to find a shopping mall, even if you got the urge to visit one), you'll get a chance to bone up on your schussing techniques before most other resorts have even launched their ski seasons.

Where To Stay

Fore the Rocks, ♥ ♥ ♥, $$, Route 58, Montgomery Center 05471, 802/326-4500. For couples looking to escape both everything and everyone, this small white stucco chalet owned by Vermont's most famous (perhaps infamous) restaurateur, Jon "Zack" Zachadnyk, is perfect. For the past 25 years, Zack has been operating Zack's on the Rocks restaurant to rave reviews. Visitors aren't just impressed that real gourmet food can be had in the Vermont hinterlands, but by Zack himself. A true eccentric, he greets guests in a purple velvet and gold threaded caftan and has a taste for decoration that might be best described as medieval Liberace.

Zack's chalet isn't quite as whimsical and weird as his restaurant, or as well known, but it's still a choice spot. The living room is large and comfortable, and has the feel of a nice country house furnished in the sixties (something Rob and Laura Petrie might have rented). The room's main feature is a grand stone fireplace. It's surrounded by a sitting area that includes a large blue upholstered couch. Walls are cream colored and adorned with an array of black and white wildlife photographs. Off the living room are a dining area and a small, tiled kitchen with wood cabinets. (Zack's doesn't serve breakfast.)

While the main rooms are pleasant enough, the chalet's pieces de resistance is its bedroom and bath. The former boasts a seven-foot, hand-carved bed that's covered with a drape that hangs from the ceiling. It sits before a large fireplace. Similarly dramatic, although far more flamboyant, is the bath which features Vegas-style silver, black, and blue wallpaper, Hollywood lights, and a sunken black bathtub.

RATES PER NIGHT: $100.

ACCOMMODATIONS: One chalet with kitchen, living room, bedroom, and bath.

AMENITIES: Two fireplaces. Television. Next door to the area's best restaurant.

RESTRICTIONS: The chalet is only rented to two people. No pets.

Rose Apple Acres Farm, ♥, $$, East Hill Road, North Troy 05859, 802/988-4300. Rose Apple isn't just a B&B that fancies calling itself a "farm."

It really is one, complete with goats, pigs, sheep, horses, and a herd of Jersey milking cows. On the day we visited, innkeepers Cam and Jay Mead were busy in their country kitchen. Jay was admiring the cider he had recently pressed that was resting in five-gallon glass drums. And Cam was dividing her time between kneading bread and watching over a lamb stew that was simmering on the stove.

The Meads operate a B&B in the truest sense. Guests actually share their home – the same living room, the same television, and even the same big, wooden kitchen table. While the sound of that much togetherness may be off-putting to some, the Meads are among the most genial and warm innkeepers we have found. Interestingly, they are amazed that their ramshackle farm and no-nonsense rooms have received such a warm reception from visitors.

It's true, the Meads may not offer fancy accommodations or Kona coffee flown direct from Hawaii. Yet they have something far more difficult to find and, to many, far more cherished – simplicity. Rose Apple Acres Farm, and the Meads themselves, remind us that there is another way of life – without time clocks, commutes, or microwave meals.

Three rooms are located above the kitchen. By far the best is the Rose Room. The only one with a private bath, it is actually two rooms, one with a double

bed, and the other with two twins. The floor is covered with rose-carpeting, and the walls are pine paneled and adorned with framed needlepoint samplers.

Guests are treated to an ample country breakfast that Cam prepares herself. Ever the low-key innkeeper, Cam is willing to heat the skillet whenever guests happen to wander downstairs. Her menu usually includes fresh fruit, homemade coffeecake and granola, and a special entree such as pancakes or omelets. Breakfast also includes the Mead's homemade jams, jellies, and syrups. (They sell these, along with their own cider and yarn.)

RATES PER NIGHT: $42-$52.

ACCOMMODATIONS: 3 rooms, 1 with private bath.

AMENITIES: Sleigh rides available.

RESTRICTIONS: No smoking. No pets.

Black Lantern Inn, ♡ ♡, $$, Route 118, Montgomery Village 05470, 802/326-4507, or 800/255-8661. On a relatively desolate stretch of Route 118, this brick, Federal style inn, with candles flickering in the windows, seems almost a mirage. But the Black Lantern is the real thing – a cozy small inn with class.

Although many people don't like staying in annexes, the Black Lantern's Burdett House, which is just next door, offers the inn's finest accommodations.

It houses six suites. Although each has its own charm, the two-floor suite is considered the best. It has a first floor sitting room with a wood-burning fireplace and a small deck. Upstairs is a bedroom with a skylight, and a bath. Outfitted with wall-to-wall nubbly beige carpeting, soft white walls, and a mix of antiques and modern furniture, it has a clean, comfortable feel.

An additional 10 rooms are located in the main inn. Although pleasant and similarly decorated—with chenille spreads, floral wallpaper, and Vermont antiques—they are small. Quarters could get cramped with you and all your ski clothes. If you must stay in the main inn, be sure to ask for the room with a sitting area.

Common rooms include a small living room with a great soapstone stove. However most guests congregate in the cozy pub, which has rough-hewn wainscoting, pale blue and tan flowered wallpaper, wooden tables and chairs, and a long bar.

The Black Lantern serves full breakfast in the pub from 8:00 A.M. to 9:00 A.M. (Yes, we think it's a little early too.) Selections include French toast, pancakes, eggs any style, and oatmeal with almonds, raisins, and brown sugar.

RATES PER NIGHT: $80-$110.

ACCOMMODATIONS: 10 rooms with private baths; 6 suites with private baths.

AMENITIES: Common room with television. Full-service restaurant serving breakfast and dinner. Full-service bar. Fireplaces in some rooms. Televisions and VCRs in some rooms.

RESTRICTIONS: No pets.

FRIDAY EVENING
Dinner

Black Lantern Inn, ♡ ♡, $$-$$$, Route 118, Montgomery Village, 802/326-4507, 800/255-8661. In transit: From Zack's, follow Route 58 back toward Montgomery, then take Route 118 north. The Black Lantern is on the left. From Rose Apple Acres, take Route 105 north to Route 101 south, to Route 242, to Route 118. The Black Lantern is on the right.

After a long drive on Friday night, the Black Lantern is the perfect spot to help you shift gears. The inn's restaurant has only seven tables, yet it's decorated with great care. Tables are dressed with starched pink and green cloths, and lit with candles.

Floors are varnished wide pine and the walls have the same blue and tan floral wallpaper found in the pub.

The menu changes nightly. Hors d' oeuvres might include herring in wine sauce, spinach ricotta stuffed mushrooms, and asparagus soup. On the night we visited, the entrees were veal with red peppers and artichokes, filet mignon with mushrooms and onions, and walnut-crusted fillet of sole. After dinner, retire to the bar for a snifter of Courvoisier. Hours: 6:00 P.M. – 9:00 P.M. No smoking.

The Inn on Trout River, ♡ ♡, $$-$$$, Route 118, Montgomery Center, 802/326-4391 or 800/338-7049. In transit: From Zack's follow Route 58 back toward Montgomery Center, then take Route 118 north. The Inn on Trout River is in the middle of town, on the left. From the Black Lantern, follow Route 118 south. The inn is a few miles down on the right. From the Rose Apple Acres Farm, take Route 105 north to Route 101 south, to Route 242, to Route 118. Follow Route 118 to Montgomery Center. The inn is on the right.

The inn was built at the turn of the century by C.T. Hall, a millionaire lumber baron. Today, innkeepers Lee and Michael Foreman are working hard to bring the Inn on Trout River back to its former Victorian elegance. A nice example of their efforts is Lemoille's (Lee's real name), the inn's dining room.

Lace curtains, a mauve Oriental rug, and working modified Rumford fireplace, give the room an old-world feel. If you can, get the table right by the fireplace – it's the best in the house.

The menu may not be adventurous, but it's surprisingly upscale for a small country inn. Appetizers include smoked salmon served with toasted rye bread, lemon, and capers; shrimp cocktail; and spinach strudel. For entrees, consider steak au poivre, pasta primavera served with a crabmeat cream sauce, or brandied chicken breast, pan-seared and topped with Vermont cheddar, bread crumbs, and a sherry cream sauce.

Chocolate lovers will appreciate Lee's selection of desserts: chocolate chip cheesecake, chocolate torte cake, chocolate mousse, and chocolate peanut butter pie. Hours: 5:30 P.M. – 9:30 P.M. (If you'd prefer a more casual meal, the Inn on Trout River also has a pub where they serve burgers, tacos, and barbecued chicken.)

SATURDAY MORNING

Go Alpine Skiing at Jay Peak, Route 242, Jay 05859, 802/988-2611 or 800/451-4449. In transit: From Montgomery, follow Route 118 north to Route 242 north to Jay Peak. Jay is about 12 miles from Montgomery. From Rose Apple Acres Farm, follow Route 105 north to Route 101 south. Follow Route 101 to Route 242. Jay is also about 12 miles from North Troy.

Jay Peak is an old-fashioned sort of ski resort. Unlike many modern resorts that look like Oz – a long winding road leading to a bright multiplex bustling with people – Jay has one main ski lodge. This lodge, the adjacent Hotel Jay, and a satellite cafeteria are cream-colored stucco buildings with sloping brown roofs that look as if they have been transplanted from a small Swiss village.

Yet this simple architecture belies Jay's sophistication: It has Vermont's only aerial tramway, which can transport 60 skiers from the base to the 3,968-foot summit in just 7 minutes. (People who have a fear of heights beware, the final chasm that the tram crosses before it reaches the craggy summit is—well, a chasm.) And unlike some of the state's more popular resorts—which make up in fancy restaurants and sizzling nightlife what they lack in natural snow—Jay's singular pride is its heavy snowfall. You won't find more of it unless you head for the Rockies.

All this snow allows Jay to offer some of the best glade skiing in the east. (Glades can only happen when enough natural snow falls in the wooded area to cover the undergrowth.) For anyone who hasn't tried it, glade skiing is a magical experience—one of the few chances in modern day skiing to experience the peaceful nature of a mountain. Although three of Jay's glades—Beaver Pond, North, and Expo—are black diamond trails, Bonaventure is for intermediates and is considered one of Jay's most pleasant glades.

Jay is also one of the few mountains in the east that allows off-trail skiing. With more than 150 acres surrounding the 40 groomed and marked trails, you should have no trouble finding your own little piece of the mountain. (Jay's only rule is that skiers must exit and enter the woods from marked trails.)

If you visit before the holidays, chances are Jay will be your first venture onto the slopes for the season. Although 25 percent of its trails are for experts, Jay isn't a mean mountain and is a great place to perfect your technique. More than half of Jay's trails are for intermediate skiers, and 20 percent for novices. (Gluttons for punishment should head straight for River Quai or Green Beret.)

What really sets Jay apart, however, isn't its accessibility to all skiers, the snowfall, or even the glades. It's the European atmosphere. Owned by the Canadian-based Mont Saint Sauveur International, and just a few miles from the Canadian border, Jay feels decidedly different from most New England ski resorts. About half of Jay's patrons are Canadian: signs are posted in both English and French and many Jay employees are bilingual. (You may want to exchange your American money for Canadian before you go. Jay accepts Canadian money at par, so you can save about 20 percent on lift tickets.)

Lunch

International Restaurant, $$, Hotel Jay, Route 242, Jay 05859, 802/988-2611 or 800/451-4449. In transit: The Hotel Jay is at the base of the mountain, connected to the base lodge.

Unfortunately, one thing Jay doesn't offer is a lot of mountainside dining opportunities. If you're looking to avoid the noon hour madness that invariably descends on all ski mountain lodges, consider the International Restaurant at the Hotel Jay. It's nothing fancy — a rather large room with lots of windows and wooden tables and chairs — but it's far more comfortable and pleasant than the main lodge. Lunch fare is standard: burgers, sandwiches, and soups. Hours: 11:30 A.M. – 2:00 P.M.

SATURDAY AFTERNOON

Continue Your Day of Skiing at Jay Peak.

If you're looking to take it easy in the afternoon, head over to Ullr's Dream, accessible only from the tramway. Ullr's is Jay's longest trail, stretching for three miles. The quintessential cruiser, it's wide at the top, narrow towards the middle, and has a final flat runout. It's the kind of trail that screams to be skied fast and furiously. Great for making you feel like Jean Claude Killy.

Aprés Ski Cocktails

The Belfry, Route 242, Montgomery Center, 802/326-4400. In transit: From Jay Peak, follow Route 242 south toward Montgomery Center. The Belfry is on a small rise on the left.

This tiny red building, formerly an old schoolhouse, is Jay's most popular après ski bar. A favorite with ski instructors, and locals, it's the perfect spot for some ex post facto bravado. If you want a little sustenance before dinner, try the Belfry's potato skins. Hours: from 4:00 P.M.

SATURDAY EVENING
Dinner

Zack's On the Rocks, ♡ ♡ ♡ ♡, $$$, Route 58, Montgomery Center, 802/326-4500. In transit: From the Black Lantern, follow Route 118 back toward Montgomery Center to Route 58. From Rose Apple Acres Farm, follow Route 105 north to Route 101 south, to Route 242, to Route 118. Just beyond Montgomery Center you'll see a sign for Route 58. Follow Route 58 for about two miles. Zack's is on the left. A giant rock painted bright purple marks the driveway.

Zack's is, in a word, unforgettable. It is, without question, the most unusual restaurant you'll ever visit. First-time patrons invariably exclaim that the place should be in Soho. But even in New York's enclave for the terminally hip and offbeat, Zack's would be one of a kind. The fact that this funky, gourmet restaurant is in such a tiny Vermont town makes it all the more fascinating.

When you first enter, you'll be ushered into the bar. (Zack prefers that guests don't glimpse the dining room until they're ready to be seated.) The tiny room is made to look even smaller by the mass of tinsel-laden tree branches suspended from the ceiling. About two thirds of the floor space is taken up with an organ that has a grand piano top built around it. Propped on a stool is a dummy in a curly black wig and a vermilion, sequined dress. (On Friday and Saturday nights, a pianist usually plays old standards.)

After you order a drink, the menu— a brown paper bag, burnt around the edges and handwritten—arrives. It has a nice mix of continental favorites. For appetizers: escargot, smoked trout, and shrimp cocktail. On our visit, entrees included veal Oscar, tournedos of beef bernaise, grilled salmon, and chicken banana (a Zack creation and surprisingly good).

Once you make your meal selections, and once Zack deems you've had enough time to unwind, "himself" breezes into the cocktail lounge— outfitted in one of his many flamboyant purple caftans and a half dozen long, clunky (and clanking) necklaces— and leads you to dinner.

To describe the dining room would be to ruin the surprise. The food is all tasty and well presented, however, it seems secondary to the decor and Zack himself. Not surprisingly, Zack's has several zany touches such as chocolate bread and butter. (You can also get "plain" bread and butter. In fact, the crusty bread Zack serves with dinner is excellent.)

Desserts are decadent. The "Jay Peaks" sundae comes in a huge, long-stemmed crystal bowl that could easily serve four. Reservations are a must. Hours: 6:00 P.M. – 9:00 P.M.

SUNDAY MORNING

Note: Some couples may choose to ski both Saturday and Sunday. But for those interested in a less strenuous schedule, the following itinerary is recommended.

Morning Sleigh Ride at Rose Apple Acres Farm, East Hill Road, North Troy, 802/988-4300. In transit: From Montgomery, follow Route 118 south to Route 242, to Route 101 north. Follow Route 101 to Route 105 east to East Hill Road. It's on the right, and Rose Apple Acres is on the left.

Most people think of sleigh rides as an evening activity. Yet watching the morning sun glisten on the blue-white snow can be equally romantic. At Rose Apple Acres, the Mead's son Courtney and his Belgian draft horse will squire you about the farm's 52 acres of woods and meadow. The ride includes great views of the Sutton and Jay mountain ranges. And you'll feel like royalty high atop the wooden sleigh, swaddled in an elk-hide blanket. After your ride, enjoy some hot cider and cookies in the Mead's country kitchen. Hours: Rides can be arranged any time, just call ahead. Admission: $20 per couple for a 45-minute ride.

Visit Downtown Montgomery.

In transit: From Rose Apple Acres, follow Route 105 west, to Route 101 south, to Route 242 to Route 118. Route 118 goes right through Montgomery, and is known there as Main Street.

With a population of about 700, it seems hard to imagine that Montgomery could be considered one of the Northeast Kingdom's commercial centers. And while it doesn't have much industry or business per se, it houses some of the region's best inns, B&Bs, and restaurants. People are also attracted to Montgomery because it's home to seven covered bridges–the most of any town in the nation! The bridges were built during Montgomery's heyday as one of the region's biggest lumber centers. During the mid 1800s, it supplied forest products to factories all around New England. While that industry may have all but died, the bridges are still in use today, supporting modern cars, trucks, and tractors.

Another remnant of Montgomery's forestry past is The Schoolhouse Inc. Located on the Montgomery village green, this is a small but thriving business that makes handcrafted wooden toys that are sold throughout the United States.

You won't find it necessary to spend a whole day in Montgomery, or even a whole afternoon for that matter. But it is pleasant to drive through one of the bridges, pick up a wooden toy, and perhaps visit a few of its shops, and its old-fashioned general store.

Following is a suggested Montgomery itinerary:

Drive through Fuller Bridge. In transit: When you're traveling on Route 118 from Rose Apple Acres, you'll come right into Montgomery. Turn right at the Black Lantern Inn, turn left on South Richford Road. From that road, you can go right through the Fuller Bridge. On your right, just before the bridge, you'll pass The Schoolhouse offices and factory.

Visit Kominsky's Bloomers, Main Street, Montgomery Center, 802/326-4505. This two-floor shop is chockablock with Victorian linens, country afghans, Vermont specialty products, and a variety of whimsical knickknacks. While the store might be a bit too frilly for some, Kominsky's does carry Schoolhouse wooden toys.

Visit Terry's Fine Woolens and Antiques, Main Street, Montgomery Center, 802/326-4118. If you're in the market for a big woolly sweater (is there anything as cozy?), Terry's is a good place to stop. It carries a large selection of handmade Icelandic sweaters, as well as hats, gloves, and alpaca shawls from Bolivia. The woolen goods are displayed around some interesting antiques, which are also for sale.

Visit Kilgore's General Store, Main Street, Montgomery Center, 802/326-4681. As soon as you walk into Kilgore's, you'll feel as if you've been transported to Mayberry R.F.D. The old-fashioned general store, complete with a soda fountain, is an interesting mix of new age, gourmet, and no-nonsense Yankee products. Flannel shirts are sold alongside imported pasta and goat's milk moisturizer. It's a great spot for browsing. Upstairs are books and a few antiques; downstairs houses food, clothing, and accessories.

Lunch

Kilgore's General Store, $, Main Street, Montgomery Center, 802/326-4681. After you've finished your perusal, sidle up to the soda fountain for lunch. The aisles of fresh baked goods, wine, and imported cheeses should be clues that Kilgore's fountain offers a lot more than cherry Cokes and tuna salad. On the day we visited, lunch selections included Cuban black bean soup, gourmet pizza, and a hummos and vegetable sandwich. Despite the up-market meals, Kilgore's hasn't forsaken its roots entirely: Finish off your lunch with a dish of pistachio ice cream and some hot cocoa, and you'll forget which decade you're living in.

SUNDAY AFTERNOON

Tobogganing at East of Eden, East Hill Road, Edens Mills, 800/639-7097 or 802/635-2700. In transit: From Montgomery Center, take Route 118 south, to 100 north to Eden Mills. You'll see the signs for East of Eden at Eden Mills.

Remember when nothing was more exciting than speeding down a snow-covered hill on a toboggan? You might think you're too big for that sort of fun now. But one of the most important aspects of romance is playfulness. At this winter fun park for adults, you can share that thrill with your partner on a groomed 1,200-foot run. The best part of it all is that you don't have to schlepp your toboggan, or yourself, back up the hill: East of Eden has a van to take you back to the top.

For speed freaks, there's also a steep, 400-foot toboggan run. East of Eden also has snowmobile trails and rentals, snowshoe and cross-country ski trails, and outdoor ice skating. Hours: 10:00 A.M. – 8:00 P.M. Admission: $8 a day for toboggans. Snowshoe and skate rentals are also $8 a day. Snowmobiles are $40 for one hour and $60 for two hours (this price includes free tobogganing).

Cut Down Your Own Christmas Tree at Lane's Tree Farm, off Route 100, Hyde Park 05655, 802/635-7702. In transit: Follow Route 100 south to route 100C. Signs for Lane's will be on your left. Simply follow the signs.

There's an indescribable pleasure in finding just the right Christmas tree.

Rather than trudging to a suburban lot to pick over sad-looking trees cut down weeks – or even months – ago, why not try cutting your own.

Lane's is a customer-friendly spot that provides saws, strings, and even candy canes. It's great fun to wade through the maze of stately spruces looking for "the one." And there's a do-it-yourself satisfaction in sawing your own tree.

One word of warning however: Don't expect to be traipsing through a wooded forest. The Lanes raise trees for a living, and as such they are grown in rows in a huge field.

An added bonus is a visit to the Lane's barn. Their animals include goats, sheep, and horses. Hours: 9:00 A.M. – 5:00 P.M. weekends only. Trees are $20. (Pre-cut trees are also available.)

Additional Activities

Breakfast at JR's Restaurant, Main Street, Montgomery, 802/326-4682. If you're staying at Zack's, you'll need to head out for your morning meal (unless you'd like to cook in). JR's is Montgomery's most popular watering hole for breakfast, lunch, dinner, and even drinks. Morning selections include most standard favorites – bacon, eggs, pancakes, hot cereal, and homemade muffins.

Go Cross-Country Skiing at Hazen's Notch, Route 58, Montgomery Center,

802/326-4708. This is considered one of the most scenic cross-country centers in Vermont. It offers spectacular views of Hazen's Notch, the Jay Range, and the Green Mountain's Cold Hollow Range. Hazen's Notch has 30 kilometers of groomed and track-set trails, along with 20 kilometers of back-country trails through both forests and open meadows. A great romantic opportunity for Nordic skiers: Hazen's Notch offers moonlight tours.

Visit the Bogner Factory Outlet, Main Street, Newport, 802/334-0135. Outlet shopping may not be the world's number one romantic activity, but for those who find it hard to resist a good bargain, this famous skiwear manufacturer has a great outlet just a half hour from Jay. Hours: 9:30 A.M. – 5:00 P.M. Monday through Saturday, 11:00 A.M. – 4:00 P.M. Sunday.

GETTING THERE

BY AIR: Burlington (VT) International Airport is about two hours from Jay Peak. Most major airlines fly into Burlington. US Air (800/468-7247) has flight and car rental packages from New York, Philadelphia, Chicago, and many other major metropolitan cities.

BY CAR: There are several ways to get to Jay Peak and Montgomery from Boston. This is the route we have found to be the least painful: I-93 north to St. Johnsbury. Then take Route 2 west to

Route 15, to Route 118. If you're staying at Rose Apple Acres Farm, and are planning to go directly there, it's easier to follow I-91 to Route 191/exit 27. Follow Route 191 to Route 105. If you're traveling from the New York/New Jersey area, take I-91 to St. Johnsbury and follow the same directions as above. Or you can take I-91 to I-89 to Route 100/exit 10. Continue along to Route 118. Or for the Rose Apple Acres Farm, continue to Route 101. Follow that north to Route 105.

BY TRAIN: Amtrak (800/USA-RAIL) offers train service to Newport, Vermont. Newport is about 45 minutes from the Jay area.

BY BUS: No direct bus service is available.

CAR RENTAL: Four car rental companies have offices at the Burlington Inter-national airport: Hertz (800/654-3131), Budget (800/787-8200), Avis (800/331-1212), and National (800/227-7368).

TAXI/LIMOUSINE SERVICE: In Newport, Kelly's Cab (802/334-6170), Northeast Limousine Service, (802/334-6601). For car rentals in Newort, call Hayes Ford (802/334-6587).

INFORMATION: Jay Peak Area Association, P.O. Box 93, Montgomery Center, VT 05471, The Association doesn't have a phone. You can write them for a brochure or call the Jay Peak Lodging Association (800/882-7460). If you'd like information on the ski area, call Jay Peak (800/451-4449). At the mountain, Jay has an information office where you can pick up brochures on various activities, restaurants, and points of interest. It's open during regular mountain hours.

Lenox and The Berkshires

*I*n the Gilded Age, any self-respecting millionaire had a summer "cottage" in Lenox. Andrew Carnegie, George Westinghouse, and Harley Proctor were just a few of the day's luminaries who were drawn to the region's peacefulness and beauty. And while the era's literati made less of an architectural splash, they too came to loll in the cool Berkshire breezes. Among them were Edith Wharton, Henry James, and Nathaniel Hawthorne.

It's this combination of affluence, art, and beauty that made Lenox the "Newport west" of the smart set. And in fact it is still this combination that makes the Berkshires a modern-day cultural mecca. The most famous events are the Tanglewood (summer home to the Boston Symphony Orchestra) concerts, and the Williamstown Theater Festival, which regularly brings Broadway stars to its stage.

Unfortunately, these activities – wonderful as they are – attract hordes of tourists during the summer and help turn the Berkshires into something of a circus. Fall is a far more serene time to visit. Although Tanglewood and Williamstown are closed for the season, most museums and tours are still operating, including The Norman Rockwell Museum, Elizabeth Wharton's home "The Mount," and Hancock Shaker Village. Moreover, sugar maples are in full regalia, a crisp bite is in the air, and fires are laid at country inns.

Fall in the Berkshires is also a great time for hiking. The region boasts some of the best trails in Massachusetts, from short rambles to strenuous treks that offer views of three states.

Hearty souls may want to enjoy baked beans by a campfire, but sophisticated palates can choose from among the Berkshires' many fine restaurants. A few places feature cuisine that rivals even Manhattan's best. (Wheatliegh in Lenox has earned raves from both the *New York Times* and *Food & Wine*.)

This combination of gourmet dining, outdoor activities, and cultural pursuits makes the Berkshires among New England's most well-rounded getaways. It's the ideal spot for couples who want it all.

Where To Stay

The Apple Tree Inn, ♡ ♡, $$-$$$$, 224 West St., Lenox, 01240, 413/ 637-1477. This inn is perhaps the most popular hotel in Lenox, if only for the fact that it's directly across the street from Tanglewood. However, Tanglewood only has a two-month season and fortunately The Apple Tree has much more than this proximity to recommend it. Set atop a high knoll dotted with craggy apple trees, it enjoys one the most panoramic locations in all the Berkshires. Views of the mountains and Stockbridge Bowl, an area lake, are magnificent from the circular dining room.

The main living room is large and elegant and has a decidedly Victorian feel, with a velvet couch, grand piano, antiques, Oriental rugs, and tulip wall lamps. The tavern is much more manly— with its exposed beams, oak-paneled walls, and stuffed water buffalo head placed prominently over the fireplace.

Guest rooms are decorated with antiques, brass and four-poster beds, and braided rugs. Room 2, a favorite, has a pine four-poster, fireplace, and private deck that overlooks the Berkshire hills. (Only a few of Apple Tree's rooms have fireplaces. So if you want one, be sure to ask.)

Although the Guest Lodge, a 20-room motel-like addition to the back of the inn, is pleasant, the 11 rooms in the main house are far more appealing.

Owners Aurora and Greg Smith are rose aficionados and grow more than 450 varieties, many of which bloom through the fall. Other amenities include an outdoor pool and clay tennis court. Complimentary continental breakfast is served daily.

RATES PER NIGHT: $80-$224 from September to October 21, $60-$200 in winter, $70-$210 in spring, and $100-$280 in summer.

ACCOMMODATIONS: 29 rooms and 2 suites. All but two rooms have private baths. Nine rooms and two suites are located in the main inn. An additional 20 rooms are in a motel-style wing.

AMENITIES: Full-service restaurant serving breakfast and dinner. Full service bar. Televisions in suites and guest lodge rooms. Clay tennis court. Swimming pool.

RESTRICTIONS: No children under 12. No pets.

Blantyre, ♡ ♡ ♡ ♡, $$$$, Route 20, Lenox 01240, 413/637-3556 or 413/ 298-3806. Blantyre is one of the most splendid hotels you're likely to visit—either here or in Europe. That said, Blantyre isn't for everyone; rooms can cost as much as $500 a night. (If you decide to go, splurge for a high-end room. When sitting in the lap of luxury, you may as well get really comfortable!)

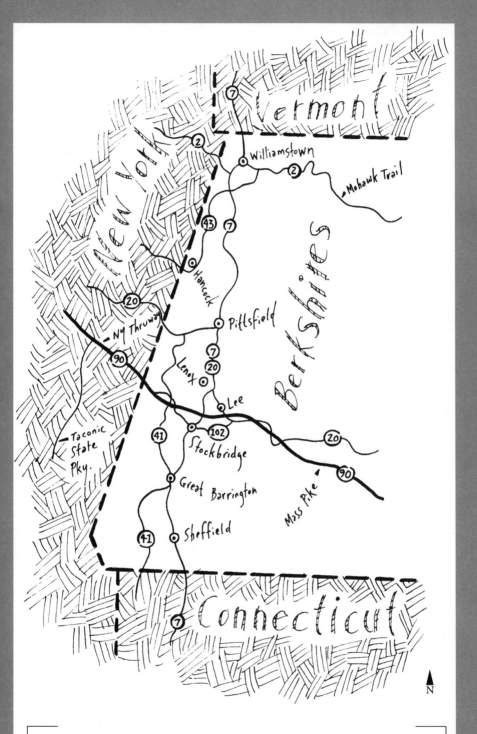

LENOX & THE BERKSHIRES

This turn-of-the-century Tudor-style mansion was once the summer home of turpentine magnate Robert Patterson. He built Blantyre for his wife, and modeled it after her family's estate in Lanarkshire, Scotland. As a premier inn of the Relais &Chateaux group, Blantyre has retained every inch of its elegance. In fact, Blantyre resembles a castle you'd imagine while reading a Gothic romance novel. The entrance room is graced with beamed ceilings, leaded windows, Oriental rugs, antique furniture, and a tremendous fireplace bound by marble and an intricately carved mantle. A sweeping oak staircase leads to the eight guest quarters in the main house.

You'll be welcomed to your room with fresh flowers, fruit and cheese trays, and a bottle of wine. The Patterson Suite is the grandest of Blantyre's offerings, but is a bit too expansive to be wildly romantic. Opt instead for the Cranwell or Laurel Suites. Each has a four-poster bed, fireplace, sitting area, dressing room, and bath. Furnishings and upholstery are exquisite – floral but regal. If these rooms aren't available, ask for any room in the main house with a fireplace; you won't be disappointed.

Although Blantyre's accommodations are all outstanding, the carriage house and cottage rooms are far less impressive. To this traveler's mind, the price can only be justified if you're staying in the main house.

Blantyre serves three meals a day. The food is as impressive as the surroundings. Room fees include a continental breakfast with fresh fruit, juice, breads, coffee, tea, and hot chocolate. Amenities include a championship bent-grass croquet lawn, tennis courts, swimming pool, hot tub, and sauna.

RATES PER NIGHT: $160-$550. Closed November-May.

ACCOMMODATIONS: 23 rooms and suites with private baths. Four suites and four rooms are located in the main building. Seven rooms and five suites are located in the Carriage House. Three additional cottages are scattered throughout the property.

AMENITIES: Television and telephone in rooms. Air conditioning. Some rooms have fireplaces, decks, and refrigerators. Full-service restaurant serving breakfast, lunch, and dinner. Full-service bar. Massage service with 24-hour notice. Four Har-Tru tennis courts (whites required), outdoor pool, sauna, and two tournament croquet lawns.

RESTRICTIONS: No pets.

Brook Farm Inn, ♡, $$-$$$, 15 Hawthorne St., Lenox 02140, 413/637-3013. What makes Brook Farm so romantic is the passion of its owners Anne and Joe Miller. Fervent poetry and literature lovers, the Millers keep more than 800 volumes. Several hundred crowd the floor to ceiling book shelves in the living room, and the rest are scattered throughout the 12 guest rooms. (Guests are even encouraged to bring along their own works for tea time readings.)

Appropriately, Brook Farm, which was named after a 19th century writers colony, has a quirky charm. The building is a grand Victorian painted a pumpkin orange with deep green shutters. As you open the door, strains of light opera waft to greet you. A fire blazes in the living room and a poem for the day is set out on a corner pedestal. A jigsaw puzzle is left half finished on an antique table. Guest rooms are also decorated with antiques, some of which were left in the house's basement by previous owners.

Be sure to ask for room 2; it has a canopy bed, fireplace, sitting area, and private bath. Should that be filled, room 4, with its beautiful chenille spread, runs a close second. Five of Brook Farm's rooms have fireplaces, and those are typically the most well appointed.

Full breakfasts are served in the dining room. Menus range from pancakes to bacon and eggs, and include juice, coffee, and muffins. Other amenities include a heated swimming pool and 1 1/4 pastoral acres.

RATES PER NIGHT: $60-$105 September and November through June, $70-$130 October, $90-$165 in summer.

ACCOMMODATIONS: 12 rooms with baths.

AMENITIES: Air conditioning (3rd floor). Outdoor pool.

RESTRICTIONS: No pets.

The Gables, ♡ ♡ ♡, $$-$$$$, 103 Walker St., Lenox 02140, 413/637-3416. Right in the middle of Lenox's mansion row, The Gables looks like just another fine country inn. However, both its history and decor, so lovingly cared for by innkeepers Frank and Mary Newton, set it apart. The Gables, originally known as Pine Acre, was once the home of Mrs. William C. Wharton, mother of Edward who was married to famed novelist Edith Wharton. In fact, Edith lived here for two years while her own cottage, "The Mount," was under construction.

If you're a Wharton fan, you'll take great pleasure in sleeping in her bedroom, which the Newtons have splendidly refurbished with a curtained four-poster bed, Oriental rug, and fireplace. In fact, Frank is more than happy to show you small details in the house for which Wharton was responsible: among them is a carved-cherub, Italianate fireplace mantle in the sitting room.

The Gables interior has an authentic Victorian elegance—lots of wood, antiques, deep red wallpaper, and fine art. The Newtons have even refurbished the eight-sided library where Wharton wrote many of her short stories. The house is in wonderful condition, and is extraordinarily clean.

Twelve of The Gables' 19 rooms have fireplaces. If you enjoy masculine elegance, consider the Teddy Wharton suite. The queen-size bed is encased in a seven-foot walnut frame with the face of William Shakespeare carved in the headboard. Other accouterments include a green marble fireplace, leather sofa, a tastefully encased television, VCR, and refrigerator, and baronial bath. For those who prefer a lighter look, ask for Wharton's room or the Edith Wharton suite.

Continental breakfast is served daily. Other amenities include an enclosed pool, tennis court, and garden.

RATES PER NIGHT: $80-$195 late May through October 31, $60-$150 November 1 through late May.

ACCOMMODATIONS: 18 rooms and suites with private baths.

AMENITIES: Air conditioning. Some rooms have fireplaces. One suite has television and VCR. Heated swimming pool. Tennis court.

RESTRICTIONS: No children under 12. No pets.

Haus Andreas, ♡ ♡, $$$-$$$$, Stockbridge Road, Lee, MA 02138, 413/243-3298. Although Haus Andreas may seem a little off the beaten path, it is less than two miles from Stockbridge center, and just a 10-minute car ride to downtown Lenox. The house was built by a Revolutionary War soldier, but its real claim to fame is that it was home to the Dutch royal family during World War II.

Haus Andreas has an elegant, but homey feel. The large living room houses a baby grand piano, well-stocked library, stereo, and fireplace. Other common areas include a television room, kitchen pantry stocked with coffee, tea, and cocoa, and a refurbished basement with an exercise area.

Guest rooms are pleasantly decorated with antiques and floral upholstery. Room 1 is Haus Andreas' prize with a lace canopy bed, fireplace, sitting area, and outstanding view. If a fireplace isn't a must, room 8 has dainty pink floral wallpaper, and colored lights that give off a dreamy glow.

Although Haus Andreas serves only breakfast, guests look forward to it with anticipation. Owner Gerhard Schmid, a world-renowned chef, bakes all the morning treats himself. Both he and his wife, Lilliane, are extraordinarily friendly and help give Haus Andreas its open-arms appeal.

RATES PER NIGHT: $105-$225, $50-$160 November through May.

ACCOMMODATIONS: 6 rooms and 2 suites with private baths. (At this writing the Haus Andreas was slated for a major facelift – new drapes, rugs, and wallpaper and should be even more pleasant that it was on our visit.)

AMENITIES: Three rooms have fireplaces. Common room with television. Guest pantry. Heated swimming pool. Tennis court. Bicycles for guest use.

RESTRICTIONS: No children under 10. No pets.

FRIDAY EVENING
Dinner

Café Lucia, ♥ ♥, $$-$$$, 90 Church St., Lenox 413/637-2640. In transit: Church Street is the main commercial thoroughfare in Lenox. It's accessible both from Main Street and from Walker Street. From Haus Andreas, follow Stockbridge Road to Route 7A/Main Street in Lenox. Turn right onto Church Street. From the Apple Tree, follow West Street east to Lenox center. West intersects with both Walker and Main streets, which in turn lead to Church. From the Brook Farm, follow Hawthorne Street east to either Walker or Main Street. You can walk from the Gables. Walk west on Walker Street and turn right on Church. And from Blantyre, follow Route 20 north to Walker Street. Turn left on Walker, then right onto Church.

This spot is a favorite with locals because it offers great Italian cuisine minus the pomp and circumstance around which so many fine-dining establishments are cloaked. Decor is unabashedly simple – tan walls, white tablecloths, wood chairs. Small oil lamps on each table provide an intimate glow. The menu is straightforward, with lots of simple pasta dishes–just as you would find in Italy. The angel hair with squid and mussels in a spicy tomato sauce is a must for shellfish lovers. Breads are warm and crusty, salad greens are fresh and dressed lightly in vinaigrette. For "Italiaphiles," Lucia offers real Tuscan Chianti and grappa, a popular and potent Italian liquor made from grape skins. Hours: 5:30 P.M. – 8:30 P.M. weekdays, 5:30 P.M. – 9:30 P.M. weekends.

Church Street Café, ♥, $$-$$$, 69 Church St., Lenox 413/637-2745. In transit: Follow directions to Café Lucia, Church Street is diagonally across the street.

Another spot with a laid-back atmosphere and exceptional food. Church Street prides itself on its eclectic menu, which includes buckwheat fettuccine, braised duck with a lentil confit, and Portuguese stew featuring chorizo, little necks, and haddock. The café has a beachy feel dressed in gray walls with small pastel prints, and wooden tables covered with white cloths.

If you want a pre-dinner cocktail, Church Street has a pleasant, quiet bar. Please note that Church Street is immensely popular and it might be wise to call for reservations. Hours: 5:30 P.M. – 8:30 P.M. weekdays, 5:30 P.M. – 9:30 P.M. weekends. (Also open for lunch.)

The Candlelight Inn, ♡ ♡, $$$, 53 Walker St., Lenox 413/637-1555. In transit: See directions for Café Lucia on Friday night. The Candlelight is just around the corner on Walker Street.

Although the Candlelight is indeed an inn, it is far better known for its restaurant, which serves continental cuisine in a quintessential country inn atmosphere. The inn has four intimate dining rooms, some with fireplaces, and all with lace curtains, white tablecloths, pale wallpaper, and a glowing candle on each table.

Given the traditional decor, the menu is surprisingly adventurous. Bouillabaisse, and pork tenderloin with apples and ginger cream are just a couple of its specialities. After dinner, repair to the cozy bar for a cognac. Hours: 6:00 P.M. – 8:30 P.M. Sunday through Thursday, 6:00 P.M. – 9:30 P.M. Friday and Saturday.

SATURDAY MORNING

Visit Hancock Shaker Village

Routes 20 and 41, Pittsfield, MA 01202, 413/443-0188. (Note that the village is on the Hancock-Pittsfield line.) In transit: Hancock Shaker Village is located at the junction of Routes 20 and 41. From the Appletree Inn and Brook Farm Inn, head back to the center of Lenox to pick up Route 7/20 north. The village is about 25 minutes away and is clearly visible on the left. From Blantyre, simply head north toward Hancock. And from Haus Andreas, travel east on Stockbridge Road to Route 20 north.

As you approach, Hancock Shaker Village – with its immense round stone barn, austere clapboard buildings, and neatly shorn grass – seems almost a mirage. Even today an aura of tranquility permeates the 1,200 acres and 20 odd buildings that remain of this Shaker community.

For those foggy on the subject, the Shakers are an American religious sect who have all but become extinct (Shakers are celibate) – only a handful of living Shakers remain in a community in Sabbath Day Lake, Maine. They acquired their name because they would dance about and "shake" as part of their prayers. And although several Shaker communities have been preserved along the East Coast, Hancock is the largest and most fully developed.

During its active years between 1790 and 1960, it was known as "The City of Peace," in the belief that it would become heaven on earth. In its peak, about 1830, more than 300 men and women lived quietly together and made their living farming, selling seeds and herbs, manufacturing medicines, and producing crafts. Their motto was "hands to work, hearts to God." Today, the Shakers are remembered best for their stunningly simple furniture.

Guides provide tours of the grounds, which include large herb gardens, and through the houses, where you can watch craftspeople weave baskets and make boxes and brooms in the same manner as the Shakers once did. Most rooms are furnished with genuine Shaker artifacts.

The most impressive part of the tour is the round barn, designed to allow one person to care for and feed 60 cows in just a morning's time.

Plan to stay at the village for several hours. A Shaker store on site sells a good array of furniture and craft reproductions. Hours: 9:30 A.M.- 5:00 P.M. May through October, 10:00 A.M. – 3:00 P.M. November and April.

Lunch

Hancock Shaker Village, $-$$, Routes 20 and 41, Pittsfield, 413/443-0188. The Village's restaurant isn't particularly fancy. But it is quietly pleasant, serves good, simple food, and overlooks the bucolic Shaker grounds. Fare includes primarily hearty soups and sandwiches.

Picnic from Crosby's, $-$$, 62 Church St., Lenox, 413/637-3396. In transit: You'll obviously have to stop at Crosby's before you head out to

Hancock Shaker Village. See directions for Café Lucia on Friday evening.

If it's a sunny day, Hancock Shaker Village's outdoor tables are the perfect spot for a gourmet picnic. And Crosby's, the most well-known caterer in Lenox, is the place to get it. Use your imagination, because Crosby's has it all – from pâtés to exotic desserts. You can call in, but it's best to make a trip and check out the delicacies first-hand. Be sure to inquire about their special picnic menus which include an entree, Brie and crackers, fruit, and brownies or cookies – even cutlery.

SATURDAY AFTERNOON

Hiking Shaker Mountain.

The Berkshires are known as a hikers' paradise. And while there's a myriad of hikes and walks to choose from, including about 90 miles of the Appalachian Trail, Shaker Mountain is particularly interesting because of its history. On the course of the 6.5-mile, 3-hour hike, you'll visit the hilltop holy sites of the Hancock and and New Lebanon (NY) Shakers as well as remnants of past villages.

The trail, maintained by a local Boy Scout troop, begins at the 1793 meeting house, which is on the north side of Route 20. It is clearly marked with a series of green triangles. But before you start your trek, alert the visitor's center. You'll be required to pay a $5 fee. The center can provide you with literature to help identify points of interest.

Among the artifacts you'll see are the remains of a 19th century dwelling, a Shaker dam, built about 1800, and old industrial sites. The trail continues to the top of Mt. Sinai, the Hancock Shaker's holy ground, to which no non believers were admitted. It then descends along an old Shaker cart path cut through a hemlock grove. From here you can go back to the village or continue the hike, which takes you to the holy ground of the New Lebanon (NY) Shaker community.

If you have an interest in stone walls, make the complete loop. Near the second holy site you will find a magnificently constructed wall that is about 18 feet long, 3 feet wide at the base, and tapered at the top. This sacred wall took the Shakers 350 man-days of labor to build.

Saturday Evening
Dinner

Gateways, ♡ ♡, $$$-$$$$, 71 Walker St., Lenox 413/637-2532. In transit: Follow directions to Café Lucia on Friday night. Gateways is just around the corner on Walker Street, which runs perpendicular to Church. Renowned for well more than a decade, Gateways consistently receives a Mobil four-star rating and consequently maintains a loyal clientele. (Only eight restaurants in New England have such a rating.) And indeed the restaurant does deserve its fine reputation.

Everything about the place – from the damask tablecloths and gilt-framed mirrors to the high-protein menu – bespeaks classic continental. No nouvelle cuisine here: Longtime Gateways devotees revel in the fact that the menu doesn't change. Filet Mignon, filet of Dover sole menuire, and shrimp Caroline (stuffed with crabmeat, breadcrumbs, and cognac) are favorites.

Desserts too are pleasingly familiar: Black Forest torte, Viennese apple strudel, grasshopper pie. Gateways also has a reputation as a friendly restaurant, unfortunately a commodity that is in short supply at many haute cuisine establishments. Hours: 5:30 P.M. – 9:00 P.M.

Blantyre, ♡ ♡ ♡ ♡, $$$$, Route 20, Lenox, 413/637-3556. In transit: From the Haus Andreas, follow Stockbridge road north to Route 7 east to Route 20 south. From Lenox center, follow Walker Street east to Route 20. Turn right at Route 20 to Blantyre.

Even if you don't decide to stay in this turn-of-the-century manor, you really should have dinner here. The atmosphere alone is worth the price of admission, which is $65 fixed price per person. Magnificent dark paneled walls, huge Oriental rugs, oil portraits, and silver candelabras are the decor's hallmarks.

The food matches the rich surroundings. Dinner is a five course affair; the menu is adventurous but not radical.

Appetizers include macadamia crusted scallops with mango chutney and white truffle pasta with grilled sweetbreads and Parmesan. Entrees range from Black Angus tenderloin to lobster and vegetable couscous with basil and orange scented olive oil. After dinner, be sure to retire to the music room and enjoy a fireside brandy. Hours: 6:00 P.M. – 9:00 P.M.

Wheatliegh, ♡ ♡ ♡ ♡, $$$$, Hawthorne Road, Lenox, 413/637-0610. In transit: From Lenox center, follow Route 7A south to Stockbridge Road. Turn right on Hawthorne Street to Hawthorne Road. From Haus Andreas, follow Stockgridge Road north to Lenox, and turn left on Hawthorne Street, which leads to Hawthorne Road.

This restaurant is best visited by real gourmets, for only a few can truly appreciate its intense formality and attention to detail (the china is coordinated with the food). The restaurant is housed in a turn-of-the-century mansion built by a Count to resemble a 16th century Italian palazzo. Although today Wheatliegh is an exclusive inn, it is most famous for its restaurant, which has received international acclaim. Its wine cellar too is considered among the world's best. The fixed price menu, which is $65 per person, is extraordinarily creative. Items might include carpaccio of Texas antelope with black truffle vinaigrette, Ossettra caviar with crème fraîche and buckwheat blinis, and loin of veal with a ravioli of sweetbreads and wild mushrooms. People either love it

or hate it – but there's no denying the food is outstanding. Hours: 6:00 P.M. – 9:00 P.M. Tuesday through Friday, 6:00 P.M. – 9:30 P.M. Saturday and Sunday.

SUNDAY MORNING

Note: Try to start your day early. If you make it to the Clark Art Institute by 10:00 A.M., you should have plenty of time for all the activities suggested.

Visit Sterling and Francine Clark Art Institute, 225 South St., Williamstown, 413/458-9545. In transit: Williamstown is about 45 minutes from Lenox. Travel on Route 7 north all the way into Williamstown. At the Williamstown Rotary, turn right onto South Street. You'll see a sign for the Institute, which is a few blocks down on the right.

For art lovers, particularly those fond of Impressionism, the Clark Art Institute is a must visit. Not only does it have an extraordinary collection of works by such masters as Renoir, Manet, Pissaro, as well as American artists Homer, Sargent, Cassat, and Remington, it is a wonderfully peaceful place to view art. Its solitude is in stark contrast to many urban museums, which are often hot, stuffy, and teaming with people invariably hunched around the paintings you want to examine.

All works are from the private collection of Sterling and Francine Clark; Sterling was the heir to the Singer sewing machine fortune. The museum, which has been open since 1955, has an intensely personal feel. Paintings are hung in relatively small rooms, just as they might have been when the Clarks owned them. Antique furniture and potted plants are scattered throughout.

Plan to spend about two hours here. Purchase headsets for your tour. Although the discussion is not thorough, it does provide a nice overview of the collection. Hours: 10:00 A.M. – 5:00 P.M. Tuesday through Sunday. Admission is free.

Visit Edith Wharton's Home, The Mount, Plunkett Street, Lenox, 413/637-1899. In transit: Take Route 7 south, continue on Route 7, even after it becomes 7/20. Continue pass the first intersection for 7A. At the southern intersection of Routes 7 and 7A, you'll see a sign for Plunkett Street and The Mount. Both signs are small; your primary marker should be that southern intersection with 7A.

Edith Wharton, the first woman to win a Pulitzer Prize, and who so aptly depicted turn-of-the-century New York society, actually preferred the hills of Lenox to the streets of Manhattan. It is here, at her summer home, that she did much of her writing, including the classic *House of Mirth.* Wharton built the house based on design and architectural precepts she advocated in her books *The Decoration of Houses,* and *Italian Villas and Their Gardens.* The

Mount–full of terrazzo and terra cotta–is a stark contrast to the heavily upholstered Victorian surroundings to which she was accustomed.

Tours last about an hour and include discussions on many aspects of Wharton's life and writing. Hours: 10:00 A.M. – 5:00 P.M. Thursday through Sunday; the last tour starts at 4:00 P.M. Admission $4, $3.50 for seniors. Closed for the season at the end of October.

Lunch

The Lion's Den, $$, at the Red Lion Inn, Main Street, Stockbridge, 413/298-5545. In transit: Follow Route 7 south to Stockbridge. It takes you directly into the center of town and right by the Red Lion Inn. The ride is about 10 minutes. Park your car anywhere downtown. It's free.

The Lion's Den isn't wildly romantic, nor is the food spectacular. But a trip to the Berkshires wouldn't be complete without visiting the Red Lion Inn, one of the grand dames of America's country inns. The white clapboard building–with its tremendous front porch lined with rocking-chairs–looks like a postcard picture. If the weather is fair, relax there and take in the panorama of downtown Stockbridge–a place that looks as if it should have been painted by Norman Rockwell, and indeed was.

The Lion's Den is the downstairs pub, complete with requisite dark wood paneling. Fare is standard, but tasty, and includes burgers, salads, soups, and sandwiches. (The inn also serves a more formal lunch in the upstairs dining room.)

SUNDAY AFTERNOON

Visit the Norman Rockwell Museum, Route 183, Stockbridge, 413/298-4100. In transit, From the Red Lion, follow Route 102 west to Route 183. There'll be a blinking light at the intersection. Turn left onto Route 183. The museum is 6/10ths of a mile on the left.

If you're not a Rockwell fan when you walk into this museum, you will be by the time you leave. The Saturday Evening Post covers, for which Rockwell was famous, in no way reflect this illustrator's real talent. Viewing his original oils is the only way to understand Rockwell's genius at detail and nuance.

The museum houses hundreds of originals, and in fact has the largest collection of Rockwell art in the world. Rockwell lived in Stockbridge for years, and many or its residents and streets appear in his work.

There's also has a room devoted to Rockwell's own art collection, which provides insight into his work. Admission: $8. Hours 10:00 A.M.- 5:00 P.M. daily through October; 10:00 A.M. – 5:00 P.M. weekends, and 11:00 A.M. – 4:00 P.M. weekdays November through April.

Stroll Stockbridge Center. Stockbridge is not a shoppers' paradise, but its Main Street is often described as the prettiest in America. It appears to be a living replica of Bedford Falls in *It's A Wonderful Life*. A few of the Main Street shops of note are:

Accents, 413/298-3882. This shop is reminiscent of ice cream parlors past. (The location was, in fact, once an ice cream parlor.) Emphasis is on gifts, art, and antiques. Merchandise ranges from plates to fireplace mantels.

Williams & Son Country Store, 413/298-3016. Hard as it might be to believe, this bona fide country store has been in continuous operation since 1795. And while it's unquestionably quaint, the products are 1990s upscale: Fortnum & Mason preserves, Jacksons of Picadilly teas, French roast coffee, and sourdough bread.

Seven Arts, 413/298-5101. Downstairs is stocked with a funky assortment of jewelry and gifts, such as you might find in Cambridge–lots of tribal and Mexican chotchkes. Upstairs, look for natural fiber clothing and artifacts.

Note: Shopping Stockbridge shouldn't take you too long. However, it is a pleasant diversion from an art-heavy day. If time permits, and you have the stamina, make a trip to Chesterwood, once the summer home of sculptor Daniel Chester French.

Tour of Chesterwood, off Route 183, 413/298-3579. In transit: From Stockbridge, take Route 102 west approximately two miles to the junction of Route 183. Turn left onto Route 183, travel one mile to a fork in the road. Turn right onto a blacktop road, travel 75 yards and turn left. Continue ½ mile to Chesterwood, which is on the right side of the road.

Although Daniel Chester French may not be known in every American household, his sculptures are world famous. He is the creator of the Seated (Abraham) Lincoln statue at the Lincoln Memorial in Washington D.C. and the Minuteman statue in Concord.

His summer home and studio, now known as Chesterwood, was donated to the National Trust for Historic Preservation in 1969. It houses nearly 500 pieces of sculpture, including two casts of the Seated Lincoln. The tour includes a gallery, French's stately home, and his studio, which is by far the most interesting part. The most unusual features of his studio are its 22-foot double doors and railroad tracks; this was French's system for taking his work outside to view in daylight. With the double doors open, assistants would push a flat car, holding the statue in-progress, down the tracks and outside.

Beyond the sculpture, Chesterwood is wonderfully peaceful, with tranquil Italianate gardens and a nature walk – a perfect spot to enjoy the last vestiges of a romantic holiday. Hours: 10:00 A.M. – 5:00 P.M. through October 31. Admission $4.

Additional Activities

Visit Arrowhead, the former home of Herman Melville, 780 Holmes Rd., Pittsfield, 413/442-1793. The author purchased this farmhouse in 1850 and moved his family to Pittsfield from New York. It is here he completed his most famous novel, Moby Dick. Admission $3.50, $3 for seniors. Hours 10:00 A.M. – 4:30 P.M. Monday through Saturday, 11:00 A.M. – 4:30 P.M. Sunday. Closed Tuesday and Wednesday from November 1 through Memorial Day.

Dinner at La Tomate, 293 Main St., Great Barrington, 413/528-3003. This bistro exudes low-key charm. Soft lights, hardwood floors, and deep red walls give this storefront restaurant a warm glow. The French menu includes a caramelized onion tart, bouillabaisse, and crème caramel. The perfect spot if you're in the mood for gourmet comfort food. Hours: 5:00 P.M. – 9:00 P.M. weekdays, 5:00 P.M. – 11:00 P.M. weekends.

Hiking Bash Bish Falls. This 7-mile hike is considered among the most spectacular in the Berkshires. The trail is rigorous, but views of the Catskills, Albany, and the Bash Bish Brook, which plunges 200-feet at the falls, are rewarding. If you're seriously considering this hike, think about taking your bikes. You can leave them in the parking lot at the top of the falls, so you can ride back to your car at Mt. Washington State Forest Headquarters instead of having to walk along the road. The headquarters is located on Mt. Washington Road, in Mt. Washington. For more information on hiking Bash Bish Falls, call the Park Supervisor at Mt. Washington State Forest, 413/528-0330.

Shopping in Lenox. Don't look for stellar shopping in The Berkshires. Lenox, however, does have some interesting craft galleries that are worth perusing. They include: Hoadley Gallery, 17 Church St.; Arkos, 66 Church St.; The Hand of Man, in the The Curtis Shops, Walker Street.

GETTING THERE

BY AIR: Lenox is only about 40 miles from the Albany, New York, airport and 70 miles from Bradley Field in Windsor Locks, Connecticut. American Airlines (800/433-7300) has direct flights from Kennedy to both Albany and Windsor Locks. However, the Berkshires is an easy drive, accessible from the Massachusetts Turnpike (I-90), which intersects with several major routes including I-91, I-87 and the Taconic Parkway.

BY CAR: From the east, take the Massachusetts Turnpike to exit 2. If you plan to stay in Stockbridge or Lee, take exit 1. From the New York City area, take the Taconic State Parkway to Route 23 east, to Route 7 north, to Lenox (south to Stockbridge or Lee), or take the New York Thruway to I-90 east to Route 7.

BY TRAIN: Amtrak (800/USA-RAIL) has service to Pittsfield, the commercial hub of the Berkshires, via Boston.

BY BUS: Bonanza (413/442-4451) has service to Pittsfield from Boston, Providence, Springfield, and New York. Greyhound (617/423-5810) has service from Boston and Albany to Pittsfield. Peter Pan (800/332-0364) has service to Pittsfield from New York, Albany, Worcester, Springfield, and other cities. And the Arrow Line (413/442-4451) has service from Albany, Hartford, and New Haven.

CAR RENTAL: Pete's Leasing Rentals, 689 East St., Pittsfield (413/445-5797), Johnson Ford Lincoln Mercury, 694 East St., Pittsfield (413/445-5795). Most major car rental companies have offices at both the Albany and Windsor Locks airports.

TAXI/LIMOUSINE SERVICE: Park Taxi in Lee (413/243-0020), Stockbridge Livery/Taxi in Stockbridge (413/298-4848), and Toby's Limousine in Lenox (413/637-0503).

INFORMATION: Stockbridge Chamber of Commerce, Stockbridge MA, 01262, 413/298-5200. Hours: 8:30 A.M. – 4:30 P.M. Monday through Friday. The Bershires Visitors' Bureau, Berkshire Common Plaza, Pittsfield, MA 01201, 413/443-9186 or 800/237-5747. This office has an excellent booklet on the region that you should send for. The Lenox Chamber of Commerce, Lenox Academy Building, 75 Main St., Lenox, MA 01240, 413/637-3646. Hours: 9:30 A.M. – 4:30 P.M. Tuesday through Saturday during fall and winter.

Portsmouth, New Hampshire

or those who enjoy culture without crowds, Portsmouth, New Hampshire, offers the perfect combination of city and country living. With a population of 26,000, Portsmouth is hardly a bustling metropolis, but more a comfortable town. Yet tucked within its center is a nationally renowned history museum, theater company, athaneum, and some of New England's best restaurants.

If these reasons alone aren't enough to visit Portsmouth, it also happens to have a lively, working seaport. Tug boats and fishing trawlers ply its waters, providing a colorful, yet very real, backdrop. And unlike many port cities where the docks are located in a remote part of town, Portsmouth's docks are in its very heart.

In fact, that's one of Portsmouth's best aspects – everything is centrally located. Its downtown – full of refurbished brick factory buildings and elegant sea captains' homes – is comprised of about a half dozen main streets. You can walk from one end to the other in 10 minutes. It's the perfect spot for couples who pre-fer to do their sightseeing on foot, and who consider a moonlit stroll an essential factor in the romance equation.

Founded in 1630 by a band of English settlers who stopped on its banks because of the profusion of wild strawberries, Portsmouth grew to be one of the nation's most thriving seaports by the mid eighteenth century. As a result, wealth poured into the city. That prosperity is evident in the many stately homes that still stand. And while Portsmouth doesn't exactly look as if it's been stored in moth balls (albeit you can still rent a horse and carriage in the center of town), it has many fine examples of colonial architecture that lend a distinctive, old-world atmosphere.

Portsmouth is no longer the commercial hub it was in its ship-building heyday. But in the 1950s local residents began efforts to preserve the city's illustrious past through restoration of historic buildings and neighborhoods. Indeed, until Strawbery Banke Inc., the nonprofit group that created a 10-acre museum, was formed, Portsmouth was just another tired city whose past glory had long since faded. Because of the group's efforts, and the renewed interest their enthusiasm sparked in other citizens, Portsmouth is today a shining example of a city that hasn't rested on its laurels, but has used its past success to create a thriving future.

Where To Stay

The Gundalow Inn, ♥ ♥-♥ ♥ ♥, $$, 6 Water St., Kittery, ME 03904, 207/439-4040. Yes, the Gundalow is in Maine. However, it's just a half mile from downtown Portsmouth and, in fact, is considered that city's best B&B. It's not that the Gundalow is particularly grand, or impeccably furnished. It's just that innkeepers Cevia and George Rosol have made the place so homey and comfortable.

The brick Victorian sits on a quiet residential street just across from Portsmouth Harbor. Although the Rosols have infused the inn with period style, it's not too heavy on the lace or velvet. The common room, a large parlor with pale pink walls and a pastel Oriental rug, is a kind of place where one could spend the afternoon; it's got a piano, shelves full of books, puzzles, and an antique table set with a tray of glasses and sherry.

All six guest rooms have private baths and are, for the most part, almost equally pleasant. The most popular room is the Royal George. Located on the third floor, it's carved out of an old attic and has sloping ceilings and a skylight. Decorated with cheery, yellow floral wallpaper and wicker furniture, it also boasts a queen-size bed and a large bath outfitted with reproduction antique fixtures.

If you don't mind being on the first floor, the Ben Butler room is lovely. It has a slightly more elegant feel, and features built-in book cases with glass doors, French-style paisley wallpaper, and a marble-top antique table. A queen-size bed is covered with a chenille spread and an antique quilt.

A full breakfast is served in the dining room, which has beamed ceilings and a raised-hearth fireplace. (In summer, guests can sit on the backyard patio.) Unlike many B&Bs, which serve meals at one long table, guests at the Gundalow dine privately. For those who really want to be alone, the Rosols will even set a separate table in the parlor. Cevia truly enjoys cooking (just get a look at her kitchen) and shows off at breakfast. Her specialties include blueberry lemon soup, cheddar herb scones, and apple puff pancakes.

Although the Rosols don't formally serve tea, guests will usually find hot cider or cocoa when they return to the Gundalow in the afternoon.

Rates per night: $75-$95.

Accommodations: 6 rooms with private baths.

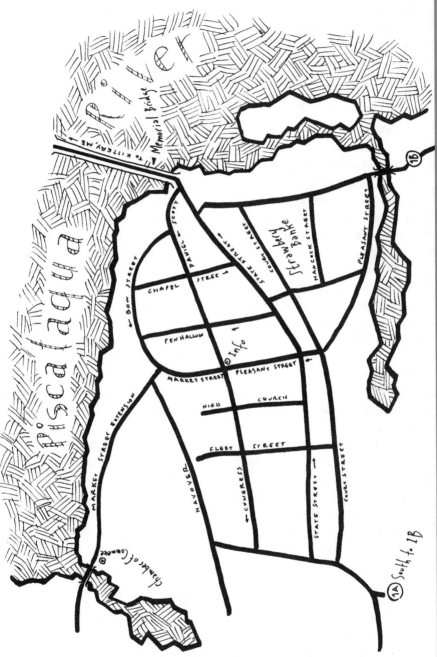

PORTSMOUTH

AMENITIES: Phone jacks are located in each room, and phones are available on request. Ceiling fans.

RESTRICTIONS: No smoking. No pets. No children under 16.

The Sise Inn, ♡♡, $$-$$$$, 40 Court St., Portsmouth 03801, 603/433-1200. Known as Portsmouth's premier inn, The Sise, owned by a Canadian resort company, is a real hybrid – an unusual cross between a bed and breakfast and a hotel. And although it lacks a touch of the homey charm one usually finds in a B&B, it does have some nice amenities – cable televisions, VCRs, and telephones in all of its 34 rooms. Moreover, it offers, for those who want it, a bit of anonymity.

From the outside, the Sise appears every inch a B&B. A grand, 1889 Queen Anne-style home, it is a "painted lady" with pale, blue-green clapboards and cream trim. The common rooms – a parlor and dining area – have gleaming oak paneling original to the house. The parlor is outfitted with a fine leather couch and wing chairs, brass lamps, and has the overall feel of being well decorated, if not quite comfortable.

Like the common rooms, the guest rooms are a pleasant mix of hotel – wall-to-wall carpeting and writing desks – and B&B. Furniture is both antique and reproduction, and most beds are covered with chenille spreads.

If you'd like to splurge, the Sise's premiere room is 302. Considered the inn's bridal suite, it has two floors; the bottom houses a sitting area and standard bath. The skylit top floor has a queen-size bed and an additional separate bath with a large, antique claw-foot tub. Sybarites might consider room 216, which has an oversize whirlpool and sauna.

Continental breakfast includes a selection of fruit, juice, hot and cold cereal, muffins, and pastries. One nice touch that the Sise Inn offers is round-the-clock coffee and snacks. The dining room – outfitted with antique oak tables and hand-carved chairs – is always open for guests to help themselves.

RATES PER NIGHT: $99-$175 late May through late October, $89-$150 off season.

ACCOMMODATIONS: 34 rooms with private baths.

AMENITIES: Televisions, telephones, and VCRs in rooms. Some rooms have whirlpools, and one room has a whirlpool and sauna.

RESTRICTIONS: No pets.

The Bow Street Inn, ♡-♡♡, $$-$$$, 121 Bow St., Portsmouth 03801, 603/431-7760. Located in an old, brick factory, perched on the edge of the Piscataqua River, Bow Street is not your typical B&B. While the exterior seems to have changed little since it served as a brewery, the interior has been spiffed up considerably and besides Bow Street, houses the Seacoast Repertory Company and several plush condominiums.

For couples interested in an unconventional B&B – no common room, no full breakfasts – Bow Street is pleasant, immaculately clean, and has an ideal downtown location and water views.

All of Bow Street's 10 rooms are located on one floor. The two most desirable rooms are 6 and 7. Both have ringside views of the Piscataqua, which flows directly into the Atlantic Ocean. Room 7 has a bit more style than 6, with pale pink walls and a rose border, a queen-size brass bed and upholstered mauve colored chairs. It is also the only room with a mini refrigerator. The other nine rooms are similarly decorated. The look is country, but the furniture is new and floors are carpeted wall to wall.

Expanded continental breakfast is served in Bow Street's dining room, an interesting spot with high windows and brick walls and ceilings. Innkeeper Jan Bova offers a good selection – cereal, granola, yogurt, English muffins, and fresh-baked goods, as well as fruit, juice, and coffee.

RATES PER NIGHT: $99-$129

ACCOMMODATIONS: 10 rooms with private baths.

AMENITIES: Televisions and telephones in rooms.

RESTRICTIONS: No smoking. No pets.

The Governor's House Inn, ♥ ♥, $$-$$$, 32 Miller Ave., Portsmouth 03801, 603/431-6546. This, one of Portsmouth's most stately 20th century homes and long-time residence of former governor Charles Dale, is now the city's newest B&B. Californian's Nancy and John Grossman, have restored virtually all the interior surfaces, from the wood floors up. Yet they've infused the place with a sense of pleasant casualness, and have foregone the heavy oils and dark Orientals that probably once played prominently in the decoration scheme.

The large common living room is graced with a beautiful grand piano that once belonged to the governor's family. A comfortable spot, the room has cream-colored walls, blue curtains, and double couches surrounding a wood-burning fireplace. Casual observers might think the tile surrounding the fireplace is original Delpht. But look closer. Nancy, an artist by profession, painted them herself.

Nancy's work can also be witnessed in all four guest rooms. Each bath features tile walls with elaborate paintings. The most impressive work is found in the Peacock Room. The shower for two (it's extra large and has two nozzles on opposite walls) features an Art Nouveau inspired painting of a woman and a peacock. The bedroom furnishings also carry out the Art Nouveau theme and feature a queen-size brass and iron bed.

If you're looking for something more traditionally romantic – lace and flowers – consider the Prescott Room. It has a grand queen-size, four-poster bed with curtains and a white eyelet cover. Other accouterments include lace pillows, wicker furniture, and blue floral wallpaper. Nancy painted the Prescott's bathroom tiles with a French folk art scene. You can enjoy it at as you lounge in the two-person Jacuzzi.

A full breakfast is served in the dining room, which is graced with a country wall mural that the Grossman's friend painted and updates seasonally. Nancy's specialties include apple puff pancakes with peach syrup, and popovers which she serves in individual custard cups.

RATES PER NIGHT: $110-$160 from June through October, $90-$140 other times of the year.

ACCOMMODATIONS: 4 rooms with private baths.

AMENITIES: Common room with television. Tennis court. Racquets and balls are available for guests. Lessons or a playing partner can be arranged.

RESTRICTIONS: No children under 14. No pets, but boarding facilities can be arranged.

FRIDAY EVENING

Note: You can walk around Portsmouth from all the inns recommended here. If the evening is pleasant, walking is an ideal way to familiarize yourself with the city. The following directions for drinks and dinner assume you're traveling on foot.

Drinks

The Portsmouth Brewery, ♡, $-$$, 56 Market St., Portsmouth, 603/431-1115. In transit: From the Gundalow, go over Memorial Bridge to Daniel Street. At Market Square turn right onto Market Street. The Brewery is near the intersection of Bow Street, on the left. From the Bow Street Inn, simply follow Bow to Market. And from the Governor's House and the Sise Inn, follow Middle Street west, turn right on Congress Street. At Market Square, turn left onto Market.

The Portsmouth Brewery may not be for those who crave dry martinis to whet their appetites. Yet this restaurant and pub, the only micro brewery in New Hampshire, has a charm of its own. Located in an old brick building, with two-story high tin ceilings and walls dressed in modern art, the Brewery is funky spot, though spanks of being "new."

All beer served is brewed right on the premises. The beer tanks are located in the back of the restaurant (Portsmouth Brewery also serves food, but it's lousy) behind a glass wall. The six varieties range from a pale ale to an Irish style stout called Black Cat. Portsmouth's Old Brown Dog was a silver medal winner at the 1989 Great American Beer Festival. Hours: from 11:30 A.M.

Dinner

The Oar House, ♡ ♡, $$-$$$, 55 Ceres St., Portsmouth, 603/436-4025. In transit: From the Portsmouth Brewery, start down Bow Street. Ceres Street is on the left, and is almost at the corner of Market and Bow Streets.

Portsmouth has other seafood restaurants. But through the years the Oar House has consistently maintained a reputation as being one of the city's best. It has a casual ambiance – brick and stone walls and wide-pine varnished floorboards. Yet it's the kind of spot where you could feel comfortable in a suit coat and tie, a dress, or a pair of jeans.

The restaurant is located on two floors. If you can, opt for a table upstairs, it's smaller and quieter. And if you get a table by the window, you might be able to glimpse the ocean.

The emphasis here is on fish, with a more limited selection of meat and chicken. Begin with something from the raw bar – cherrystones, oysters, or shrimp. Appetizers include escargot, steamed mussels, and baked stuffed clams. If you're not in the mood for shellfish, you might choose baked Brie wrapped in pastry or artichoke hearts au gratin.

Entrees are similarly simple, but well prepared–broiled scallops, baked haddock, and twin boiled lobsters. A more elaborate dish is fruit de mer, which is scallops, shrimp, lobster, and fresh fish sautéed with mushrooms, scallions, black olives, and tomatoes, served over pasta, blended with crème fraîche and parmesan cheese.

If your partner isn't a fish lover, the Oar House also offers tournedos of beef, New York sirloin, and a chef's chicken, which is prepared differently every night. (If you're not a beer lover, the Oar House has nice bar where you can get mixed drinks.) Hours: 5:30 P.M. – 10:00 P.M. Friday and Saturday, 5:30 P.M. – 9:00 P.M. Monday through Thursday.

Guido's Trattoria, ♡ ♡, $$-$$$, 67 Bow St., Portsmouth, 603/431-2989. In transit: From the Portsmouth Brewery, start down Bow Street. It veers to the right off Market. Guido's is at the end of the first block of stores, on the left.

Although the name might lead you to believe that this is a "spaghetti and meatballs" restaurant, Guido's serves authentic Tuscan cuisine. In fact, the chef/owner of this second-story, waterside café makes regular pilgrimages to Italy for new menu ideas. Although selections change often, some appetizers you might find include crostini with chicken liver paté with sage and sautéed mushrooms, and grilled shrimp with garlic and olive oil.

Like most restaurants in Italy, Guido's offers both a pasta course and a meat/fish course. But chances are, particularly if you get an appetizer, you will only be able to eat one or the other. Selections here include homemade gnocchi (pasta dumplings) with a tomato basil sauce; risotto alla Milanese, which is rice with saffron, onion, and prosciutto; and roasted chicken served with prosciutto, olive oil, and sage. Hours: 6:00 P.M. – 9:30 P.M. Tuesday through Sunday.

Saturday Morning

Visit the Strawbery Banke Museum, Marcy Street, (P.O. Box 300), Portsmouth 03802, 603/433-1100. In transit: You can walk to the museum from every inn included here. From the Gundalow, go across Memorial Bridge and turn left on Marcy Street. From the Sise Inn and Governor's House, follow Court Street to the end. Then turn right on Marcy Street. From the Bow Street Inn, follow Bow Street east. Marcy Street will be right before you, after you traverse State Street.

Far more than just a single building containing historical artifacts, Strawbery Banke encompasses 10 acres of land on which sit 8 furnished houses of different time periods. They offer wide ranging exhibits on social history, traditional trades, and architecture, as well as historical gardens and landscape.

All the houses located at Stawbery Banke are original structures that have been refurbished. The earliest dates back to the 1690s. The museum's goal is to give visitors a picture of the people who helped shape the city of Portsmouth, from its earliest days. Not coincidentally, the museum is located on a plot that was the site of the area's first English settlement. In 1630, Captain Walter Neal and a small band of Englishmen sailed up the Piscataqua. They were so impressed with the land and the thick growth of wild berries along the river's bank that they chose the site for a settlement, which they appropriately named Strawbery Banke. (Strawberry with only one "r" is the original English spelling.)

Strawbery Banke enjoyed its share of prosperity over the centuries. But by the 1950s it had become a shanty town, known as Puddle Dock, where once fine homes served as four and five family tenements. The area had become so decrepit it was slated for demolition and urban renewal. It was saved, however, when a group of local citizens banded together to form Strawbery Banke Inc. Through the efforts of these historically minded residents, Puddle Dock dwellers were relocated and renovation and rediscovery of Portsmouth's heritage began.

It has been nearly three decades since Strawbery Banke first opened to the public, and it seems with each passing year that its popularity increases. One reason is that the museum is vigilant about offering a wide array of educational programs to the public, including on-site excavation projects.

Visitors may tour the grounds and houses with a well-versed guide, or by themselves. We toured alone, and found that the written information provided in each house was plentiful, and that being on our own allowed us to take a leisurely pace. The entire tour will probably take you anywhere from three to four hours.

Be sure not to skip the William Pitt Tavern. Originally built in 1766, it has been magnificently restored. Its three floors of exhibits, depicting the central role taverns played in colonial life, give the best insight into our forefathers' world.

For those who enjoy active exhibits, Strawbery Banke also has a working boat building shop, blacksmith, and pottery.

Before you leave, be sure to visit the Museum Shop. It's got a particularly interesting selection of books, crafts, and gifts. Hours: 10:00 A.M. – 5:00 P.M. daily from May 1 through October 31. It's also open for a candlelight Christmas stroll the first two weekends in December, 3:30 P.M. – 8:30 P.M. The gift shop is open year-round.

Admission $9, $8 for seniors. Tickets are good for two consecutive days.

Lunch

Karen's, $-$$, 105 Daniels St., Portsmouth, 603/431-1948. In transit: From Strawbery Banke, turn left on Marcy Street, then left on Court Street, then left on Atkinson Street. Cross State Street to Chapel Street; it's directly across from Atkinson. Then turn left on Daniels Street. Karen's is on the left. The entire walk shouldn't take much more than five minutes.

One of Portland's more popular casual restaurants, Karen's is a bohemian spot with a laid-back atmosphere. The dining room is simply decorated – wooden tables and chairs, and pale pink walls decorated with work from local artists. Offerings are quasi healthy and eclectic. Selections include black bean burritos, stir-fried vegetables served with brown rice and tamarind ginger sauce, and spinach salad. However, Karen's isn't above offering a hearty BLT, as well as other more traditional sandwiches, and gooey desserts. On our visit, sweets included pumpkin cheesecake and chocolate cake with raspberry cream. Hours: 11:30 A.M. – 3:00 P.M. On Sunday brunch is served from 8:00 A.M. – 2:00 P.M. Lunch is served until 2:30 P.M. on weekdays.

Old Ferry Landing, $-$$, 10 Ceres St., Portsmouth, 603/431-5510. In transit: From Strawbery Banke, turn left on

Marcy Street, then left on State Street. Turn right on Wright Avenue, which is the first street on the right. This becomes Bow Street. Follow Bow Street, then turn right on Ceres Street. The Old Ferry Landing is on the right.

Originally built as a ferry terminal, The Ferry Landing has one of the most popular outdoor bars in Portsmouth. Its patio, directly on the Piscataqua and actually almost level with the water, is the best in town. The inside dining room has great views as well. It is the place to go for those who consider a trip to the seashore incomplete without some fried clams. Hours: from 11:30 A.M. (Note: The Old Ferry Landing is only open seasonally and closes at the end of October.)

SATURDAY AFTERNOON

Shopping around Downtown Portsmouth.

In transit: One of the most pleasant things about Portsmouth is its walkability. With a detailed map, free at virtually all shops, you can easily negotiate the six or seven streets that comprise downtown.

While Portsmouth is a fun place to shop, don't expect designer clothing or priceless antiques. Merchants here purvey an interesting hodgepodge of crafts, antiquarian books, jewelry, and chotchkes. Following are some of the better stores:

N.W. Barrett Gallery, 53 Market St., 603/431-4262. Arguably the best craft gallery in Portsmouth, Barrett stocks an interesting selection of items—hand-painted lamp shades, whimsical pottery, and funky jewelry. Don't forget to visit the upstairs art gallery.

Randall Poquette, 65 Daniel St., 603/436-0345. If department stores leave you cold, Randall Poquette has an interesting selection of locally designed and made women's clothes. The look is simple and spare – no flowers or frills – and the quality is good, although not detailed.

Macro Polo, 89 Market St., 603/436-8338. Silly is the best way to describe this shop. Great place for buying each other dumb, cheap gifts. Look for all kinds of whirligigs, T-shirts, and rubber balls.

City & Country, 50 Daniels St., 603/433-5353. This is a top-notch housewares store, where you'll find all kinds of unusual glasses, plates, tablecloths, and pillows, to help make your home feel special. It will be hard not to buy *something.*

The Portsmouth Book Shop, 110 State St., 603/431-0694. A great stop for book lovers. This shop carries a large selection of used and antiquarian books from classics to cooking guides. Also an excellent selection of antique maps, advertisements, and magazine covers.

The Trunk Shop, 23 Ceres St., 603/431-4399. Antique sea captains' chests hold a certain mystique. And at this shop, you'll find some beautifully refurbished chests, wooden trunks, and small boxes. Even if you're not in the market, it's worth a visit.

SATURDAY EVENING

Sunset Horse and Buggy Ride around Portsmouth, Portsmouth Livery Company, Market Square, Portsmouth, 603/427-0044. In transit: Market Square is the very center of Portsmouth– impossible to miss. It is where the two main thoroughfares, Market and Congress Streets, converge.

Yes, horse and buggy rides can be hokey. But in colonial Portsmouth with its old brick factory buildings, clapboard houses, and gas lights, it seems a fitting way to see the city. Portsmouth Livery operates its service right from Market Square, by the old North Church. You may choose from one of the livery's three routes, 15, 30, and 40 minutes in length. The 40-minute ride is the most interesting and the only one that goes into the Strawbery Banke museum. You can also hire a buggy to "drive" you to dinner, or to another special destination. Hours: from 12:00 noon daily May 1 through October 31. If you're visiting in the off season, call for reservations.

Dinner

Strawbery Court, ♡ ♡ ♡, $$$-$$$$, 20 Atkinson St., Portsmouth 603/431-7722.

In transit: From Market Square, turn down Daniel Street – it's essentially the continuation of Congress Street. Then turn right on Chapel Street. Once you cross State Street, Chapel becomes Atkinson Street.

Arguably the best restaurant in Portsmouth, Strawbery Court is a treat for food lovers who enjoy dining in an elegant, yet unstuffy atmosphere. Decor is refined and simple – oyster colored walls, round tables with starched white linens adorned with a small bouquet of fresh flowers and a single white candle. With only 11 tables, the feeling is intimate. Nine of these are located in the main dining room, and an additional two tables in a small adjoining room. If you're making a reservation, ask for the main sitting area; it's more festive and always has a gorgeous spray of fresh flowers in the middle of the room.

Strawbery Court serves haute French cuisine. Food, service, and presentation are all impeccable. On our visit, an appetizer of crêpes was filled with chicken, grilled shitake mushrooms, and walnuts, then tied on with a scallion and served on a clear plate made red with paprika. Other appetizers included a chicken liver pâté with black bean sauce, and Norwegian smoked salmon served with capers and onion.

The menu changes regularly, but always reflects things very French. It might include fillet de bouef bordelaise, served with grilled peppers, mushrooms, bacon, and veal sausage, or roast loin of pork stuffed with tomatoes, kale, and garlic and served with wild rice and a sweet corn sauce.

Although the fresh bread served with meals changes regularly too, the warm, crusty Parmesan bread we had was positively addictive. Don't eat too much though, or you won't have room for crème caramel or chocolate mousse.

The menu sounds expensive, and indeed is. If you want, you can order a la carte or pay $38 for a fixed price meal which includes an appetizer, salad, entree, and dessert. Budget conscious travelers who still appreciate good food should note that Strawbery Court also offers a $19.50 fixed price meal that includes an appetizer, salad, and a choice of a few selected entrees. Hours: 6:00 P.M. – 9:00 P.M. Tuesday through Saturday.

(There's a small park just outside the Strawbery Court, with a grassy area and a couple of swing sets. It's a great spot for a little after-dinner conversation.)

Blue Strawbery, ♡ ♡ ♡, $$$$, 29 Ceres St., Portsmouth, 603/431-6420. In transit: From Market Square, walk down Market Street toward Bow Street. At Bow Street, turn left onto Ceres Street. The Blue Strawbery is on the left.

Blue Strawbery is somewhat of a legend among New England epicures. It was one of the region's first real gourmet restaurants, when that trend began sweeping the country more than 20 years ago.

Blue Strawbery is still considered a top-notch restaurant, and is a favorite among those who take their eating seriously. It has steadfastly retained its formal service, fixed price ($39 per person without liquor or gratuities), and single-hour seating.

Located in an odd place for a fine dining restaurant – an old ship's chandlery with brick and stone walls – it still has a decidedly formal flavor. Menu selections are relatively limited. Dinners are usually offered a selection of three appetizers, a salad, and three entrees – always one meat, fish, and fowl.

Appetizers might include snails baked in a garlic scotch-whiskey butter and served with toast rounds, or artichoke heart cream soup with champagne and thyme. For the entrees, maybe roast duck with green peppercorns and a honey lemon glaze, a seafood medley of salmon, sea scallops, and shrimp baked in a duxelles with a Pernod lime butter, and beef Wellington with lightly gingered Madeira wine and mushroom sauce. Desserts include a varying selection of sweets, and always their signature dessert, fresh strawberries with brown sugar and cream. Hours: 7:30 P.M. seating Thursday through Saturday, 6:00 P.M. seating Sunday. Be sure to call for reservations and note that in season Blue Strawbery offers two seatings and is open Tuesday and Wednesday.

SUNDAY MORNING

Visit the U.S.S. Albacore, Albacore Park, Market Street, Portsmouth, 603/436-3680. In transit: Located at the far end of Market Street, just before the entrance of I-95, Albacore Park is easy to find. From Bow Street, head west. Turn right on Market Street. The park is on the left, just beyond the Chamber of Commerce. From the Sise Inn and the Governor's House Inn, follow Middle Street north toward the center of town. Turn right on State Street, then left on Pleasant Street. At Market Square, continue straight onto Market Street. At the intersection with Bow Street, you'll have to veer left to stay on Market Street. And from the Gundulow, cross Memorial Bridge and turn right on Wright Avenue. Cross Daniel Street and follow Bow Street to Market Street. Turn right on Market. (Note: Even though you could walk to the Albacore, it's more sensible to drive.)

Built at the Portsmouth Naval Shipyard, the U.S.S. Albacore served with the U.S. Navy from 1953 to 1972. Unlike most vessels, however, the Albacore never fired a weapon, and was never even outfitted with torpedo tubes. It was built, not to fight, but to serve as a prototype vessel to help develop high speed propulsion characteristics to be used in future submarines.

The Albacore's tear-drop-shaped hull was so efficient it became the standard design for all future subs. In fact, in February 1966, the Albacore was recorded as the fastest moving submarine in history. That record has never been broken and the exact speed is still classified information.

Today visitors can tour the 205-foot submarine which, while in commission, housed 50 crew members. Visitors over six feet tall beware: quarters are cramped. You'll have to crouch, but it will be worth it. Getting a look inside a real Navy submarine isn't an opportunity that comes along often.

Be sure to watch the short film before your tour. It gives good background information about the Albacore, particularly how it was maneuvered into its dry dock, and will help you appreciate your visit. Hours: 9:30 A.M. – 5:30 P.M. May 1 through Columbus Day, 9:30 A.M. – 3:30 P.M. Thursday through Monday off season. Admission $4, $3 for senior citizens.

Walk Along the Portsmouth Trail.

In transit: The walk starts at the Moffatt Ladd House on Market Street, right in the center of town. You might be able to find a parking space on a main street. Or you can head to the downtown municipal lot. The entrance is on Hanover Street. From the Albacore, follow Market Street back toward town. Turn right on Hanover Street. The lot is on the left.

The Portsmouth Trail is a 1½-mile historic walking tour produced by the Historic Associates at the Greater Portsmouth Chamber of Commerce. It encompasses six historic houses that are open to the public for guided tours. Each house is restored and has its own distinct flavor. Even if you don't want to visit every house, it's interesting to walk the entire trail, then pick and choose the places you want to explore.

The Moffatt-Ladd House (1763) is a mansion overlooking the Piscataqua, and was built by Captain John Moffatt, who had no formal architectural training. The John Paul Jones House (1758) contains a valuable collection of late 18th century clothing, glass, ceramics, guns, glass, silver, portraits, and documents. Next on the tour is the Rundlet- May House (1807). Furnished with many pieces from the original family, it is a fine example of Federal architecture.

George Washington called the next house, the Governor John Langdon House (1784), the finest home in Portsmouth. This Georgian mansion boasts some of the best and most intricate interior wood carvings in the city. The Wentworth Gardner House (1760) is considered one of the nation's finest examples of Georgian architecture. It was once owned by the Museum of Modern Art, which planned to move the house to Central Park.

The last house on the tour is also the oldest. The Warner House was built in 1716 and the murals on its walls are thought to be the oldest of their kind in the United States.

Maps of the Portsmouth Trail are available at the Chamber of Commerce and also at the information kiosk in Market Square. The kiosk is open daily from Memorial Day through Columbus Day. And the Chamber of Commerce (500 Market St., 603/436-1118) is open weekends 10:00 A.M. – 2:00 P.M. through Columbus Day. It's open year-round 8:30 A.M. – 5:00 P.M. Monday through Friday.

Hours (for historic houses): John Paul Jones, 10:00 A.M. – 4:00 P.M. Monday through Saturday, 12:00 P.M. – 4:00 Sunday (from July 15), Gov. Langdon House and Rundlet-May, 12:00 P.M. – 5:00 P.M. Wednesday through Sunday, Warner House 10:00 A.M. – 4:00 P.M. Tuesday thorough Saturday, 1:00 P.M. – 4:00 P.M. Sunday; Moffatt-Ladd House, 10:00 A.M. – 4:00 P.M. Monday through Saturday, 12:00 P.M. – 5:00 P.M. Sunday; Wentworth-Gardner House, 10:00 A.M. – 4:00 P.M. Tuesday through Sunday. All historic houses are open from May 1 through mid October. The John Paul Jones House is sometimes open in April. Admission: $4 per house.

Lunch

The Stock Pot, $-$$, 53 Bow St., Portsmouth, 603/431-1851. In transit: If you finish at the Warner House, you'll be on the corner of Daniel and Chapel Streets. From there, head down Chapel Street, toward Bow Street. Turn left on Bow. The Stock Pot is on the right.

The Stock Pot is an institution in Portsmouth. Originally housed on Market Street, it has new digs at a waterfront building. Yet the menu and atmosphere stay reassuringly the same. The downstairs houses the main dining room, which is casual and has brick and wood walls. But if the upstairs bar area isn't too crowded, it is a much cozier spot. Try to get a table right by the window, or if you're really beat, on the couch across from the bar.

This restaurant's motto is "good food cheap." And that's precisely what the Stock Pot serves, nothing too fussy, but decidedly eclectic. Its lunch menu includes Sara's vegetarian salad, with lentils, rice, black beans, artichoke hearts and greens served with vinaigrette dressing, as well as a hommus platter. For the less adventurous, the Stock Pot also has sandwiches and hamburgers. Sweet tooths will appreciate the dessert menu that includes a dozen homemade treats – from fudge brownies to banana cream pie. Hours: from 11:30 A.M.

Take-out from Belle Peppers, $, 41 Congress St., Portsmouth, 603/427-2504. In transit: Follow Daniel Street to Market Square. At Market Square, continue straight ahead onto Congress Street. Belle Peppers is on the right. This may be Portsmouth's only gourmet take-out shop, but it's truly top notch. If the weather is good, you might consider a picnic at Odiorne Point State Park (your first stop of the afternoon). Belle Peppers will pack you an absolutely princely lunch. How about a lemon crusted chicken breast sandwich with lettuce, tomato, and cheddar? Vegetarians might consider avocado, Boursin, and sprouts. If you're looking for something sweet, try a slice of Belle Peppers' chocolate outrage. Hours: 8:00 A.M. – 6:00 P.M. Monday – Saturday, 12:00 P.M. – 5:00 P.M. Sunday.

SUNDAY AFTERNOON

Visit Odiorne Point State Park, Route 1A, Rye, 603/436-8043. In transit: From the parking garage, turn left on Hanover Street, then left on Maplewood Avenue to Middle Street. At Miller Street, turn left and follow signs to Route 1A. Odiorne State Park is a few miles down on the left. The entire ride should take no more than 15 minutes. This 350-acre park is directly on the Atlantic and offers miles of nature trails for visitors to explore. In the early 1900s, this seaside spot housed about six mansions. However, the government took over the land in World War II to protect Portsmouth Harbor. History buffs might enjoy checking out the reinforced concrete bunker right near the parking lot: It's still camouflaged to look like a grassy hill.

Although the mansions have all been torn down, some remnants remain. One of the loveliest spots for a picnic is on the park's north side amidst remnants of a formal garden and water fountain. Also, a cluster of picnic benches is located on a grassy lawn right by the ocean. The science center, which has several marine exhibits as well as information on Odiorne's history, provides maps. Hours: 10:00 A.M. – 5:00 P.M. Tuesday through Sunday, also 12:00 P.M.–5:00 P.M. Monday in summer.

Visit Fort Constitution, Route 1B, New Castle, no phone. In transit: From Odiorne Point, follow 1A back towards Portsmouth. Then turn right on Wentworth Road/1B. You'll see a sign on the right leading you to Fort Constitution. The entire ride shouldn't take more than 10 minutes.

You won't find a visitors center, a gift shop, or a tour guide. But those interested in the American Revolution will enjoy a trip to Fort Constitution, the site of the first organized assault on a royal fortress.

Four months before Paul Revere made his historic ride from Boston to Lexington, he road to Portsmouth to warn colonists that British troops were moving to reinforce Fort William and Mary. Four hundred people stormed and captured the fort, which is now known as Constitution.

Visitors are free to tour the remnants of the fort. Several informative plaques are located on the site, describing its history.

Also located here is Portsmouth Light. Still in operation today, it was the 10th lighthouse built in North America.

SUNDAY EARLY EVENING

Snack at Café Brioche, 14 Market Square, Portsmouth, 603/430-9225. In transit: From Fort Constitution, retrace your path back down Route 1B. At the intersection of Route 1A, turn right. Follow 1A back into Portsmouth. As you enter town, 1A will become Miller Street. Follow Miller, bear right at Middle Street, then turn right on State Street. Park on the street. Café Brioche is right in Market Square.

Café Brioche is a tiny spot that feels like a slice of Paris in downtown Portsmouth. This fine bakery makes exquisite brioches, criossants, and other pastries and sweets. It also serves cappuccino, teas, and coffee, as well as a small selection of soups and sandwiches. Order two steaming cups of cappuccino topped with some shaved chocolate cinammon, and enjoy the last vestiges of your weekend.

Additional Activities

Have a Soak in Hot Tub at the Tub Shop, 62 Market St., Portsmouth, 603/431-0994. This place has private hot tubs that you can rent by the hour. It sounds sleazy, but it's not. Atmosphere is like an upscale health club. This company also has a location in Portland, ME. (See Portland chapter.)

Take in a Play at the Seacoast Repertory Company, 125 Bow St., Portsmouth, 603/433-4472. Since it set up shop more than five years ago, the theater company has garnered great praise from the local press. It typically produces Broadway hits. Recent offerings have included "Evita," "Love Letters," and "La Cage Aux Folles."

See a Movie at the Music Hall, 28 Chestnut St., Portsmouth, 603/436-9900. Movie buffs will enjoy taking in a show at this 900-seat theater cum music hall. It shows movies on a huge screen – a nice switch from the mini versions multiplexes use nowadays.

See a Musical Production at the Music Hall, 28 Chestnut St., Portsmouth, 603/436-2400. When the Music Hall isn't screening movies, it offers a wide range of musical shows from operettas like The Mikado to Mario Bauza and his Afro-Cuban jazz orchestra.

Visit The Press Room, 77 Daniels St., Portsmouth, 603/431-5186. Pub lovers will appreciate this spot's dark and cozy ambiance. It's a local favorite.

Getting There

By Air: Portsmouth is just an hour from Boston. All major carriers fly into Logan International Airport. The Manchester (NH) Airport and the Portland (ME) Jetport are also less than an hour from Portsmouth. Most major airlines fly into Manchester. However, the flights are less frequent and many make stops in Boston before arriving in Manchester or Portland.

By Car: Portsmouth is easily accessible by car. From I-95 take exit 7, which leads directly to downtown Portsmouth.

By Train: No train service is available.

By Bus: C & J Trailways (800/258-7111) offers almost hourly service from Boston's Logan International Airport. Service is also available from Boston's South Station at the Peter Pan Bus Terminal.

Car Rental: All major car rental companies are located at Boston's Logan International Airport. They include Avis (800/331-1212), Dollar Rent-A-Car (617/569-5300), Hertz (800/654-3131), Thrifty (617/569-6500), National (617/227-6687), Budget (617/787-8200), and Sears (617/787-8220). Four rental companies are located at the Portland Jetport: Avis, Hertz, Budget Rent-A-Car (207/774-8642), and Thrifty (207/772-4268). And at the Manchester Airport, there are Avis, Hertz, National (603/627-2299), and Budget (603/668-3166). Merchants (603/431-1999), Agency (603/436-1647), National (603/431-4707) and Thrifty (603/431-5506) are all located in Portsmouth.

Taxi/Limousine Service: First Class Limousines (603/626-5466) has service from the Manchester Airport. Several taxi services are available in Portsmouth. They include A-1 Taxi (603/431-2345) and Allied Taxi (603/436-7177).

INFORMATION: Greater Portsmouth Chamber of Commerce, 500 Market St., Portsmouth 03802, 603/436-1118. The chamber is easily accessible, but it is not located right downtown. If you're driving and get off at exit 7, you'll be right on the beginning of Market Street. Head for downtown Portsmouth, and the chamber is on the right. Hours: 8:30 A.M. – 5:00 P.M. Monday through Friday, on weekends 10:00 A.M. – 2:00 P.M. from Memorial Day through Columbus. An information kiosk is also open in Market Square from Memorial Day through Columbus Day.

Winter

Jackson, New Hampshire

Nantucket, Massachusetts

Portland, Maine

Stowe, Vermont

Sugarloaf & Kingfield, Maine

Jackson, New Hampshire

New Hampshire and Vermont may sit side by side, but these states, and particularly their ski resorts, have two vastly different atmospheres. As rural as Vermont might be, its tourist towns have a certain caché. It's not uncommon for general stores to sell goat cheese, shops to carry imported sweaters, and slopeside restaurants to offer $8 salads of radicchio and arugula.

In the Granite State, however, things are more down to earth, more relaxed. You won't find chic boutiques or gourmet groceries. But you will find lots of down-home country inns, funky restaurants, and majestic scenery. New Hampshire ski resorts are for people who want to leave their one-piece designer ski suits at home and enjoy a weekend free from the trappings of urban sophistication.

No other resort town in the state is better suited to such a pursuit than Jackson. Unlike some New Hampshire communities that have been all too anxious to attract the tourist dollar with motels, fast-food restaurants, and outlet stores, Jackson has maintained its pristine beau-

ty. Tucked in a small pocket at the base of the White Mountains, it is postcard perfect with a snow-covered village green, an old stone bridge, and a white steepled church. In fact, this town of 600, which is entered from the south via an old covered bridge, looks much the same as it did in the 1800s when its cool mountain breezes made it a popular summer retreat.

Although Jackson attracts many warm weather tourists, it's primarily known as a ski resort. Indeed, Esquire magazine named the Jackson Ski Touring Foundation, with its 150 kilometers of trails, one of the four best cross-country ski centers in the world. In addition, downhill skiing is available at four nearby areas: Wildcat, Black Mountain, Attitash, and Cranmore. Combined they offer more than 100 trails, from gentle cruising runs for the novice, to steep, bumpy descents for the mogul aficionado.

WHERE TO STAY

The Nestlenook Farm, ♡ ♡ ♡, $$$-$$$$, Dinsmore Road, Jackson 03846, 603/383-9443. In this rustic New Hampshire town, The Nestlenook

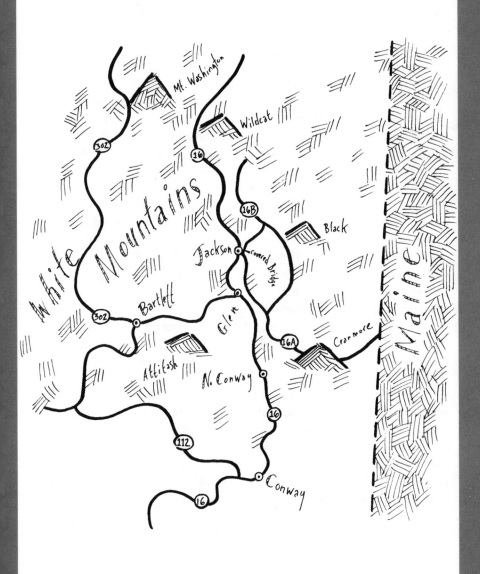

Mt. Washington

Wildcat

302

16

16B

Black

White Mountains

Jackson · covered bridge

Bartlett
302

Glen

16A

Cranmore

Maine

Attitash

N. Conway

16

112

16

Conway

N

JACKSON

seems almost a mirage, or perhaps a movie set. A gingerbread Victorian inn, it's whimsically painted pink and green, and surrounded by green lawns dotted with swag-trimmed bridges and lattice-work gazebos. In fact, local innkeepers secretly refer to it as "Disneynook." And although the inn suffers just a touch from the cutes, these remarks are probably made out of jealousy, for The Nestlenook is the most well-appointed and amenity-laden property in Jackson.

Completely rehabbed in 1986 by new owners Robert and Nancy Cyr, the inn's seven rooms have an updated "old world" look. All are furnished with modern plush carpets, phones, and two-person spa tubs, as well as not-so-modern fine antiques, including hand-carved bed frames and parlor stoves.

The most impressive room is the C.C. Murdoch Suite, which encompasses the entire third floor. In addition to a bedroom and sitting room, it boasts a Jacuzzi room with wet bar and panoramic view. Another interesting room is the Myke Morton. Slightly more rustic looking, it's located in the oldest part of the house and has the original beamed ceiling, as well as pine floors, an Oriental rug, parlor stove with brick hearth, queen-size bed, and side porch.

The common rooms carry out the Victorian theme with velvet settees and well-restored antiques. One pleasant and unusual amenity is a small lounge where guests may mix drinks from a complimentary liquor cabinet. Although breakfast is served daily, The Nestlenook also provides a spacious guest kitchen that boasts a spectacularly refurbished cast iron stove. The refrigerator is stocked with wine, Ben & Jerry's ice cream, and other treats, to which guests are encouraged to help themselves.

The Nestlenook sits on 65 bucolic acres, which includes a pond maintained for skating. (Skate rentals are available.) Cocoa is served in the "warming hut", a glass-enclosed gazebo, complete with fireplace.

Cross-country ski rentals and lessons and are also available. Although Nestlenook has several kilometers of its own trails, the inn's land abuts the Jackson Ski Touring Center. Guests can purchase tickets at the inn and ski virtually straight from the door.

In addition, Nestlenook offers sleigh and dog sled rides. And for animal lovers, the farm has a complement of horses, sheep, deer, chicken, and ducks. Barn tours can be arranged.

RATES PER NIGHT: $144-$196.

ACCOMMODATIONS: Six rooms with private baths, two suites with private baths. One suite has separate Jacuzzi room and wet bar.

AMENITIES: Lounge with free access to drinks. Ice skating pond and cross-country skiing trails on property. Sleigh rides.

RESTRICTIONS: No children under 12. No smoking. No pets.

Paisley & Parsley, ♥ ♥ ♥, $$, 16B, Jackson, 03846, 603/383-0859 or This three-room bed and breakfast is an intimate spot, truly reminiscent of an old-fashioned B&B, but with a high-fashion flair. Owners Bea and Chuck Stone have always enjoyed pampering and entertaining family and friends. But it wasn't until 1989 that they decided to pull up their New Jersey stakes, move to Jackson (a favorite family vacation spot), and turn their love into a livelihood.

Although the Stones searched for an old home to house their impressive collection of antiques, quilts, and folk art, they ended up with a modern structure, complete with cathedral ceilings, sky lights and picture windows. But, given the location – a birch-covered hill overlooking Mt. Washington – the oversize glass windows are a big plus. And the house's smooth white walls offer a perfect backdrop for the fine antiques.

The downstairs bedroom's showpiece is a queen-size, hand-painted, salmon-colored wood-framed bed, with a Battenburg lace duvet. A pink and white antique quilt hangs on the wall.

The large bathroom is graced with Oriental rugs and a two-person Jacuzzi. One upstairs bedroom is similarly well appointed, and also offers a view of Mt. Washington. Although the third room is also lovely, it has two double beds and a private bath down the hall.

Bea cooks a full gourmet breakfast each morning, complete with Kona coffee from Hawaii. It's served at a community table off the living room, where she keeps the fireplace roaring – even at 8 A.M.

If you're looking to be anonymous, Paisley & Parsley may not be the place for you. However, if you want fine accommodations, excellent breakfasts, and gracious hosts, this small B & B is a true find.

RATES PER NIGHT: $65-$95, $85-$115 from mid September to mid October.

ACCOMMODATIONS: Three rooms with private baths.

AMENITIES: Telephones. Cable television and VCR available.

RESTRICTIONS: No children under 12. Smoking on outside porches only. No pets.

The Inn at Thorn Hill, ♥ ♥, $$, Thorn Hill Road, Jackson 03846, 603/383-4242. Set atop a knoll on Thorn Hill, this inn offers Jackson's most majestic views of the Presidential Mountain Range.

Designed by renowned architect Stanford White (he designed the original Madison Square Garden), Thorn Hill was constructed as a private residence in 1895. The building – yellow clapboard, green shutters, and a front porch – looks more farm house than manse. However, current owners Peter and Linda LaRose – corporate refugees from Washington D.C. – have chosen to capture the flavor of that era with Victorian furnishings. The main parlor has authentic period furniture, including velvet chairs and couches, and a soapstone wood stove. Antique wedding dresses, hung on models, decorate the room. But the parlor's most impressive feature is views of Mt. Washington.

The 10 guest rooms in the main house are similarly outfitted. Although they, like the main areas, have some elegant furnishings, including floral wallpaper and Oriental rugs, the overall feel is "homey." Unlike some Victorian style inns that are decorated within an inch of their lives, Thorn Hill, looks like – and is – a real country inn.

Room 10 has the most scenic views, as well as a king-size brass bed, chenille spread, and antique dresser and table. However, the Ramsey Suite is the inn's most popular. Its queen-size bed with ruffled canopy, spread, and window curtains, appeals to those who prefer a feminine look.

In addition, Thorn Hill has a carriage house and three cottages that offer a more secluded, and slightly more rustic, setting.

Full breakfast and dinner are served in the inn's 42-seat dining room, which is wonderfully cozy with wood chairs, deep green walls, and a fireplace. A small bar is also open in the afternoon and evenings.

Thorn Hill's property is adjacent to the Jackson Ski Touring network, and guests may purchase tickets at the inn and ski directly from the front door. For those who prefer to take their outdoor excitement sitting down, Thorn Hill has old-fashioned wooden toboggans and maintains a hill next to the inn.

RATES PER NIGHT: $60-$100, $68-$106 Christmas week and foliage season, $55-$95 spring and autumn. (Rates include full breakfast. Packages that include dinner are available.)

ACCOMMODATIONS: 10 rooms with private baths in main house; 7 rooms with private baths in carriage house; 3 cottages.

AMENITIES: Restaurant serving breakfast and dinner. Lounge. Cable television and vcr in sitting room. Outdoor swimming pool (summer only).

RESTRICTIONS: No smoking. No pets.

The Notchland Inn, ♥ ♥, $$-$$$, Route 302, Hart's Location 03812, 603/374-6131 or 800/866-6131. Although The Notchland is not right in Jackson, but about 15 minutes away, it is ideal for those who want a complete country escape. Located amidst 400 acres, on a fairly desolate section of Route 302, the Notchland is a granite country manor set high atop a hill overlooking the Saco River Valley.

Built in 1862 by Samuel Bemis, a Boston dentist and lifelong bachelor, the interior was designed by the famous Gustave Stickley, creator of the Mission Style. Bemis bequeathed the estate to his caretaker who passed it down through his family who occasionally used the place as a rooming house. However the home had been abandoned and boarded up when innkeepers Pat and John Bernardin bought it in 1983. It had no electricity, no water, and no septic system.

The Bernardins have spent years refurbishing the home. And it now offers nine guest rooms and two suites, all are extraordinarily spacious, with high ceilings, private baths, and working fireplaces. (Note that if a working fireplace is a prerequisite for your romantic getaway, this is the only inn around Jackson where you'll be assured of getting one.) Furnishings, which are pleasant and comfortable but not elegant, typically include wing chairs near the fireplace, double or queen-size beds with brass or wood frames, and armoires or chests.

Common rooms include a living room (with rough hewn paneling, cast-iron chandelier, and tremendous terra-cotta tile fireplace), as well as a library, dining room, and atrium. But perhaps the best amenity, particularly for weary skiers, is the outdoor hot tub in a gazebo behind the inn.

Full breakfast and dinner are served daily. Rates are typically based on the Modified American Plan, and include breakfast and dinner. A bed-and-breakfast-only option is sometimes offered. However, because the Notchland Inn is relatively secluded, you might appreciate the meal package.

The Bernardins also run a sanctuary for the preservation of endangered species. They're happy to show off their collection of Pygmy goats, Karakul and Jacob's sheep, as well as the more ordinary llamas, miniature horses, and Belgian Draft horses. (The Belgians are used for guest sleigh rides.)

RATES PER NIGHT: $136-$166, $95-$105 B&B rates.

ACCOMMODATIONS: Nine guest rooms and two suites, all with private baths.

AMENITIES: Outdoor hot tub. Fireplaces in all rooms. Sleigh rides.

RESTRICTIONS: No smoking. No pets.

Friday Evening
Dinner

The Wildcat Inn, ♥ ♥, $$, Route 16A, Jackson, 603/383-4245. In transit: From Route 16, take 16A into downtown Jackson. The Wildcat is Jackson's downtown landmark. You can't miss it.

Although the Jackson area has several fine restaurants, most locals say that the Wildcat has the best kitchen around. And in fact, the inn is known for its food, rather than its accommodations. The candle-lit dining room is rustic and convivial, with hardwood floors and softly-colored cotton tablecloths. A nice touch—each table is graced with a fresh rose bloom floating in a (fake) snow-filled brandy snifter. If you can, opt for the porch, it is the most intimate of the restaurant's three rooms.

The menu is serious, but unpretentious. An adventurous standard is chicken martini, which is chunks of chicken breast, artichokes, olives, mushrooms, and sun-dried tomatoes, baked in butter with garlic, white wine, and balsamic vinegar. More traditional items include lasagna, tavern steak, and baked scallops. The chef offers several daily specials and, if by chance one is crab cakes, order them. They're the best you'll eat this side of the Chesapeake Bay. All breads and desserts are baked fresh daily. (One note: The house white wine is a bit sweet. If you prefer something dry, order a bottle. The wine selection isn't extensive, but

serviceable.) Hours: 6:00 P.M. - 9:00 P.M. Sunday through Thursday, 6:00 P.M. - 10:00 P.M. Friday and Saturday.

The Thompson House Eatery, ♥, $$, Route 16 A, Jackson, 603/383-9341. In transit: From Route 16, take 16A into Jackson. Follow 16a through town. The Thompson is just beyond the center of town, on the left.

Most restaurants with the word "eatery" in their titles are suspect. However, The Thompson House Eatery is an exception. This restaurant, housed in an unprepossessing red clapboard building, has an eclectic menu with emphasis on Italian cuisine. One of the favorites is seafood Francesca, a melange of scallops, sole, shrimp, and crab with mushrooms and scallions, in a garlic and wine sauce, flavored with tomato, and served with linguine. If you prefer a real stick-to-your ribs meal, try Lorenzo's Loaf, made with ground beef, vegetables, and herbs, and served with mushroom gravy.

The Thompson House has several dining rooms, all of them casual, with an antique country motif. The most intimate area is a small room off to the right of the front door. It has a low ceiling, dark paneling, and a painted wood floor. The main dining area, with its vaulted ceiling, sky lights, and expanse of glass, is more spacious and airy. Hours: 5:30 P.M. - 10:00 P.M.

SATURDAY

Note: This day isn't broken out into morning and afternoon activities because you'll probably spend the entire day skiing. Instead, it offers suggestions for both the downhill and cross country enthusiast.

The Nordic Day: Cross-Country Skiing at the Jackson Ski Touring Foundation, Route 16A, Jackson, 603/383-9355. In transit: The main ticket office is impossible to miss. It's smack in Jackson center, right on 16A across from the Wildcat Inn and next to the Jack Frost Ski Shop.

The Jackson Ski Touring Foundation, is a nonprofit organization, chartered in 1972. It exists through the generosity of 77 private land owners, the towns of Jackson and Bartlett, and the White Mountain National Forest. Today, the organization maintains a 160-kilometer network of 60 trails spanning three river valleys, the largest in the eastern United States.

Even if you've never skied before, you can enjoy yourself at Jackson. More than 20 trails are marked for novices. In fact, the Ellis River Trail (7.7 km) is rated easiest and is considered among the most scenic.

For experienced Nordic skiers, the Wildcat Valley trail, which starts at the summit of the Wildcat ski area, offers 17.8 kilometers of harrowing, heart-stopping fun. The easiest access is via the Wildcat gondola, for which a $3.50 ticket must be purchased. (This is good for one gondola ride.) Hours: 8:00 A.M. TO 4:30 P.M. Tickets: $9, $6 weekdays. Equipment rentals (available through the Jack Frost shop, right next door to the center): $12 per day, for skis, boots, and poles. Lessons: $10-$25.

Lunch

Note: One of the nice things about Jackson is that you can actually ski in and out of several different inns and restaurants. (The center doesn't have food service.)

Christmas Farm Inn, $-$$, Route 16B, Jackson 603/383-4313. On winter weekends, the Christmas Farm Inn serves lunch in its barn. This 200-year-old building with its hand-hewn beams, mortise and peg joints, and soaring fieldstone fireplace, is a great spot to refuel after a morning on the trails. Atmosphere is casual; comparable to a nice lodge at an alpine resort. The menu isn't extensive, but features homemade soups, chili, pizza, and sandwiches. There is also a small bar with a full liquor license.

Conveniently, the Christmas Farm Inn is just 1.6 kilometers from the Jackson Ski Touring center. And it is on what Jackson has dubbed its "hot chocolate loop." This five-mile trail, of easy to moderate difficulty, goes by six of

Jackson's inns or restaurants where skiers may stop for a cocoa break. Hours: 11:30 A.M. - 3:00 P.M. for lunch; open until 10:00 P.M.

Eagle Mountain House, $-$$, Carter Notch Road, Jackson, 603/383-9111. The Eagle Mountain House, which opened in 1879, is one of Jackson's grand dames. With a front porch longer than a football field, it has a commanding presence. Refurbished in 1986, the inn now boasts 94 rooms and a condominium center. Lunch is served in the Eagle Landing Tavern, a small bar with wood paneling, chairs, and tables. The menu offers basic sandwiches, soups, and burgers. Among the most popular sandwiches is the Watson Special, broiled marinated chicken served on a bulkie roll with lettuce, tomato, and horseradish sauce.

Direct access is available from the Jackson ski touring trails. For less experienced skiers, the easiest route is via the Eagle Mountain Golf Course trail. Hours: 11:30 A.M. until closing.

The Alpine Day: Downhill Skiing at One of Four White Mountain Resorts: Attitash, Cranmore, Black Mountain, and Wildcat.

Following are four descriptions of the alpine areas closest to Jackson. Although all offer trails for both novices and experts, each has its own personality and distinct reputation. Lunch spots are

not suggested because the only sensible option is to eat at the resort lodge. If you're lucky enough to ski on a warm, sunny day, most places will offer outdoor barbecues.

Attitash, Route 302, Bartlett 03812, 603/374-2368. In transit: From 16 north, take Route 302 west. Attitash is on the left.

If you can only visit one ski area around Jackson, it should be Attitash. It has the most varied terrain, with 5 beginner, 12 intermediate, and 10 expert trails. And although all area mountains have extensive snow making, Attitash is noted for its extraordinary attention to making– and grooming – the white stuff when Mother Nature isn't doing her share. (*Ski* magazine rated Attitash fourth in the nation for snow making.)

In addition, Attitash is a sunny mountain, which is big plus when you're planning on spending six hours in subfreezing temperatures. The lodge has a great sun deck for fine-tuning your tan in warmer weather. Tickets: $34, weekdays $27.

Wildcat, Route 16, Pinkham Notch 03846 603/466-3326. In transit: Wildcat is right on Route 16, just north of Jackson.

Wildcat, as its name implies, is the "meanest" of the local ski areas. Not only is it considered one of the coldest, windiest resorts, with the highest lift-served summit and longest vertical plunge in the Mt. Washington Valley, it is also among the most challenging. If you're both advanced skiers, you won't find a better spot to test your mettle. Don't miss the Wildcat trail, the mountain's bumpiest and steepest descent.

Fortunately, the mountain's physical and climatic severity is tempered by its scenery, the most magnificent in the valley with unobstructed views of Mt. Washington. Polecat, a top-to-bottom 2 3/4-mile cruiser is a must for nature lovers. Tickets: $34 Saturdays and holidays, $29 Sundays, and $27 weekdays.

Cranmore, Snowmobile Road, North Conway 03860, 603/356-5543. In transit: From Jackson take Route 16 south, turn left onto Kearsage Street. At then end of Kearsage turn left, then right into Cranmore. (They'll be signs from Route 16.)

Cranmore is a classic family mountain. A full 70 percent of the trails are devoted to beginners and intermediates. In addition, it's relatively sunny and calm, and doesn't have the hubbub of Attitash. Tickets: $34, $27 weekdays.

Black Mountain, Route 16B, Jackson 03846, 603/3383-4490. In transit: Black is on Route 16B, just above Jackson center.

Black bills itself as affordable and un-stressed. And with 22 trails and a vertical drop of 1,100 feet, it is indeed the smallest ski area in the valley. However, with $29 weekend lift tickets and $12 weekday tickets, you may not mind the limited acreage. If you have an aversion to crowds, and dream of finding a trail that the two of you will have to yourselves, Black is your best bet.

SATURDAY EVENING
Drinks

The Wildcat Tavern, ♡, $-$$, Route 16A, Jackson 603/383-4245. In transit: From Route 16, take 16A into Jackson center. The tavern is inside the Wildcat Inn, right in the center of town.

For après ski relaxation, there is no better spot in Jackson than the Wildcat. With dark wood floors, two roaring fireplaces, a few scattered well-worn chairs and a couch, this refuge is heaven to a tired body. But don't expect an intimate setting where you can whisper compliments about each other's telemarking technique; save that for your country inn dinner.

Skiing, both cross country and downhill, is the kind of activity that fosters a camaraderie with fellow enthusiasts. Rather than relax quietly at the end of the day, most people prefer to share the pain and pleasure with kindred spirits. The Wildcat is just the spot to chat up some compatriots. Hours: 11:30 A.M. – 12:30 A.M.

Dinner

The Bernerhof, ♡ ♡, \$\$, Route 302, Glen 603/383-4414. In transit: head south on Route 16 to the intersection of Route 302. The Bernerhof is about five minutes down the road on the right.

For more than 35 years the Bernerhof has had a fine reputation for its Swiss cuisine. "A Taste of the Mountain" cooking school, which operates from the inn, also adds to its cachet. And like most fine restaurants in Jackson, the casual setting belies the seriousness of the kitchen. The unfinished wainscoting and heavy wood chairs, are given just a touch of elegance by white linen tablecloths and candle-lit tables.

Although the menu, which changes monthly, includes a selection of international dishes, the best choices are Swiss offerings. Fondue seems to be the food of choice among skiers, and the Bernerhof has a fine Fondue Bernese—made with a blend of Emmenthal and Gruyère, Riesling wine and Kirsch—accompanied by fresh vegetables. Other entrees include Wiener schnitzel, and smoked salmon with horseradish cream, capers, lemon, and red onion.

Be sure to take an after-dinner cup of espresso or cappucino in the Zumstein Room, the Bernerhof's intimate, dark-paneled bar. One wall is graced with a black bear skin (complete with head). Hours: 5:30 P.M. - 9:30 P.M.

The Inn at Thorn Hill, ♡ ♡- ♡ ♡ ♡, \$\$-\$\$\$, Thorn Hill Road, Jackson, 603/383-4242. In transit: Thorn Hill Road is off 16A, on the south side of Jackson Village.

If you're planning to make a reservation, request a table near the fireplace at Thorn Hill's lovingly-decorated dining room. Lace curtains, forest green floral wallpaper, white tablecloths and authentic Victorian oil lamps, give the place a slightly more formal look than other local restaurants.

The continental menu includes steak au poivre, roast prime rib, and lobster pie, which is served with a brandy Newburg sauce in a puff pastry shell. Hearty desserts include homemade apple pie and Louisiana bread pudding with lemon sauce and Chantilly cream.

Sipping cognac in Thorn Hill's small bar, outfitted with authentic Victorian pieces, is a perfect way to end your meal. Hours: 5:30 P.M. - 9:30 P.M.

SUNDAY MORNING
Brunch

Yesterday's, ♡, \$, Route 16A, Jackson, 603/387-4457. In transit: From Route 16, take 16A to Jackson center. Yesterday's is just beyond the Wildcat Inn.

Most inns recommended in *Romantic New England Getaways* offer wonderful breakfasts. But sometimes it's fun to experience the local haunts. Yesterday's is the quintessential country restaurant—the kind of place that serves donuts instead of croissants. The waitresses know almost everyone who walks through the door. And even if they don't, they act as if they do.

Decor is unfussy: wood tables, white walls, frilly yellow curtains, and a great wood bar with stools for those on the go.

Breakfasts are simple, well-cooked and come out piping hot. The blueberry pancakes served with pure maple syrup are delicious. Or, if you're particularly hungry, try the Countryman's Special: two eggs any style, French toast or pancakes, ham or sausage, home fries, and coffee. Imagine, all for $4.95. Other items include omelets, waffles, bagels, and cold and hot cereals. Hours: 6:15 A.M. - 3:00 P.M.

Walk to Jackson Falls. In transit: From Yesterday's, turn right on Route 16, follow the signs for 16B. Signs for the Falls are on the left.

This cascade, part of the Wildcat River, is renowned as the most scenic spot in Jackson Village. Not surprisingly, it's the site of many marriage proposals. The Falls is a perfect short jaunt to help you digest breakfast.

SUNDAY AFTERNOON

Ice Skating at Nestlenook Farm, Followed by a Dogsled or Sleigh Ride, Dinsmore Road, Jackson, 603/383-9443.

In transit: From Route 16A south (heading toward North Conway) turn left onto Dinsmore Road.

Nestlenook perfectly combines the smooth ice and amenities of a posh private rink with the beauty and tranquility of a country pond. Glide along Emerald Lake, past the Victorian arched bridges and onto a small island where you can warm up beside a crackling bonfire. Old-fashioned music wafts through the air, and guests are served hot cocoa in a lakeside glassed-in gazebo, complete with fireplace. Skating fees: $5 per day. Skate rentals: $8 per day, or $5 for an hour.

This amenity-laden resort also offers rides in authentic Austrian sleighs. The trip lasts about a half hour and meanders along the Ellis River and through Nestlenook's woodlands. Usually the driver makes one stop to give passengers a glimpse of the farm's reindeer. For an ultimately romantic ride, reserve a whole sleigh and sit in the rumble seat. Dusk is a perfect time because you can watch the moon rise in the sky.

If you're interested in something a bit more invigorating, consider a dogsled ride—a hard to find adventure, even in New England's north country. You'll be whisked through the woods by eight Eskimo dogs. Rides, however, are available only on Sundays, during holiday weekends, and weekly on Friday and Saturday between 4:00 P.M. and 8:00

P.M. Sleigh rides $11.50 per person.
Dogsled rides $10 per person.

SUNDAY EVENING
Early Dinner

Red Parka Pub, ♥, $$, Route 302
Glen, 603/383-4344. In transit: The Red
Parka is just west of the Routes 16/
302 intersection.

The Red Parka has been an institution
in the Jackson area since it opened in
1972. Appropriately dark (as all pubs
must be) and done up in reds and blues
with ice cream parlor chairs, it's a
perfect spot for a good, quick meal
before you make the trek home. The
menu is made for carnivores, with no
less than seven meat selections from
barbecued pork spare ribs to
Delmonico steak. Also a selection of
seafood, chicken, salads, burgers, and
munchies. Locals claim you can make a
meal of the cheesy baked potatoes.
Hours: 4:30 P.M. - 10:00 P.M.

Additional Activities

Outlet shopping in North Conway.
While you might not consider this a
truly romantic activity, it's a great
option in foul weather. Home to more
than 100 outlet stores, including Ralph
Lauren, J. Crew, Patagonia, and L.L.
Bean (yes, even they have an outlet),
this town is a bargain lover's paradise.
If the two of you enjoy shopping for
lingerie together, Natori (Route 16,

Settler's Green 603/353-7367) also has
an outlet here.

**Indoor Rock Climbing at the Mt.
Cranmore Recreation Center,**
Cranmore Mountain, North Conway,
603/356-6316. This is another great foul
weather option. If you've always want-
ed to try rock climbing, but would feel
more comfortable within the confines
of a safe environment, Mt. Cranmore
has the largest indoor climbing wall
in the Northeast. A great opportunity
to learn a new sport or bone up on an
old favorite. Climbing instruction is
available. (Ice climbing is also popular
in this area. Among the outfits that give
lessons is Eastern Mountain Sports at
603/356-5433.)

Skating on Echo Lake. If you're look-
ing for an old-fashioned skating experi-
ence–a huge deserted pond set amidst a
dense forest of evergreens, head to Echo
Lake in North Conway. The pond isn't
maintained for public skating (it's a
beach in summer), but residents do use
it regularly. To make sure the lake is
safe for skating, call the White
Mountain National Forest 603/374-
2241 or the Mt. Washington Valley
Chamber of Commerce 603/356-3171.

Visit local art galleries. Jackson isn't
an art colony per se, but there are
several popular local artists. If checking
out the local art scene is a must for you,
following is a list of galleries: Denis
Chasse, Route 16, Jackson, 603/

383-6294; Mary Sage Gilman, Route 16 at 16A, Jackson, 603/383-4451; Myke Morton, Route 16A, Jackson 603/383-9258; State of the Art, Route 16A, Jackson Village, 603/383-9441.

GETTING THERE

BY AIR: The closest commercial airport (1½ hours by car) is the Portland (ME) International Jetport. It's serviced by Continental (800/525-0280), Delta (800/221-1212), Northwest Airlink (800/225-2525), United (800/241-6522), and US Air (800/428-4322). Boston's Logan International is 2½ hours away and Manchester (NH) Airport is 2 hours. If you live in or close to New England, it's probably more sensible to drive: You'll need a car while you're there anyway.

BY CAR: From the south take I-95 north to Portsmouth, NH. Then head north on the Spaulding Turnpike, to Route 16 north to Jackson. Jackson can also be reached from I-93 north, to exit 32. Turn left at the end of the exit onto the Kancamagus Highway. (The Kancamagus can be treacherous in bad weather. Take that into consideration when planning your drive.) Follow to end. Head north on Route 16 to Jackson. Or, take I-93 north, to Route 3 north to Route 302 east, to Route 16 north.

(The latter route is longer, but it avoids traffic on Route 16.)

From the north take I-91 or I-89 to Route 302 east, to Route 16 north.

BY TRAIN: Amtrak has no nearby service.

BY BUS: Concord Trailways (800/258-3722) has daily service from Boston.

CAR RENTAL: Two rental companies are located at the Portland Jetport: Budget Rent-a-Car (207/774-8642) and Thrifty (207/772-4268). In North Conway, call, Crest Chevrolet (603/356-5401).

TAXI/LIMOUSINE SERVICE: Lilley's Limousine in Cornish, ME – it's close by – (207/773-5765). For cabs, try Harris Taxi in North Conway (603/356-5577), Valley Taxi Service in Bartlett (603/374-2453).

INFORMATION: Mt. Washington Valley Chamber of Commerce, Route 16, P.O. Box 2300-G, North Conway, NH 03860, 800/367-3364, or 603/356-3171. Hours: 10:00 A.M. - 4:00 P.M. Monday through Thursday, until 5:00 P.M. Friday, 9:00 A.M. - 5:00 P.M. Saturday, 9:00 A.M. - 3:00 P.M. Sunday. There's also a visitor information booth in Jackson on Route 16 (603/383-9356) Hours: 10:00 A.M. - 4:00 P.M. Monday, Tuesday, and Thursday-Saturday. Closed Wednesday and Sunday.

Nantucket, Massachusetts

artha's Vineyard may be the island of choice for Hollywood celebrities. But Nantucket, which sits 30 miles off the Massachusetts shore and is little more than 14 x 3 miles around, offers a visit to another place and time. Imagine silver-gray shingled houses weathered by a century of salt-water breezes, brown cobblestone streets, fields of purple heather, and stands of pines.

Despite its relative inaccessibility – it takes nearly 2½ hours to reach by boat–Nantucket enjoys an international reputation for its muted beauty, serenity, and timelessness. The island's architecture is virtually unchanged from the mid 19th century when it was the most prosperous whaling port in the world. In summer, its population swells from 7,000 to nearly 40,000.

A far less crowded, and equally beautiful, season is winter. The first weekend in December, when the island conducts its annual Christmas Stroll, is unquestionably the most magical time to visit. Streets are dotted with twinkling Christmas trees, whimsically decorated by local children with painted walnuts and paper ornaments.

Merchants serve hot cider, sugar cookies, and other holiday treats. Santa rides through town in his sleigh. And carolers serenade visitors, encouraging them to sing along.

Begun in 1972 as a tactic to get islanders to Christmas shop at home rather than at mainland malls, the Stroll has burgeoned into an "event," attracting people from all over the country.

Several thousand visitors come to Nantucket for Christmas Stroll weekend, but don't let the numbers alarm you; the crowds in no way approach the summertime madness. Moreover, many people fly over just for Saturday, leaving the island wonderfully deserted on Sunday. You will, however, have to plan ahead. Because many inns and restaurants are closed for the season, an excessive strain is put on the year-round facilities. Consequently, it's not unusual for people to book inn and restaurant reservations up to a year in advance.

If you don't have this much forethought (who but a few among us does), be assured that you can usually get into your favorite restaurant if you call in the early afternoon. Those overly

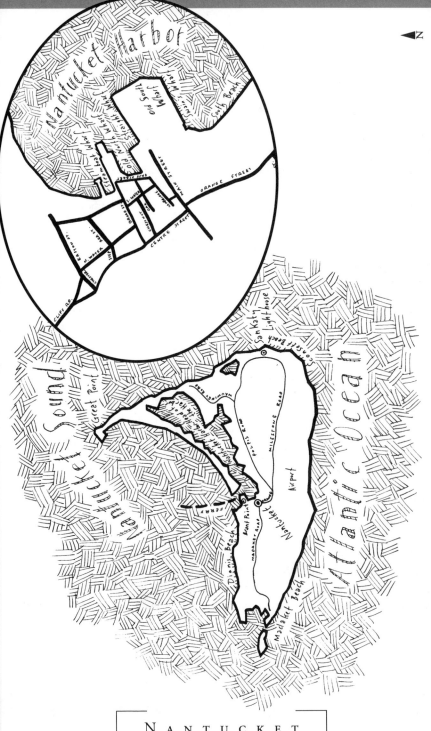

NANTUCKET

organized tourists frequently make two or three reservations for one night and then cancel the others once they decide.

Finding an inn on short notice isn't quite so easy. Your best bet is to call the Information Bureau (508/228-0925), a clearing house for room cancellations.

Nantucket plans lots of activities for Christmas Stroll weekend, more than are suggested here. To get a listing of the entire weekend's happenings, call the *Nantucket Beacon* (508/228-8455), and ask them to send you a copy of *The Caroler*, the Beacon's free Christmas magazine.

WHERE TO STAY

The Centerboard Guest House, ♥ ♥ ♥ ♥, $$$, 8 Chester St. 02554, 508/228-9696. From the outside, this sweet, white Victorian looks like a simple B&B. However, it is one of the most elegant and romantic small inns on the island. With pickled pine floors, white walls, white shutters, laced-trimmed pillow shams, and handmade quilts, the six guest rooms are pristine. Each is equipped with a television, telephone, and mini refrigerator. And on those cold December nights, you can cuddle up on the downy featherbeds that lie atop every mattress.

The grandest accommodation is the first floor suite: a large sitting room with parquet floors, eggplant-colored walls, and fireplace; a marble bath; and a bedroom with a four-poster bed draped in a lace canopy. On a smaller scale, room 2 has a wonderful pastel wall mural of the Nantucket moors, and a pale pink wedding ring bed quilt.

A homemade continental breakfast is served daily. Common rooms have a similarly light, airy–almost California– feel. As one Centerboard regular put it, "New Yorkers love this place. It's got everything they need: style, class, and amenities."

RATES PER NIGHT: $135-$225 (all double rooms are $135 expect for suite and small apartment), $85-$150 off and mid season.

ACCOMMODATIONS: 6 rooms with private baths.

AMENITIES: Telephone, televisions, and mini refrigerator in rooms.

RESTRICTIONS: No pets.

Cliff Lodge, ♥ ♥ ♥, $$$, 9 Cliff Rd. 02554, 508/228-9480. Set on a quiet residential street, just outside the bustle of downtown, Cliff Lodge was once the home of an 18th century sea captain. But today's Laura Ashley-inspired interior and funky, paint-splattered wood floors, give little indication of its former incarnation. Brightly papered walls and colored floors give Cliff Lodge– even in winter–a beachy ambiance. Most double rooms have nonworking fireplaces and king-size beds. All have eyelet-lace bedding and mohair throws.

Although all the rooms have a similar flavor, room 5 is particularly whimsical with a wonderful wooden folk-art angel that hangs above the bed. Room 2 is exceptionally large; an antique sea captain's chest sits at the foot of the bed, and the fireplace is graced with a large spray of peach silk tulips. If you want to splurge, the first floor apartment has a sitting room with a working fireplace, kitchenette, bath, and separate bedroom.

Live-in manager Gerri Miller makes and serves continental breakfast daily. Her granola is a favorite with guests, and many have suggested that she sell it commercially. In the afternoon, Miller serves snacks by the fireplace in the living room. (On Christmas stroll weekend, you'll get to taste her famous wassail.)

RATES PER NIGHT: $100-$190, $50-$120 off and mid season.

ACCOMMODATIONS: 11 rooms with private baths.

AMENITIES: Television and telephones in rooms.

RESTRICTIONS: No children under 10. No pets.

The Corner House, ♡ ♡, $$-$$$, 49 Centre St. 02554, 508/228-1530. If you're looking for the feel of an 18th century Nantucket seaport house – complete with original wide pine floorboards, paneling, and fireplaces – the Corner House should be your choice. Unlike many Nantucket B&Bs that gussy up their quarters, owners Sandy and John Knox-Johnston have maintained a colonial, Yankee flavor. Rooms are simple, but have an old-world charm, with deep-colored walls, antiques, and down comforters. All have private baths, although some are tiny. (It takes creative reconstruction to put modern amenities in a 220-year-old house.)

The Elderberry room is the most impressive, with a fireplace (nonworking), berry-colored walls, queen-size four-poster canopy bed covered with a red, green and peach paisley duvet. If bubble baths are on your itinerary, opt for the Beach Plum room which has an antique clawfoot tub.

In addition to the eight rooms in the main house, the Swan's Nest, just down the street, has four more rustically furnished rooms that include beamed cathedral ceilings, skylights, and sleeping lofts.

Part of the Corner House's charm is Sandy and John's hospitality. They, even more than the furnishings, give the Corner House a homey feel. Sandy enjoys cooking and it shows; breakfast includes an array of homemade muffins, coffeecake, sticky buns, juices, and fruit. In the afternoon, Sandy usually feeds guests one of her famous pâtés. Fires in the common rooms are always blazing, and the Knox-Johnstons are eager to chat or offer travel trips.

RATES PER NIGHT: $80-$130, $55-$110 off and mid season.

ACCOMMODATIONS: 8 rooms with private baths in the main house. The Swan's Nest has 4 rooms with private baths. Rose Cottage (open only in summer and early fall) has 2 rooms and a suite, all with private baths.

AMENITIES: Some rooms have televisions and refrigerators. Television in common room.

RESTRICTIONS: No children under 8. No pets.

Four Chimneys Inn, ♥ ♥ ♥, $$$-$$$$, 38 Orange St. 02554, 508/228-1912. Once the mansion of a wealthy sea captain, Four Chimneys is the most architecturally grand inn on Nantucket. Since she purchased the place in 1989, 30-year-old Bernadette Mannix has been working hard to give Four Chimneys the elegant ambiance it deserves. Rooms are outfitted with richly upholstered furniture and bed coverings. The Gardner Room is the inn's most luxurious, with a curtained canopy bed, working fireplace, bathroom with an antique clawfoot tub, and a private deck. The Lindlely Room, on the first floor, offers 8-foot windows, 10-foot ceilings, a working fireplace, and an original hand-carved Civil War era four-poster bed.

The inn's common areas include double parlors with fireplaces and crystal chandeliers. It is here Mannix serves a homemade continental breakfast that includes fresh juice, fruits, muffins, and pastries. If you're feeling decadent, Four Chimneys is glad to deliver your breakfast in bed. Tea and hors d'oeuvres are served daily at 5:00 P.M. And fresh baked choclate chip cookies usually find their way into the living room in the evening.

RATES PER NIGHT: $115-$185.

ACCOMMODATIONS: 10 rooms with private baths.

AMENITIES: Half the rooms have working fireplaces (a hard to come by commodity on Nantucket). Television and VCR in living room.

Restrictions: No pets. Children are welcome, but only two people are allowed in each room, so they would have to get their own room.

Ten Lyon Street, ♥ ♥ ♥, $$$, 10 Lyon St. 02554, 508/228-5040. Set on a tiny, quirky street filled with unprepossessing weathered shingled houses, Ten Lyon, at first glance, appears a modest B&B. The common rooms are small and have low ceilings. But as soon as innkeepers Ann Marie and Barry Foster open the staircase door and lead you to the upstairs guest chambers, you'll be in awe of the inn's simplistic beauty.

Barry completely refurbished the house with white plaster walls, pine floorboards, and ceiling beams. It is in no way austere, but rather graceful and elegant.

Ann Marie has filled the seven immaculately clean rooms with spectacular country antiques, among them sleigh beds, clawfoot tubs, and handmade quilts. But the rooms are really brought to life by Ann Marie's small touches— an unusual cache pot or mirror, a cluster of pine boughs carefully draped on a windowsill.

Room 1 is Ten Lyon's most elegant, with an antique French tester bed draped in diaphanous mosquito netting. Porcelain cupids hang on either side of the bed, and a dark red Oriental rug graces the wood floor. Room 5 is another winner, with a pine sleigh bed, fireplace, and large bath. In fact, all of Ten Lyon's bathrooms are among the biggest and best on the island.

Continental breakfast is served daily, as well as afternoon snacks.

RATES PER NIGHT: $120-$160 mid June to mid September and holidays, $85-$120 mid season, and $75-$95 off season.

ACCOMMODATIONS: 7 rooms with private baths.

AMENITIES: None

RESTRICTIONS: No children under 16. No pets.

FRIDAY EARLY EVENING

Note: Nantucket's downtown is so small, it is virtually impossible to get lost. But just in case, maps can be easily found in the town newspaper, which you can pick up at the ferry or airport, as well as at nearly every store. For this reason no in-transit notations are included in this chapter.

Christmas House Tour. Each year, Friends of the Nantucket Public Schools sponsor this tour, which takes visitors through five or six of the island's finest homes, typically sea captain's mansions. In addition to a fascinating glimpse inside these showplaces, you'll also learn about Nantucket's illustrious past. (The selection of houses changes every year.) A reception follows at the Thomas Macy Warehouse on Straight Wharf. Hours: tour starts at 4:00 P.M. Methodist Church, Center Street. Tickets: $15.

Dinner

The Second Story, ♥ ♥ ♥ ♥, $$$-$$$$, 1 South Beach St., 508/228-3471. Perhaps the most urbanely chic restaurant on Nantucket, the Second Story is a dark, intimate spot that sits above a French gift shop. Large hurricane lamps grace each table, providing the only light. An eclectic mix of art—from quilts to traditional ship oils to modern paintings—hang on forest green walls.

Decor reflects the menu's similarly adventurous mix. Favorites include grilled swordfish in garlic sauce, served over puréed squash with creme fettucini. The hors d'oeuvres are at least as, if not more, interesting that the entrees: lobster and spinach pâté in red pepper vinaigrette is sublime, and the shrimp cakes are among the best you'll eat. Hours: 7:00 P.M. - 9:15 P.M. (They usually accept later reservations on Stroll weekend.)

American Seasons, ♥ ♥ ♥ ♥, $$$-$$$$, 80 Centre St., 508/228-7111. With Pasty Cline playing softly in the background, champagne available by the glass, hand-painted tables, and walls covered with farm-scene murals, American Seasons is the funkiest restaurant on Nantucket, if not the best. The menu is inventive without being pretentious; it includes venison with buttered sweet potatoes and roast loin of pork with bacon gravy and country biscuits. For noncarnivores, American Seasons grills a near perfect salmon. The relative simplicity of the dishes belies the panache and expertise with which they are presented. Desserts too are at once upscale and down home – sweet potato pie, banana split with espresso chip ice cream and chocolate sauce. If you're a real gourmet, don't miss this gem. Hours: 6:00 P.M. - 10:00 P.M.

The Brotherhood of Thieves, ♥ ♥ ♥, $$, 23 Broad St., no phone. Don't give yourself away as an off-islander by calling this Nantucket institution by its full name. It is simply known as "The Brotherhood." It's included as a Friday dinner suggestion primarily because it is the only place you can get a meal until midnight. And if you take the 8:15 P.M. ferry, you won't get on island until 10:30 P.M. Beyond its convenience, however, The Brotherhood is a fantastically romantic, albeit rustic, spot. (Also a great spot for lunch, but daylight diminishes its mystique.)

As you descend into this English-style pub, you'll find a blazing fire, low (very low) beamed ceilings, and dark paneling. A jazz or folk musician will probably be playing softly in a corner. Fare is simple and hearty – burgers, fish and chips, chowder. Whatever you choose, you may want to order a side of shoestring fries, for which The Brotherhood is famous. The drink selection is bigger than the food menu. Try a hot concoction; the cider with rum, cinnamon, and cloves is delicious. Hours: 11:30 A.M. - 12:00 A.M. Friday and Saturday, 12:00 P.M. - 11 P.M. Sunday, 11:30 A.M.-11:00 P.M. Monday through Thursday.

SATURDAY MORNING

Historic Walk through Nantucket.

Starts at Jared Coffin House, 29 Broad St. This one-hour tour is one of the many yearly events that takes place over Christmas Stroll weekend. A guide, dressed in 1800s garb, assumes the persona of a long-dead Nantucketer and takes you through a one-hour tour of the island streets, explaining life as it was. The tour guide provides a colorful overview of Nantucket's impressive history and dispenses little known facts of its whaling years. Among the more interesting facts is that most whaling voyages lasted between three and five years. This dearth of men created a community essentially run by women, including virtually all the town's shops. Who would have thought such feminism existed in the 1850s? Hours: Tour starts at 10:00 A.M. Tickets: $5.

Shopping Nantucket's Boutiques.

Since the original purpose of the Christmas Stroll was to encourage islanders to shop at home, it's no surprise that one of the weekend's primary activities is shopping. You do have to do your Christmas shopping sometime.... Virtually all shopkeepers offer free cider, cocoa, cookies, and other holiday snacks to entice visitors. It's common for strangers to trade information on which shops are offering the best food. The decorated trees and strolling carolers add to the festive mood.

Visiting all the stores could take your entire weekend. Chances are you won't be able to – or even want to. Although half the fun is just browsing, following is a list of spots that you should make a special point to visit:

Spectrum, 26 Main St., 508/228-4606 This arts and crafts gallery is the best of its kind on the island. You'll find unusual pottery, glass lamps, furniture, jewelry, and high-quality Nantucket lightship baskets. All artists represented at Spectrum are American.

Nantucket Looms, 16 Main St., 508/228-1908. If you enjoy fine woolens, you'll be duly impressed here, where you can actually watch weavers at work. Look for a high-quality selection of handmade sweaters, scarves, and mittens, as well as hand-loomed blankets and throws, made from mohair, wool, and silk. There is also a selection of folk art. Be warned, prices are high.

Four Winds Craft Guild, 6 Straight Wharf, 508/228-9623. This store boasts that it has the largest selection of Nantucket lightship baskets and collector scrimshaw on the island. And although the store is small, it is chockablock with merchandise. Four Winds craftsmen are still using sperm whale bone that they had collected prior to 1972 when the U.S. government banned its importation and classified the whale as an endangered species. (Investors take note: Four Winds claims it only has a short supply left. You can expect that prices will only go up.)

Zero Main Street, O Main St., 508/228-4401. There's no funkier women's clothes shop. Lots of great hats, socks, and other accessories. In addition to name fashions from the likes of Kikit and Episode, Zero also carries an array of lesser known "arty" labels.

The Lion's Paw, O Main St., 508/228-3837. This upscale home accessories shop seems as if it's a Madison Avenue transplant. That possibly explains why the store is filled with so many women in fur coats. Merchandise includes fine linens, hand-painted trays, lace pillows, and French pottery.

The Artists Association's Little Gallery, Straight Wharf, 508/228-0294. For art collectors, this is the place to shop the local artists. As you might expect, there are a great many landscapes.

Lunch

Note: Unfortunately, Saturday lunch on the Stroll weekend can present a problem. Many visitors make day trips, and lunch is the excursion's focal point. Consequently, most restaurants are packed, requiring that you wait 15 minutes to an hour. If you have late dinner reservations, you could wait till about 3 P.M. – by that time you can be seated almost immediately. Otherwise, go with the flow, sidle up to the bar, and order some hot cider.

The Atlantic Café, $, 15 South Water St., 508/228-0570. One of the local hangouts, the Atlantic Café is great for a casual meal. Simple food, such as tuna melts, chili relejanos, and quahog chowder are among the menu's highlights. The atmosphere is nautical, and even on sunny days the restaurant's dark wood bar and booths gives you the feeling that you're eating in a ship's lower deck. Be sure to wait for your

table at the bar and catch a bit of island gossip. Hours: 11:30 A.M. - 12:00 midnight.

The Tap Room, $, 29 Broad St., 508/228-2400. Located downstairs at the Jared Coffin House, the Tap Room is a cozy restaurant and bar, with wooden tables and low, beamed ceilings, from which hang an array of wooden whales. The lunch menu includes hearty sandwiches and burgers. "Lite bites," such as chowder, steamers, and fried clams are served until closing. Hours: 11:30 A.M. - 2:30 P.M. Lite bites are served until 9:30 P.M.

Provisions, $, Straight Wharf, 508/228-3258. This gourmet café may not be fancy, but it has some of the best light fare on Nantucket. Service is primarily take out. However there are several tables spaciously arranged. Sandwiches are inventive, such and turkey breast on onion-dill bread, with stuffing and cranberry sauce. And the mini pizzas are sensational. Don't forget to finish off the meal with one of Provisions' lunch-dish size oatmeal cookies. This is the perfect spot if you don't have the temperament to wait at one of the "sit-down" restaurants. Hours: 9:00 A.M. - 4:00 P.M.

Note: If you didn't go to The Brotherhood for a late meal last night, be sure to stop in for lunch. It would be a shame to miss such an island classic. Don't be put off by the queue outside; there's no room to wait indoors and the line moves fast.

Saturday Afternoon

Visit the Whaling Museum, Broad Street at Steamboat Wharf, 508/228-1984. If you only visit one historical site on your trip to Nantucket, make sure it's the Whaling Museum. What makes this museum so good is that guides supplement historical artifacts – among them a 43-foot whale skeleton – with colorful insight into the rise and fall of the whaling era, and the men who made and lost their fortunes from it.

Appropriately, the museum is housed in a building that was once used for refining whale oil. Begin your tour with the 20-minute lecture that discusses the treacherous life on board a whaling vessel. If the guide doesn't offer, ask for an additional talk on the adventures of Captain Pollard. Usually, he or she will be more than happy to offer it.

Captain Pollard became infamous when it was discovered that he ate his nephew to stay alive while he was shipwrecked on a deserted island after a whale had gored his vessel. The museum has a replica of the ship, and a wall-size map of Pollard's course. Gory, but interesting nonetheless!

Also, don't miss the room filled with curiosities that whaling captains brought back from far off voyages. Hours: 10:00 A.M. - 5:00 P.M. Admission $3.

Witness Tree Lighting Ceremony, Main Street, in front of Pacific National Bank. This is another traditional Stroll event. What makes it so much fun is the caroling that goes along with it. Local singers, in 19th century garb, lead the crowds in traditional Christmas songs. With all this atmosphere – the singing, the lights, the cobblestone streets – you'll feel as if you're in a Walt Disney movie. (As precious as this scene might sound, it really is a charming event.) Hours: Starts at dusk; about 5:00 P.M.

Saturday Evening

Candlelight Ecumenical Service, United Methodist Church, Centre Street and Main Street.

It's easy to forget, but Christmas isn't a secular holiday. And while the message of Christmas may not be about romance, it is about love. This service, which is typically celebrated by representatives from most of the island's Christian churches, is a wonderful way to rekindle the holiday's true spirit. The service lasts about an hour and consists of prayers, readings, singing, and a homily. It's punctuated by a ceremony in which the clergy members walk through the church and light candles distributed to the congregation. Hours: Starts at 7:00 P.M.

Dinner

Le Languedoc, ♡ ♡, $$$-$$$, 24 Broad St., 508/228-2552. Although Le Languedoc is an inn and restaurant, its fine reputation is based strictly on its cuisine. The place is named after a province in the south of France and, not surprisingly, decor is reminiscent of a French country inn. Several small rooms, each with four or five tables, are decorated with pine antiques filled with faïence china and dried flowers. The menu shows a similar influence: beef bourguignon with winter vegetables, oyster stew with truffle butter toast, and desserts such as crème brûlee and apple raisin pudding. Hours: 6:00 P.M. - 9:00 P.M.

India House, ♡ ♡ ♡, $$$, 37 India St., 508/228-9043. Other restaurants may be more gracious, or urbane, but India House wins hands down for rustic, country – yes, romantic – charm. Housed in an authentic turn-of-the-18th century inn, the three small candle-lit dining rooms have wide pine floorboards and low ceilings; one has an enormous fireplace. Tables are set with linen and fresh flowers, which provide an interesting contrast to the rooms' natural rough-hewn appearance. The food here is among the best on the island, and is a favorite among residents, perhaps because of its unself-conscious style.

Although the menu changes weekly, during Christmas Stroll weekend, items might include venison chops with cognac mustard sauce, marinated scallops with roasted red pepper sauce, and escargots en croute with roquefort cream sauce. Desserts are simple but elegant: fresh fruit tarts, country pies, and chocolate pecan bourbon cake. Hours: 6:30 P.M. - 9:30 P.M. Closed Wednesdays.

After Dinner Drinks

The Club Car, ♡ ♡, $$, 1 Main St., 508/228-1101. In the late 18th century, when Nantucket was just testing the tourism waters, the island built a railroad to carry visitors from one end of the island to the other. In World War I, the cars and tracks were torn up for scrap metal. Today, the lone remaining rail car – still used to attract tourists– is now a part of a restaurant known appropriately as the Club Car. This old, slightly cramped Nantucket Railroad car serves as the restaurant's bar and main entrance. The perfect spot for history buffs to take their nightcaps. Piano entertainment. Hours: 11:00 A.M. - 1:00 A.M.

SUNDAY MORNING
Brunch

Note: Although all the inns recommended here have wonderful continental breakfasts, one of the most enjoyable and relaxing meals on a romantic getaway is Sunday brunch. And because there are so many fine restaurants on Nantucket – more than can be explored in two evening meals – you should get out and sample some morning fare.

Jared's, ♡, $$-$$$, 29 Broad St., 508/228-2400. If you're looking for a traditional brunch in a traditional setting, you'll love the Jared Coffin House's restaurant. Buy the *Boston Globe* or *New York Times* at the front desk and head into the inn's living room. Grab a seat by the fire and relax while you're waiting for a table. (Chances are the wait won't be longer than 20 minutes.)

Unlike some smaller inns' dining rooms, Jared's is large, airy, and lit by the room's many windows. Walls are a deep peach color, and wooden chandeliers, dressed in Christmas swags, hang from the ceiling.

If you're a lobster fan, don't miss Jared's version of eggs Benedict, which uses fresh boiled lobster instead of ham. Waffles with hot apple and cranberry compote are also delicious, as is the Grand Marnier French toast, made with Portuguese bread. But what makes Jared's truly stand out is its accommodating and friendly wait staff. On our visit, when one guest waffled about a particular item, a waitress offered to bring out a sample to test. Hours: 7:00 A.M. - 11:00 A.M.

21 Federal, ♡ ♡-♡ ♡ ♡, $$$ 21 Federal St., 508/228-2121. With polished pine floorboards, spruce-colored wainscoting, and fireplaces, 21 Federal's six small dining rooms have a subdued elegance. A great spot for the sophisticated palate, 21 Federal offers traditional egg dishes, but also a wide selection of nontraditional entrees. They include a half chicken with cranberry and chestnut sauce, Nantucket Bay scallops in garlic butter, and bouillabaisse with salmon, mussels, and rouille. One of the best kitchens on the island, you shouldn't go back to the mainland without trying a meal here. Hours: 11:30 A.M. - 2:30 P.M.

SUNDAY AFTERNOON

Nantucket Harbor Seal Cruise, Straight Wharf Slip #12, 508/228-1444. This hour-long motorboat cruise is the perfect way to spend a sunny winter afternoon. But be sure to bundle up – although the captain offers wool blankets – seating is strictly outside. The tour travels out to the jetties, where hundreds of seals who migrate yearly from Canada, reside. If you've never seen these animals up close, you owe it to yourself to go. They are silly looking creatures, who appear startlingly clumsy on land, yet are graceful in the water. Curious by nature, it's not uncommon for several seals to swim right up to the boat. An added bonus: You won't get a better view of Nantucket Harbor. Hours 1:00 P.M. and 3:00 P.M., but call to verify. Admission: $12.50.

Jeep Ride through Nantucket Beaches.

If you come without a car, it might seem that Nantucket *is* its main streets of commerce. However, some argue that the real Nantucket lies outside the center of town. For an unforgettable trip to Nantucket's deserted winter beaches, rent a jeep and go for a ride: Driving on the beach is permitted.

Although you can rent from many dealers around town (see Car Rentals under the Getting There section), we found Affordable Rentals, 6 South Beach St., 508/228-3501, unusually helpful. All rental companies, however, provide maps and directions to beaches.

One of the most picturesque rides is to Great Point. Until severe storms hit in the fall of 1991, you could drive all the way out to the lighthouse. At this writing, however, access was limited. But it's still worth a trip.

Another destination, on Nantucket's south side is Sankete Head Light. Be careful if you're unfamiliar with driving a jeep in sand. South side sand is much softer than that on north beaches, and people frequently get stuck. Thankfully, rental jeeps are equipped with shovels and ropes.

Of the northern beaches, consider a trip to Eel Point at the tip of Dionis Beach.

Additional Activities

Visit Theatre Workshop of Nantucket, 62 Centre St., 508/228-4305. Every year the island's own production company stages a popular play for Christmas visitors. (The 1991 production was By the Skin Of Our Teeth.) Performances are held Friday, Saturday, and Sunday of Christmas Stroll weekend.

Rafael Osona Antique Auction, American Legion Hall, Washington Street, 508/228-3942. It may not be easy to get your purchases off island, but if you're an antique lover, don't miss this. Although Osona has auctions throughout the year, bidding is known to remain unusually low at the Christmas auction because most people who attend are tourists. (If you really get a deal, you won't mind paying the freight.) Merchandise typically consists of American and English furniture, decorative accessories, paintings, Oriental and hooked rugs, quilts, jewelry, crystal, and silver.

GETTING THERE

BY AIR: Because ferries to Nantucket take more than two hours one way, many people prefer to fly. Several airlines offer service: Delta Business Express (800/345-3400) has daily flights from Boston and New York. Northwest Airlink (800/225-2525) has daily flights from Boston and Newark. Nantucket Airlines (508/228-6234 or 800/635-8787) has 12 round-trip flights a day (from Hyannis) from 6:35 A.M. to 7:20 P.M. (to 8:30 on Friday). Two charter services also operate to Nantucket: Coastal Air Services (508/693-5942) and Rainbow Air (609/921-3867), which is based in New Jersey.

BY CAR: Obviously you can only drive as far as Hyannis, then must take either a ferry or plane to Nantucket: From

Boston, take Route 3 south to Route 6 east. Take exit 6/Route 132 and follow to Hyannis. At the downtown rotary, take the second right off the rotary. At the fork, take a right. Turn right onto Main Street, then left on Ocean Street. At the Shell station, turn left onto South Street. The Steamship Authority is on South.

From the New York area, take I-95 north to I-195 east to Route 6.

To the airport: Hyannis Airport is right off Route 132 at the Hyannis Rotary. You'll see signs at the rotary for the airport.

BY TRAIN: No train service is available.

BY BOAT: Barring foul weather, the ferry can be fun. Everyone is in a festive mood. And somehow, any place you must travel to by boat seems clandestine. Bring a thermos of rum cider to sip while you're gazing at the rolling, black sea.

In winter, the only ferry available to Nantucket is through the Steamship Authority in Hyannis. There are three crossings daily at 9:15 A.M., 2:45 A.M., and 8:15 P.M. From Nantucket to Hyannis, scheduled crossings are 8:45 A.M., 12:00 noon, and 5:30 P.M. No reservations are needed for walk-on passengers. Round trip cost is $19.

Cars are truly unnecessary (and indeed unwanted) on Nantucket. All inns are located either in town, or within a three- to five-minute walk from the center. Besides, taking your car on the ferry is expensive – $94 round-trip. The steamship has parking lots where you may leave your car. However, a lot directly across the street from the docks is cheaper, and just as convenient.

If you decide you must take a car, be sure to make ferry reservations early – preferably several months in advance – space is at a premium. You can also rent cars on the island.

BY BUS: Although buses do travel to Hyannis, you'll have to take a cab from the terminal to the Steamship Authority. If you can arrange for another mode of transportation, do so. But if you must, Bonanza (800/343-9330) has service from New York, Providence, and Boston. Plymouth & Brockton (800/328-9997) offers service from Boston, including from Logan airport.

Car Rental: Many national car rental companies have offices on Nantucket. The airport has National (508/228-0300), Budget (508/228-5566), and Hertz (508/228-9421). Companies at Steamboat Wharf include Ford Rent-a-Car (508/228-1151), and Nantucket Four Wheel (5508/228-6040). Others on island are Affordable Cars & Jeeps (508/228-3501), Barrett's (508/228-0174),

Harbor Sales (508/228-5585), Nantucket Jeep Rentals (508/228-1618), and Windmill Auto Rental (508/228-1227).

TAXI/LIMOUSINE SERVICE: Barretts Tours & Taxi, 508/228-0174.

INFORMATION: Nantucket Island Chamber of Commerce, Pacific Club Building, Lower Main Street, Nantucket 02554, 508/228-1700. Hours: 9:00 A.M. - 5:00 P.M. Monday through Friday, 11:00 A.M. - 3:00 P.M. Saturday in summer and on Christmas Stroll weekend. The Visitors Information Center is located at 25 Federal St., 508/228-0925 or 0926. Hours: 9:00 A.M. - 5:30 P.M. Monday through Saturday. Open Sunday in summer and on Christmas Stroll weekend.

Portland, Maine

*P*ortland is a city that can easily be forgotten. Just 90 minutes from Boston, many visitors think of it as the Hub's poor relation. And while Boston may cast a long shadow, it has not shrouded Portland – a thriving seaside mini-metropolis with a symphony, two theater companies, world-class restaurants, and an I.M. Pei-designed art museum.

Surprised? So are most first-time visitors. Who would have thought Maine could be so cosmopolitan, you say. Well, unfortunately, a few have already uncovered this little jewel. In the past decade, greater Portland's population has grown by 10 percent to 186,000. (Central Portland's population is 64,000.)

A healthy portion of that increase is due to the influx of the much maligned young urban professional. For city dwellers looking to escape the hustle, dirt, and crowds without forsaking bagels and good book stores, Portland is nothing short of perfect. It is at once rural and cultural.

While primarily known as a summer destination, Portland is equally beautiful in winter and far less crowded. Moreover, it's a great cold weather escape alternative– imagine traveling to northern New England without having to lug your skis.

Part of Portland's charm (and claim to fame) is its working port, refreshingly still alive, and bustling with fishing trawlers. But equally, if not more, important to its overall appearance is its architectural integrity. You can find Renaissance Revival state buildings, Italianate mansions, grand Federal style homes, and Victorian gingerbread cottages – all amazingly well preserved.

What you won't find in Portland are skyscrapers, blocks of brownstones, or even much traffic. For it is not modern, retro-chic, or home to the business world's wheelers and dealers. It is simply a thriving, working city, that is trying to be nothing but itself.

WHERE TO STAY

The Pomegranate Inn, ♡ ♡ ♡ ♡, $$, 49 Neal St. 04102, 207/772-1006 or 800/356-0408. It is difficult to describe the Pomegranate Inn without sounding like a paid advertisement, for this is one of the finest, if not the finest, B&B in New England. Owners Isabelle and Alan Smiles have created an aesthetically invigorating showplace filled with original modern and classical art, antiques, and quality furniture. The overall effect is something just short of magical.

Isabelle gave up her interior design work in Greenwich, Connecticut, to run the Pomegranate, and her professional experience shows. The main entrance area has hand-painted wood floors that resemble black and white marble tiles. And the hall walls are a vibrant mustard yellow, also hand-painted, and covered with art.

The eight guest rooms show similar panache. They too have hand-painted walls, some with a wild tropical theme, others more subdued. All have modern amenities that include telephones, televisions, and large baths, as well as down comforters and feather pillows.

Room five is particularly elegant with its cranberry and mauve striped walls and a teal Grecian design border (unusual, but surprisingly tasteful). It also boasts a queen-size four-poster bed draped in a white swag, an antique dresser, Oriental rug, and original oil paintings. There's even art in the bathroom.

Breakfast is served in the living room at a large table hand painted in deep hues of purple, green, and gold. Isabelle and Alan do the cooking themselves, and are as concerned about the food as they are about the inn's decoration. A typical breakfast includes coffee, juice, fruit, eggs, scones, and toast and jam. Ever meticulous, Alan bakes fresh bread for toast.

All the gushing said, the Pomegranate may not suit all tastes. The Smiles don't run a cute country inn – there are no hand-stitched quilts or dried flower arrangements. It is rather a sophisticated respite for the urban traveler.

RATES PER NIGHT: $85; $95-$125 late May through October.

ACCOMMODATIONS: Eight rooms with private baths, including one suite with a sitting area and kitchen.

AMENITIES: Telephones and televisions in rooms.

RESTRICTIONS: No children. No smoking in guest rooms. No pets.

The West End Inn, ♡ ♡, $$, 146 Pine St., 04102, 207/772-1377. Located in a stately brick townhouse on a quiet street in the Western Promenade, The West End Inn is a cozy place that could be a stage set for a BBC mini series. Tom and Hilary Jacobs (Hilary is, in fact, from England), who opened the West End four years ago after retiring, have infused the place with a sense of rumpled gentility.

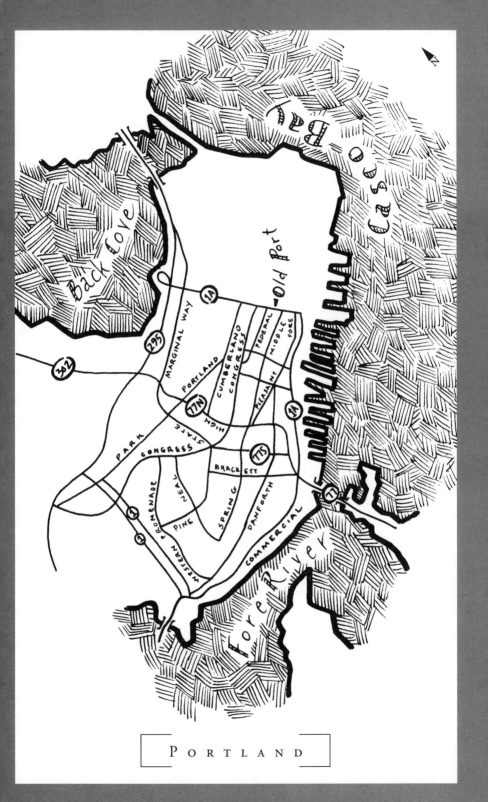

PORTLAND

The living room is painted a soft cream and is outfitted with overstuffed couches, landscape paintings in ornate wooden frames, scatter rugs, and delicate lamps on silver pedestals.

Each of the four guest rooms, all with lovely new modern baths, has a similar feel. The King room boasts a king-size four-poster bed with a chenille spread, a beige rug, pink floral wallpaper, and an antique sea-captain's trunk. The Queen room is also a good choice. Although a bit smaller, it's situated in the corner of the building and gets both morning and afternoon light.

Hilary has a friendly manner and makes you feel more like a guest in her home than a customer. To that end, she likes to add a few extra touches: a small bowl of fresh fruit in each room, along with a couple of bottles of water, and a dish of candy.

She and Tom make a full breakfast for guests every morning. Their repertoire includes homemade breads, muffins, pancakes, scambled eggs, and waffles. The meal is served at a large wooden table in the dining room, which is filled with paintings and knickknacks, including Hilary's collection of porcelain and silver teapots. The pots are put to good use as well – the Jacobs also serve tea in the afternoons.

RATES PER NIGHT: $80, $90 in summer and fall.

ACCOMMODATIONS: 4 rooms with private baths.

AMENITIES: None.

RESTRICTIONS: No smoking. No pets. No children under 8.

The Portland Regency, ♡-♡♡, $$-$$$, 20 Milk St., Portland 04101, 207/774-4200. For those who enjoy big hotel amenities, but with personal service and charm, the Portland Regency is a perfect choice. This family-owned, 4-story, 95-room hotel sits in the heart of the Old Port. Prior to its present incarnation, it was a National Guard armory.

Because of its former service, each of the guest rooms has a different configuration. Rooms on the fourth floor have skylights, and the two suites both have turrets. These suites are the Regency's choice rooms and are worth the little bit extra you'll pay for them. They have brick fireplaces, high ceilings and windows, sitting areas, and king-size four-poster beds. Both are decorated in shades of gray, peach, pink, and white, and have matching floral curtains and bedspreads.

The Regency's standard king rooms are similarly outfitted, although a bit smaller, and have no couch or fireplace. Amenities in all rooms include two telephones, cable television, and a stocked mini bar.

Among the Regency's homey touches are free newspapers and complimentary morning coffee served in rooms. Coffee is also available in the lobby until 10:00 P.M. every night. Although breakfast isn't included in the room rate, the hotel has a full-service restaurant that serves three meals a day. Interestingly, the restaurant, which has red and white marble tile floors, was once a drill room where the Guard practiced their maneuvers.

In addition, the hotel has a lounge, called Salutes, which is a popular local hangout, as well as a full-service health club.

RATES PER NIGHT: $95-$110, $150 for suites. $100-$130 (for standard rooms) in spring, $115-$140 in summer and fall.

ACCOMMODATIONS: 93 rooms with private baths, and 2 suites with private baths.

AMENITIES: Telephones, cable television, and mini bars in rooms. Full service restaurant serving three meals, as well as a cocktail lounge. Full service health club. Complimentary coffee and newspapers. Free shuttle to and from the airport. No-smoking rooms available.

RESTRICTIONS: None.

FRIDAY EVENING

Note: Portland has a lively downtown. And if the weather isn't too cold, it's fun to walk to dinner. From the west end, where both the Pomegranate and West End Inn are located, it should take no more than 15 minutes. The Regency is right in the heart of the city. Although directions are provided here, it's always wise to have a street map. Ask for one at your inn.

Alberta's Café, ♡ ♡, $$, 21 Pleasant St., 207/774-0016. In transit: From the West End, walk east on Pine Street to State Street. Turn right on State, then left on Spring Street, then left onto Pleasant Street. From the Regency, turn left onto Market Street, then right onto Fore Street, which becomes Pleasant.

This casual, eclectic restaurant with delicious raspberry-colored walls attracts an arty crowd. The menu, best described as New American, is a mix of many different cuisines. Appetizers, though tasty, are almost absurdly adventurous – try stir-fried scallops and vegetables served in a poppadum taco shell with a lemon grass, cilantro, and tomato cream sauce. Entrees are just slightly more tame. If you like shrimp, try the sautéed black tiger shrimp with andouille sausage and tomatoes in a pistachio, parsley, and garlic sauce. The pan-fried chicken breast on a bed of mustard greens in a pancetta and onion sauce is also a winner.

If you've got a light appetite, Alberta's suggests ordering an appetizer, and for an additional $4 they'll provide a salad, vegetable, and rice or potato to make a complete meal.

Service is fast, but customers are never rushed. It's the perfect spot for a good meal when you have other plans for the evening. Hours: 5:00 P.M. - 10:30 P.M. Monday through Thursday, 5:00 P.M. - 11:00 P.M. Friday and Saturday, 5:00 P.M. - 10:00 P.M. Sunday.

Katahdin, ♡ ♡, $$-$$$, Spring and High streets, 207/774-1740. In transit: From the West End, head east on Pine Street, then turn right onto State Street, then left onto Spring Street. From the Regency, turn left onto Market Street right onto Fore Street, which becomes Pleasant Street. Then turn right onto High Street.

Katahdin looks like a dive bar. And, in fact, that's precisely what this one-story corner brick storefront was before it was turned into Portland's hottest new restaurant. Katahdin is relentlessly funky, with a simultaneously down home and high haute flavor. Brick walls are painted white and decorated with everything from patchwork quilts to tribal art. Tables are hand painted a deep blue, and are complimented by a dull blue ceiling that resembles a twilight sky. The long bar that anchors the middle of the restaurant is painted to look like it might be from an old-stone hunting lodge.

The menu is similarly eclectic. Katahdin's shtick is to the blur the lines between home cooking and haute cuisine. The end result is food that is always interesting, if not always first rate.

Appetizers include lobster spring rolls with grilled duck sausage and goat cheese flans. These gourmet treats are offered side-by-side with nightly blue plate specials, which on some nights might be as simple as pot roast. More sophisticated entrees include vegetarian lasagna with smoked gouda and sweet peppers in a cream sauce. All Katahdin's meals are served with buttermilk biscuits, salad, and a starch, and vegetable of the day. Hours: 5:00 P.M. - 9:00 P.M. Monday through Wednesday, 5:00 P.M. - 10:00 P.M. Thursday through Saturday. Closed Sunday.

Coffee and Jazz

café no, $, 20 Danforth St., 207/772-8114. In transit: Danforth intersects High Street and is two blocks north of Commercial Street, which is on the water.

This nightclub and restaurant, located in a renovated factory space, is a little bit of Soho in Portland. Offering the only live jazz in the city, café no is also one of the city's most popular night spots. The atmosphere is coffee house casual – old brick walls, high ceilings, and long large windows. (You might feel out of place in a coat and tie.)

Although café no does serve food, primarily Middle Eastern specialties, many people come just for the music. Eating isn't required, and food isn't served after 9:00 P.M. anyway (8:00 P.M. on Sunday). Café no serves beer and wine only. Hours: 11:00 A.M. - 9:00 P.M. Tuesday and Wednesday, 11:00 A.M.- 12:00 midnight or 1:00 A.M. Thursday through Saturday. Live music starts about 9:00 P.M. and is available Thursday through Saturday. Closed Monday.

SATURDAY MORNING

Self-Guided Walking Tour of the Western Promendade.

In transit: Begin your tour at the Thomas Brackett Reed statue, which is on Western Promenade (the street) at West Street. From the Regency, take a cab. In cold weather, you probably won't feel like taking the 25-minute hike to the statue, then taking the tour. Both the West End Inn and Pomegranate are just blocks from the statue. Neal and Pine streets both intersect West. Head west on West Street to the Western Promenade

This suggested tour is outlined in Greater Portland Landmarks Inc.'s wonderful architectural walking-tour maps. Each of Portland's four major neighborhoods is accorded its own booklet in which it's described in detail. Your innkeepers should have a copy they can lend you. If not, the guides can be purchased at several downtown book shops, including Little Nemo's

World of Books (420 Fore St., 207/ 874-2665). Or if you want to plan ahead, call Greater Portland Landmarks (165 State St., Portland 04104, 207/774-5561) and ask them to send you one.

Since the 1850s, Portland's Western Promenade neighborhood has been considered the city's most fashionable. The area was so named because it was originally planned as a public walk and carriage way that commanded then unspoiled views of the Atlantic Ocean and White Mountains.

Although Portland has gone through many changes since its development, the "Western Prom" (as residents call it) remains Portland's choicest section. The people living here today reside in the very same homes that were showplaces a century ago. In fact, the Western Promenade is considered one of America's best-preserved Victorian residential neighborhoods: The whole area was entered into the National Register of Historic Places in 1982.

The Portland Landmark tour will take you by fine examples of Gothic Revival, Italianate, Federal, Queen Anne, Mansard, and Stick and Shingle style architecture. Plan to take at least two hours. The entire walk is only about 1.5 miles long, but you'll want to do plenty of lingering.

Lunch

Gritty McDuff's, $, 396 Fore St., 207/ 772-2739. In transit: Assuming you've completed the end of the architectural tour, you'll end up on Vaughn Street. Turn right onto Pine Street, then right onto Congress Street, then right onto Exchange Street. Turn left onto Pleasant Street, which runs into Fore Street. Gritty's is in the middle of Portland's Old Port district. The walk should take you about 20 minutes. If you decide to take a taxi, the nearest phone is at the Maine Medical Center. To get there, turn left on Pine, then right on Western Promenade. The center will be right in front of you.

In any city, it's always fun to visit a favorite local hang out. And in Portland, Gritty's is just such a place. It brews its own beer right in the basement, and feels very much like an authentic English pub – down to the kidney pie and common dining tables. It's a great spot for picking up insider travel tips from friendly locals.

The menu is simple and hearty, and includes sandwiches, soups, and pub-style meals. A favorite is the ploughman's lunch: liver, Gloucester cheddar cheese, chutney, pickle, and peasant bread. If you like burgers, Gritty's has some unusual and delicious choices. Both the mint-spiced lamb burger and vegetarian lentil burger are nice twists on an old standard.

Don't forget to sample one of Gritty's six brews, among them, a low-alcohol ale. Hours: from 11:30 A.M. Food is served until 8:00 P.M.

Walter's, $$, 15 Exchange St., Portland, 207/871-9258. In transit: From Vaughn Street, where you'll end up at the end of the architectural tour, turn right onto Pine Street, then right onto Congress Street, the right onto Exchange Street.

Walter's is one of Portland's newest and best restaurants. This bright airy café has a great simple atmosphere and top-notch food. It's no wonder that there's usually a wait to get in, even at lunch on weekdays. (If you do have to wait, you can always poke around the shops on Exchange Street.)

The restaurant is long and narrow with high, ornate tin ceilings, brick walls, plants in terra cotta pots, and lots of sunlight. The menu serves standard fare, but all done with a light and elegant touch. Sandwiches include grilled chicken with pecans, and bacon, lettuce, and tomato served in a flour tortilla with sweet Cajun mayonnaise. Among the salads is a delicious Chinese chicken salad with freshly grilled chicken, cashews, crispy noodles, and lots of dark greens in sesame ginger dressing. If you've worked up a big appetite, Walter's also has a good selection of pizzas (thin style) and hot entrees. The latter includes lots of fresh fish, such as steamed mussels, and angel hair pasta with lobster, mushrooms, and scallions. (Walter's also has a good dinner menu.) Lunch hours: 11:00 A.M. - 3:00 P.M.

SATURDAY AFTERNOON

Shopping in the Old Port.

In transit: Both Gritty McDuff's and Walter's are in the middle of the Old Port. You only need to walk out the door and start browsing through the colorful shops. The general area is bounded by Commercial Street to the south and Congress Street to the north, and encompasses Exchange, Milk, Market, Middle, Union, and Fore streets.

The Old Port is the jewel of Portland's commercial district. What makes it particularly exciting is its blend of old and new. Although many of the old brick warehouses have been restored (a la Boston's Faneuil Hall) and now house art galleries, clothing stores, and trendy cafés, just as many are home to sail makers and chandlers. The area has at once authentic patina and a modern spit and polish.

You could spend your entire weekend shopping in the Old Port, but the city has so much more to offer. One afternoon should satisfy all but the most ardent, shop-happy couples. Most stores are open until 5:00 P.M. , and a few remain open until 6:00 P.M. Following are some stores and galleries that should not be missed:

Joseph's, 410 Fore St., 207/773-1274. *The* high-end, high-fashion (men's and women's) clothing store in Portland. If you like Armani, Max Mara, and clothes made to order, this is the place. You'll find styles and accessories that the big stores don't carry. Even if you don't think you can afford the merchandise – you will see $400 women's pants – it's worth a look see. Besides, they have some great winter sales.

Little Nemo's World of Books, 420 Fore St., 207/775-5841. This shop has a fine selection of antique and rare books and maps. Bibliophiles could spend hours here. If you're looking for an out-of-print book, Little Nemo's offers a search service.

African Imports, New England Arts, 1 Union St., 207/772-9505 Great selection of interesting and unusual collectible objects, from tribal masks to brilliant painted-fabric wall hangings. Also a selection of jewelry, pottery, and small sculptures

Congress Square Gallery, 42 Exchange St., 207/774-3369. If you're looking for modern interpretations of "landscape paintings," check out Congress Square, arguably the most progressive gallery in Portland. Gallery artists include Phillip Barter, Gina Werfel, and Margaret Gerding.

West Port Antiques, 8 Milk St., 207/774-6747. This small homewares antique shop, filled with beautiful lace, quilts, china, and fabrics is a step above most stores of its kind.

Thos. Moser Cabinetmakers, 415 Cumberland Ave., 207/774-3791. This store isn't quite in the Old Port, but, if you appreciate fine furniture, you should make a trip here. Thomas Moser is one of the country's most renowned and respected furniture makers. He lives, works, and has a showroom in Portland. His style is early American, almost Shaker like. Moser works only in American-grown woods, primarily cherry and ash. Merchandise is expensive (close to $5,000 for an "entertainment" unit), but well worth it.

Dinner

Note: Plan an early meal so you can enjoy one of Portland's cultural offerings, either the symphony or theater.

Café Always, ♡ ♡ ♡ ♡, $$$, 47 Middle St., Portland, 207/774-9399. In transit: From the West End, head east on Pine Street, then turn right onto State Street, then left onto Spring Street. Spring Street turns into Middle Street. Café Always is on the far edge of the Old Port, on the left. From the Portland Regency, walk up Market or Pearl Streets (away from the water), and turn right on Middle Street.

Simply, Café Always is Portland's best restaurant. In fact, it's probably one of the best restaurants in New England. Chef/owner Cheryl Lewis' philosophy of food is "no rules." Hence she combines elements of many cuisines – Italian, French, African, Japanese, Cajun, Thai, and Mexican – to create what she describes as modern American food.

Appetizers include salmon cakes sautéed and served with Japanese wasabi and beurre blanc, and a salmon and cilantro quesedilla filled with mozzarella, cheddar, and Parmesan cheese, served with salsa, and sour cream. As heavy-handed as these dishes might sound (particularly the latter), Lewis's style is to kiss with flavor rather than smother. Everything is treated with a light and, indeed, artistic hand.

Among the most popular entrees is lobster served with mango salsa and lime beurre blanc. Other favorites include fettucine tossed with grilled squid, olives, tomatoes, garlic, Parmesan cheese, and sweet onions.

If you're a chocolate fan, be sure to save room for dessert. Café Always offers several dangerous treats. If the chocolate roulade filled with ricotta and hazelnuts and served with dark chocolate sauce is offered, don't pass it up.

The space is intimate – not much more than a dozen tables, and decor is sophisticated and spare. Walls are handpainted with a pale peach design; tables are covered with white clothes and white butcher paper, and decorated with a single votive candle. Hours: from 5:00 P.M. Reservations are recommended and usually accepted until about 10:00 P.M. Closed Sunday and Monday.

Back Bay Grill, ♥ ♥ ♥, $$$, 65 Portland St., 207/772-8833. In transit: You'll probably want to drive here. From the West End, travel north on Neal Street to Congress Street. Turn right on Congress, then left onto Mellen to Park Avenue. Turn right onto Park, which goes into Portland Street. From the Portland Regency, travel north onto Pearl Street, then turn left onto Cumberland Street. Turn right onto Premble Street, then left onto Portland Street.

Despite the fact that the Back Bay Grill is located in one of Portland's less savory neighborhoods, it's a favorite spot for the city's power executives. As soon as you walk through the door and catch a glimpse of the stainless-steel bar, you'll understand why. The Back Bay Grill is sleek. The two dining rooms have high ceilings and glistening white walls covered with large, modern oil paintings. From the front room, dinners can watch the chefs at work in the open kitchen. (If you're looking for quiet, you should try to reserve a table in the back room. However, the front room, where the bar is located, is more of a scene.)

The menu, which changes weekly, is as stylish as the surroundings, and nearly rivals Café Always in preparation and presentation. Appetizers might include such inventive offerings as lobster won tons in chili sauce, or carpaccio with celery root remoulade. Entrees

emphasize grilled items. But all are served with unusual flair. For example, a grilled veal chop might be served with peppercorn sauce and braised endive, and chicken with root vegetables and cumin in a roasted pepper sauce.

Desserts usually include some decadent chocolate offerings. On our visit it happened to be a delicious chocolate rum torte with mocha butter cream and espresso creme anglaise. Or, for the ultimate comfort dessert, try a Back Bay Grill standard, crème brûlée. They're famous for it. Hours: 5:30 P.M. - 9:30 P.M. or 10:00 P.M. Monday through Saturday.

After Dinner Entertainment

Portland Symphony Orchestra, 30 Myrtle St., 207/773-8191 or 800/638-2309. In transit: Drive or take a cab from the Back Bay Grill. The Symphony is no more than a 10-minute walk from Café Always. Walk onto Middle Street, back toward the center of the Old Port. Then turn right onto Market Street, then left onto Congress. The symphony performs in the Portland City Hall auditorium, which is on the corner of Congress and Myrtle streets.

The Portland Symphony offers a wide range of entertainment that includes both a pop and classical series. Special guests run the gamut from the flamboyant, Grammy-award winning Doc Severinsen to world renowned cellist Janos Starker.

During its regular season, which runs from October to April, only popular music concerts are given on Saturday evenings. Seven classical performances are given on selected Tuesday evenings. Chamber orchestras perform on four Sunday afternoons. Over the holidays, there are 11 Christmas concerts.

If visiting the symphony is a must on your visit, call ahead to make sure a concert is planned. Although you'll have the best seating selection if you order ahead, it is usually possible to get tickets on the day of a performance.

Saturday performances begin at 8:00 P.M. Admission: $10-$30, depending on seating and performers.

Portland Stage Company, 25A Forest St., 207/774-0465. In transit: Drive or take a cab from the Back Bay Grill. The Stage Company is only a 10-minute walk from Café Always. Head north onto Middle Street. Turn left onto Federal Street, then left onto Congress, then right onto Forest Street.

In operation since 1974, the Portland Stage Company is the city's premiere professional theater organization. (The Mad Horse Theatre Company is Portland's neophyte theater troupe and performs only sporadically.) The company's mainstay are contemporary plays and reinterpretations of classics. Two recent productions that exemplify its range are Sam Shepard's *Fool for Love* and Machiavelli's *The Mandrake*.

The company's season runs from November through March, and includes seven plays. Each has at least 21 performances. Saturday performances start at 9:00 P.M. Admission: $12-$26.50. If the play isn't sold out within 10 minutes of curtain time, tickets can be purchased at the door for 50 percent off.

Late Evening Hot Tub Soak

The Tub Shop, 30 Market St., 207/774-7491. In transit: From the symphony turn left onto Congress Street, then right onto Market Street. From the Portland Stage Company, head south on Forest Avenue, then left onto Congress Street, then right onto Market Street.

What could be more relaxing than spending an hour in a secluded candle-lit room lounging in your own private hot tub? Nothing, you might say. Most people consider renting a hot tub by the hour a bit tawdry, but after one visit to the immaculately clean and pleasant Tub Shop, even the most skeptical traveler will be convinced that this in an entirely respectable and wholeheartedly romantic endeavor.

The ambiance is one of an upscale health club. Each of the four private rooms is wood paneled, and has a private shower, dressing area, radio/cassette player, and a wooden deck that is decorated with plants. Water is heated to 104 degrees and spas are equipped with hydro therapy jets and an air bubbler.

Room 4 is particularly pleasant because it has a window. What a great treat to relax in a steaming tub and watch the snow fall. Hours: 12:00 P.M. - 2:00 A.M. Thursday through Saturday, 12:00 P.M. - 12:00 A.M. Sunday through Wednesday. Cost: $25 per hour.

SUNDAY MORNING

Boat Trip to, and Hike Around, Peaks Island, Casco Bay Lines, Casco Bay Ferry Terminal, Commercial and Franklin streets, 207/774-7871. In transit: From the West End, take a cab to the Ferry Terminal. Or, if you're checking out of your inn, you can drive. The Terminal is on the east end of Commercial Street. If you follow Clark Street south, it intersects with Pine and runs into Commercial Street. From the Portland Regency, walk down Market or Pearl streets toward the water. Turn left onto Commercial Street.

Peaks Island – a 15-minute ferry ride from downtown Portland – is just five miles in circumference and has about 1,000 year-round residents. Dotted with a melange of Victorian style cottages, it's a treat to walk around the perimeter of the island: It takes about 1½ hours and the paved roads are flat. The island provides some great views of Casco Bay and the Atlantic.

Even though it's virtually impossible to get lost, buy a map at Down Front, an ice cream and candy shop. It's the blue building just beyond the ferry dock at the corner of the first main thoroughfare (Island Avenue). Hours: Ferries travel roughly on the hour. Call ahead for a schedule. Round-trip tickets: $6.

Boat Trip Around the islands on Casco Bays Mail Boat Run, Casco Bay Lines, Casco Bay Ferry Terminal, Commercial and Franklin Streets, Portland, 207/ 774-7871. In transit: (See above).

If you're not up for a hike, consider a trip on the islands' mail boat. The longest operating service of its kind in America, the boat carries commuters, freight, and mail to the islands in Casco Bay. You'll have dockside views of Cliff, Chebeaque, Long, and Little and Great Diamond islands. The entire trip takes 2 hours and 45 minutes. Indoor seating is available. Hours: 10:00 A.M. and 2:45 P.M. daily. Tickets: $8.50.

Lunch

The Seamen's Club, $$, 1 Exchange St., 207/772-7311. In transit: From the ferry terminal, walk west on Commercial street, then turn right onto Exchange Street.

After a morning "at sea," you'll probably feel compelled to have some fish for lunch, and the Seamen's Club is among

Portland's best spots for a good, traditional meal. The fresh crab meat sandwiches on homemade bread are outstanding – just the right amount of mayonnaise to hold the meat together without overpowering the crab's delicate flavor. Or, if you can't leave Maine without having a boiled lobster, Seamen's serves a fine specimen. Its chowders, unfortunately, are less than inspired. (Yet it's an item for which they are known.)

Atmosphere is casual. Ambiance (which relies on the oldstandby: exposed brick and plants) is drawn primarily from its second floor perch and expansive windows with views of the Old Port and harbor. Be sure to ask for a table by the window. Hours: from 11:00 A.M.

SUNDAY AFTERNOON

Visit The Portland Museum of Art, 7 Congress Square, 207/773-2787. In transit: Head north on Exchange Street, then turn left onto Congress Street. The museum is a few blocks up on the left, and is about a 10-minute walk from the restaurant.

The architectural style alone is reason enough to visit this post-modern building, designed by Henry Cobb of I.M. Pei. Built in 1983, the new structure essentially replaced the museum's original buildings, which were more than a century old. (These buildings are still standing, but closed pending renovation.) Winner of international architectural awards, the interior is unusually light and airy because of its sky lit domes and stark white walls.

Regular collections include paintings by Renoir, Degas, Monet, and Picasso. Maine artists represented include Andrew Wyeth, Marsden Hartley, and Winslow Homer. The museum has one of the world's largest Homer collections.

Don't forget to check out special exhibits. Hours 10:00 A.M. - 5:00 P.M. Tuesday, Wednesday, Friday, Saturday, 10:00 A.M. - 9:00 P.M. Thursday, 12:00 noon - 5:00 P.M. Sunday. Admission: $3.50. Free admission Saturday 10:00 A.M. - 12:00 noon.

Dinner

Pepperclub, ♥, $-$$, 78 Middle St., 207/772-0531. In transit: The restaurant is about a 10-minute walk from the museum. Head west on Congress Street, then turn left onto High Street. Turn left onto Middle Street.

If you're looking for a quick, light bite before you head home, the Pepperclub is a good choice. Atmosphere is casual – walls are painted vivid colors, seating is a mixture of white plastic tables (really, they don't look that bad) and wooden booths.

The menu concentrates on healthy foods – vegetarian dishes, organic meats, and seafood. Offerings are extensive and eclectic, ranging from miso soup to pesto lasagna. For New Age carnivores, Pepperclub even has organic hamburgers.

Despite its primarily holistic cuisine, Pepperclub is not above gooey desserts. You might want to save room for cream puffs with chocolate sauce or Key lime pie. Hours: 5:00 P.M. - 9:00 P.M. Sunday through Wednesday, 5:00 P.M. - 10:00 P.M. Thursday through Saturday.

Additional Activities

Visit Polly Peters Antiques, 26 Brackett St., 207/774-6981. Calling this spot an antique shop is somewhat of a stretch. The dusty three-room store on the west side of the Old Port is filled with old furniture and knickknacks – some junk, some antiques. But everything is interesting. Merchandise runs the gamut–lamps with bear-paw pedestals, gargoyles, and old wooden tables. This shop is one of Isabelle Smile's (Pomegranate's innkeeper) favorite haunts. Given her fine taste, this spot must house some real treasures. Hours: 10:00 A.M. - 5:00 P.M. Monday though Thursday. If you want to visit on a weekend, call ahead and Polly might open the store for you.

Visit L.L. Bean, Main Street, Freeport, 207/865-4761. If you've got some really foul weather, plan a car trip to L.L. Bean, the nation's most renowned sportswear and equipment manufacturer. (It's about a half-hour drive from Portland.) Bean's only full retail store is huge, carrying everything from fish bait to spandex biking shorts. Hours: 24 hours a day, 365 days a year. (Shopping in a near empty store at 3:00 A.M. has an inexplicable Twilight Zone quality.)

Visit the Nantucket Lightship, #112, Maine Wharf, 207/775-1181. History buffs will enjoy touring America's largest floating lighthouse. Decommissioned in 1975 after 40 years of service, it is the only remaining native lightship. Tours explore the pilot house, crews quarters, galley, and other compartments Hours: 10:00 A.M. - 4:00 P.M. Saturday, 12:00 noon - 4:00 P.M. Sunday. Extended hours in summer. Admission: $4.

GETTING THERE

BY AIR: The Portland International Jetport is serviced by five major carriers: Continental (800/525-0280), Delta (800/221-1212), Northwest Airlink (800/225-2525), United (800/241-6522), and US Air (800/428-4322). From there you can catch a cab into the city – it's less than 10 minutes away – or rent a car. A car, however, isn't necessary in Portland. It's an unusually walkable city, and if you don't mind a little exercise, you can really get a feel for this seaport if you travel by foot.

BY CAR: From I-95 take I-295 to the Congress Street exit for downtown Portland.

By Train: No train service is available.

By Bus: Greyhound (207/772-6587) has daily service into Portland from Boston.

Car Rentals: Four rental companies are located at the airport: Budget Rent-A-Car (207/774-8642), Avis (207/874-7500), Hertz (207/774-4544), and Thrifty (207/772-4268). Also, American International Rent-a-Car (9 Johnson Rd., 207/772-5955) has pick-up service at the airport.

Taxi/Limousine Service: Chances of stepping off a sidewalk and hailing a taxi are virtually nil. Better call ahead: Town Taxi (207/773-1711).

Information: Portland has a great information center: The Greater Portland Convention and Visitor's Bureau, 305 Commercial St., 207/772-5800. Hours: 9:00 A.M. - 5:00 P.M. Monday through Friday. From May through October the center is open seven days a week. If you can't make it, call and they'll send you information.

Stowe, Vermont

ther New England ski resorts have bigger mountains, better restaurants, and more quaint country inns, but what sets Stowe apart, and makes it one of the best ski destination in these six states, is its relentless charm.

The center—with its white steepled church, 100-year-old general store, and 18th century red brick inn—is a Currier and Ives incarnate. Cars may travel its main street today, but it's easy to imagine horses and buggies trotting Stowe's first tourists through town more than 150 years ago.

In those days, summer visitors came to Stowe for its cool mountain breezes. It wasn't until the 1930s, with the invention of the ski lift, that Stowe became known as a winter retreat. Through the years, the town has grown, as has its reputation. Now it's an internationally recognized ski resort that even attracts a few Hollywood celebrities. (Julia Roberts made a big splash recently.)

The mountain itself (whose real name is Mt. Mansfield, but is commonly just called Stowe) is known as a haven for the serious skier. It boasts some of the toughest mogul runs in the country. Yet it has enough gentle, cruising slopes to keep even the most reticent novice satisfied.

Stowe's popularity, however, isn't based solely on its ski resort. People come to Stowe for the village itself—a place that, in spite of its urban sophistication, has managed to retain the patina of a simple, Yankee community. Of course, you'll find stores that carry $400 imported German ski sweaters. But next door will probably be a small shop that purveys hand-dyed wool and fresh lamb meat!

Simply, Stowe is the perfect winter vacation spot for those who want urban panache and amenities surrounded by rustic charm.

WHERE TO STAY

Ten Acres Lodge, ♡ ♡, $$-$$$$, Luce Hill Road, Stowe 05672, 802/253-7638 or 800/327-7357. Best known as one of the area's finest restaurants, visitors might not think of staying at Ten Acres. That would be a mistake. Under the direction of innkeepers Curt and Cathy Dann, this small country inn is becoming one of Stowe's coziest and most comfortable spots. The common rooms – small bar, living room, and den – are quietly elegant, outfitted with Shaker reproductions, antiques, Orientals, and beamed ceilings. They've got the kind of ambiance that makes you want to curl up by the fire and spend the day reading. (A minor problem: One of our spys had to ask the innkeeper to light the fire three times before it was done.)

Of the 10 inn guest rooms, 2 have been newly decorated, and are thus the most popular. Room 10 has a king-size brass bed, pale green wall-to-wall carpeting, and a pastel, flowered couch. If you're looking for a country motif, room 11 has pine paneling, a chenille bedspread, antique dresser, and needlepoint rug.

Although annexes are usually undesirable, Ten Acres' Hill House offers eight large suites with fireplaces, some with cathedral ceilings. All have king- or queen-size beds, sitting areas, baths, cable televisions, and phones. Although, Hill House is newly constructed, the rooms are furnished with antiques and nice reproductions. Hill House's real selling point, however, is its outdoor hot tub that has a grand view of the Green Mountains. (All Ten Acres guests have free use of the hot tub, it's just so much more convenient if you're staying in Hill House.)

Ten Acres also has two cottages, one with two bedrooms, and another with three. Both are equipped with a kitchen, living room with fireplace, dining area, and bath.

Full breakfasts are included in the room charge. Dinner is available for an extra charge.

RATES PER NIGHT: $75-$135, Hill House $140-$160, cottages $225-$275.

ACCOMMODATIONS: 10 rooms with private baths, and 8 suites in an annex. Two cabins reserved for families or people traveling in groups are also available.

AMENITIES: Full-service bar and restaurant serving dinner. Outdoor hot tub. Suites have fireplaces, telephones, and cable television. (In summer: outdoor pool, tennis court, air conditioning.)

RESTRICTIONS: No pets. Smoking allowed only in cabins.

The Green Mountain Inn, ♡-♡♡, $$-$$$, Main Street, Stowe 05672, 802/253-7301 or 800/445-6629. Set on the town's busiest intersection, The Green Mountain is Stowe's premier anchor and landmark. Built as a private residence in 1833, it has operated as a hotel for more than 100 years. Completely refurbished for its 100th anniversary, the Green Mountain is a lovely combination hotel/country inn – the perfect spot for people who want all the modern amenities, without sterility and blandness.

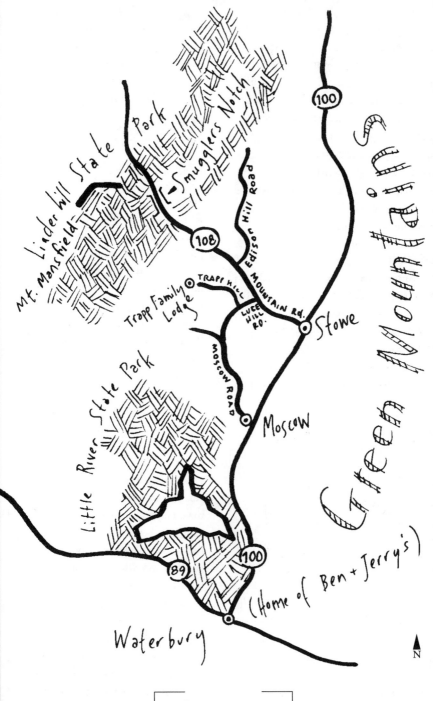

Linder hill State Park

Mt. Mansfield

Smugglers Notch

Edison Hill Road

100

108

MOUNTAIN Rd.

TRAPP HILL

Trapp Family Lodge

LUCE HILL RD.

Stowe

Moscow ROAD

Little River State Park

Moscow

Green Mountains

89

100

(Home of Ben + Jerry's)

Waterbury

N

S T O W E

All of Green Mountain's 53 rooms are appointed in classic country motif: canopy beds specially made for the inn from 18th century designs, chenille spreads, braided wool rugs, stenciled wallpaper, and folk art reproductions. Modern amenities include televisions, phones, updated baths, and toiletries. Housekeeping is immaculate. (One note: Even though the rooms are large, the building is old and halls are narrow. Hall noise is virtually unavoidable, but not too disturbing.)

Common rooms, surprisingly small and homey, are finely furnished with Orientals, oil paintings, floral drapes, and federal-style furniture. The main living room has a fireplace, usually kept stoked. Complimentary continental breakfast is served here, as well as afternoon cookies and hot cider.

In addition, the inn has two restaurants, and a full service health club that includes pool, sauna, steam room, and Jacuzzi.

RATES PER NIGHT: $95-$99, $115-$139 for suites. Prices are higher during the Christmas holiday, and lower off season. When making reservations, be sure to ask for a room in the main inn. Green Mountain has a pleasant motel-like annex, but the inn offers far more charm.

ACCOMMODATIONS: 54 rooms and suites with private baths.

AMENITIES: Two restaurants serving breakfast lunch and dinner. Full-service health club. Televisions and telephones in rooms. (In summer: outdoor pool.) No-smoking rooms are available.

RESTRICTIONS: None.

The Inn at the Brass Lantern, ♥, **$$-$$$,** 717 Maple St. (Route 100), Stowe 05672, 802/253-2229 or 800/729-2980. This 1800s farmhouse and attached carriage barn have been completely restored by innkeepers Mindy and Andy Aldrich. Now it's a casual, down-home inn, the place to stay if you're looking for a low-key getaway. The common living room has wood floors, beamed ceilings, lace curtains, well-stocked bookshelves, and country oak furniture.

The nine guest rooms are furnished simply but comfortably: All have wood floors, private baths, and handmade quilts. Three rooms have fireplaces. The choice of these is the Honeymoon Room (number 9). It has a a queen-size brass and iron bed with a heart-shaped iron headboard, sitting area, and fireplace. Most importantly it has grand views of Mt. Mansfield. If this room is booked, ask for room 6 or room 7, they are both pleasant and have fireplaces.

Mindy and Andy are extraordinarily friendly innkeepers, without being cloying. They'll do anything possible to simplify your stay, including making reservations for dinner, sightseeing, and even plane travel.

Mindy does all the cooking, and serves a hearty, full breakfast such as blueberry pancakes or bacon and eggs. Each afternoon she faithfully puts out sweets and tea. And, after you return from dinner, it's not unusual to find coffee and dessert waiting in the living room.

RATES PER NIGHT: $70-$115. Prices are lower off season.

ACCOMMODATIONS: 9 rooms with private baths.

AMENITIES: Some rooms have fireplaces.

RESTRICTIONS: No smoking. No pets.

Edson Hill Manor, ♡ ♡, $$$, 1500 Edson Hill Road, Stowe 05672, 802/253-7311 or 800/253-0284. This country mansion turned inn, set on 200 rolling acres, enjoys the most pastoral setting and magnificent views of any place in Stowe. Owned and operated by the Heath family for more than 40 years, Edson Hill was recently purchased by Eric and Jane Lande, maple syrup manufacturers from nearby Johnson. Although it had had devotees, Edson Hill had fallen into disrepair under the Heaths, and the new innkeepers have undertaken a grand-scale renovation project.

The Landes have traveled extensively through Europe and are infusing Edson

Hill with a French Provincial style. The main living area – the nicest of all Stowe's inns – is rustically grand. Original oil paintings, Oriental carpets, and dried delphinium and hydrangea arrangements provide elegance. Yet the hand-hewn ceiling beams (from Ira and Ethan Allen's Burlington, Vermont, barn), and pine floors and walls add country charm. Tile aficionados should take note that those around the fireplace are original Delpht, imported from Holland.

All told, Edson Hill has 25 rooms: 10 are in the manor, and the remaining are scattered throughout the several carriage houses on the property. Although the latter provide more seclusion, the manor rooms – five of which have fireplaces – are far more romantic.

Room 3 is the manor's largest and finest, with a queen-size bed that sits under a skylight, as well as a fireplace, sitting area, pine paneling, and picture windows with views of Mt. Mansfield. Room 2, which has been newly renovated, has a more formal feel, with an Oriental rug and dark maroon floral wall paper. It also has a fireplace and a pencil post bed.

Full breakfast and dinner are served in Edson Hill's dining room, which has slate floors and fireplace and a hand-painted ceiling.

Other amenities include 40 kilometers of cross-country ski trails, a skating pond, and sleigh rides.

RATES PER NIGHT: $158-$178, includes breakfast and dinner for two. B&B rates are $108-$128. Off-season rates are lower.

ACCOMMODATIONS: 25 rooms with private baths; 10 located in the manor house and the remaining are located in 4 separate carriages houses.

AMENITIES: Full service restaurant serving dinner. Fireplaces in some rooms. Cross-country ski trails, skating pond, and sleigh rides. (In spring through fall: stables that offer trail rides and lessons. Also, trout fed pond.)

RESTRICTIONS: No pets.

FRIDAY EVENING
Drinks

Mr. Pickwick's Pub, ♥, $$, at Ye Old England Inne, Mountain Road, Stowe, 802/253-7558. In transit: From Route 100 turn onto Mountain Road (it's the intersection with street lights in the center of town). The inn is about ½ mile north on the left.

Beer aficionados will think they're in heaven at Mr. Pickwick's, an English-style pub. It offers more than 150 selections from over 23 countries, including Africa, Czechoslovakia, and India. Twelve brews are on tap, among them John Courage, Whatney's, and Whitbread.

Decor is appropriately casual and dark, with stucco and stone walls, wooden benches and tables, and a fireplace across from the bar. Hours: 11:00 A.M. - 2:00 A.M. (Many travelers won't get to Stowe until late evening. But this is a nice place to unwind for couples who want to relax before dinner.)

Dinner

Villa Tragara, ♥ ♥, $$-$$$, Route 100, Waterbury, 802/244-5288. In transit: Head south on Route 100, Villa Tragara is six miles from Stowe village. Although Stowe has several fine Italian restaurants, none is as good as Villa Tragara. In fact, Tragara will stand up to most top-notch Northern Italian restaurants. Located in a white clapboard farmhouse, and decorated with candles, red tablecloths and posters of Italy, the restaurant is unpretentious and cozy. Although there are several small dining rooms, try for a table on the enclosed porch.

Entrees are hearty, large, and mostly traditional. But a few unusual choices include the crespelle ai quattro formaggi (a pasta crêpe with four cheeses, raisins, pine nuts, and lemon peel), and vitello scallopini Vermontenese (sautéed veal served with grilled apples, maple syrup, and mustard seed). For seafood lovers, the linguine fra Diavalo – a large plate of pasta smothered with mussels, clams, scallops, and lobster, in a spicy tomato sauce – is superb.

Fresh, crusty bread, baked at the restaurant daily, is served with all meals. The wine list is extensive and appropriately Italian. Chances are you'll be too full for dessert, but don't miss a cup of espresso or cappuccino made from imported beans (it will help you digest). Hours: 5:30 - 9:30 P.M. Closed Monday.

Ten Acres Lodge, ♡ ♡, $$$, Luce Hill Road, Stowe, 802/253-7638. In transit: From Route 100 turn onto the Mountain Road, then left onto Luce Hill.

When most locals are pressed to name Stowe's best fine dining room, they'll usually mention Ten Acres Lodge. Decor is simple and pretty – candle-lit tables with white cloths, green wood wainscoting, and pale pink walls. The menu is similarly unfussy, yet elegant. Longtime chef Jack Pickett prides himself on regional food and produce.

Although the menu changes weekly, winter selections might include roast loin of lamb with sweet onion crust, and stuffed breast of chicken with spinach and mascarpone cheese. Appetizers tend to be a bit more adventurous. Among them are eggplant caponata with artichoke and Parmesan dressing, and pan fried oysters with bacon and horseradish.

Desserts can run the gamut from fruit sorbets to mud pie with a cookie crust, ice cream filling, and hot fudge sauce. The wine list is impressive and includes an array of rare vintages and ports. Hours:

6:00 P.M. - 9:30 P.M. nightly. Weekends only November to mid December.

SATURDAY

Note: This day isn't broken out into morning and afternoon activities, because you'll probably spend the entire day skiing. Stowe has such great alpine and Nordic skiing, it's the perfect vacation spot for people who enjoy both.

Alpine Skiing at Mt. Mansfield, Mountain Road, Stowe 802/253-6617. In transit: From Route 100 turn onto Mountain Road. Mt. Mansfield is about 8 miles north.

With a vertical drop of 2,360 feet, Mt. Mansfield is Vermont's highest ski resort. And with more than 45 trails, covering 378 acres, it is also one of its largest. But Stowe offers more than just "big." It has terrain for all types of skiers. Of course, many New England resorts make that claim, but few have the bumps to satisfy true experts.

Stowe has the legendary Front Four: Star, National, Goat, and Nosedive. All are double black diamond slopes and considered among the most difficult in the United States. In fact, Olympian Billy Kidd says of National, "You have to be a good skier just to survive it. To enjoy it, you have to be superb."

The beauty of Stowe is that alongside these slopes are some wonderful cruising runs. A full 59 percent of Stowe's trails are for intermediates, and 16 percent for beginners. The Toll Road provides novices with nearly four miles of top to bottom skiing.

Both intermediate and expert slopes are often serviced by the same lift, which makes things simple for couples who may want to take different trails to the bottom. (Sometimes it's better for the relationship to take separate but equal trails!)

Among Stowe's other impressive features is its new high-speed gondola, the fastest in the world. A trip to the top of the mountain takes just 6 minutes and 20 seconds.

Be sure to find yourself at the peak around lunch time. Although Stowe has several restaurants, the most pleasant and picturesque is the Cliff House located at the summit, just past the gondola. It offers an international buffet, with pasta, salads, meats, and desserts. Hours: 11:00 A.M. - 3:00 P.M.

Tickets: $39 weekends and weekdays. Equipment rental: (including skis, boots, and poles) $19 a day. Lessons: 2-hour group $24, 1-hour private $45.

SATURDAY EVENING

A Hot Tub Soak at the Spa at Top Notch, at The Top Notch Resort, Mountain Road, Stowe, 802/253-8585. In transit: The club is just behind the inn, which is at the intersection of Mountain Road and Route 100.

Forget the après ski cocktail. Stop off at your inn, enjoy a few complimentary hors d'oeuvres (all the inns listed offer afternoon snacks), then head straight to the Spa at Top Notch, one of the nation's most famous health spas. The place is expensive and ridiculously plush: the locker rooms are equipped with fireplaces. Although it has no outdoor whirlpool, the indoor Jacuzzi sits next to floor-to-ceiling windows, and has a pulsating waterfall that will do wonders for your aching shoulder muscles. Also enjoy a coed sauna, or a leisurely swim in the pool. Daily fee: $25 or $40 for two. Massages, manicures, pedicures, facials, and other beauty treatments are offered for an additional fee.

Dinner

Stowehof Inn, ♡ ♡, $$$, Edson Hill Road, Stowe, 802/253-9722. With floor to ceiling windows that provide wonderful meadow and mountain views, the Stowehof has the town's most scenic dining room. In the evening you can watch the inn's horse-drawn sleigh trot through the snow. (If you don't spend too much time at Top Notch, you might be able to fit in a ride as well. Dinner and sleigh ride packages are available for $80 per couple.)

The room has low ceilings with rough hewn beams, a fireplace, candle-lit tables with white cloths and pewter serving pieces. Waiters are dressed formally in black vests and white aprons. A classical pianist, who works the inn's antique Steinway baby grand, adds to the atmosphere.

Although the menu changes regularly, you can expect hearty continental dishes with French influences. Appetizers might include seafood sausage with grilled leeks and cilantro shrimp sauce, or terrine of smoked salmon with fresh avocado remoulade. Entrees range from New England bouillabaisse to pork loin stuffed with fresh South American peaches and homemade granola with citrus-yogurt sauce.

For coffee and dessert (a dazzling array of tortes, tarts, and cakes are featured on a traditional cart), retire to Stowehof's living room, where you can either sit by the fire or get cozy among one of the many intimate seating clusters. Hours: 6:00 P.M. - 9:00 P.M.

Copperfield's, ♡, $$$, at Ye Old England Inne, Mountain Road, Stowe, 802/253-7064. In transit: From the intersection of Route 100 and the Mountain Road, Copperfield's is about ¼ mile north, on the left.

Copperfield's is one of Stowe's most formal dining rooms and is in stark contrast to most of the local spots, where people wear their ski sweaters and "post game" bravado at the dinner table. Part of Ye Old England Inne, the restaurant is housed in a small, candle-lit, Tudor-style room with low ceilings and beamed stucco walls. Tables are adorned with white linens and fresh flowers.

In keeping with the inn's atmosphere, Copperfield's menu is Anglo with European touches. Appetizers include paté of mixed venison, duck, and pheasant with herb-infused aspic, and fried Brie, which is lightly breaded and served with fresh fruit. Entrees favor meat lovers and include beef Wellington, broiled venison steaks topped with a wild mushroom cabernet demi glace, as well as pheasant and game sausage.

Copperfield's prides itself on its unusual and extensive wine list—it offers mostly Australian varieties—and it was recently the recipient of the *Wine Spectator's* award of excellence.

The dessert menu has such traditional favorites as aged Stilton with port and English trifle. Hours: 6:30 P.M.-9:30 P.M. (No smoking.)

SUNDAY MORNING

Brunch at the Gables Inn, ♡, $$, Mountain Road, Stowe, 802/253-7730. In transit: Traveling from the intersection of Route 100 and the Mountain Road, the Gables is about two miles north on the left.

After a full day on the slopes, you may decide to sleep in on Sunday. Why rush out of bed to grab the last croissant at your inn–most stop serving by 10:00 A.M.–when you can enjoy a delicious and leisurely meal at the Gables, the place for breakfast in Stowe.

Don't be put off by its simple atmosphere – brown carpet, wood tables, and painted plates decorating the walls. The Gables is appealing precisely because it's a little country spot that serves good food.

Start off with some fresh squeezed orange juice. Then choose from the Gables' surprisingly extensive menu, which runs the gamut from traditional blueberry pancakes served with real maple syrup, to sautéed chicken livers with onions and scrambled eggs. One of the dishes for which the Gables is famous is its stuffed French toast: raisin bread filled with cream cheese, walnuts, and molasses, and served with maple syrup. While too sugary and gooey for this French toast lover's palate, it's perfect for those with an insatiable sweet tooth. Hours: 8:00 A.M. - 12:30 P.M. weekends, and 8:00 A.M. - 10:30 AM. weekdays.

Nordic Skiing at the Trapp Family Lodge, Trapp Hill Road, Stowe, 802/253-8511 or 800/826-7000. In transit: From the Mountain Road, head north toward Mt. Mansfield. Turn left onto Luce Hill Road, then left on to Trapp Hill Road.

As corny as it might sound, you can't help but hum, "The hills are alive... ,"

when you take your first look at the Trapp Family Lodge and Cross Country Center. Its location, set high atop a hill, overlooking the valley and Green Mountains, is awe-inspiring. In complete contrast to the hip hop of Mt. Mansfield (and to downhill skiing itself), Trapp is the essence of peacefulness and pastoral charm.

Ski through forests of hardwoods and evergreens, along old farming roads, or on trails overlooking Stowe Valley. If you're an advanced skier, Trapp even has off-track wilderness skiing.

Take a hot cocoa break at the Alpen Rose Tea Room: part of the Trapp complex, it's conveniently trailside. The huge glass windows offer spectacular mountain views. Or, if you're destination oriented, ski to the Slayton Pasture Cabin, a muscle-warming 5-kilometer trek (one way). Inside this rustic log cabin, set in an open meadow, you can sit by the fire and enjoy a hot drink, or soup and a sandwich.

Tickets: $8. Equipment rental: (including boots, skis, and poles) $12 a day. Lessons: ½-hour group $12, 1-hour private $40.

SUNDAY AFTERNOON

Shopping Stowe Village. Nordic devotees may choose to spend the rest of the day at Trapp, but for those who've had their fill of the great outdoors after about three hours (cross-country skiing is exhausting), a stroll through Stowe village is a treat. Following are some special shops:

Shaw's General Store, Main Street, 802/253-4040. If you only visit one store in Stowe, it should be Shaw's. It has occupied the same space on Main Street for nearly 100 years. And while its product mix has changed to accommodate modern life, it still has the same "if you can't find it here you don't need it" atmosphere. A good spot to find basic winter apparel, including after-ski boots, fleece jackets, and rabbit-fur hats.

Joan Rankin Sweaters, The Carriage House, Main Street, 802/253-4445. This place has a nice selection of fine quality, hand-knit and hand-loomed sweaters made from wool, alpaca, silk, cotton, and linen. Styles for both men and women. Prices are high – some sweaters are well over $200 – so take a big swallow before you enter.

Exclusively Vermont, Mountain Road, 802/253-8776. (Walk over the covered bridge just off Main Street. Exclusively Vermont is on the right.) As its name suggests, this shop specializes in Vermont handcrafts. Look for hand-rolled beeswax candles, Simon Pierce glass, as well as local pottery, quilts, and food products.

Green Mountain Chocolate, Main Street, 802/253-8973. If you're a chocoholic, don't miss this spot.

Owned and operated by Albert Kumin, formerly the White House pastry chef under Jimmy Carter, Green Mountain makes all its sweets by hand. Truffles, nut barks, cakes, cookies and other treats are available.

Emotional Outlet, Mountain Road, Stowe Center Shops, 802/253-7407. (If you're traveling north, it's on the right.) You'll have to take your car to get to this shop, which is just five minutes from the village center, but the Emotional Outlet is the best fine crafts store in Stowe. Merchandise includes hand-painted furniture, wood-framed mirrors, whimsical pottery, hand-woven rugs, and jewelry.

SUNDAY EVENING
Dinner

The Restaurant Swisspot, ♡, $$, Main Street, Stowe, 802/253-4622. In transit: The Swisspot is right in Stowe Village, on the north side of the road.

The perfect spot if you're looking for a casual, relaxing, yet relatively quick, meal before you depart. The restaurant's interior was moved from the Swiss Government Pavilion at the 1967 Montreal World's Fair to this Main Street site. Decor is simple with polished wood tables, and Swiss flags and photographs decorating the walls.

Although the Swisspot offers fish, pasta, and steaks, its specialties are fondues and quiches (all baked to order). Try the Swiss cheese fondue for two, made with Emmentaler and Gruyère, cooked in a dry white wine with a dash of Kirsch, and served with French bread. Or, you might consider the quiche St. Gallen, with cheese, onion, tomato, mushroom, and broccoli.

No matter what you order, save room for dessert. Who could pass up chocolate fondue with fruit and marshmallows, or a Matterhorn sundae with hot Tobler chocolate sauce? Hours: 5:00 P.M. - 9:00 P.M.

Additional Activities

Cold Hollow Cider Mill, Route 100, Waterbury Center, 802/244-8771. Cold Hollow is Vermont's largest producer of fresh apple cider. It offers self-guided factory tours where you can watch cider being pressed. And while the tour is less than impressive, the plethora of apple products Cold Cider makes and sells at its gigantic factory store is worth the trip. Chutneys, sauce, jelly, syrup, chips, and more. Don't leave without purchasing a few samples. Hours: 8:00 A.M. - 6:00 P.M. daily.

Ben & Jerry's Ice Cream Factory Tour, Route 100, Waterbury Center, 802/244-5641. Some people consider ice cream an aphrodisiac. If this is indeed so, none could be more potent than Ben & Jerry's, arguably the best ice cream on the planet. At this factory, where all the ice cream (save the Peace

Pops and a few other bar snacks) is made, you can take a half-hour, guided tour that includes a sample of fresh ice cream. One note: Since no ice cream is produced on Sunday, it's best to take the tour on another day when you can actually see the production process. Tours given 9:00 A.M. - 4:00 P.M. daily, on the half hour. Admission: $1.

Dinner at Le Cheval D'Or, Windridge Inn, Main Street, Jeffersonville, 802/644-5556. Mimi Sheraton included this in her 1992 selection of the 50 best American restaurants. The interior looks entirely Colonial, but the menu is very French. Chef-owner Yves Labbe's specialties include escargot, rabbit civet (in a sauce of wine and onions), and pan-gilded quail. Hours: 6:30 P.M. - 8:30 P.M. Closed Wednesdays.

Visit Mabel Wilson, Fine Antiques & Americana, Route 100, Stowe, 802/253-7826. You might not be able to afford anything here – prices are mostly four and five digits – but if you appreciate antiques and folk art, you'll enjoy looking. Amazing selection of working clocks, hand-painted mirrors, and other unusual pieces.

GETTING THERE

BY AIR: Burlington (VT) International Airport is only 45 minutes from Stowe, and is served by most major airlines. US Air (800/428-4322) has flight and car rental packages from New York,

Philadelphia, Chicago, and many other major metropolitan airports.

Should you choose to rent a small, private plane, the Morrisville-Stowe Airport has a small asphalt runway.

BY CAR: From Eastern Massachusetts, take I-95 north, to I-93 north, to I-89 north to exit 10/Route 100. Head north on Route 100 to Stowe. The Main Street of Stowe is Route 100. From New York, Connecticut, and New Jersey, take I-95 north, to I-91 north, to I-89 north to exit 10/Route 100. Head north on Route 100 to Stowe.

BY TRAIN: Amtrak (800/872-7245, USA-RAIL) offers daily service to Burlington/Essex Junction from Boston, New York, and other regional cities.

BY BUS: Vermont Transit Lines (802/253-7131) offers service to Stowe from Burlington. Greyhound (617/423-5810) has daily service to Burlington from New York, Hartford, and Boston.

(If you don't own a car and are contemplating taking a bus, you're better off renting a car and driving to Stowe. You'll need one once you're there.)

CAR RENTAL: Four car rental companies have offices at the Burlington International Airport: Hertz (800/654-3131), Budget (800/787-8200), Avis (800/331-1212), and National (800/227-7368). In Stowe, you can rent a car at Stowe Auto Service (207/253-7608).

TAXI/LIMOUSINE SERVICE: Should you need a taxi or limo to take you to or from the airport or train station, contact Sullivan Transportation (207/253-9440) in Stowe.

INFORMATION: Stow has an excellent information center right on Main Street, across from the Green Mountain Inn. The Stowe Area Association (802/253-7321) is open 9:00 A.M. - 9:00 P.M. Monday through Friday, 10:00 A.M. - 6:00 P.M. Saturday, 10:00 A.M. - 5:00 P.M. Sunday.

Sugarloaf & Kingfield, Maine

&ven crowd-loathing "Mainiacs" think that Sugarloaf is in the wilderness. A Friday night drive will find you negotiating dark, uninhabited roads that require all the light your high-beams can throw. And while the last leg of the trip might make you edgy, the morning light will show your reward – snow covered fields, towering pines, and Sugarloaf itself - one of the East's best mountains for serious skiers.

Yet this ski area doesn't have the plethora of quaint country inns, gourmet restaurants, and upscale shops found in most resort communities. In fact, Sugarloaf doesn't even have a community! Kingfield, which is the closest village, is 16 miles away.

But what it lacks in sophistication (some might say ruination) and alternative activities, it makes up for in uncrowded slopes and nonexistent lift lines. Sugarloaf also has one of the highest snowfalls in New England, averaging nearly 170 inches annually. It also has the only snow field skiing this side of the Rockies.

That warning given, Sugarloaf isn't completely devoid of amenities. It's got a great slopeside hotel, an impressive continental restaurant, as well as several accommodation and restaurant choices in Kingfield, considered Sugarloaf's commercial center. (To put "commercial" in perspective, Kingfield's population is 1,000.)

The best time to visit is late March or early April. Sugarloaf is notoriously cold, windy, and snowy. On our visit in early February, the crystal blue day was deemed nothing short of miraculous by astonished locals. In early spring, the weather is warmer and days are typically sunnier. In fact, the mountain usually doesn't close until the third week in April. Also, the snow fields are more likely to be open later in the season: Snow making doesn't extend to the fields so they usually aren't skiable until March.

WHERE TO STAY

The Sugarloaf Mountain Hotel, ♥-♥♥, $$-$$$$, Carrabasset Valley 04947, 207/237-2222 or 800/526-9897. This modern, six-story brick slopeside hotel looks like it belongs to another ski

SUGARLOAF & KINGFIELD

resort—one that caters to people who wear fur-trimmed ski suits. The bell service, valet parking, and in-room microwaves and refrigerators will please creatures of comfort. Yet the decor, though definitely hotel-like, will attract couples looking for country charm.

All 120 rooms have pine furniture, down comforters, and colonial-style wing chairs and/or couches, as well as phones, televisions, and VCRs. But best of all, you can walk out the door, get into your skis, and hop on the chairlift. The inn could only be more convenient if a lift ran through the lobby.

Although the Sugarloaf Mountain Hotel has no central common area, guests can relax in the second-floor library, which is well stocked and has comfortable leather chairs that surround a wooden meeting table. The health club, for guests only, boasts floor-to-ceiling windows that afford views of this Bigelow Mountain Range. Amenities include a hot tub, cold plunge, sauna, and steam room.

If you're really in the mood to splurge, or if you're traveling with another couple (albeit a questionable romantic holiday), consider the hotel's penthouses. These three-story, three-bedroom suites have spectacular mountain views, full kitchens, living rooms, saunas, and best of all—hot tub rooms. What could be more pleasant than sipping champagne in your own private hot tub, while gazing at the grooming-machine lights twinkling on the mountain?

RATES PER NIGHT: $100-$150, $165-$210 for one-bedroom suites, $225-$265 for two-bedroom suites, and $350-$500 for penthouses. Prices are lower in non-ski seasons.

ACCOMMODATIONS: 120 rooms with private baths, including a three-bedroom penthouse, and one- and two-bedrooms suites.

AMENITIES: All rooms have televisions and telephones. Most have mini refrigerators and microwaves. Full service restaurant serving breakfast, lunch, and dinner. Health club.

RESTRICTIONS: No pets.

The Inn on Winter's Hill, ♥ ♥, $$-$$$, Winter's Hill Road, Kingfield 04947, 207/265-5421 or 800/233-9687. This Georgian revival mansion, set atop a hill overlooking downtown Kingfield, appears far too regal for its country setting. Built by the Stanley brothers (of Stanley Steamer fame) for Amos G. Winter, it was the first house in Maine to have central heat. Winter wanted a grand house for his wife Julia, who grew up in New York City: It was the only way he felt he could get and keep her in the Maine wilderness.

Current innkeepers Richard and Carolyn Winnick, who purchased

Winter's Hill in 1989, have spent several years restoring the home to its original grandeur. And indeed the main house gleams with the care the Winnicks have shown it. The living room has wonderfully restored oak floors, original tin ceilings, a fireplace flanked by Greek pillars, and a grand carved staircase leading to three guest rooms on the second floor.

The Winnicks also rebuilt the old barn to original specifications and have 16 pleasant yet motel-like rooms there; however, the three rooms in the main house are far more elegant and luxurious. For a good view of Sugarloaf, ask for William's room: It has tin ceilings, a king-size iron-framed bed, and is decorated in shades of green. As in all the main rooms, toiletries and bathrobes are provided.

One note: Don't be put off by Winter Hill's entrance. Because the house is so hard to heat, guests enter through the side door in winter. This check-in area has a small motel-style front desk that seems incongruous with the rest of the house. The same goes for Winter Hill's modern lounge, which you must also walk through to get to the mansion. Although these features diminish the inn's overall appearance, it does not take away from the fact that the Winnicks have put their hearts into refurbishing the main house.

For hot tub aficionados, Winter Hill's tub is on a pleasant outdoor deck which affords panoramic views. In addition, the tennis court is flooded for skating, should you have enough energy after your day on the slopes.

A full breakfast and dinner is served in the main dining room, known as Julia's. This elegant spot has restored cherry floors, pale pink walls, green upholstered chairs, and a working fireplace.

RATES PER NIGHT: $85-$150. Breakfast is served from 8:00 A.M. - 9:00 A.M. and is not included in the room rate. It costs about $5 per person. For MAP rates add $30 per person. Two-night minimum.

ACCOMMODATIONS: 3 rooms with private baths in main house; 16 rooms with private baths in barn.

AMENITIES: Restaurant serving breakfast and dinner. Lounge. Outdoor hot tub. Barn rooms have cable televisions and telephones. Outdoor pool/ice skating rink. In summer, Winter Hill offers a clay tennis court, and crocquet and bocce courts.

RESTRICTIONS: No pets.

The Herbert Hotel, ♥, $$, Main Street, Kingfield 04946, 207/256-2000 or 800/ 843-4372. If Mayberry had a hotel, it would look just like The Herbert. As its promotional literature boasts, there is "no frou-frou here, and not a Laura Ashley print in sight just comfortable things your grandmother may have had."

Actually, The Herbert is a bit more grand than granny's house. Built in 1917 by Herbert Wing – a Maine politician, gubernatorial aspirant, and lumber baron – it was originally used as his private residence. Wing spared no expense in the building's construction: it boasts oak woodwork, Italian marble floors, and brass lighting fixtures.

Today the common rooms retain the original style. The living room is graced with Oriental rugs, velvet Victorian furniture, and – to give the place a country touch – taxidermic wildlife. The moose head, which has become the inn's "logo," sits above the fireplace mantle. In addition, the dining room still has the original wash sink, where guests, dusty after a stagecoach ride, refreshed themselves before dinner.

Unlike many inns that have a recreated look, the Herbert somehow seems as if it's in a time warp. It is no surprise then that the 33 rooms are pleasant and comfortable, in an old-fashioned way. The bed frames are brass, the antiques are simple (read old furniture), and the bedspreads are typically chenille. One surprise of note: Although the baths are 1950s style modern, all are equipped with whirlpool baths.

The rooms have no televisions, but there is a television lounge on the main floor, as well as a bar, which once served as the town barber shop. (Antique lovers can admire the bar's

original Frigidaire ice box on display.) The Herbert also has a hot tub (indoor) and sauna for guest use.

A complimentary continental breakfast of homemade muffins, juice, and coffee is served daily.

RATES PER NIGHT: $65-$100, $110 for two-room suite, $140 for three-room suite.

ACCOMMODATIONS: 33 rooms with private baths.

AMENITIES: Television in common room. Restaurant serving breakfast, lunch, and dinner. Lounge. Sauna and hot tub.

RESTRICTIONS: None.

FRIDAY EVENING
Dinner

The Herbert, ♡ ♡, $$, Main Street, Kingfield, 207/365-2000 or 800/743-4372. In transit: On route 27 in the middle of Kingfield. If you're traveling north and staying at the Sugarloaf Mountain Hotel, you may want to go to dinner before you check in, as the hotel is 16 miles north, and you drive right by the Herbert to get there.

To a weary traveler, the Herbert is an oasis of both civilization and civility in the midst of Maine's western mountains. The dining room's decor has a remarkably authentic feel. It includes two reproduction Hunter ceiling fans with French crystal shades, and a display of antique cut glass and whiskey bottles. Phone jacks are still visible on the walls: In the 30s, it was the only dining room north of Boston in which guests could receive tableside phone calls. Lace cloths and curtains, candles, and fresh flowers add to the flavor.

The menu emphasizes Maine cuisine. Specialties include Carrabasset rabbit, baked with cider and apples and finished with a light cream sauce; Pork Cumberland, tenderloin of pork sautéed with cream Dijon mustard and capers; and venison (preparation varies daily). Although the menu is meat heavy, the Herbert does have some nice selections for vegetarians and fish lovers, including dilled haddock and daily specials caught directly from the Gulf of Maine. Desserts are old-timey: homemade pies, cordial parfaits, ice cream and sherbert. Hours: 5:30 P.M. - 9:00 P.M. Monday through Saturday, 5:30 P.M. - 8:00 P.M. Sunday.

Hugs, ♥ ♥, $$, Route 27, Carrabasset Valley, 207/237-2392. In transit: Hugs is north of Kingfield, between the town and the mountain. Traveling south from Sugarloaf, Hugs is on the right side of Route 27, next to the Touring Center entrance.

Named after the former owner's wife (Hugette), Hugs is an unassuming, bright green, one-story shack that looks more like a "do-drop" bar than a restaurant. But don't be put off by the exterior; Hugs is a good Italian restaurant and cozy to boot – dark walls and floors, wood tables, and candlelight.

The menu is simple and concentrates primarily on pasta: with pesto, sausage, Alfredo, or with tomatoes, garlic, and oil. Other Italian favorites include veal scalopinne and shrimp scampi. All meals are served with great warm pesto bread and salad. (The lettuce is, unfortunately, iceberg.)

Although the appetizers are interesting– Hug's offers a decent foccaccia – you might want to hold off. Portions are huge: one bowl of pasta could easily feed two or even three. If you have room for dessert, consider a cannoli stuffed with chocolate frozen yogurt and topped with a raspberry sauce. It may not be authentically Italian, but it is tasty. Hours: 5:00 P.M. - 9:00 P.M.

SATURDAY MORNING

Alpine Skiing at Sugarloaf/USA, Carrabasset Valley 04947, 800/843-5623. In transit: Sugarloaf/USA is 16 miles north of Kingfield, off Route 27. You'll see signs on 27 for the mountain.

In winter, there is nothing to do in the Carrabasset Valley but ski. (You could count snowmobiling and ice fishing,. but we are, after all, discussing romantic holidays.) And although the area has some fine Nordic trails, you can find those in New Hampshire and Vermont. Of course you can find downhill skiing elsewhere too, however, few other mountains can claim Sugarloaf's impressive snowfall or its uncrowded slopes.

Statistically, Sugarloaf is Maine's highest ski mountain, and second highest peak, with an elevation of 4,237 feet and a vertical drop of 2,637. Of Sugarloaf's 70 trails, nearly 50 percent are for experts. And in fact, it's one of the few areas in New England that has double black diamond slopes: Sugarloaf's got six, including the snow fields.

If you're both advanced or expert skiers, head straight to the Spillway East chair, which is accessible from the Skidway lift at the bottom of the mountain. Spillway provides access to most of Sugarloaf's serious bump runs. For those who want something challenging, but not necessarily life threatening, the King Pine chair on the far east side of the mountain is your best bet. Cruisers should head to the west side, for the Bucksaw lift.

Unfortunately, there aren't any lifts that service both beginner and expert trails. But then again, if one of you is a real novice, you're better off at another mountain. Tickets: $37, $34 weekdays. Equipment rental: $18 per day. Lessons: $45 for one-hour private, $25 for one-hour semi-private. Multi day packages available.

Lunch

Gepetto's, $, West Village, Sugarloaf/USA, Carrabassett Valley, 207/237-2192. In transit: This restaurant is in the Sugarloaf complex at the bottom of the lifts.

One of Sugarloaf's biggest assets is its base village, reminiscent of those found in Rocky Mountain resorts. Gepetto's is among several restaurants in this complex, all of which offer a respite from overpriced, under-spiced ski lodge food.

Atmosphere is casual, with pine paneling, wooden booths and tables, lots of plants, and large windows that look onto the mountain. Food is similarly low key, but good. Items include deli sandwiches like Monte Christos and French dips, hamburgers, pizza, homemade soups, and chili. For the upscale eater, there's even a blackened scallop salad.

What a treat not to have to schlep a damp tray through a lodge lunch line. Hours: 11:00 A.M. - 3:00 P.M.

Gringo's, $, Base Lodge, Sugarloaf/USA, Carrabasset Valley, 207/237-2000. In transit: Gringo's is on the second floor of the base lodge, in the Widowmaker Lounge.

Gringo's is Sugarloaf's newest restaurant addition. Located within the popular Widowmaker Lounge, it boasts vaulted ceilings and impressive views of

Sugarloaf and the Bigelow Mountain Range. Mexican hats, blankets, and dried chili peppers hanging from the walls provide a festive, lively look. The menu includes such south-of-the-border basics as chimichangas, enchiladas, and burritos. You won't find much over $7; a good deal when you consider the price of most ski lodge food. Hours: 11:00 A.M. - closing.

SATURDAY AFTERNOON

Continue Day of Alpine Skiing at Sugarloaf/USA. Sugarloaf's lifts don't close until 4:00 P.M. after February 1. If you're trying to follow the sun, and take it easy after lunch, head to the Bucksaw lift.

Outdoor Hot Tub Soak, Sugartree Club, Sugarloaf/USA, Kingfield, 207/237-2701. In transit: From the Sugarloaf mountain parking lot, turn right onto the Mountain Road as if you're heading back to Route 27. Then turn right onto Mountainside Road. The Sugartree Club is on the right.

The Sugartree is the perfect anecdote for a hard day on the slopes. The club's two outdoor hot tubs face the mountain and are just a few steps from the building. The indoor swimming pool and hot tub enjoy equally good views from an arched glass ceiling and glass walls.

Both men's and women's locker rooms are equipped with additional hot tubs,

sauna, and showers. And the lounge, although not particularly intimate, is a good spot for a quiet drink before you start your evening. Rates: $10 for a one-day pass, $26 for a three-day pass.

Note: If you're staying at the Inn on Winter's Hill, you might prefer to take a soak in your own hot tub. It's equally nice and is probably a bit less populated. Besides, you've already paid for it.

SATURDAY EVENING

Moonlight Dogsled Ride with the Howling Express, T.A.D. Dog Sled Services, Route 27, Stratton, 207/237-2000 or 207/246-4461. In transit: T.A.D. is 1/10 mile north of Sugarloaf's Mountain Road on Route 27.

Imagine being whisked through a starlit forest on a high, wooden sled by a team of 10 furry white dogs. The experience is not only fun, but other worldly. Owner and musher Tim Diehl captains these strong, beautiful, and speedy Samoyeds through dense forests and open glens by calling out directions that the dogs miraculously understand and follow.

Sleds are long and slim and accommodate two people, one in front of the other. Before the half-hour ride, Diehl introduces visitors to his beloved dogs. (Virtually all were rescued from unwanted homes and pounds.) Then he carefully swaddles passengers in leopard-print faux furs, hops on the back runners, gives a hoot, and the dogs –and you–are off.

Diehl is extraordinarily friendly and willing to help you plan a special ride. Consider bringing along a bottle of champagne and, for whimsy, some marshmallows. Diehl will be happy to set a post-ride bonfire.

Those concerned about animal cruelty, should know that Samoyeds need an inordinate amount of activity. They enjoy running and relish the weight of the sled behind them. In fact, Diehl says that the reason so many Samoyeds end up in animal pounds is that most people don't realize just how much exercise these dogs need. If they don't run regularly they become destructive, gnawing at anything their mouths can reach. Diehl's dogs are rambunctious but friendly. Bring a camera and have your picture taken with them. Rates: $25 per person.

Dinner

One Stanley Avenue, ♡ ♡, $$, 1 Stanley Ave., Kingfield, 207/265-5541. In transit: Traveling south on Route 27, turn left in the center of Kingfield, right before Longfellow's restaurant. Go over the bridge, then turn right onto Riverside Street, then left onto Stanley Avenue.

One Stanley alludes to graciousness, yet it isn't a fancy spot. The restaurant is housed in an old Victorian home; furnishings though fine are a bit worn. The wood tables are graced with flowers and candles and peach-colored cloths. But more importantly, chef/ owner Dan Davis serves the best and most inventive food in town. Emphasis is on regional cuisine: Davis relies on the likes of rhubarb, maple syrup, and fiddleheads to give his meals panache.

Among Davis' most acclaimed dishes are roast duck with rhubarb, red wine, and cinnamon glaze, and alluvial chicken, which is sautéed in a white sauce with fiddleheads, juniper berries, and hemlock needles.

After coffee and dessert (usually a simple affair, such as chocolate cake or blueberry pie), retire to a velvet couch in the lounge for a liqueur. Hours: 5:00 P.M. - 9:30 P.M. Tuesday through Sunday.

The Truffle Hound, ♡ ♡, $$, West Village, Sugarloaf/USA, Carrabasset Valley, 207/237-2355. In transit: At the base of Sugarloaf mountain, if you walk up the steps past the Sugarloaf Mountain Hotel, it is on the right.

The Truffle Hound is Sugarloaf's original gourmet restaurant. In operation for more than 20 years, it still has a fine reputation. Escargot, roast duck l'orange, filet mignon with bordelaise sauce and truffles are items that typify the conventional, albeit elegant, menu. Desserts too are continental and rich: The chocolate truffle mousse cake is outstanding.

Decor mixes the rustic with the refined. Ceilings are vaulted and beamed, and walls have a rough-hewn wainscoting. Tables are set with white cloths and candles in crystal holders. If possible, try for a seat on the restaurant's second floor. The room has just a few tables, and is dim and intimate. Hours: 5:30 P.M. - 9:30 P.M.

SUNDAY MORNING

Note: Because Sugarloaf is primarily a downhill resort, chances are that most people who visit will want to ski alpine both days. But if you'd like to try something different, here's an alternative plan:

Breakfast

Seasons, $, The Sugarloaf Inn, off Mountainside Rd., Kingfield, 207/237-2000. In transit: From Kingfield, head north on Route 27, turn left onto Sugarloaf's Mountain Road. Turn left onto Mountainside Road. Turn right at the sign for the Sugarloaf Inn.

If you're looking for a good breakfast in pleasant surroundings, Seasons is the only game in town. (The Herbert offers a nice Sunday Brunch, but it doesn't start until 11:30 A.M.) Located inside the Sugarloaf Inn, a standard but pleasant hotel, Seasons offers mountain views in a greenhouse-style setting.

The menu is ordinary but extensive, and includes pancakes, waffles, omelettes, and oatmeal. Everything is well cooked and hot, and if you ask for toast well done, it indeed comes out that way. (That may seem like no small feat, but it's amazing how few restaurants truly oblige such requests.) Coffee is bottomless and the help never rushes. Be sure to get a seat by the window, relax, and enjoy the view.

Nordic Skiing at Carrabasset Valley Ski Touring Center, Route 27, Carrabasset Valley, 207/237-2205. In transit: From Sugarloaf's Mountain Road, head south on Route 27. The touring center is about a mile down the road on the right.

The largest ski touring center in Maine, Carrabasset Valley offers more than 85 kilometers of groomed double-tracked trail loops for both skating and classic cross-country skiing. Carrabasset prides itself on having trails away from civilization and, in fact, boasts that you're more likely to spot a moose than a car. If you've never skied before, Carrabasset is a good place to start. It offers a 13-kilometer beginners loop. Or, if you're both advanced skiers and are looking for some serious exercise, you can try the 7.5-kilometer competition loop or Carrabasset's steepest trail, which is 750 vertical feet from top to bottom. Tickets: $8. Equipment rental: $10 per day. Lessons: $10-$20. Hours: 9:00 A.M. - 4:00 P.M. until January 30, 9:00 A.M. - 5:00 P.M. until the end of the season.

Note: If you're not interested in cross-country skiing, Carrabasset also has a large skating rink that's open 9:00 A.M. - 4:00 P.M. nonholiday weeks and until 8:00 P.M. weekends and holidays. Rates: $3 per day.

SUNDAY AFTERNOON
Lunch

Klister Kitchen, $, Carrabassett Valley Ski Touring Center, Route 27, Carrabassett Valley, 207/237-2205.

It's not fancy, but this solar heated lodge is just right for relaxing after a few hours in the great outdoors. Decor is early picnic table, but the grand views and large wood stove give the place some up-country ambiance. Enjoy a bowl of homemade soup or chili, and finish off with one of Klister's famous brownies.

Visit the Stanley Museum, School Street, Kingfield, 207/265-2729. In transit: Take Route 27 south through Kingfield. Turn left onto School Street (look for the Kingfield Variety). The museum is on the left.

Kingfield is proud of its most illustrious residents, twins Francis Edgar (F.E.) and Freeland Oscar (F.O.) Stanley, made famous by their invention of the "Stanley Steamer," a car powered by steam.

The museum is a tribute to the Stanley family, exemplars of Yankee ingenuity and stick-to-it-ivenss. Although the Stanleys were essentially self-taught, in addition to inventing the steamer, they made contributions to the worlds of art, music, and engineering.

F.E. invented the dry plate formula for making photographic images. Chansonetta, the twins' sister, was among the most creative photographers at the turn of the century. Her daughter, Dorothy Stanley Emmons, distinguished herself as a fine artist. And after the Stanley Motor Carriage Company went out of business in 1924, F.O. and his nephew Carlton Stanley went back to an old family tradition of making violins. That business lasted until 1953.

Among the museum's collections are an authentic and refurbished Stanley Steamer car, photographs, violins, books, and other memorabilia. Admission free. Hours: 1:00 P.M. - 4:00 P.M. Closed Monday.

Note: Sugarloaf is a long drive for most people. Rather than having dinner in town, you'll probably choose to start for home. If you'd like to pick up a snack for the road, the most well stocked store is Tranten's (207/265-2202), right on Route 27 in Kingfield. It's just north of town. (You could always stop in Portland for dinner. See Portland, Maine, chapter for dining suggestions.)

Additional Activities

Dancing at the Widowmaker Lounge, Base Lodge, Sugarloaf/USA, 207/237-2000. *Ski* magazine considers the Widowmaker's reggae (usually Saturday) night one of the top action spots in U.S. ski country. While that's debatable, the Widowmaker has the best (did someone say only) live music in Sugarloaf. It's worth a look-see if you still have enough energy to dance all night after skiing all day. Live entertainment starts at 9:30 P.M. Open until 1:00 A.M.

Visit the Goldsmith Gallery, Village South, Sugarloaf/USA, Kingfield, 207/235-2405. Sugarloaf doesn't have much in the way of shopping, save the Goldsmith Gallery. This spot features unusual gold and silver jewelry handmade by Maine artisans. Other items include pottery, baskets, and gourmet food. Hours: 10:00 A.M. - 5:00 P.M.

GETTING THERE

BY AIR: Portland (ME) International Jetport, about two hours away, is the closest airport to Sugarloaf. It is serviced by Delta (800/221-1212), US Air (800/428-4322), United (800/241-6522), Continental (800/525-0280), and Northwest Airlink (800/225-2525.)

BY CAR: From the south, take I-95 north to Augusta, then Route 27 north through Farmington to Kingfield and Sugarloaf. Or take the Maine Turnpike to the Auburn exit and follow Route 4 north through Farmington. Then pick up Route 27 and proceed to Kingfield and Sugarloaf.

BY TRAIN: No train service is available.

BY BUS: No bus service is available.

CAR RENTAL: Avis (207/874-7500), Budget (207/772-6789), National (207/773-0036), and Hertz (207/774-4544) all have offices at the Portland Jetport.

TAXI/LIMOUSINE SERVICE: None. Riverbend Express (207/628-2877) provides transportation to the Portland Jetport. Advance reservations are required.

INFORMATION: For Sugarloaf itself, write or call Sugarloaf/USA, Carrabassett Valley, ME 04947, 207/237-2000. For geneneral information on the area, try the Carrabbasset Valley Chamber of Commerce, Route 27, Kingfield 04947, 207/235-2100. Hours: 9:00 A.M. - 5:00 P.M. Monday through Friday.

Activities Index

AIR BALOON RIDES
Litchfield Hills, Connecticut

ANTIQUE AUCTIONS
Nantucket, Massachusetts

ANTIQUE SHOPPING
Cape Ann, Massachusetts
Down East – Blue Hill and
Deer Isle, Maine
Lake Champlain Islands, Vermont
Litchfield Hills, Connecticut
Mystic and Stonington, Connecticut
Newport, Rhode Island
Portland, Maine
Stowe, Vermont
Wellfleet, Massachusetts

APPLE CIDER MILLS
Stowe, Vermont

APPLE PICKING
Grafton and Weston, Vermont

ART GALLERIES
Boston, Massachusetts
Cape Ann, Massachusetts
Down East – Blue Hill and
Deer Isle, Maine
Grafton and Weston, Vermont
Wellfleet, Massachusetts

ART SCHOOL TOURS
Down East – Blue Hill and
Deer Isle, Maine

BASEBALL GAMES
Boston, Massachusetts

BEACH GOING
Wellfleet, Massachusetts
Litchfield Hills, Connecticut
Martha's Vineyard, Massachusetts
Lake Champlain Islands, Vermont
Cape Ann, Massachusetts
Block Island, Rhode Island
Nantucket, Massachusetts

BICYCLE RIDING
Wellfleet, Massachusetts
Martha's Vineyard, Massachusetts
Lake Champlain Islands, Vermont
Cape Ann, Massachusetts
Mystic and Stonington, Connecticut
Block Island, Rhode Island

BOAT CRUISES
Block Island, Rhode Island
Boston, Massachusetts
Cape Ann, Massachusetts
Lake Champlain Islands, Vermont
Mystic and Stonington, Connecticut
Portland, Maine

BOATING
Concord and Lexington, Massachusetts
Lake Champlain Islands, Vermont
Litchfield Hills, Connecticut

CANDLELIGHT ECUMENICAL SERVICES
Nantucket, Massachusetts

CARRIAGE RIDES
Litchfield Hills, Connecticut
Portsmouth, New Hampshire

CHRISTMAS TREE SHOPPING
Jay and Montgomery, Vermont

CHRISTMAS TREE LIGHTING CEREMONIES
Nantucket, Massachusetts

DANCING
Martha's Vineyard, Massachusetts
Sugarloaf and Kingfield, Maine

DOG SLED RIDES
Jackson, New Hampshire
Sugarloaf and Kingfield, Maine

DOWNHILL SKIING
Jackson, New Hampshire
Jay and Kingfield, Vermont
Stowe, Vermont
Sugarloaf and Kingfield, Maine

GARDEN VISITS
Litchfield Hills, Connecticut

HIKING
Block Island, Rhode Island

Down East – Blue Hill and Deer Isle, Maine
Grafton and Weston, Vermont
Litchfield Hills, Connecticut
Lenox and the Berkshires, Massachusetts
Wellfleet, Massachusetts

HISTORICAL SITES
Boston, Massachusetts
Concord and Lexington, Massachusetts
Grafton and Weston, Vermont
Lenox and the Berkshires, Massachusetts
Mystic and Stonington, Connecticut
Newport, Rhode Island
Portland, Maine
Portsmouth, New Hampshire

HORSE SHOWS
Lake Champlain Islands, Vermont

HORSEBACK RIDING
Martha's Vineyard, Massachusetts

HOT TUBBING
Portland, Maine
Portsmouth, New Hampshire
Stowe, Vermont
Sugarloaf and Kingfield, Maine

HOUSE TOURS
Nantucket, Massachusetts

ICE CREAM FACTORIES
Stowe, Vermont

ICE SKATING
Jackson, New Hampshire

Mansion Tours
Newport, Rhode Island
Lenox and the Berkshires,
Massachusetts

Maple Sugar Houses
Grafton and Weston, Vermont

Monastaries
Grafton and Weston, Vermont

Museums
Boston, Massachusetts
Cape Ann, Massachusetts
Concord and Lexington, Massachusetts
Grafton and Weston, Vermont
Lenox and the Berkshires,
Massachusetts
Litchefield Hills, Connecticut
Martha's Vineyard, Massachusetts
Mystic, Connecticut
Nantucket, Massachusetts
Portland, Maine
Portsmouth, New Hampshire
Sugarloaf and Kingfield, Maine
Wellfleet, Massachusetts

Musical Events
Boston, Massachusetts
Cape Ann, Massachusetts
Litchfield Hills, Connnecticut
Mystic and Stonington, Connecticut
Portland, Maine
Portsmouth, New Hampshire

Nature Preserves
Concord and Lexington, Massachusetts
Down East – Blue Hill and
Deer Isle, Maine
Lake Champlain Islands, Vermont

Nordic Skiing
Jay and Montgomery, Vermont
Jackson, New Hampshire
Sugarloaf and Kingfield, Maine
Stowe, Vermont

Picnics
Block Island, Rhode Island
Cape Ann, Massachusetts
Grafton and Weston, Vermont
Lake Champlain Islands, Vermont
Lenox and the Berkshires,
Massachusetts
Newport, Rhode Island

Rollerblading
Boston, Massachusetts

Sailing Charters
Martha's Vineyard, Massachusetts

Sand Dune Buggy Rides
Wellfleet, Massachusetts

Scenic Drives
Mystic and Stonington, Connecticut
Newport, Rhode Island

Scenic Walks
Boston, Massachusetts
Concord and Lexington, Massachusetts
Nantucket, Massachusetts
Newport, Rhode Island
Portland, Maine

Sea Kayaking
Block Island, Rhode Island
Down East – Blue Hill and
Deer Isle, Maine

SEAL CRUISES
Nantucket, Massachusetts

SHOPPING
Block Island, Rhode Island
Boston, Massachusetts
Cape Ann, Massachusetts
Concord and Lexington, Massachusetts
Grafton and Weston, Vermont
Jay and Montgomery, Vermont
Lenox and the Berkshires,
Massachusetts
Litchfield Hills, Connecticut
Martha's Vineyard, Massachusetts
Mystic, Connecticut
Nantucket, Massachusetts
Newport, Rhode Island
Portland, Maine
Portsmouth, New Hampshire
Stowe, Vermont

SLEIGH RIDES
Jay and Montgomery, Vermont
Jackson, New Hampshire
Stowe, Vermont

SWIMMING
Litchfield Hills, Connecticut
Wellfleet, Massachusetts

THEATRE
Cape Ann, Massachusetts
Nantucket, Massachusetts
Portland, Maine
Portsmouth, New Hampshire
Wellfleet, Massachusetts

TOBOGGANING
Jay and Montgomery, Vermont

TRAIN RIDES
Grafton and Weston, Vermont

VINEYARD TOURS
Down East – Blue Hill and
Deer Isle, Maine
Martha's Vineyard, Massachusetts
Mystic and Stonington, Connecticut

WHALE WATCHING
Cape Ann, Massachusetts
Wellfleet, Massachusetts

General Index

Romance Index

Paisley & Parsley –
Jackson, New Hampshire

Pilgrim's Inn –
Down East – Blue Hill
and Deer Isle, Maine

Rowell's Inn –
Grafton and Weston, Vermont

Sea Cliff –
Martha's Vineyard, Massachusetts

Ten Lyon St. –
Nantucket, Massachusetts

Terrace Townhouse –
Boston, Massachusetts

Thorncroft Inn –
Martha's Vineyard, Massachusetts

♡ ♡– ♡ ♡ ♡

Antiques & Accommodations –
Mystic and Stonington, Connecticut

Goose Cove Lodge –
Down East – Blue Hill and
Deer Isle, Maine

Gundalow Inn –
Portsmouth, New Hampshire

Manor House, The –
Litchfield Hills, Connecticut

♡ ♡

Addison Choate Inn –
Cape Ann, Massachusetts

Apple Tree Inn –
Lenox and the Berkshires,
Massachusetts

Black Lantern Inn –
Jay and Montgomery, Vermont

Boston Harbor Hotel –
Boston, Massachusetts

Breakfast at Tiasquam –
Martha's Vineyard, Massachusetts

Cahoun Hollow Bed & Breakfast –
Wellfleet, Massachusetts

Corner House –
Nantucket, Massachusetts

Eaglebrook at Grafton –
Grafton and Weston, Vermont

Eden Pines Inn –
Cape Ann, Massachusetts

Edson Hill Manor –
Stowe, Vermont

Governor's House Inn –
Portsmouth, New Hampshire

Haus Andreas –
Lenox and the Berkshires,
Massachusetts

Hawthorne Inn –
Concord and Lexington, Massachusetts

Inn at Thorn Hill –
Jackson, New Hampshire

Inn on Cove Hill –
Cape Ann, Massachusetts

Inn on Winter's Hill –
Sugarloaf and Kingfield, Maine

Notchland Inn –
Jackson, New Hampshire

Old Tavern at Grafton –
Grafton and Weston, Vermont

Randall's Ordinary –
Mystic and Stonington, Connecticut

Shiverick Inn –
Martha's Vineyard, Massachusetts

Sise Inn –
Portsmouth, New Hampshire

Ten Acres Lodge –
Stowe, Vermont

West End Inn –
Portland, Maine

Wilder Homestead Inn –
Grafton and Weston, Vermont

♡–♡ ♡

Bow Street Inn –
Portsmouth, New Hampshire

Green Mountain Inn –
Stowe, Vermont

Hilltop Haven –
Litchfield Hills, Connecticut

Inn at Castle Hill –
Newport, Rhode Island

North Hero House –
Lake Champlain Islands, Vermont

Portland Regency –
Portland, Maine

Shore Acres Inn –
Lake Champlain Islands, Vermont

Sugarloaf Mountain Hotel –
Sugarloaf and Kingfield, Maine

♡

Brehmer Graphics –
Wellfleet, Massachusetts

Brook Farm Inn –
Lenox and the Berkshires,
Massachusetts

Colonial Inn –
Concord and Lexington, Massachusetts

Herbert Hotel –
Sugarloaf and Kingfield, Maine

Inn at the Brass Lantern –
Stowe, Vermont

Longfellow's Wayside Inn –
Concord and Lexington, Massachusetts

Rose Apple Acres Farm –
Jay and Montgomery, Vermont

Seacrest Manor –
Cape Ann, Massachusetts

Thomas Mott Homestead –
Lake Champlain Islands, Vermont

RESTAURANTS

♡ ♡ ♡ ♡

Aigo Bistro –
Concord and Lexington, Massachusetts

American Seasons –
Nantucket, Massachusetts

Blantyre –
Lenox and the Berkshires,
Massachusetts

Café Always –
Portland, Maine

Cielo Gallery –
Wellfleet, Massachusetts

Hampshire House –
Boston, Massachusetts

Hungry i –
Boston, Massachusetts

Mannisses, The –
Block Island, Rhode Island

Second Story –
Nantucket, Massachusetts

Wheatleigh –
Lenox and the Berkshires,
Massachusetts

Zack's on the Rocks –
Jay and Montgomery, Vermont

♡ ♡ ♡

Back Bay Grill –
Portland, Maine

Biba –
Boston, Massachusetts

Bistro and 2 Main St. –
Cape Ann, Massachusetts

Blue Strawbery –
Portsmouth, New Hampshire

Brotherhood of Thieves –
Nantucket, Massachusetts

Captain Daniel Packer Inne –
Mystic and Stonington, Connecticut

Captain Higgins –
Wellfleet, Massachusetts

Commodore Inn –
Newport, Rhode Island

Firepond –
Down East – Blue Hill and
Deer Isle, Maine

Harborview Restauraunt –
Mystic and Stonington, Connecticut

Hopkins Inn –
Litchfield Hills, Connecticut

India House –
Nantucket, Massachusetts

Jasper's –
Boston, Massachusetts

L'etoile –
Martha's Vineyard, Massachusetts

La Petite Auberge –
Newport, Rhode Island

Mayflower Inn –
Litchfield Hills, Connecticut

Old Tavern at Grafton –
Grafton and Weston, Vermont

Strawbery Court –
Portsmouth, New Hampshire

West Street Grill –
Litchfield Hills, Connecticut

White Horse Tavern –
Newport, Rhode Island

White Rainbow –
Cape Ann, Massachsuetts

Winfield's –
Block Island, Rhode Island

♡ ♡ – ♡ ♡ ♡

Inn at Thorn Hill –
Jackson, New Hampshire

♡ ♡

Chantecleer, The –
Grafton and Weston, Vermont

Café Lucia –
Lenox and the Berkshires,
Massachusetts

Gateways –
Lenox and the Berkshires,
Massachusetts

The Oar House –
Portsmouth, New Hampshire

Guido's Trattoria –
Portsmouth, New Hampshire

Black Lantern Inn –
Jay and Montgomery, Vermont

Inn on Trout River –
Portsmouth, New Hampshire

Wildcat Inn –
Jackson, New Hampshire

Bernerhof, The –
Jackson, New Hampshire

Herbert, The –
Sugarloaf and Kingfield, Maine

Hugs –
Sugarloaf and Kingfield, Maine

One Stanley Avenue –
Sugarloaf and Kingfield, Maine

Truffle Hound –
Sugarloaf and Kingfield, Maine

Le Languedoc –
Nantucket, Massachusetts

Alberta's Café –
Portland, Maine

Katahdin –
Portland, Maine

Villa Tragara –
Stowe, Vermont

Ten Acres Lodge –
Stowe, Vermont

Stowehof Inn –
Stowe, Vermont

Davio's –
Boston, Massachusetts

The Raven –
Boston, Massachusetts

Village Forge Lounge –
Concord and Lexington, Massachusetts

Il Capriccio –
Concord and Lexington, Massachusetts

Flood Tide –
Mystic and Stonington, Connecticut

Randall's Ordinary –
Mystic Stonington, Connecticut

Puerini's –
Newport, Rhode Island

Déjà Vu Café –
Lake Champlain Islands, Vermont

Shore Acres Inn –
Lake Champlain Islands, Vermont

Daily Planet –
Lake Champlain Islands, Vermont

Jonathan's –
Down East – Blue Hill and
Deer Isle, Maine

Freshfields –
Litchfield Hills, Connecticut

Savoir Faire –
Martha's Vineyard, Massachusetts

Le Grenier –
Martha's Vineyard, Massachusetts

Aesop's Table –
Wellfleet, Massachusetts

Adrian's –
Wellfleet, Massachusetts

♡–♡ ♡

The Wayside Inn –
Concord and Lexington, Massachusetts

♡

Bayside Lobster Hutt –
Wellfleet, Massachusetts

Black Dog –
Martha's Vineyard, Massachusetts

Blue Coyote –
Grafton and Weston, Vermont

Church Street Café –
Lenox and the Berkshires,
Massachusetts

Colonial Inn –
Concord and Lexington, Massachusetts

Copperfields –
Stowe, Vermont

Gables, The –
Stowe, Vermont

Homeport –
Martha's Vineyard, Massachusetts

Mohegan Café –
Block Island, Rhode Island

Mr. Pickwick's Pub –
Stowe, Vermont

North Hero House –
Lake Champlain Islands, Vermont

Pappa Razzi –
Concord and Lexington, Massachusetts

Pepper Club –
Portland, Maine

Portmouth Brewery –
Portsmouth, New Hampshire

Red Parka Pub –
Jackson, New Hampshire

Restaurant Swisspot –
Stowe, Vermont

Rudder, The –
Cape Ann, Massachusetts

Skipper's Dock –
Mystic and Stonington, Connecticut

South Wellfleet Clam Shack –
Wellfleet, Massachusetts

Thompson House Eatery –
Jackson, New Hampshire

Yesterday's –
Jackson, New Hampshire